Ethics in Mental Health–Substance Use

Ethics in Mental Health–Substance Use aims to explore the comprehensive concerns and dilemmas occurring from mental health and substance use problems, and to inform, develop, and educate by sharing and pooling knowledge, and enhancing expertise, in this fast developing region of ethics and ethical care and practice. This volume concentrates on ethical concerns, dilemmas, and concepts specifically interrelated, as a collation of problem(s) that directly or indirectly affect the life of the individual and family. While presenting a balanced view of what is ethically best practice today, this title challenges concepts and stimulates debate, exploring all aspects of the development in treatment, intervention and care responses, and the adoption of research-led best practice.

David B Cooper has specialized in mental health and substance use for over 36 years. He is currently an associate editor for the *Journal of Substance Use*. He also served as an editor-in-chief of *Mental Health and Substance Use*. Seminal work includes *Alcohol Home Detoxification* and *Assessment and Alcohol Use*, both published by Radcliffe Publishing, Oxford. Mr. Cooper (2011) edited a series of six textbooks with the series title of Mental Health–Substance Use.

D0061121

About the Mental Health–Substance Use Series

The seven books in this series are:

1 Introduction to Mental Health–Substance Use
2 Developing Services in Mental Health–Substance Use
3 Responding in Mental Health–Substance Use
4 Intervention in Mental Health–Substance Use
5 Care in Mental Health–Substance Use
6 Practice in Mental Health–Substance Use
7 Ethics in Mental Health–Substance Use

The series is not merely for mental health professionals but also for substance use professionals. It is not a question of 'them' (the substance use professionals) teaching 'them' (the mental health professionals). It is about sharing knowledge, skills and expertise. We are equal. We learn from each fellow professional, for the benefit of those whose lives we touch. The rationale is that to maintain clinical excellence, we need to be aware of the developments and practices within mental health and substance use. Then, we make informed choices; we take best practice, and apply this to our professional role.

Generically, the series *Mental Health–Substance Use* concentrates on concerns, dilemmas, and concepts specifically interrelated, as a collation of problems that directly or indirectly influence the life and well-being of the individual, family, and carers. Such concerns relate not only to the individual but also to the future direction of practice, education, research, service development, interventions, and treatment. While presenting a balanced view of what is best practice today, the books aim to challenge concepts and stimulate debate, exploring all aspects of the development in treatment, intervention and care responses, and the adoption of research-led best practice. To achieve this, they draw from a variety of perspectives, facilitating consideration of how professionals meet the challenges now and in the future. To accomplish this, we have assembled leading international professionals to provide insight into current thinking and developments, related to the many varying and diverse needs of the individual, family and carers experiencing mental health–substance use problems.

Ethics in Mental Health–Substance Use

Edited by

DAVID B COOPER

Sigma Theta Tau International: The Honor Society of Nursing; Outstanding Contribution to Nursing

Routledge
Taylor & Francis Group

NEW YORK AND LONDON

First published 2017
by Routledge
711 Third Avenue, New York, NY 10017

and by Routledge
2 Park Square, Milton Park, Abingdon, Oxon, OX14 4RN

Routledge is an imprint of the Taylor & Francis Group, an informa business

© 2017 Taylor & Francis

Library of Congress Cataloging in Publication Data
A catalog record for this book has been requested

ISBN: 978-1-138-67249-9 (hbk)
ISBN: 978-1-4987-6723-1 (pbk)
ISBN: 978-1-315-19862-0 (ebk)

Typeset in Minion
by Florence Production Ltd, Stoodleigh, Devon, UK

Dedication

Dedicated to Harvey (Hogan) Appel (2016) long-time friend, cousin-in-law. Our children, Phil, Marc and Caroline, looked forward to seeing Uncle Harvey as he always brought a smile to their faces with his sense of humor and jokes. Hogan will be greatly missed by our family. Our thoughts are now with Barbara, Harvey's wife and our cousin.

Dedicated to Jo Cooper, without whose support, guidance and encouragement this book would never have been written. With whom my life is worthwhile.

Dedicated to Audrey (Derry) Keryk, my sister, for her love and care.

Contents

About the editor

David B Cooper
Sigma Theta Tau International: Honor Society of Nursing
Outstanding Contribution to Nursing
Associate Editor – dual diagnosis: *Journal of Substance Use*
Author/Editor/Writer
Apartment 43
Manton Court
Kings Road
Horsham
West Sussex
England
RH13 5AE

David has specialised in mental health and substance use for over 36 years. He has worked as a practitioner, manager, researcher, author, lecturer, and consultant. He has served as editor, or editor-in-chief, of several journals, most recently as editor-in-chief of *Mental Health and Substance Use*. David is currently an Associate Editor: dual diagnosis for the *Journal of Substance Use*. He has published widely and is 'credited with enhancing the understanding and development of community detoxification for people experiencing alcohol withdrawal' (Nursing Council on Alcohol; Sigma Theta Tau International citations). Seminal work includes *Alcohol Home Detoxification and Assessment* and *Alcohol Use*, both published by Radcliffe Publishing, Oxford.

Other books by the editor

Cooper DB, *Alcohol Home Detoxification and Assessment*. Boca Raton, Florida: CRC Press; 1994 – reprinted 1996.

Cooper DB, editor. *Alcohol Use*. Boca Raton, Florida: CRC Press, 2000 – reprinted 2008.

Cooper DB, editor. *Introduction to Mental Health–Substance Use*. Boca Raton, Florida: CRC Press, 2011.

Cooper DB, editor. *Developing Services in Mental Health–Substance Use*. Boca Raton, Florida: CRC Press, 2011.

Cooper DB, editor. *Responding in Mental Health–Substance Use*. Boca Raton, Florida: CRC Press, 2011.

Cooper DB, editor. *Intervention in Mental Health–Substance Use*. Boca Raton, Florida: CRC Press, 2011.

Cooper DB, editor. *Care in Mental Health–Substance Use*. Boca Raton, Florida: CRC Press, 2011.

Cooper DB, editor. *Practice in Mental Health–Substance Use*. Boca Raton, Florida: CRC Press, 2011.

Cooper DB, Cooper J, editors. *Palliative Care within Mental Health: principles and philosophy*. Boca Raton, Florida: CRC Press, 2012.

Cooper DB, Cooper J, editors. *Palliative Care within Mental Health: care and practice*. Boca Raton, Florida: CRC Press, 2014.

Cooper DB, editor. *Ethics in Mental Health–Substance Use*. New York/Oxon: Routledge/Taylor & Francis, 2017.

Contributors

CHAPTER 1
David B Cooper
See About the editor

CHAPTER 2
Dr. Michael Robertson
Clinical Associate Professor
Centre for Values, Ethics and the Law in Medicine
University of Sydney
New South Wales
Australia

Michael Robertson is a Clinical Associate Professor of Mental Health Ethics and a visiting Professorial Fellow at the Sydney Jewish Museum. He works as a clinical and forensic psychiatrist and worked previously in community psychiatry for 20 years. He has previously coordinated a clinical service for survivors of psychological trauma. Dr. Robertson completed his PhD in the area of psychiatric ethics and traumatic stress. He has published in the area of psychological trauma, philosophy and psychiatry, and brief psychotherapy. He has interests including the depiction of psychiatry in cinema and human rights abuses perpetrated by psychiatrists under National Socialism in Germany.

Dr. Edwina Light
Researcher
Centre for Values, Ethics and the Law in Medicine
University of Sydney
New South Wales
Australia

Edwina Light is a postdoctoral research affiliate at the Centre for Values, Ethics and the Law in Medicine (VELIM) at the University of Sydney, NSW, Australia.

Her research interests include mental health ethics and policy, including involuntary treatment, social justice, disability rights, and the relationship between psychiatry and the state. Based on research into community treatment orders (CTOs), her recent publications include a review of involuntary treatment in Australian mental health policies, a survey of rates of CTO use, a study of the experiences and perspectives of patients, carers, clinicians and tribunal members of the involuntary community treatment system in NSW and factors associated with its use. Dr Light is a Visiting Fellow of the Sydney Jewish Museum. She is also an editor of Ethics and Health Law News (www.ehln.org), a resource run by VELIM and the Centre for Health Governance, Law and Ethics.

CHAPTER 3

Professor Cynthia MA Geppert

Chief of Consultation Psychiatry and Ethics, New Mexico Veterans Affairs Health Care System.
Professor and Director of Ethics, University of New Mexico School of Medicine
Albuquerque
New Mexico
USA

Cynthia Geppert is Chief of Consultation Psychiatry and Ethics at the New Mexico Veterans Affairs Health Care System, and has been an Acting Health Care Ethicist at the VA's National Center for Ethics in Health Care since 2014. She is also Professor of Psychiatry and Director of Ethics Education at the University of New Mexico School of Medicine and Adjunct Professor of Bioethics at the Albany March Bioethics Institute of Albany Medical College. She is board certified in psychiatry, psychosomatic medicine, addiction medicine, hospice and palliative medicine, and pain medicine and her clinical work is at the interface between ethics, psychiatry, and internal medicine. Cynthia is a Distinguished Fellow of the American Psychiatric Association, a Fellow of the Academy of Psychosomatic Medicine, and the American Society of Addiction Medicine. She currently serves as Editor-in Chief of *Federal Practitioner* and the Ethics Section Editor for *Psychiatric Times*. Cynthia has published over 100 book chapters, articles, and other writings in her areas of clinical ethics interest: ethics consultation, mental health, palliative care, addiction, and chronic pain. She has been actively engaged in the education of medical students, residents, fellows, and other health care professionals for two decades.

CHAPTER 4

Professor Larry Purnell

Professor Emeritus, University of Delaware, Newark, Delaware USA

Adjunct Professor Foreign Educated Physician Program, Florida International University, Miami, Florida, USA
Adjunct Professor and Consulting Faculty, Excelsior College, Albany, NY, USA
Maryland
USA

Dr. Purnell is Emeritus Professor from the University of Delaware where he coordinated the graduate programs in nursing and healthcare administration and taught culture. His Model, the Purnell Model for Cultural Competence has been translated into Arabic, Czech, Flemish, Korean, French, German, Japanese, Portuguese, Spanish, and Turkish. His textbook, *Transcultural Health Care: A Culturally Competent Approach* won the Brandon Hill and American Journal of Nursing Book Awards. Dr. Purnell has over 100 refereed journal publications, 100 book chapters, and 14 textbooks. He has made presentations throughout the United States as well as in Australia, Colombia, Costa Rica, England, Italy, Korea, Panama, Russia, Scotland, Spain, and Turkey. He is the U.S. Representative to the European Union's Commission on Intercultural Communication resulting from the Salamanca, Sorbonne, Bologna, and WHO Declarations. He has been on the International Editorial Board, for six journals. Dr. Purnell is a Fellow in the American Academy of Nursing, a Transcultural Nursing Scholar, Luther Christman Fellow, and is on the Rosa Parks Wall of Fame for Teaching Tolerance.

CHAPTER 5

Dr. Alyna Turner
Senior Clinician/Research Fellow
Centre for Translational Neuroscience and Mental Health
Faculty of Health and Medicine
University of Newcastle
Callaghan
New South Wales
Australia

Dr. Alyna Turner is a Research Fellow at Deakin University; Senior Clinician at the University of Newcastle and the NHMRC CRE in Mental Health and Substance Use; and Honorary Fellow in the Department of Psychiatry at the University of Melbourne, Australia. She has been a fully registered psychologist since 2001 and holds endorsement as a Clinical Psychologist, previously working within psychiatric rehabilitation, liaison psychiatry, and chronic disease services in Australia. Dr Turner's clinical and research focuses on mental health and comorbidity, spanning substance misuse, psychotic illness, CVD risk behaviours, depression, anxiety, heart disease, stroke, and diabetes. She has been involved in the development and evaluation of individual, group-based, online, and telephone delivered psychological interventions for people with comorbid conditions.

Ms. Nola M Ries
Senior Lecturer
Research Director and Deputy Dean
Newcastle Law School
Faculty of Business and Law
University of Newcastle
Callaghan
New South Wales
Australia

Nola M Ries, BA (Hons), JD, MPA, LLM, is Deputy Dean and Research Director at the University of Newcastle Law School. Her research focuses on health law and policy, especially legal aspects of health system reform, public health law, law and the ageing population, and the governance of biomedical research. Nola is a recipient of a 2016 Australian Fellowship in Health Services and Policy Research. She has published over 45 peer-reviewed articles and chapters and 20 major reports. She practiced law in Canada in the areas of human rights and constitutional law, was a consultant to organisations such as the Canadian Academy of Health Sciences and the National Panel on Research Ethics, and has served on research ethics committees.

Professor Amanda L Baker
Senior Research Fellow
Faculty of Health and Medicine
Centre for Translational Neuroscience and Mental Health
University of Newcastle
New South Wales
Australia

Professor Amanda Baker is a senior clinical psychologist who has worked in mental health, alcohol, and other drug and forensic settings in the UK and Australia. She is Co-Director of the NHMRC Centre of Research Excellence (CRE) in Mental Health and Substance Use. She is an expert in the treatment of co-existing mental health and substance use problems and has a special interest in smoking cessation treatment research and healthy lifestyle interventions. She leads an internationally renowned program of clinical research trialling novel interventions targeting co-existing mental health, substance use, and health risk behaviours.

CHAPTER 6
Professor Cynthia MA Geppert
See Chapter 3

CHAPTER 7

Dr. Geraldine S Pearson
Associate Professor
University of Connecticut
School of Medicine Department of Psychiatry
Farmington
Connecticut
USA

Dr. Pearson is a graduate of the University of Cincinnati College of Nursing and Health with her BSN and MSN. She received her PhD in nursing from the University of Connecticut School of Nursing. She is currently an associate professor in the Child and Adolescent Division of the Department of Psychiatry, University of Connecticut School of Medicine. She is also an elected trustee of the Committee on Publication Ethics (COPE) and acts as the co-vice chair of this UK charity trust. She is the editor-in-chief of the *Journal of the American Nurses Association* and was previously editor of *Perspectives in Psychiatric Care*. Her interests are chronic psychiatric illness in paediatric populations and clinical care outcomes in outpatient psychiatric populations.

CHAPTER 8

Dr. Barbara J Russell
Senior Bioethicist
University Health Network and Women's College Hospital
Assistant Professor
Dalla Lana School of Public Health
Member of Joint Centre for Bioethics
University of Toronto
Toronto
Ontario
Canada

Barbara Russell PhD MBA is a senior bioethicist at University Health Network and Women's College Hospital in Toronto, Canada. She is a member of WCH's Research Ethics Board. As an Assistant Professor in the Dalla Lana School of Public Health at the University of Toronto, Dr. Russell also teaches undergraduate and graduate courses in bioethics.

Professor WJ Wayne Skinner
Assistant Professor
Department of Psychiatry
Adjunct Senior Lecturer
University of Toronto

Deputy Clinical Director and Head of Problem Gambling
Institute of Ontario
Centre for Addiction and Mental Health
Toronto
Ontario
Canada

Wayne Skinner, MSW, RSW, is an Assistant Professor in the Department of Psychiatry and Adjunct Senior Lecturer in the Faculty of Social Work at the University of Toronto. He was Clinical Director of the Concurrent Disorders Program at the Center for Addiction and Mental Health in Toronto, Canada between 1998 and 2005, and more recently Head of the Problem Gambling Institute of Ontario. He has written and edited books on addictions, concurrent disorders, and motivational interviewing, as well as co-authoring many peer review articles on addiction and mental health. He was Associate Editor (Canada) for the journal *Mental Health–Substance Use*. Active as a consultant and educator, he is a member of the Motivational Interviewing Network of Trainers.

CHAPTER 9

Professor Louise Nadeau
Professor
Fellow at the Canadian Academy of Health Sciences
Department of Psychology
Université de Montréal
Centre-Ville
Montréal
Québec
Canada

Louise Nadeau, Professor in the Department of Psychology at the Université de Montréal and associate researcher at the Douglas Mental Health University Institute, University McGill, is an elected fellow of the Royal Society of Canada and the Canadian Academy of Health Sciences. Her research focuses on the prediction of recidivism among high-risk drivers convicted for driving under the influence, on co-occurring disorders in addictions, gambling and the history of addictions. She is the Chair of the Board of Éduc'alcool and is Co-chair of the Canadian Centre on Substance Abuse Low-Risk Gambling Guidelines Group. She was Chair of the Working Group on Online Gambling for the Minister of Finances Qc, Vice-chair of the Canadian Institutes of Health Research (CIHR) Governing Council. She is a member of the Board of l'Institut national d'excellence en santé et en services sociaux, served on the Advisory Committee of the Institute of Neurosciences, Mental Health and Addiction and the HIV/AIDS Research Initiative, CIHR.

CHAPTER 10

Jacqueline Talmet
Advanced Nurse Clinical Services Coordinator/Regional Manager
Drug and Alcohol Services South Australia (DASSA)
Norther and Inner Northern Country Services
Adelaide
South Australia
Australia

Jacky Talmet is a registered nurse with over 35 years' experience working in mental health and drug and alcohol nursing. Jacky has a special interest in ethical practice and how it related to people with alcohol and other drugs and mental health comorbidity and has worked with colleagues over many years to address discrimination and stigmatisation and ensure people have the right to equitable access to services that provide supportive and appropriate care in which their rights for self-determination are upheld.

CHAPTER 11

Dr. John Richard Ashcroft
Substantive Consultant Psychiatrist
5 Boroughs Partnership NHS Foundation Trust
Winwick
Warrington
Lancashire
England, UK

John R Ashcroft is a Consultant Psychiatrist in North West England. He has special interests in Neuropsychiatry, Addiction, and Mental Health Law. He has authored a number of chapters for CRC Press covering aspects of assessment in mental health and substance use. He is a member of the Neuropsychoanalysis Society and is a keen supporter of an integrative approach towards the understanding of the neurosciences.

Dr. Siân Bensa
Clinical Psychologist
Brooker Centre
Runcorn
Cheshire
England, UK

Siân Bensa is a clinical psychologist who currently works in acute mental health in the North West of England. Her role is to provide psychological services for two inpatients units within 5 Boroughs Partnership NHS Trust serving North Cheshire. Prior to this she has worked in other acute and step-down mental health rehabilitation units within the NHS and independent sectors. She has particular interests in trauma, psychosis, and psychological formulation. She undertook her Doctorate in Clinical Psychology at Royal Holloway, University of London, and subsequently trained as a Systemic Practitioner at Birmingham Parkview.

CHAPTER 12

Dr. Siân Bensa
See Chapter 11

Dr. John Richard Ashcroft
See Chapter 11

CHAPTER 13

Scott Macpherson
Lecturer
School of Nursing and Midwifery
Faculty of Health and Social Care
Robert Gordon University
Aberdeen
Grampian
Scotland, UK

Scott Macpherson is a lecturer in Mental Health at Robert Gordon University in Aberdeen. Scott has an academic background in Psychology and Cognitive Behavioural Psychotherapy. Scott qualified as a Mental Health Nurse from Dundee University in 1999 and worked primarily in the field of substance use prior to moving into teaching in 2013. During that time Scott worked in both private and statutory organisations. Scott has presented work on stigma at conferences at both a national and international level. Scott's teaching and research interests include substance misuse, spirituality, and cognitive behavioural therapy. In his time away from work Scott enjoys football, music, films, and adventuring with his children Jayden and Cally.

Dan Warrender
Lecturer
School of Nursing and Midwifery
Faculty of Health and Social Care
Robert Gordon University
Aberdeen
Grampian
Scotland, UK

Dan Warrender is a lecturer in Mental Health at Robert Gordon University in Aberdeen. Dan has an academic background in philosophy and, prior to his chosen area of Mental Health, a working background in learning difficulties. He qualified as a Mental Health Nurse from Robert Gordon University in September 2011. Gaining a place on the Early Clinical Career Fellowship (ECCF) 2012, he began an MSc Nursing at the University of Aberdeen, while continuing to work in acute mental health. An interest in borderline personality disorder (BPD) and mentalization-based treatment (MBT) became the focus of an MSc and primary research which was disseminated at national and international conferences throughout 2014. Dan's research and teaching interests include: Borderline Personality Disorder, Mentalization-Based Treatment, Acute Mental Health Wards and Ethics.

CHAPTER 14

Professor Agnes Higgins
Professor of Mental Health
School of Nursing and Midwifery
Trinity College Dublin
University of Dublin
Dublin
Ireland

Agnes Higgins PhD, MSc, BNS, RPN, RGN, RNT, FTCD is Professor in Mental Health Nursing at the School of Nursing and Midwifery Trinity College Dublin, Ireland, where she teaches and assesses across program at undergraduate and postgraduate level, and supervises Masters and PhD students. Her research interests are in the area of mental health recovery, service user involvement, gender and sexualities and is widely published in these areas. She has completed studies on service users' recovery journeys, impact of different models of recovery on users' and family members' experiences of recovery, factors influencing recover-oriented education and impact of peer-support on recovery outcomes.

Ailish Gill
Researcher
School of Nursing and Midwifery
Trinity College
Dublin
Ireland

Ailish Gill RPN, MCAT is a registered psychiatric nurse, creative arts therapist, and academic with over 25 years' experience of mental health clinical practice and education in Australia, where she has managed major projects in adolescent, adult, and perinatal mental health. Since her return to Ireland in 2014 she has been involved in a number of research projects and e-learning initiatives in mental health at Trinity College Dublin.

CHAPTER 15

Dr. MJM Verhaegh
Senior researcher
Board member of Foundation 'Family as an ally'
GGz Eindhoven; Dr. Poletlaan 40
Eindhoven
Noord-Brabant
The Netherlands

Giel Verhaegh is a health scientist and works as a teacher at the academy for nurse specialists and as senior researcher at the Mental Health Care Institute Eindhoven (GGzE) in the Netherlands. He is the leader of research programs focussing on rehabilitation, participation, and recovery of persons that cope with severe mental illnesses. In recent years he introduced family involvement policy in the daily practice of GGzE. He teaches professionals how to cooperate in triads (family-client-professional) and is a board member of 'Familie als Bondgenoot' ('family as partner in recovery'). In 2009 he got his PhD in 'Effectiveness of Assertive Community Treatment in Early Psychosis'. It was an important contribution to the awareness that family involvement is essential in the recovery process of severely mentally ill clients.

Dr. DPK Roeg
Senior researcher at GGzE and Tilburg University, Tranzo
GGz Eindhoven; Dr. Poletlaan 40
Eindhoven
Noord-Brabant
The Netherlands

Diana Roeg is a health scientist and works as senior researcher at Tilburg University, department Tranzo and at the Mental Health Care Institute: GGzE in the Netherlands. She is involved in research focussing on rehabilitation, participation, and recovery of persons that cope with mental illness. She has finished a number of projects on assertive outreach programs for persons with complex and combined psychiatric problems, and on an international project focusing on user involvement in health care innovation for persons with dementia. Recent projects include an effect study on the Dutch Strengths-based rehabilitation method CARe, the development and effect study of Victoria: a conversation method paying attention to the influence of victimization on participation of persons with severe/combined mental illnesses, and an effect study on the DIARI: a structured need assessment to improve the care for and our understanding about victims of partner violence.

CHAPTER 16

Philip D James
Clinical Nurse Specialist/Co-ordinator,
Louth/Meath Adolescent Substance Use Service
St. Bridget's Hospital Complex
Ardee
Co. Louth.
Ireland

Philip James trained as a psychiatric nurse in Dublin 1999 and was appointed as the first Clinical Nurse Specialist in Adolescent Substance Misuse in 2006. Since then he has worked full time in substance use services for adolescents. In April 2016 he was appointed as Clinical Nurse Specialist and Co-ordinator of the adolescent substance use service for counties Louth and Meath. He completed a Master's Degree in 2005 and is a qualified cognitive behavioural therapist. In addition to his clinical work he has been involved in a number of research projects and publications. He has published various research articles and is co-author of *The Handbook of Adolescent Substance Use* which was published by Radcliffe Publishing, Oxford in 2013. He has acted as reviewer for a number of academic journals and provides lectures on a variety of addiction and mental health related topics with a number of third level institutions.

CHAPTER 17

Dr. Sarah Wadd
Directory of Substance Misuse and Ageing Research Team (SMART)
Tilda Goldberg Centre
University of Bedfordshire
Luton
Bedfordshire
England, UK

Dr. Sarah Wadd is programme director of the Substance Misuse and Ageing Research Team (SMART) at the University of Bedfordshire. Her seminal 'Working with Older Drinkers Study' identified best practice based on interviews with alcohol practitioners who specialise in working with older people and older people receiving alcohol treatment. Sarah is the academic lead for the £25m Big Lottery funded 'Drink Wise Age Well' Programme which aims to reduce alcohol-related harm in people aged 50+. Her other research studies have included alcohol misuse that co-exists with cognitive impairment in older people, drug use in older people, 'wet' care homes for older people and accessibility and suitability of residential alcohol services for older people. Sarah has provided advice on substance misuse among older people to various government and national bodies including the Home Office, Public Health England, Alcohol Research UK, Drugscope and Age UK.

CHAPTER 18

Professor Sunita Simon Kurpad
Professor, Department of Psychiatry
Professor, Department of Medical Ethics
St John's Medical College
Bengaluru
Karnataka
India

Professor Sunita Simon Kurpad gained her MBBS from St John's Medical College, Bengaluru, India and MRC Psychiatry from Cambridge University, United Kingdom. After obtaining DNB Psychiatry she has been a faculty member at St John's for 20 years, where she is currently Professor, Department of Psychiatry and Professor and Head, Department of Medical Ethics. She is actively involved in clinical work, teaching, and research. She has been involved in teaching psychiatry and ethics to medical graduates, postgraduates, interns, paramedical, and health management students. She has published in scientific journals. She is currently involved in international collaborative research with the Consortium on Vulnerability to Externalizing Disorders and Addiction (cVeda). She has made a short film on sexual harassment. She is currently Co Chairperson of the Task Force for Boundary Guidelines of the Indian Psychiatric Society and has been instrumental in Drafting guidelines for doctors on sexual boundaries in India.

CHAPTER 19

Kevin Reel
Practicing Healthcare Ethicist
Joint Centre of Bioethics
University of Toronto
Toronto
Ontario
Canada

Kevin Reel is a practicing healthcare ethicist in Toronto, Canada. He obtained his Master of Science in medical ethics from Imperial College, London, England and his Bachelor of Science in occupational therapy from the University of Toronto (UofT). He completed his Fellowship in Clinical and Organizational Ethics through the Joint Centre for Bioethics' (JCB) at UofT, where he is a member of the JCB Task Force on Implementing Medical Assistance in Dying. Kevin has worked as the ethicist at Mackenzie Health, Southlake Regional Health Centre and the Centre for Addiction and Mental

Health. He is an assistant professor in the Department of Occupational Science and Occupational Therapy and a faculty member with the Global Institute for Psychosocial, Palliative and End-of-Life Care at UofT. He is a regular ethics columnist for Hospital News.

Jean-François Crépault
Senior Policy Analyst
Centre for Addiction and Mental Health
Toronto
Ontario
Canada

Jean-François Crépault is a Senior Policy Analyst at the Centre for Addiction and Mental Health (CAMH). He leads CAMH's public policy efforts in the area of substance use, communicating evidence-based public policy to government and other stakeholders as part of CAMH's organizational commitment to "driving social change". He is the lead author of the CAMH Cannabis Policy Framework, which made the case for legalization and health-focused regulation of cannabis and has shaped debate around public health approaches to substance use in Canada.

Gavin S MacKenzie
Legal Counsel at the Centre for Addiction and Mental Health
Toronto
Ontario
Canada

Gavin S MacKenzie is legal counsel to the forensic program at the Centre for Addiction and Mental Health (CAMH) in Toronto. He represents the hospital before the Ontario Review Board in hearings for individuals found unfit to stand trial or not criminally responsible of criminal offences on account of a mental disorder. Gavin also regularly represents CAMH before the Court of Appeal for Ontario and the Ontario Superior Court of Justice, and provides legal advice to CAMH clinicians and senior leadership. Gavin is also involved in policy work at CAMH, and assisted the hospital to draft its medical marijuana policy. Prior to joining CAMH in 2013, he spent six years as a criminal defence lawyer in Toronto.

Professor Bernard Le Foll
Laureate of the French Academy of Medicine
Medical Head, Addiction Medicine Service and Medical Withdrawal Service, Ambulatory Care and Structured Treatments, CAMH
Head, Alcohol Research and Treatment Clinic, Addiction Medicine Service, Ambulatory Care and Structured Treatments, CAMH

Head, Translational Addiction Research Laboratory, Campbell Family Mental Health Research Institute, CAMH
Professor, Department of Family and Community Medicine, Pharmacology Psychiatry and Institute of Medical Sciences
University of Toronto
Centre for Addiction and Mental Health
Toronto
Ontario
Canada

Bernard Le Foll, MD PhD MCFP is a clinician-scientist specialized in drug addiction. He is the Medical Head of the Addiction Medicine Service and Medical Withdrawal Service at the Centre for Addiction and Mental Health (CAMH). He is the Head of the Translational Addiction Research Laboratory within the Campbell Family Mental Health Research Institute of CAMH. He is a Professor at University of Toronto and holds several graduate faculty appointments. He received specialized training in drug addiction and behavioral and cognitive therapy in France, has written addiction treatment guidelines and various reviews on neurobiology and treatment of drug addiction. His research is funded by the Canadian Institutes of Health Research, the National Institutes of Health (NIH) and other funding agencies. He has been a consultant/advisor for CAMH, the Canadian Centre on Substance Abuse, the NIH and Health Canada.

CHAPTER 20

Kevin Reel
See Chapter 19

Rosanna Macri
Clinical and Organizational Ethicist
Whitby
Ontario
Canada

Rosanna Macri is currently the Ethicist at Ontario Shores Centre for Mental Health Sciences where she leads the Ethics subcommittee of the Medical Advisory Committee on Medical Assistance in Dying. She is also a member of the University of Toronto, Joint Centre for Bioethics' (JCB) Medical Assistance in Dying Implementation Task Force. Rosanna earned a Master of Health Science in Bioethics and completed an academic fellowship in Clinical and Organizational Ethics with the JCB. Rosanna holds a Bachelor of Science in Radiation Sciences and has worked as a Medical Radiation Therapist internationally. She has volunteered with a number of organizations including the Editorial Review Board for the American Society of

Radiation Technologists and is on the board of directors for St. Clair West Services for Seniors. Rosanna is a Lecturer in the Department of Radiation Oncology and the Dalla Lana School of Public Health at the University of Toronto.

Dr. Justine S Dembo
Psychiatrist
Los Angeles
California
USA

Justine S Dembo, MD, FRCPC is a psychiatrist trained at the University of Toronto now working in Los Angeles in private practice and at an intensive outpatient trauma program. Her research focus has been on medically assisted dying in patients with psychiatric illness, since 2009. She has several related publications and regularly gives talks on this topic. She is a member of Compassion and Choices in the United States, and of several Canadian organizations related to assisted dying, including the Physician Advisory Council at Dying With Dignity Canada. In her practice, she specializes in psychotherapy and medication management for Obsessive-Compulsive Disorder, anxiety disorders, and trauma-related disorders.

Sally Bean
Senior Ethicist and Policy Advisor
Toronto
Ontario
Canada

Sally Bean is the Director of the Ethics Centre and Policy Advisor at Sunnybrook Health Sciences Centre, an Adjunct Lecturer in the Dalla Lana School of Public Health and the Institute of Health Policy Management and Evaluation, and an Associate Member of the School of Graduate Studies at the University of Toronto. Sally is the co-chair of the University of Toronto Joint Centre for Bioethics Medical Assistance in Dying Implementation Task Force. Her research areas of interest pertain largely to health institution and health system ethics with an emphasis on health law and policy.

Dr. Ruby Rajendra Shanker
Fellow in Clinical and Organizational Bioethics
Joint Centre for Bioethics
University of Toronto
Toronto
Ontario
Canada

Ruby Shanker is an internationally trained physician with clinical experience in general and community medicine. She is a graduate of the Master of Health Sciences in Bioethics program at the University of Toronto's Joint Centre for Bioethics (JCB), where she is currently pursuing a Fellowship in Clinical and Organizational Bioethics. Ruby is a member of the JCB Medical Assistance in Dying Implementation Task Force and its mental health and addictions subgroup. Her wide range of bioethics interests include disability and rehabilitation ethics, organ donation and transplant ethics, clinical ethics in the acute care setting, research ethics, professional ethics, and medical ethics education. She is passionate about exploring cross-cultural competencies in healthcare, public engagement in healthcare via social media, as well as standards of practice and training related to the professionalization movement within healthcare ethics.

Lucy Costa
Deputy Director
Empowerment Council
Toronto
Ontario
Canada

Lucy Costa is a systemic advocate in a large psychiatric institution. Her work is focused on promoting the rights of mental health service users, as well as encouraging critical analysis about service user inclusion in the mental health sector. She sits on a number of advisories and has been involved with the consumer/psychiatric survivor community for over 20 years. She is currently completing her Master of Laws (LLM) at Osgoode Hall Law School, York University, Toronto, Canada.

Dr. Robyn Waxman
Geriatric Psychiatrist
Ontario Shores Centre for Mental Health Sciences
700 Gordon Street
Whitby
Ontario
Canada

Robyn Waxman is the medical director of the Geriatric and Neuropsychiatry Program and the electroconvulsive therapy service at Ontario Shores Centre for Mental Health Sciences. She received her medical degree from the University of Ottawa in 2005 and graduated as a geriatric psychiatrist from the University of Toronto in 2010, where she is now a lecturer in geriatric Psychiatry in the Department of Psychiatry. Robyn is a member of the Ontario Shores Medical Advisory Committee's Ethics Subcommittee on Medical Assistance in Dying.

CHAPTER 21

Jo Cooper
Macmillan Clinical Nurse Specialist in Palliative Care (retired)
Author and Editor
Horsham
West Sussex
England, UK

Jo Cooper spent 16 years in Specialist Palliative Care, initially working in a hospice inpatient unit, then 12 years as a Macmillan Clinical Nurse Specialist in Palliative Care. She gained a Diploma in Oncology at Addenbrooke's Hospital, Cambridge, and a BSc(Hons) in Palliative Nursing at The Royal Marsden, London, and an Award in Specialist Practice. Jo edited *Stepping into Palliative Care* (2000) and the 2nd Edition, *Stepping into Palliative Care 1: relationships and responses* (2006) *and Stepping into Palliative Care 2: care and practice* (2006), both published by Radcliffe Publishing, Oxford. Jo has been involved in teaching for many years and her specialist subjects include management of complex pain and symptoms, terminal agitation, communication at the end-of-life, therapeutic relationships, and breaking bad news. Current publications include: Cooper DB, Cooper J, editors. *Palliative Care within Mental Health: principles and philosophy.* Boca Raton, Florida: CRC Press; 2012. Cooper DB, Cooper J, editors. *Palliative Care within Mental Health: care and practice.* Boca Raton, Florida: CRC Press; 2014.

CHAPTER 22

David B Cooper
See About the editor

Special acknowledgement

Thank you to Jo Cooper, who has been actively involved with this project throughout – supporting, encouraging, listening, and participating in many practical ways. Thank you for all your hard work on these chapters . . . your key points are second to none! Jo is my rock who looks after me during my physical health problems, and I am eternally grateful. Thank you for managing my physical health challenges and making life worthwhile. Jo is the most caring, thoughtful, and compassionate person I know, and for that I am truly grateful.

Acknowledgements

I am grateful to all the contributors for having faith in me to produce a valued text and I thank them for their support and encouragement. Thank you to those who have commented along the way, and whose patience has been outstanding.

Many people have helped me along my career path and life – too many to name individually. Most do not even know what impact they have had on me. Some, however, require specific mention. These include Larry Purnell, a friend and confidant who has taught me never to presume – while we are all individuals with individual needs, we deserve equality in all that we meet in life. Thanks to Martin Plant (who sadly died in March 2010), and Moira Plant, who always encouraged and offered genuine support. Phil and Poppy Barker, who have taught me that it is okay to express how I feel about humanity – about people, and that there is another way through the entrenched systems in health and social care. Keith Yoxhall, without whose guidance back in the 1980s I would never have survived my 'Colchester work experience' and the dark times of institutionalisation, or had the privilege to work alongside the few professionals fighting against the 'big door'. He taught me that there was a need for education and training, and that this should be ongoing – also that the person in hospital or community experiencing our care sees us as 'professional' – we should make sure we act that way. Thank you to Phil Cooper, who brought the concept of this series of books to me. It was then I realised that despite all the talk over too many years of my professional life, there was still much to be done for people experiencing mental health–substance use problems. Phil is a good debater, friend, and reliable resource for me – thank you.

To George Zimmar, Senior Editor, Routledge, my sincere thanks. Thank you to Meira Bienstock, Editorial Assistant, for putting up with my too numerous questions! Thank you to the many others who are nameless to me as I write but without whom these books would never come to print; each has his or her stamp on any successes this book has.

My sincere thanks to all of you named, and unnamed, my friends and colleagues along my sometimes broken career path: those who have touched my life in a positive way – and a few, a negative way (for we can learn from the negative to ensure we do better for others).

Finally, any errors, omissions, inaccuracies or deficiencies within these pages are my sole responsibility.

Terminology

Whenever possible, the following terminology has been applied. However, in certain instances, when referencing a study and/or specific work, when an author has made a specific request, or for the purpose of additional clarity, it has been necessary to deviate from this applied 'norm'.

MENTAL HEALTH–SUBSTANCE USE

Considerable thought has gone in to the use of terminology within this text. Each country appears to have its own terms for the person experiencing a mental health and substance use problem – terms that include words such as dual diagnosis, coexisting, co-occurring, and so on. We talk about the same thing but use differing professional jargon. The decision was set at the beginning to use one term that encompasses mental health *and* substance use problems: *mental health–substance use.* One scholar suggested that such a term implies that both can exist separately, while they can also be linked (Barker, 2009)

SUBSTANCE USE

Another challenge was how to term 'substance use'. There are a number of ways: abuse, misuse, dependence, addiction. The decision is that within these texts we use the term *substance use* to encompass all (unless specific need for clarity at a given point). It is imperative the professional recognises that while we may see another person's 'substance use' as misuse or abuse, the individual experiencing it may not deem it to be anything other than 'use'. Throughout, we need to be aware that we are working alongside unique individuals. Therefore, we should be able to meet the individual where he or she is.

ALCOHOL, PRESCRIBED DRUGS, ILLICIT DRUGS, TOBACCO OR SUBSTANCES

Throughout this book *substance* includes alcohol, prescribed drugs, illicit drugs and tobacco, unless specific need for clarity at a given point.

PROBLEM(S), CONCERNS AND DILEMMAS OR DISORDERS

The terms *problem(s)*, *concerns and dilemmas*, and *disorders* can be used inter-changeably, as stated by the author's preference. However, where possible, the term 'problem(s)' or 'concerns and dilemmas' has been adopted as the preferred choice.

INDIVIDUAL, PERSON, PEOPLE

There seems to be a need to label the individual – as a form of recognition. Sometimes the label becomes more than the person! 'Alan is schizophrenic' – thus it is Alan, rather than an illness that Alan experiences. We refer to patients, clients, service users, customers, consumers, and so on. We need to be mindful that every person we see during our professional day is an individual – unique. Symptoms are in many ways similar (e.g. delusions, hallucinations), some interventions and treatments are similar (e.g. specific drugs, psychotherapy techniques), but people are not. Alan may experience an illness labelled schizophrenia, and so may John, Beth, and Mary, and you or I. However, each will have his or her own unique experiences – and life. None will be the same. To keep this constantly in the mind of the reader, throughout the book we shall refer to the **individual, person or people** – just like us, but different to us by their uniqueness.

PROFESSIONAL

In the eyes of the individual, we are all professionals, whether students, nurses, doctors, social workers, researchers, clinicians, educationalists, managers, service developers, religious ministers – and so on. However, the level of expertise may vary from one professional to another. We are also individuals. There is a need to distinguish between the person experiencing a mental health–substance use problem and the person interacting professionally (at whatever level) with that individual. To acknowledge and to differentiate between those who experience – in this context – and those who intervene, we have adopted the term **professional.** It is indicative that we have had, or are receiving, education and training related specifically to help us meet the needs of the individual. We may or may not have experienced substance use and/or mental health problems but we have some knowledge that may help the individual – an expertise to be shared. We have a specific knowledge that, hopefully, we wish to use to offer effective intervention and treatment to another human being. It is the need to make a clear differential, and for that purpose only, that forces the use of 'professional' over 'individual' to describe our role – our input into another person's life.

REFERENCE

Barker P. Personal communication; 2009.

Cautionary note

Wisdom and compassion should become the dominating influence that guide our thoughts, our words, and our actions.

(Ricard M, 2003)

Never presume that what you say is understood. It is essential to check understanding, and what is expected of the individual and/or family, with each person. Each person needs to know what he or she can expect from you, and other professionals involved in his or her care, at each meeting. Jargon is a professional language that excludes the individual and family. Never use it in conversation with the individual, unless requested to do so; it is easily misunderstood.

Remember, we all, as individuals, deal with life differently. It does not matter how many years we have spent studying human behaviour, listening and treating the individual and family. We may have spent many hours exploring with the individual his or her anxieties, fears, doubts, concerns and dilemmas, and the ill health experience. Yet, we do not know what that person really feels, how he or she sees life and ill health. We may have lived similar lives, experienced the same ill health but the individual will always be unique, each different from us, each independent of our thoughts, feelings, words, deeds and symptoms, each with an individual experience.

REFERENCE

Ricard Matthieu. As cited in: Föllmi D, Föllmi O. *Buddhist Offerings 365 Days*. London: Thames and Hudson, 2003.

CHAPTER 1

Setting the scene

David B Cooper

PRE-READING EXERCISE 1.1

Time: 20 minutes

When preparing to read this book you may wish to undertake the following exercise.

Write a brief description of your thoughts and feelings in relation to mental health–substance use problems and ethical issues that you think could arise. When you have read the book repeat the exercise, taking note of the following:

- Have your thoughts and feelings changed? If yes, in what way?
- What information do you feel most influenced that change? What did not?
- Are there any areas that you feel you need to investigate further? If yes, what are they? What resources will you need?
- Make a plan of action to develop your learning and understanding of mental health–substance use.

INTRODUCTION

The difficulties encountered by people who experience mental health–substance use problems are not new. The individual using substances presenting to the mental health professional can often encounter annoyance and suspicion. Likewise, the person experiencing mental health problems presenting to the substance use services can encounter hostility and hopelessness. 'We cannot do anything for the substance use problem until the mental health problem is dealt with!' The referral to the mental health team is returned: 'We cannot do anything for this person until the substance use problem is dealt with!' Thus, the individual is in the middle of two professional worlds and neither is willing to move, and yet, both professional worlds are involved in 'caring' for the individual.

SELF-ASSESSMENT EXERCISE 1.1

> **Time: 20 minutes**
> In your area of practice or management, how would you proceed in changing
> the above situation? What would you need:
> - to consider?
> - in terms of resources to change practice?

For many years, it has been acknowledged that the two parts of the caring system need to work as one. However, this desire has not developed into practice. Over recent years, the impetus has changed. There is now a drive towards meeting the needs of the individual experiencing mental health–substance use problems, pooling expertise from both sides. Moreover, there is an international political will to bring about change, often driven forward by a small group of dedicated professionals at practice level.

Some healthcare environments have merely paid lip service, ensuring the correct terminology is included within the policy and procedure documentation, while at the same time doing nothing, or little, to bring about the changes needed at the practice level to meet the needs of the individual. Others have grasped the drive forward and have spearheaded developments at local and national level within their country to meet such needs. It appears that the latter are now succeeding. There is a concerted international effort to improve the services provided for the individual, and a determination to pool knowledge and expertise. In addition, there is the ability of these professional groups to link into government policy and bring about the political will to support such change. However, this cannot happen overnight. There are major attitudinal and ethical changes needed – not least at management and practice level. One consultant commented that to work together with mental health–substance use problems would be too costly. Furthermore, the consultant believed it would create 'too much work'! Consequently, there is a long way to go – but a driving force to succeed exists.

Obtaining in-depth and knowledgeable text is difficult in new areas of change. One needs to be motivated to trawl a broad spectrum of work to develop a sound foundation – the background detail that is needed to build good professional practice. This is a big request of the hard-worked and pressured professional. There are a few excellent mental health–substance use books available. However, this series of seven books, of which this is the last, is ground-breaking, in that each presents a much needed text that will introduce the last, but vital, step to the interventions and treatments available for the individual experiencing mental health–substance use problems.

These books are educational. However, they will make no one an expert! In mental health–substance use, there is a need to initiate, and maintain, education and training. There are key ethical principles and factors we need to bring out and explore. Some we will use – others we will adapt – while others we will reject. Each book is complete. Conversely, each aims to build on the preceding book. However, books *do not* hold all the answers. Nothing does. What is hoped is that the professional will participate in, and collaborate with, each book, progressing through each to the other. Along the way, hopefully, the professional will enhance existing knowledge or develop new concepts to benefit the individual.

The books offer a first step, relevant to the needs of professionals – at practice level or senior service development – in a clear, concise, and understandable format. Each book has made full use of boxes, graphs, tables, figures, interactive exercises, self-assessment tools, and case studies – where appropriate – to examine and demonstrate the impact mental health–substance use can have on the individual, family, carers, and society as a whole.

A deliberate attempt has been made to avoid jargon, and where terminology is used, to offer a clear explanation and understanding. The terminology used in this book is fully explained at the beginning of each book, before the reader commences with the chapters. By placing it there the reader will be able to reference it quickly, if needed. Specific gender is used, as the author feels appropriate. However, unless stated, the use of the male or female gender is interchangeable.

BOOK 7: ETHICS IN MENTAL HEALTH–SUBSTANCE USE

The ability to learn and gain new knowledge is the way forward. As professionals we must start with knowledge, and from there we can begin to understand. We commence using our new-found skills, progressing to developing the ability to examine practice, to put concepts together and to make valid judgements. This knowledge is gained through education, training and experience, enhanced by own life experiences.

Those we offer care to, and their family members, bring their own knowledge, skills and life experiences, some developed from dealing with ill health. Therefore, in order to make interventions and treatment outcome effective requires mutual understanding and respect.

KEY POINT 1.1

Listening fully to the pain of another enables understanding. Understanding and acknowledging the person, pain or problems enables us to practice the art of truly helping and caring. Ultimately, this is the fundamental principal of the therapeutic encounter (Jo Cooper, 2016, Personal Communication).

In this book, primarily we:

➤ explore the comprehensive concerns and dilemmas occurring from, and in, mental health–substance use practice, management, service development and professionally

➤ inform, develop and educate by sharing knowledge and enhancing expertise in this fast-developing interrelated experience of ethical, psychological, physical, social, legal and spiritual need.

The analogy of the house purchaser sums up the approach of the editor and authors when writing this book. Once a property is identified, we need to find out more before we invest further – the first step is to visit the property. On arrival, we quickly grasp a view of the surrounding area, the look of the outside of the house and its grounds. Here we make the decision to enter the property to find out more – or we leave. It is hoped that the reader of this book will stay! The book takes the reader through the front door of mental health–substance use, for some that will be all that is needed, for a decision to be made, and they will proceed to *own the property*. Others will need more information or guidance on the many and diverse approaches to mental health–substance use.

Once we have decided to purchase the property, we look closer and decide what needs updating to meet our needs, what has to be removed, and what needs rebuilding. We decide not to paper over the cracks because this is our property! Providing and developing services in mental health–substance use is not different to this approach. We need to explore what is good about the service provided to date, how this can be improved, what needs revamping, what services, and people, do we need to make the vision work, what must be replaced, and who is best placed to undertake this work effectively.

We look at what is around – we shop for concepts and the functions and facilities that are best for the people we meet, and to whose needs we must relate to. We then plan how we are going to undertake this organisation and when, and how, the changes can be implemented. Once we have a clear idea what is required, we implement – put into practice – the plans.

Then we leave it for years on end untouched! Do we? Should we? Services, like properties, need constant monitoring – they cannot merely be left until we are forced to do something – until they are damaged. Therefore, we must continually monitor and evaluate the service provision. From here, we can develop, build on new services, and update existing services. What we must not forget is that there are people at the end of these change processes who need us, the professionals, to make the right decision, for and with them, at all stages.

We can never know all there is to know. There is always the need to remain open-minded in the approaches to the individuals needs and expectations. It is essential that we are open minded to the many differing ways we can bring about change, and how we can access new information and knowledge. This applies in terms of both self-learning, and the way we approach interventions with those who are in need of advice, and guidance. In this book, each chapter provides direction to further learning, and exploration.

Many learned professionals are willing to share what they know, and listen to the knowledge and advice of others. It is hoped that this introduction to ethics in mental health–substance use will stimulate us to 'purchase the property', to take full ownership of service delivery, concerns and dilemmas for the individual in need of therapeutic interventions and treatments resulting from problems related to his or her, or someone else's, experiences of mental health–substance use.

From the outset, and at all levels of the health and social care process, the manager and the service developer play a pivotal role in ensuring that care and quality interventions and treatment are achieved. What he or she does at that point depends on his or her knowledge, skills, and attitudes. Moreover, it requires that these professionals acknowledge their responsibility to use the knowledge of others when providing the best services for the individual experiencing mental health–substance use problems.

To have knowledge and skill, there is a need to know something about the bigger picture, and how that fits into the care of the individual, the family, and carer(s) on whose lives it will impact. Once we have that information, there is a need to know how to develop these services so as to maximise the intervention. To fully comprehend, and understand, we then need to appreciate what it is like to be on the receiving end of these interventions – only then can a service be developed to address the individuals' needs.

It is one thing to look after the person with the physical, psychological, emotional, spiritual, social, and/or legal problems, but there is an inbuilt need to care for the professional who provides that care. By so doing, the good manager has a direct impact on the professionalism of the person providing the intervention.

These books are primarily for the student, junior and senior manager, administrator, and service developer, policy providers and commissioners. In addition, the ward manager, team manager, and clinician need to have some knowledge of how services come to being, the impact that has on them, what steps he or she can take to improve the lot for his- or her-self, others, and the individual with the health issue. Therefore, these books have relevance to educators and students as well as those providing and developing services in mental health–substance use that focus on the therapeutic relationship (*see* Book 4, Chapter 2).

Senior managers, service developers, and ward-based professionals need to understand the experiences of the individual and family, and accept their individual needs without judgement. Moreover, there is a need to understand what factors, beyond the mental health–substance use concerns and dilemmas, affect their lives and influence the services they need. This cannot be achieved without involving the individual, the family, and the carer(s) who also experience the concerns and dilemmas associated with mental health–substance use, at all levels of the service development, provision, and ongoing practices.

There is a trend towards 'targets'. This appears to have taken over from the care of the individual to the extent that meeting the target(s) takes precedence. A recent number of experiences highlighted this fact for the author while on an orthopaedic ward. The professionals involved in the care were excellent. However, the demands for bed space precluded care of the individual. The responsibility to 'clear beds', lay heavily with the ward professionals, who had a number of people in a cramped space waiting for 'the bed'. This meant that the individual could progress to theatre without knowing where he or she would eventually be. The anxiety this provoked to vacate beds was the primary focus – taking care away from the individual. Hence, we employ the ward-based professional to 'bed care' and not 'individual care'. When planning services, the good manager ensures that the ward-based professional is employed to do what he or she is best trained to do – otherwise 'care' becomes counter-productive.

In this seventh book we examine the ethical issues, from an international perspective, facing the professional on a daily basis, and the development of ethical care and practice. This cannot be done by merely saying 'this is ethically correct'. To consider what is ethically correct – or not – we do need to take into account our culture and belief systems. There is no internationally accepted way of deciding what may be ethically correct – or not - which can complicate the subject for the professional and those deciding what services can and should be provided.

Chapters 2 and 3 review practical ethical frameworks that can be used to guide practice and ensure that the best interests of the individual are always the focus of our care.

This book, as a whole, looks at these aspects of ethical practice. It does not take into account your own belief systems or consideration you might have to make to decide on ethical practice. What is hoped is to provide the reader with an overview of ethical practice, from an individual professional perspective, and how these concerns and dilemmas may be encountered, what considerations need to be given to that ethical practice and overcome our anxieties of what ethics means to us on a daily basis.

CONCLUSION

Referring to the analogy above, it is hoped that this book is helpful and informative. One would hope that we feel sufficiently stimulated to proceed, having extended and developed this grounding in mental health–substance use. Now that the basics have been explored, we can build upon our knowledge using the 'To Learn More', section in each chapter as a guide to further study and knowledge. As one enters each new area of knowledge (each new room), so understanding improves of what is needed – and what is not. With that comes the ability to use an open, non-judgemental, and accepting approach to the problems identified by the individual presenting for intervention, treatment, advice, or guidance.

Our knowledge and understanding constantly change. What we believe to be ethically correct one day may be unethical on the next, as does the way we look at our ethical practices. The challenge is to remain open and accessible to the knowledge and information that will help each of us provide appropriate therapeutic interventions:

➤ at the appropriate level of expertise
➤ at the appropriate time
➤ at the appropriate level of understanding of the individual, and her or his presenting concerns and dilemmas
➤ at the appropriate cost.

We cannot afford to be cocooned in our belief that all individuals are the same. If this book encourages us to be wise in the development and provision of services, then it has achieved its aim. If it helps us to appreciate some of the problems encountered by the individual, family, and carer(s) – we have 'purchased the property', and can now bring about much needed changes for the individual experiencing mental health–substance use problems.

REFERENCE

Adapted with the kind permission of the editor from © Cooper DB. 2011. Setting the Scene. In *Mental Health–Substance Use book series,* edited by DB Cooper. Chapter 1. Boca Raton, Florida: CRC Press.

CHAPTER 2

What is ethics?

Michael Robertson and Edwina Light

INTRODUCTION

Since antiquity, humans have grappled with the question 'how do I live a good life?' Socratic dialogues, Confucian teachings or Qur'an texts, inter alia, have offered some guidance over time, although what we now endorse as Western moral philosophy is a product of the European Enlightenment. The descriptor 'ethical' has connotations of rectitude, goodness, legality or right-eousness, yet these are fallacies.

KEY POINT 2.1

In a number of circumstances, the issue of 'what is ethical' is at odds with 'what is legal'.

In essence, ethics is a process of formulating thought and action in accord-ance with a notion of a set of values. Whether these values are acquired by religion or secular rational thought is not critical, but rather how they enable the moral agent to formulate responses to questions of moral deliberation.

Values are conceptually prior to ethics. As such, the maxims or rules out-lined in professional, organisational or institutional codes of ethical conduct require a clear and coherent conceptualisation of values. Examples of such values in a health care setting have included respect for the individual's autonomy, tenets of best practice, and advocacy. From these emerge moral prescriptions such as 'always utilise best practice' or 'always respect a person's right to refuse or modify consent to treatment'.

Theories of ethics are either descriptive or normative. Descriptive ethical theories aim to define 'what is', whereas normative theories aim to define 'what should be'. A relatively new discipline of empirical ethics allows analysis of the ethical conduct of different groups or communities in order to provide a comprehensive description of what is regarded as ethical conduct of exemplary or typical members of the group. This enables an 'idiographic' (unique to individuals or specific groups) model of values (axiology) to be developed and support the formulation of maxims or codes of conduct. By contrast, the grand normative theories of ethics, such as utilitarianism or deontic ethics, seek to generate 'nomothetic' (generalizable) accounts of moral philosophy

While descriptive ethics are problematic in that they may lack solid foundations other than what has emerged out of a culture or society as it 'is', normative ethics suffer the problem of justifying 'shoulds' and 'oughts'. The Scottish philosopher David Hume argued that most humans act ethically in response to their emotions, not their thoughts or values and as such, 'shoulds' and 'oughts' could not be defined (Hume 1751/1998). Normative ethics do, however, attempt rational definitions of 'shoulds', based upon various methods of reasoning, a process that the English utilitarian philosopher RM Hare described as 'prescriptivism' (Hare 1963).

In this chapter we will consider how descriptive ethics can be formulated and then provide brief accounts of the most commonly applied normative ethical theories in mental health and drug and alcohol practice.

DESCRIPTIVE ETHICS

Athenian philosopher Aristotle's *Nicomachean Ethics* (Aristotle 1998) was the first attempt at empirical ethics. Aristotle's project sought to identify the habits and dispositions of great men in Athenian society. Contemporary descriptive ethics rely on more evolved empirical methods of enquiry from a range of disciplines, such as sociology, psychology, medicine, public health, epidemiology, and economics (Borry et al. 2004). In a typical approach to empirical ethics, a selection of members of a particular group participates in interviews, focus groups or other techniques of data acquisition. This data is then analysed using methods that attempt to systematically refine the observations into a more structured account of the values evident in their speech or written acts. Through a process of further analysis, the data is used to construct an idiographic account of the value system of the group. Empirical ethics seeks to focus on 'ethics in action' (Borry et al. 2004), bringing us closer to the 'detail of everyday life' (Carter 2009).

KEY POINT 2.2

Empirical ethics seeks to inform, contextualize, and challenge normative claims by providing insights into what 'is', rather than solely dictating what 'ought' to be.

Case Study 2.1

A professional organization of drug and alcohol counsellors resolves to publish a code of ethics for their members. The executive of the group decides to apply an empirical approach to the process and a research group is recruited to conduct the research. After a series of in-depth individual interviews and focus groups of a sample of the organization that is varied for numerous demographic, professional, and clinical practice descriptors, the research group analyzes the data and refines a series of thematic categories that reflect a set of values for the group. This draft set of values is circulated to all members of the group for comment. The executive committee drafts a series of maxims based upon the themes identified in the research that form the basis of a published code of ethics for the group.

A common value identified among professional groups is that of respect for a person's right to refuse treatment.

Case Study 2.2

A member of the aforementioned professional group is the subject of a written complaint by the family of a person participating in counselling for problem drinking. In the course of therapy, the counsellor identified that the person was competent in that they did not exhibit features of an organic brain syndrome based on alcohol abuse. The person stated that he did not have any motivation to change his drinking behaviour and that he was only attending counselling at the insistence of his family. He was aware of deranged liver function tests and at least one episode of pancreatitis, however he indicated that he had no wish to change his drinking behaviour and that he saw no point in continuing therapy. His therapist discharged him from therapy, much to the chagrin of the family. The professional organisation's disciplinary committee considered the situation and agreed that the therapist had, in respecting the man's right to refuse, acted in accordance with the principle of 'respecting client choices' in their code of ethics.

NORMATIVE ETHICS

Normative ethical theories posit generalizable rules for moral conduct based upon core, inviolable assumptions. These vary from theory to theory, although all of the currently endorsed normative theories have emerged since the European Enlightenment and are based upon human rationality and the assumption of autonomy as a form of rational self-governance. Robertson and Walter (2013) have argued for a taxonomy of different normative ethical theories (*see* Box 2.1).

BOX 2.1 Normative ethical theories – taxonomy

A Instrumental approaches
These apply a particular method to enable a decision or 'output':
1 Utilitarian ethics – based upon maximising preferences;
2 The ethics of duty – based upon fulfilment of duties in good will;
3 The four principles – based upon deliberating prima facie conflicts between principles;
4 Casuistry – similar to legal case-based reasoning and normative analogy;
5 Common morality theory – based upon evaluation in light of a series of values held generally in the community.

B Reflective approaches
These promote reflection upon a situation and developing an approach to a problem coherent with the moral agent's value system:
6 Virtue ethics – based upon a process of arriving at a 'golden mean' of actions in light of a series of defined virtues;
7 The ethics of care – a process of reflecting on a principle of emotional or filial bonds rather than impersonal rules;
8 The ethics of the 'Other' – an approach derived from post-War continental philosophy that emphasises obligation to the 'Other' as a moral imperative.

C Integrative approaches
These place a series of foundational ideas into a particular political or socio-cultural perspective.
9 'Political' ethics and the Rawlsian approach to justice in mental health – applying principles of social contract and Kantian ethics into a process of distributive justice;
10 'Post-modern' ethics or 'Anti-modern' ethics – challenge Enlightenment based ideas and seek to emphasis the individual's capacity to evolved individual and contextualised, relative ethical systems.

UTILITARIANISM

One of the questions that has challenged moral philosophers over time is that of defining the 'good life'. For Aristotle, the '*summum bonum*' (highest good) was human reason, although more fundamental formulations, such as that of pre-Socratic philosopher Epicurus (1926), have involved maximising pleasure, best considered as an 'absence of pain', what is now considered 'ethical hedonism'. The philosophy of 'consequentialism' takes the position that the merit of any act is evident in its ultimate consequences. When integrated with ethical hedonism, this approach to moral philosophy held that the merit of any act was the amount of overall pleasure it generated. This was the philosophy of utilitarianism. Utilitarianism was first articulated by English philosopher Jeremy Bentham (1970/1823), who argued that all humans were beholden to a form of hedonism, and as such, any moral and political philosophy should aim to maximize pleasure within the population. Bentham's, somewhat vulgar, form of utilitarianism argued it was better to be a contented pig than an unhappy human. It may be that there is a survival advantage for species which practice utilitarian approaches in that elevating collective over individual needs may help groups thrive in challenging settings of threat or environmental adversity (Singer 1981). Indeed, Canadian philosopher Kymlicka has argued utilitarianism has been so dominant as a moral philosophy in the modern era, that it represents the theoretical starting point for all ethical considerations (Kymlicka 2002).

One of the main problems with Bentham's hedonistic utilitarianism is the 'quantification problem' (Williams 1973). That is, how do we quantify the level of pleasure achieved by a moral act? English philosopher John Stuart Mill tried to grapple with this problem by emphasising that cultural, intellectual, and spiritual pleasures are of greater value than physical pleasures in the eyes of a 'competent judge' (Mill 1968, 1859/1975), whereas English philosopher GE Moore argued that maximising 'ideals', like aestheticism or love, are preferable to mere pleasure (Moore 1903/1988). The solution to the quantification problem came with the emergence of the notion of 'preference utilitarianism', advanced largely by controversial Australian philosopher Peter Singer (1993). Singer argued that an individual's or group's preferences should be the focus of a utilitarian deliberation, rather than the simple gratification of pleasures.

Preference utilitarianism is not without its problems, particularly the challenges of 'adaptive preferences', whereby gratification of people's preferences is compromised in that they tend to accept less, because of modest expectations (such as the 'parable of the contented slave' – Elster 1982). 'Unexperienced preferences' (i.e. ones we will never know existed) and 'harmful preferences' (Kymlicka 2002) also create problems in utilitarian deliberations. The 'replaceability problem' (Foot 1967) is based upon a thought experiment involving the utilitarian justification of one healthy person being killed to provide transplant organs for a half a dozen others in need – clearly a situation where the preferences of six people exceed that of the 'donor' (Williams 1973).

English philosopher RM Hare, a prominent utilitarian, distinguished between two levels of utilitarian thinking. The first is the 'critical' level of thinking, applying the 'golden-rule argument' (do unto others that which you would have done to you). The second level of utilitarian thinking is the 'intuitive' level that utilizes simple consequentialist principles (Hare 1997).

The distinction between intuitive and critical levels has evolved into 'Act' and 'Rule' utilitarianism (Smart 1973). Act utilitarianism is where the moral agent decides to act on the basis of what is most likely to maximise utility in a particular instance. 'Rule utilitarianism', by contrast, is more prescriptive and has the moral agent acting relative to the notion of maximising preferences generally, rather than in regards to the specific instance.

Case Study 2.3

A director of a mental health service faces budget constraints and is tasked with winding down clinical services to contain costs. She has to deliberate between an early intervention program for pregnant women with chemical dependency or a court diversion program for offenders with substance use problems. Both programs are well regarded and effective, however, it is clear that the high long-term recidivism rate for individuals passing through the court diversion program indicates that it is not as cost effective as the early intervention program for pregnant women. After a cost analysis, the service director arrives at a decision that the preferences of the community are best gratified through continuing the preventative maternal and infant health program. The court diversion program is discontinued, to considerable protest within the service and the families of many of the young offenders who engage the court diversion program.

DEONTIC ETHICS

The term 'Deontic' refers to one's duty. The ethics of duty, or deontic ethics, emerge from the work of the eighteenth century Köningsberg philosopher, Immanuel Kant. Kant's moral philosophy is outlined in his three main works: *Groundwork for the Metaphysics of Morals* (1785) (Kant 1785/1997); *Critique of Practical Reason* (1787) (Kant 1787/1997); and *Metaphysics of Morals* (1797) (Kant 1797/1996). Kant's primary ethical question was, 'what ought I do?'. Kant viewed human reason as the essence of the good life. Kant sought principles of action, which could be adopted by anyone in any context. Kant differentiated between so-called 'perfect' duties, which are required of all moral agents at all times, and 'imperfect duties'. The latter refers to not neglecting our duties to others in need.

KEY POINT 2.3

Kant defined 'autonomy' as the capacity for free, rational moral choice – the ability of a person to formulate his or her own laws of morality, what he referred to as 'practical reason'.

In Kant's 'Kingdom of Ends' each moral agent is both a moral self-legislator and beholden to a common law. Kant did not believe individual autonomy trumped the rule of law. Kant rejected any other basis of moral agency, such as emotions or filial bonds. To Kant, the moral agent acts upon 'good will' or dedication to duty. The moral worth of an act is its basis in good will. Kant had no concern for intentions or consequences.

Duty is defined in Kant's ethics as the 'Categorical Imperative' (CI), articulated in the *Groundwork*. Kant argued that we develop maxims that guide our moral decisions. The universalizability of any moral maxim is tested against the CI.

The Categorical Imperative (CI) has multiple formulations

1   The First Formulation articulates the principle of universalizability by directing:
    'Act only according to that maxim whereby you can at the same time will that it should become a universal law' (421).
2   The Second Formulation of the CI is the injunction:
    'Act as if the maxim of your action were to become through your will a universal law of nature' (421).
3   Kant's Third Formulation of the CI is often dubbed 'the formula of humanity'. It reads:
    'Act in such a way that you treat humanity, whether in your own person or in the person of another, always at the same time as an end and never simply as a means' (429).
    The latter is usually acknowledged as the most important of Kant's ethics.

In an appendix to *Critique of Practical Reason* Kant (1787/1997) wrote of the specific example of lying. The article, 'On a supposed right to lie from altruistic motives', poses the question of the 'enquiring murderer'. Kant argues that a well-intentioned lie to the murderer may have unintended harmful consequences, even though the lie was to protect the murderer's intended victim. In this instance, the truth has been diminished and the consequences catastrophic.

KEY POINT 2.4

For Kant, a lie (or any other violation of a maxim of duty) may have desirable consequences, but does not occur in accordance with good will and is therefore unethical.

Case Study 2.4

A professional caring for a patient with a history of intravenous opiate abuse becomes aware that she has shared a needle with another user. The woman is psychologically quite fragile and does not tolerate bad news well. The professional is concerned about the possibility of *human immunodeficiency virus* (HIV) infection and orders a test to confirm his suspicions, with her consent. The result returns positive; however, she becomes profoundly anxious waiting for the result. When asked if the result is available, the physician decides to delay by telling the woman the result is still pending, in order to help build her resilience. The person then shares a needle with another user who is HIV negative, who as a result acquires HIV.

PRINCIPLES BASED ETHICS

The Scottish physician and philosopher WD Ross argued that ethical duties were related to a clinician's responsibilities to particular irreducible ethical principles (Ross 1939). Building on this foundation, American bioethicists Beauchamp and Childress (2001) outlined four principles upon which to deliberate moral dilemmas:

1 **Respect for autonomy**: respecting the decision-making capacities of people and enabling individuals to make reasoned informed choices
2 **Beneficence**: considering the balance of benefits of treatment against the risks and costs so as to act in a way that benefits the individual
3 **Non-maleficence**: avoiding causing harm to the person, or at least harm disproportionate to the benefits of treatment
4 **Justice**: distributing benefits, risks, and costs fairly and treating individuals in similar positions in a similar manner.

Any ethical quandary involves the formulation of two of the four principles in a *prima facie* conflict. Most of the conflicts mediated by the four principles involve clashes between the principal of autonomy versus beneficence. As noted in the previous section on 'Deontic ethics' and Kant, autonomy is the principle of individual self-rule or self-governance. It is now enshrined in the liberties and rights of modern liberal states. In the moral philosophy of Beauchamp and Childress there are at least four aspects to autonomy (Feinberg 1989):

1 The capacity to govern oneself
2 The actual condition of self-government
3 A personal ideal, and
4 A set of rights expressive of one's sovereignty over oneself.

Beauchamp and Childress (2001) contend that all theories of autonomy accord with the issues of liberty and agency. While autonomy is ostensibly on a par with the other principles, it tends to prevail in *prima facie* conflicts (Dawson and Garrard 2006).

Case Study 2.5

A drug and alcohol professional provides care and support for an older man who is alcohol dependent. The man demonstrates increasing neglect of his health and his finances and has been ejected from a number of accommodations. His alcohol use affects his judgement and rational thinking and it is becoming increasingly apparent that he does not intend to cease his drinking behaviour. The professional suspects that the man is not capable of making competent decisions, but is troubled by the situation. Applying the four principles approach, she sees a prima facie tension between her obligations to respect the man's autonomous choice to drink and compromise his welfare and her obligation to act beneficently. She arranges a medical examination, which determines the man is not competent to administer his affairs due to alcoholic dementia and she proceeds to place his financial affairs under a form of guardianship or power of attorney.

VIRTUE ETHICS

The concept of virtue is clearly outlined in Aristotle's *Nicomachean Ethics* (Aristotle 1998) as: 'a settled disposition of the mind determining the choice of actions and emotions, consisting essentially in the observance of the mean relative to us . . . as the prudent man would determine it' (*see* Aristotle, *The Nicomachean Ethics*, Book 2, Ch. 6).

Aristotle determined that the definitive character of mankind was the capacity for reason. Happiness was found in the life of rational excellence. The good life was that of the good citizen, who strove for excellence in his or her particular role. The Aristotelian concept of virtue is a habit of choosing the 'golden mean' between the extremes. In the case of justice, for example, the golden mean lies between being excessively generous or forgiving and being excessively harsh or austere. The four cardinal virtues of antiquity were justice, temperance, prudence, and phronesis (practical wisdom).

More modern conceptions of virtue ethics are found in the work of Scottish philosopher Alisdair MacIntyre (1984, 1988, 1990), who developed further the concept of the socially situated, contextualized virtue. MacIntyre noted that in Athenian society, the concept of the 'good' related to a citizen's discharging of their allotted social functions within the *polis*. MacIntyre's concept of practical wisdom considers practices, which are the exercise of human excellence in the pursuit of a collectively defined good.

Others writing in the clinical ethics space have elaborated checklists of desirable virtues in clinicians, for example Beauchamp and Childress (2001) list compassion, discernment, trustworthiness, integrity, and conscientiousness, whereas Engelhardt (1996) lists tolerance, liberality, and prudence as virtues required of a clinician.

ETHICS OF CARE

American psychologist Lawrence Kohlberg conducted a series of studies of latency age and adolescent boys to identify patterns of moral development (Kohlberg 1981). Kohlberg argued that younger children behave according to socially acceptable norms under threat of punishment. Older children exhibit a form of psychological egoism before evolving understanding of a social contract.

KEY POINT 2.5

Gilligan argues that morality is better defined as occurring within a network of caring relationships, or what she terms 'situation attuned perceptions' to the needs of others.

Carole Gilligan (1982, 1987) argued against Kohlberg's finding, stating that his entirely male sample provided misleading findings and that moral development in females revealed that they are more focused on caring and social relationships. Beyond this, Nel Noddings (1984) focused upon the limits of abstract moral theories and how the 'ethics of care' may add to the perspective of the moral agent. Moral actions are motivated by care and not by abstract notions of what is right, which revisits Hume's original argument (*see* 'Introduction' Chapter 2). From the perspective of care ethics, the moral agent reflects upon a network of caring relationships as a context to moral agency and in particular, acknowledges its motivating and shaping influences on ethical behaviour.

PROFESSIONAL ETHICS

Over the past few decades, health care has evolved into a major economic enterprise, representing one of the major public spending commitments in many communities. As a consequence, clinical practice is subject increasingly to legal or governmental regulation, often overshadowing ethical deliberation. From this has emerged the necessity for reformulation of professional ethics. The *Oxford English Dictionary* (1993) defines a profession as:

An occupation whose core element is work, based on the mastery of a complex body of knowledge and skills. It is a vocation in which knowledge of some department of science or learning, or the practice of an art founded on it, is used in the service of others. Its members profess a commitment to competence, integrity, morality, altruism, and the promotion of the public good within their domain. These commitments form the basis of a social contract between a profession and society, which in return grants the profession autonomy in practice and the privilege of self-regulation. Professions and their members are accountable to those served and to society.

Within this comprehensive account are the elements of professional ethics – a group possessed of certain knowledge and skills, and the beneficent application of those skills in exchange for autonomous self-regulation and social status. This interrogates the concept of social contract theory.

Social contract theory ('contractarian ethics') is predicated on the notion that humans will ultimately act in their self-interest – an approach referred to as 'psychological egoism'. Professional ethics represent a variant of this contractarian approach to moral agency. Social contract ethics involves rational individuals choosing to abide by agreements about modes of conduct in a social system.

The original notion of social contract theory came from the work of English philosopher Thomas Hobbes in his most significant work, *Leviathan* (Hobbes 1651/(1985)). Hobbes postulated that without a social contract – a condition described as 'the state of nature' – life would be characterised by anarchy, murder, conflict, theft, and other depredations. In this state of nature, no one competitor is likely to triumph. In the light of this, rational choosers would realise their self-interest to be best served by entering into agreements with other competitors to renounce their right to predation and submit to the authority of the sovereign to enforce the contract.

Professional ethics involves a social contract between the profession and society, involving the service of the collective good through the practice of a craft in a desirable or laudable manner (Cruess and Cruess 1997).

KEY POINT 2.6

Professional ethics, arguably, has three core components: specialized training and the acquisition of specialized skills; the provision of expert assistance to those in need and the vulnerable; and the virtues of trustworthiness, efficacy, and knowledge which ultimately enhance the common good and aggregate well-being (Fullinwider 1996).

A particular problem with this approach is what is defined as a common or collective good. There is potential for significant ethical tension as it is possible that an expected action in the interests of a collective good may be deleterious to the individual. History is littered with many examples of malignantly populist, authoritarian or totalitarian regimes that co-opt professions into a process of exclusion or oppression of groups. The use of psychiatric labels to discredit political opponents of the regime in the former Soviet Union (Bloch and Reddaway 1983) or the murder of the disabled in Nazi Germany (Friedlander 1995) are two particular examples of the use of professional skills to serve the collective 'good' of a community at the expense of a smaller group within the community.

Case Study 2.6

A professional receives a request from a probation and parole officer to provide counselling for a man convicted of repeat drink-driving offences. The man's conditional release from custody involves his regular participation in such counselling and his maintaining sobriety. As part of the request, the professional is expected to report on progress and specifically to notify the parole board of any default on attendance or resumption of drinking. In the course of therapy, the man discloses to the professional that he has had a small amount of alcohol on several occasions, but requests that this not be disclosed. The professional, realising he faces a clear dilemma is compelled to report the man by law, clearly in conflict with the ethical principle of confidentiality. The professional reports the indiscretion otherwise he would be guilty of a breach of the law and would face criminal sanction himself.

CONCLUSION

In this chapter we have attempted to identify the concept of 'what is ethics' and demonstrate through case examples how different approaches to moral deliberation may assist clinicians working with people living with mental illnesses and dealing with addictions and chemical dependency syndromes. More specific consideration of applied ethical dilemmas are found in later chapters.

REFERENCES

Aristotle. 1998. *The Nicomachean Ethics*. Translated by D Ross. Edited by J Akrill and J Urmson. Oxford: Oxford University Press.

Beauchamp TL and JF Childress. 2001. *Principles of Biomedical Ethics* (5th ed.). New York: Oxford University Press.

Bentham J. 1970/1823. *An Introduction to the Principles of Morals and Legislation*, edited by JH Burns and HLA Hart. London: Althone Press.

Bloch S and P Reddaway. 1983. *Soviet Psychiatric Abuse*. London: Gollancz.

Borry P, P Schotmans and K Dierickx. 2004. "What is the role of empirical research in bioethical reflection and decisionmaking? An ethical analysis." *Medicine, Health Care and Philosophy* 7: 41–53.

Carter S. 2009. "Beware Dichotomies and Grand Abstractions: Attending to Particularity and Practice in Empirical Bioethics." *The American Journal of Bioethics* 9: 76–7.

Cruess R and S Cruess. 1997. "Teaching medicine as a profession in the service of healing." *Academic Medicine* 72: 941–52.

Dawson A and E Garrard. 2006. "In defence of moral imperialism: four equal and universal prima facie principles." *Journal of Medical Ethics* 32: 200–4.

Elster J. 1982. "Utilitarianism and the genesis of wants." In *Utilitarianism and Beyond*, edited by A Sen and B Williams, 219–38. Cambridge: Cambridge University Press.

Engelhardt HT. 1996. *The Foundations of Bioethics* (2nd ed.). New York: Oxford University Press.

Epicurus. 1926. "Letter to Menoeceus." In *The Extant Remains*. Oxford: The Clarendon Press.

Feinberg J. 1989. "Autonomy." In *The Inner Citadel: Essays on Individual Autonomy*, edited by J Christman, 27–53. New York: Oxford University Press.

Foot P. 1967. "Abortion and the doctrine of double effect." *Oxford Review* 5: 28–41.

Friedlander H. 1995. *The Origins of Nazi Genocide: From Euthanasia to the Final Solution*. Chapel Hill, NC: University of North Carolina Press.

Fullinwider R. 1996. "Professional codes and moral understanding." In *Codes of Ethics and the professions*, edited by M Coady and S Bloch. Melbourne: Melbourne University Press.

Gilligan C. 1982. *In a Different Voice: Psychological Theory and Women's Development*. Cambridge, MA: Harvard University Press.

Gilligan C. 1987. "Moral orientation and moral development." In *Women and Moral Theory*, edited by E Feder-Kittay and D Myers. Ottawa: Rowman and Littlefield.

Hare RM. 1963. *Freedom and Reason*. London: Oxford University Press.

Hare RM. 1997. "A Philosophical Self Portrait." In *The Penguin Dictionary of Philosophy*, edited by T Mautner, 234–5. London: Penguin.

Hobbes T (Ed.). 1651/1985. *Leviathan*. Edited by C Macpherson. London: Penguin.

Hume D. 1751/1998. *An Enquiry Concerning the Principles of Morals – The Clarendon Edition of the Works of David Hume*. Edited by TL Beauchamp. Oxford: Oxford University Press.

Kant I. 1785/1997. *Groundwork for the Metaphysics of Morals*. Translated by M Gregor. Cambridge: Cambridge University Press.

Kant I. 1787/1997. *Critique of Practical Reason*. Translated by M Gregor. Cambridge: Cambridge University Press.

Kant I. 1797/1996. *The Metaphysics of Morals*. Translated by M Gregor. Cambridge: Cambridge University Press.

Kohlberg L. 1981. *Essays on Moral Development, Vol. I: The Philosophy of Moral Development*. New York: Harper and Row.

Kymlicka W. 2002. *Contemporary Political Philosophy*. New York: Oxford University Press.

MacIntyre A. 1984. *After Virtue*. Notre Dame, IN: University of Notre Dame Press.

MacIntyre A. 1988. *Whose Justice? Which Rationality?* Notre Dame, IN: University of Notre Dame Press.

MacIntyre A. 1990. *Three Rival Versions of Moral Enquiry: Encyclopaedia, Geneology and Tradition.* Notre Dame, IN: University of Notre Dame Press.

Mill JS. 1859/1975. *On Liberty.* Edited by D Spitz. New York: WW Norton.

Mill JS. 1968. *Utilitarianism, Liberty, Representative Government.* Edited by A Lindsay. London: JM Dent and Sons.

Moore GE. 1903/1988. *Principia Ethica.* Amherst, NY: Prometheus Books.

Noddings N. 1984. *Caring: A Feminine Approach to Ethics and Moral Education.* Berkeley, CA: University of California Press.

Oxford English Dictionary. 1993. 2nd ed. Oxford: Clarendon Press.

Robertson M and G Walter. 2013. *Ethics and Mental Health – The Patient, Profession and Community.* Boca Raton, FL: CRC Press.

Ross W. 1939. *The Foundation of Ethics.* Oxford: Clarendon Press.

Singer P. 1981. *The Expanding Circle: Ethics and Sociobiology.* New York: Farrar, Straus and Giroux.

Singer P. 1993. *Practical Ethics* (2nd ed.). Cambridge: Cambridge University Press.

Smart JJC. 1973. "Act-utilitarianism and Rule-utilitarianism." In *Utilitarianism: For and Against,* edited by JJC Smart and B Williams, 9–12. Cambridge: Cambridge University Press.

Williams B. 1973. "A Critique of Utilitarianism." In *Utilitarianism: For and Against,* edited by JJC Smart and B Williams, 75–150. Cambridge: Cambridge University Press.

CHAPTER 3

Practical and professional ethics

Cynthia MA Geppert

INTRODUCTION

Practical and professional ethics comprise of two primary questions. 'What is ethics?' and 'Can ethics be taught?' are two of the oldest questions in philosophy. And while there will likely never be universal agreement on the answer, there is general consensus that will be presented here. This chapter will provide an overview of the branches of ethics, ethical theories and principles, and virtues, and ethical codes that serve as the primary sources of ethics knowledge for health care professionals. A method of ethical decision making will be introduced and resources for further learning offered. The accompanying case studies, and self-assessment and reflective practice exercises are intended to enhance the clinical care of individuals with mental health–substance use problems.

SELF-ASSESSMENT EXERCISE 3.1

Time: 20 minutes

Perhaps the most important aspect of becoming a serious moral person is to identify the source of personal and professional ethical values and their origins.

- Do your values come from religious teaching, community consensus, influential role models, or spiritual experience?
- Do your professional and personal values cohere or conflict and how do you resolve those differences?
- Finally, briefly describe what living an ethical life as a health care professional means to you.

The task of ethics (moral philosophy) is to answer systematically a range of questions concerning right and wrong conduct.

(Pascalev, 2014)

Scholars of ethics recognize three main divisions of the discipline: normative, metaethics, and practical ethics each with its own specific area of ethical concerns and issues. The first and third of these will be the focus of this discussion. Normative ethics is the ethics of Socrates, Plato, and Aristotle and asks what does it mean to be a morally good person? What is the good life for a human being? How should a good professional act? Each individual must conceptualize and internalize their own answers to these questions in order to guide their ethical thinking and conduct.

Normative ethics has over centuries developed systematic responses to these age-old questions. These responses are generally formulated into ethical theories that provide norms for moral deliberation and action. Normative ethics can be an abstract enterprise.

In contrast, practical ethics addresses moral issues and concerns in a specific area with the aim of assisting individuals to analyse and resolve ethical dilemmas that have a real-time human impact in everyday life. Practical ethics applies normative theories to the conduct of human activities and professions such as science, journalism, and the military (Slote, 2014).

> **KEY POINT 3.1**
>
> The normative branch of ethics is more abstract and poses general ethical theories, whereas practical ethics is more concrete and particularized.

Medical ethics is such an applied ethics and is as old as Hippocrates and found in almost every culture. In the 1960s and 1970s traditional norms of medical ethics were challenged with unprecedented medical discovery, a rising consciousness of human and civil rights, and exposure of the abuses of a nascent and previously unimaginable scientific power. From the coalescence of social, political, legal movements came a marriage of ancient humanities and modern science that the great historian of ethics Albert Jonsen called, 'the birth of bioethics' (Jonsen, 1998).

ETHICAL THEORIES

These theories often purport to be systematic, to be complete and comprehensive but each has its own logical strengths and conceptual limitations that suggest a professional should choose the best-fit theory for a particular problem. For example, utilitarianism is often employed to resolve ethical issues in the arenas of public policy and resource allocation. It behoves professionals confronted with a complicated ethical concern to analyse the issues from multiple theoretical perspectives as a kind of rational checks and balances of the coherence and cogence of ethical thinking. While most professionals will naturally gravitate toward one theory or another, working familiarity with

Table 3.1 Ethical Theories

Ethical Theory	Distinguishing Aspects	Case Application
Virtue Ethics ➤ Places more emphasis on the character of the person making the decision than the actual decision. ➤ Internalized virtues such as faithfulness, justice, discernment guide the professional.	➤ Ethical decisions express the qualities and habits of a virtuous person. ➤ A good action is what a person of virtue would do in a similar situation.	➤ A compassionate professional working with homeless population builds enough trust with a teenager whose parents threw him out of the house for using drugs to persuade him to enter a residential treatment program.
Casuistry ➤ Focuses the way general norms are applied to the specific facts of a case. ➤ Used in legal and medical education and practice.	➤ Analogical reasoning about what is the same and different in paradigm cases. ➤ Emphasizes context and precedent over abstract theory and general principles.	➤ When an individual with *human immunodeficiency virus* (HIV) and schizophrenia who has been ostracized from his church asks the professional to pray with him, the professional recalls similar situations in which he has or has not prayed with persons under his care.
Consequentialism ➤ What is normative is what attains the most goodness (happiness, health) for the most people. ➤ Utilitarianism most well known in health care circles.	➤ Calculates a risk or burden/benefit analysis as the basis for decision-making. ➤ Most ethically justifiable action is that which maximizes the outcome for the greatest number than other actions or no action.	➤ A public health professional with a limited budget provides housing to homeless persons with mental illness and substance use whether or not they are sober or in treatment because research has shown such harm

Deontology

▶ Uses a rights or duty based framework for ethical analysis.

▶ There are near moral absolutes that do not depend on context or consequences such as not lying or killing.

▶ It is the intention of the person doing the action, not the consequences of the action that make it morally right or good.

▶ Individuals have rights and duties that justify their actions and decisions.

▶ When a middle-aged woman who has struggled with eating and mood disorders for decades asks a professional for physician-assisted death or euthanasia, the professional states that such actions are never acceptable for a healer to perform.

Principlism

▶ The most widely utilized ethical approach.

▶ General principles and rules govern ethical decisions and actions.

▶ Four principles of autonomy, non-maleficence, beneficence, and justice.

▶ Principles are weighed, balanced and specified to resolve ethical dilemmas.

▶ A professional treats the medical problems of an individual with chronic alcohol dependence and anxiety even when the individual refuses to consider treatment.

Feminist/care ethics

▶ Developed as a critical response to principlism and other male dominated rational approaches.

▶ Primacy of emotions and relationships over reason and law.

▶ Commitment to family and community good over individual self-determination.

▶ Emphasizes caring relationships and moral values as means of resolving ethical dilemmas.

▶ A professional working with a gay youth whose family has rejected him resulting in a suicide attempt connects the individual to a community group that provides counseling and advocacy for lesbian, gay, bisexual and transgender (LGBT) persons.

reduction approaches are overall more positive for public health than requiring abstinence or treatment engagement as a condition of being housed.

several different normative theories can help identify biases and strengthen ethical justifications for actions. Ethical theories provide a framework to organize moral deliberation and structure ethical analysis (Kuhse and Singer, 2012). Table 3.1 summarizes the theories and provides applications to the mental health and substance use practice (Udovic et al., 2002).

KEY POINT 3.2

Ethical theories offer different ways of approaching ethical dilemmas and ordering ethical reflection.

SELF-ASSESSMENT EXERCISE 3.2 – ANSWERS ON P. 35

> **Time: 40 minutes**
> Choose two theories from Table 3.1 and apply them to Case Study 3.1.
> • Why did you select those particular theories?
> • Identify both one strength and one limitation of each theory
> • Indicate how combining them could provide a more comprehensive analysis of the case than utilizing either theory alone.

Case Study 3.1 – Robert

Robert is a person experiencing bipolar disorder who uses drugs intravenously. When stabilized on his psychotropic medications, Robert is kind and cooperative but when he uses drugs Robert stops his prescribed medications and becomes angry and violent. Robert develops a serious infection in his heart from injecting drugs. Robert needs several weeks of intravenous antibiotics in order to cure the infection. Robert would like to stay in a residential setting or even a medical ward because it allows him greater freedom. The administrators of the hospital system feel Robert is too dangerous to be placed on a medical or residential ward and should be placed on a locked psychiatric unit. Nurses on the psychiatric unit do not feel they have the competency to handle Robert's daily infusions of antibiotics while nurses on the medical wards do not feel they have the training to manage Robert's behaviour. The residential programme staff feel Robert will leave their open unit and inject drugs through his intravenous line risking his health and life and creating potential liability for their practice licenses and the institution. As the social work executive, you have been charged with making the decision regarding Robert's clinical placement and must consider Robert's needs and wishes as well as the concerns of the respective staff members.

Codes of Ethics

Professions possess special knowledge and skill gained through long and arduous education and training. Society rewards these efforts and accomplishments with great privilege and power that unless it is exercised responsibly and altruistically can lead to the exploitation of vulnerable individuals and the aggrandizement of self-interest. This is where Codes of Ethics have a crucial role to play in the self-governance that is a hallmark of a profession. Whether the reader is a social worker, addiction counsellor or therapist it is highly likely that the professional organization to which they belong has a code of ethics (National Center for Ethics in Health Care, 2012).

REFLECTIVE PRACTICE EXERCISE 3.1

Time: 15 minutes

Using the Internet or a library locate the code of ethics or statement of ethical principles of a professional organization to which you belong such as a nursing association or a medical society. Read the code and ask yourself which principles you may not have fully honoured or even values you may have breached during your career.

- First, ask yourself why there was an ethical lapse and what you can do to prevent a similar erosion of values in the future.
- Second, identify two values or principles from your respective code you could more closely follow to improve the ethical quality of your practice and develop a strategy for how you will change your practice.

Codes of Ethics are aspirational documents of the learned professions that express its normative ideals; where the law or regulation sets the floor of acceptable behaviour, a code of ethics establishes the ceiling. Codes of ethics are a means of accountability; the guidelines for the exercise of the unique privileges of the healing professions and the standards for evaluating the behaviour of members of these groups. Uniting the diverse provisions of the various professional health care codes of ethics are a central tenet: the good of the individual being cared for must hold primary over all other interests be they personal, social, economic or political.

KEY POINT 3.3

The central tenet of all professional ethics codes is that the good of the person being treated must take precedence over all other interests.

Ethics committees and ethics consultation

In addition to codes of ethics, almost every institution whether it is a large university medical hospital or a small community nursing home, has some methods for resolving ethical dilemmas. These mechanisms can be of immense assistance to the professional facing a difficult ethical decision or needing information and guidance regarding an ethical issue. Ethics Committees are usually multidisciplinary groups with broad representation from the professions often along with community members. Professional organizations such as nursing associations and medical societies frequently have their own ethics committees or boards that set discipline or specialty specific rules and often adjudicate breaches of those rules.

Ethics committees generally have three main functions: first, educating individuals and their families who receive health care services, the professional staff who provide these services, and students learning to serve. The second function is developing and implementing policy regarding crucial ethical procedures and processes, such as rules and approaches for withdrawing or withholding life-sustaining care at the end-of-life. This ensures privacy and confidentiality of personal health information. The final function ethics consultation, 'is a set of services provided by an individual or group in response to questions from patients, families, surrogates, healthcare professionals, or other involved parties who seek to resolve uncertainty or conflict regarding value-laden concerns that emerge in health care' (American Society for Bioethics and Humanities Task Force on Standards for Bioethics and Humanities, 2011).

KEY POINT 3.4

The three functions of ethics committees are: ethics education, policy development, and ethics consultation.

Ethical values and virtues

Ethical theories, codes, and committees are all ways and means of acculturating and socializing, assuring and ensuring that health care professionals have access to the ethical knowledge and skill they need to practice according to the highest values and priorities of the profession. All the health care professions from nursing to chaplaincy share core principles and virtues listed in Table 3.2 along with illustrative mini case scenarios. Principles express general rules and norms what Beauchamp and Childress call, 'action guides' such as respect for autonomy and beneficence that dictate the kinds of actions that are permitted, required, or prohibited when faced with ethical concerns and dilemmas (Beauchamp and Childress, 2013). Virtues are qualities of character such as compassion, honesty, and courage. These are the dispositions that a virtuous person cultivates until they become the habits that constitute moral excellence (Pellegrino and Thomasma, 1993). Principles help the moral person know what is good and reason about what is right. Virtues help us choose to do what is good and be attracted to what is right.

Principles and virtues are obviously central to the two theories examined above that bear their names but they also constitute a shared set of concepts and language that is used in most ethical analysis. Important ethical practices such as the informed consent process and confidentiality protections, and professional boundaries are based upon and derived from these concepts. Informed consent for example fulfils the principle of autonomy and the virtue of respect. Principle and virtues express our deepest most sacred values as professionals, values being those things we find most important in life and prioritize in decisions.

KEY POINT 3.5

Principles guide the mind to be aware, and virtues direct the heart and will to practice according to the professional values.

ETHICAL DILEMMAS

Ethical dilemmas present choices between two values or decisions both in themselves good and right. But both cannot be simultaneously and completely honoured. This creates a conflict between the values and often within the professional. Such a conflict may result in an experience of moral distress for the professional.

When the choice is between right and wrong, there is no dilemma. A person under your care for post-traumatic stress disorder and alcohol use disorder calls. He is intoxicated and tells you he is going to shoot the boss who last night fired him from his job as a security guard after he had an episode of disassociation. It is your ethical and legal duty to protect the person's confidentiality yet there is a higher obligation to save the individual's life, which likely means you will have to disclose some information to emergency personnel dispatched to the home. In disclosing you take the chance the individual is not really serious about killing his boss but only disinhibited from alcohol and expressing his anger about losing his job. If you breach his privacy, he may be alienated from care or even take legal action. Ethical dilemmas come in many shades of grey, the 'ought' situations. In contrast, it is wrong and often illegal to have a romantic or sexual relationship with an individual who has a mental ill health or substance use problems you are treating, as a professional. These are 'must' situations, the black and white of the law.

Table 3.2 Ethical Principals and Virtues

Principles	Definition	Mini-Case Scenario
Autonomy	Literally, 'self-rule'. The right of the individual to make their own health care decisions.	A social worker offers a homeless person struggling with mental illness in the middle of winter a bed in a shelter but respects when the patient refuses and provides him with a blanket.
Beneficence	'To do good'. The primary obligation of the professional to act so as to benefit the patient.	The professionals in a free-clinic for persons with *human immunodeficiency virus* (HIV) provide comprehensive integrated medical and mental health care.
Fidelity	'Being faithful'. The quality and duty of keeping promises, telling the truth, and honoring responsibilities within the therapeutic alliance.	When a young prostitute with heroin addiction relapses for several days but then returns to the treatment program, all the members of her care team work together to develop a recovery plan.
Justice	Fair and equitable distribution of burdens and benefits with a specific population. 'Similar persons and situations are treated similarly', unless there are substantive differences.	The nurse manager of a residential program for persons with co-occurring disorders advocates that patients with criminal histories adhering to the program should be given the same privileges as other individuals.
Non-Maleficence	The primary obligation of health care professionals to 'do no harm'. To prevent pain and suffering when possible and to minimize the adverse effects of treatment.	A patient with a psychotic break has developed diabetes from antipsychotic medication. The physician believes that heavy marijuana use triggered the psychosis and so tapers down the medication in favor of evidence based therapy for addiction.

Virtues	Definition	Mini-Case Scenario
Altruism	Giving of oneself for the good of another.	A nurse working in a hospice for the mentally ill stays up all night long after her shift has ended to comfort a dying person who has no friends or family.
Compassion/ Empathy	Feeling 'for' not 'with' another's suffering. Active regard for the welfare of another person or animal and responding to alleviate another's pain with kindness and mercy.	A chaplain never leaves the side of a teenager with bipolar disorder hospitalized under police guard after stealing and crashing a car while high on methamphetamine.
Courage	Standing up for principles even at risk to livelihood and even life.	The director of a substance use program for women who are victims of domestic violence stands up to an angry husband demanding his wife be handed over to him.
Honesty	Telling the truth without omission, deception or misrepresentation and with sensitivity to the needs and desires of the individual.	A physician kindly but firmly tells an individual with childhood trauma that if he does not stop drinking alcohol, he will die of liver failure and that he feels frustrated he cannot help him stop.
Integrity	Consistence, soundness, and coherence in intention and action. A person who is responsible, fair, dependable.	The priest who directs a street ministry to lesbian, gay, bisexual and transgender (LGBT) run-away youths that operates only on donations refuses money from a conservative foundation that has supported legislation against marriage equality.

A true ethical dilemma presents a choice between two rights, not between a right and a wrong.

Ethical decision making models

In order to resolve ethical dilemmas a number of ethical decision making methods and models have been developed. As with ethical theories each has its own pros and cons. There are models specific to a discipline such as business or a situation such as end-of-life. Many share common steps. What is most important is for the professional to become familiar with a method she can make her own. Box 3.1 summarizes and adapts a model that combines several mental health decision making methods (Fisher, 2005).

BOX 3.1

1 ASSESS
a Determine whether the problem is an ethical one. Use Codes of Ethics and other professional guidelines to identify the specific ethical issues.
b Describe and clarify the clinical components of the issue.
c Consider any legal requirements, contractual obligations, or agency considerations that might influence your decision or limit your options.
d Consider any relevant personal values that might affect your objectivity, introduce bias or otherwise influence your decision.
e Evaluate the rights, vulnerabilities, and responsibilities of all parties involved and your respective relationship and obligations to each.
f Obtain consultation from a trusted colleague or supervisor about the ethical, legal, and personal issues involved. If needed obtain a formal ethics, legal, or medical consultation.
g Consider whether other members of your team or practice group should be collaboratively engaging in the decision process with you.

2 PLAN
a Generate a list of possible decisions/solutions: consider every possible course of action.
b Eliminate from the list, any options that are clearly unethical, illegal or clinically inappropriate.
c Articulate, consider, and weigh the consequences of each of the remaining options.

3 IMPLEMENT
a Make a decision and decide how to best carry it out.
b Carry out the decision.

4 EVALUATE
a Document your decision-making process and actions.
b Evaluate the process, decision, and its outcome.

Case Study 3.2 – Jane

Jane, who experiences severe borderline personality disorder, was just recently discharged from the psychiatric hospital for suicidal ideation. She is the mother of three small children under the age of seven. Jane is dependent on benzodiazepines, which while initially prescribed for her anxiety, she now abuses, doctor shopping and buying them off the street. Jane is admitted to the emergency medical unit after having taken an overdose of her antidepressant medications along with the anxiolytics. She reports the overdose was intentional in the wake of a fight with her husband. Her husband learned she had an online relationship with another man and now threatens to take the children to his parents in another state and divorce her. The psychiatrist insists that Jane be readmitted involuntarily if necessary to the inpatient unit. If she is admitted she will have no chance to try and work things out with her husband or if they cannot reconcile to see the children before he takes them away. The nurse mentions that Jane's mother is now with her in the room and perhaps she could stay with Jane to keep her safe. The social worker believes she can arrange an appointment with Jane's therapist the next day and if the couple wishes, get them into marriage counselling. The psychiatrist rejects the plan saying it will place Jane at risk of harm and that if Jane kills herself he and the hospital will be legally liable. You are the psychologist on the team and have yet to voice an opinion.

SELF-ASSESSMENT EXERCISE 3.3

Time: 20 minutes
Imagine you are the psychologist asked to give an opinion. Use the mental health ethical decision-making model to systematically work through the case presented. Briefly write or type answers to all the applicable elements of each section. Ask yourself how your responses might have been different before reading this chapter.

CONCLUSION

There are persons, even professionals, who believe ethics is relative, that 'ethics is whatever is convenient or you want it to be'. Such a viewpoint eschews the presumption of this chapter that there are some foundational values that we as professional healers hold in common even if as individual professions or persons we may contextualize and particularize them differently. Ethical diversity is not equivalent to ethical relativism. The nature of our role as healers requires some values to be nearly universal such as never doing intentional harm to a person under our care and respecting the self-determination of capable individuals even when they make a choice that may not be in their best interest.

Similarly, there are very smart and good people who believe that you are either born and brought up to be moral or you are not and nothing you can learn from a book or in a class or even from a wise mentor can make you more ethical. The position of this author is that ethics can be both taught and learned and while some individuals from a combination of nature and nurture may be more or less ethically inclined than others, with dedication and effort, each of us can be better than we are as people and as professionals. And such striving is what all of us are called to do if we are to deserve the trust of those we serve and society places in us.

REFERENCES

American Society for Bioethics and Humanities Task Force on Standards For Bioethics And Humanities. 2011. "Core Competencies for Health Care Ethics Consultation". *The Report of the American Society of Bioethics and Humanities.* 2nd ed. Glenview, IL: American Society of Bioethics and Humanities.

Beauchamp TL and JF Childress. 2013. *Principles of Biomedical Ethics.* New York: Oxford University Press.

Carter L. 2002. "A Primer to Ethical Analysis." Queensland, Australia: University of Queensland, Office of Public Policy and Ethics Institute for Molecular Bioscience.

Fisher MA. 2005. Ethical Decision-Making Model. www.centerforethicalpractice.org/publications/models-mary-alice-fisher-phd/ethical-decision-making-model/.

Jonsen AR. 1998. *The Birth of Bioethics.* New York: Oxford University Press.

Kuhse H and P Singer (Eds.). 2012. *A Companion to Bioethics.* Oxford: Blackwell.

National Center for Ethics in Health Care 2012. *The Place of Ethics Codes in Ethics Consultation.* Washington, DC: Department of Veterans Affairs.

Pascalev A. 2014. Task of Ethics. In: *Bioethics*, edited by B Jennings. 4th ed. Farmington Hills, MI: Gale, Cengage.

Pellegrino ED and DC Thomasma. 1993. *The Virtues in Medical Practice.* New York: Oxford University Press.

Slote MA. 2014. History of Ethics. In: *Bioethics*, edited by B Jennings. 4th ed. Farmington Hills, MI: Gale, Cengage.

Udovic D, D Morris, A Dickman, J Postlethwait and P Wetherwax. 2002. Workshop biology: Demonstrating the effectiveness of active learning in an introductory biology course. *BioScience* 52: 272–281.

TO LEARN MORE

Jonsen AR, M Siegler and W Winslade. 2010. *Clinical Ethics: A Practical Approach to Ethical Decisions in Clinical Medicine,* 7th ed. New York: McGraw-Hill.

Lo B. 2014. *Resolving Ethical Dilemmas: A Guide for Clinicians*, 5th ed. Philadelphia, PA: Lippincott, Williams, & Wilkins.

Macklin R. 1999. *Against Ethical Relativism: Cultural Diversity and the Search for Ethical Universals in Medicine.* New York: Oxford University Press.

USEFUL CONTACTS

Makkulla Center for Applied Ethics. www.scu.edu/ethics
Ethical Codes & Practice Guidelines. http://kspope.com/ethcodes/

ANSWER TO SELF-ASSESSMENT EXERCISE 3.2 – *SEE* P. 26

A deontological type of ethics might say that once Robert requests transfer back to the medical unit, it is unethical to keep him on the psychiatric ward. Since Robert is capable his autonomous choices must be respected no matter the potential risk to staff, other individuals in the hospital or himself. A consequentialist thinker might argue that since the outcome of the stay on the psychiatric unit was positive it is most ethically justifiable to attempt a transfer. However, if Robert decompensates with the freedom of the medical unit and threatens staff then he will need to be transferred back to psychiatry.

CHAPTER 4

Collectivism versus individualism

Larry Purnell

INTRODUCTION

The ethnic, racial, and cultural composition of the world is continuing to evolve, perhaps more so now with a recent surge in asylum seekers, refugees, immigrants, emigrants, and migrants. Consequently, many mental health professionals are caring for more diverse populations. Whereas there is value on knowing cultural values of specific populations for whom healthcare professionals provide care, it is impossible to know the beliefs and values of all groups. Therefore, having a general framework for collectivistic and individualistic cultures is a starting point for assessment, the first step for counselling and planning care for individuals and their families. Regardless of a person's culture and diagnosis, professionals are ethically bound by codes of conduct. Health disparities and inequities between the majority and ethnically and racially diverse and underserved are well documented. A modern, yet familiar, adage common in the United States is that when America catches a cold, minority and other vulnerable groups get pneumonia because of the disparate burden of illness for ethnic minorities, the underserved, and other vulnerable and marginalized groups (Giger, et al., 2007). This adage is probably true around the world, especially when one considers the social determinants of health. One of the ways to decrease health and health-care disparities and inequalities and provide ethical care to people with substance use and mental health issues is through cultural competence.

Many countries have ethical codes or codes of conduct for healthcare professionals, including those specific to psychiatric/mental health and substance use, paediatrics, midwifery, and others. Many countries use the International Council of Nurses Code of Ethics rather than developing their own. For decades, professional organizations have unsuccessfully tried to develop codes of ethics or codes of conduct that meet the needs of Western (primarily individualistic) and Eastern (primarily collectivistic) philosophies and worldviews. Moreover, to date, one code of ethical standards has not been adopted by all nations.

Professionals must make a concerted effort to remain non-judgmental and optimize relationships to maximize quality care for all peoples.

ESSENTIAL DEFINITIONS AND LEVELS OF CULTURE

Before defining, comparing, and contrasting collectivistic and individualistic cultural values, the professional must have an understanding of essential terminology related to culture. Anthropologists and sociologists have proposed many definitions of culture. For the purposes of health and health-care, **culture** is defined as the totality of socially transmitted behavioral patterns, arts, beliefs, values, customs, lifeways, and all other products of human work and thought characteristics of a population of people that guide their worldview and decision making. These patterns may be explicit or implicit, are primarily learned and transmitted within the family, are shared by most (but not all) members of the culture, and change in response to global phenomena (Purnell, 2013a). In addition, culture has three levels:

> ➤ a tertiary level that is visible to outsiders, such as things that can be seen, worn, or otherwise observed
> ➤ a secondary level, in which only members know the rules of behavior and can articulate them and
> ➤ a primary level that represents the deepest level in which rules are known by all, observed by all, are implicit, and are taken for granted (Purnell and Pontious, 2014).

Culture is largely unconscious and has powerful influences on health and ill health. Mental health professionals must recognize, respect, and integrate people's cultural beliefs and practices into health recommendations.

Cultural beliefs, values, and practices are learned from birth: first at home, then in religious institutions, schools, and other places where people congregate. This process is called **enculturation**. The terms cultural awareness, cultural sensitivity, and cultural competence are often confused and sometimes used interchangeably. However, there is a difference. **Cultural awareness** has more to do with an appreciation of the external signs of diversity, such as arts, music, dress, and physical characteristics. **Cultural sensitivity** has more to do with personal attitudes and not saying things that might be offensive to someone from a cultural or ethnic background different from the professional's background.

REFLECTIVE PRACTICE EXERCISE 4.1

Time: 30 minutes
- Who in your family had the most influence in teaching you cultural values and practices?
- Outside the family, where else did you learn about your cultural values and beliefs?
- What cultural practices did you learn in your family that you no longer practice?

Cultural competence in health care is having the knowledge, abilities, and skills to deliver care congruent with the persons' cultural beliefs and practices.

KEY POINT 4.2

Increasing one's knowledge of cultural diversity improves the potential for professionals to provide culturally competent care.

One progresses from unconscious incompetence (not being aware that one is lacking knowledge about another culture), to conscious incompetence (being aware that one is lacking knowledge about another culture), to conscious competence (learning about the persons' culture, verifying generalizations about the persons' culture, and providing culturally specific interventions), and finally, to unconscious competence (automatically providing culturally congruent care to persons' of diverse cultures). Unconscious competence is difficult to accomplish and potentially dangerous because individual differences exist within specific cultural groups. To be effective, culturally competent care must be integrated into the overall plan of care in mental health in order to benefit from the recommendations and interventions (Purnell, 2013a).

An understanding of one's own culture and personal values, and the ability to detach oneself from 'excess baggage' associated with personal views, are essential to cultural competence and is commonly referred to as cultural **self-awareness**. Even then, traces of ethnocentrism may unconsciously pervade one's attitudes and behavior. **Ethnocentrism** is the universal tendency of human beings to think that their ways of thinking, acting, and believing are the only right, proper, and natural ways. Ethnocentrism, a concept that most people practice to some degree, perpetuates an attitude in which beliefs that differ greatly from one's own are strange, bizarre, or unenlightened and, therefore, wrong.

When people migrate to a new location, they **acculturate** to some degree and selectively take on the dominant values and beliefs of the majority culture (Markus, et al., 1991). Those who willingly migrate acculturate more easily than those who are forced to migrate. People who spend the majority of their time in ethnic enclaves such as in a China Town or Little Italy enclave, may not have the need or desire to acculturate and may become more traditional than people in their home country. The stronger the **enculturation**, the process by which an individual learns the traditional culture and incorporates its practices, values, and worldview, the more difficult it becomes to acculturate (Greenfield, et al., 2003).

The controversial term race must be addressed when learning about culture. **Race** is genetic in origin and includes physical characteristics that are similar among members of the group, such as skin color, blood type, and hair and eye color. Although there is less than a 1 percent difference among the races, this difference can be significant when conducting physical assessments and prescribing medication (Human Genome Project, 2012). People from a given racial group may, but not necessarily, share a common culture. Race is also seen as a social concept and is sometimes more important than race as a biological concept. Race can assign status, limit or increase opportunities depending on the setting, and influences interactions between people and professionals in mental health and substance use.

Any **generalization**, a research principle, reducing numerous characteristics of an individual or group of people to a general form can render them indistinguishable. When a generalization relates less to the actual observed behavior than to the motives thought to underlie the behavior (that is, the why of the behavior), it is likely to be oversimplified. Thus, generalizations can lead to **stereotyping**, an oversimplified conception, opinion, or belief about some aspect of an individual or group of people. Stereotyping is an endpoint; generalizing is a starting point for assessment. One of the problems with stereotyping is that people outside and inside the culture might believe them. The more a professional knows about a cultural group, the better the assessment can be conducted resulting in improved counselling.

REFLECTIVE PRACTICE EXERCISE 4.2

Time: 20 minutes
- What evidence of racism or stereotyping have you seen in your community?
- Is there an age or educational difference among those who made racial or ethnic slurs?
- Have you addressed them to the person who made the comments?

Even in relatively homogeneous cultures, there are subcultures that may not hold all the values of their dominant culture. **Subcultures** are groups who have experiences different from those of the dominant culture. Subcultures include gangs, punks, bikers, gays and lesbians, transgendered people, alcoholics anonymous, weight lifters, athletes, as well as other groups. The distinction here is that each group can include people from many different cultures and ethnicities; therefore, they form their own culture. For example, bikers may include people of Bangladeshi, Filipino, Italian, Spanish, Norwegian, British, German, cultures etc. and form a subculture.

REFLECTIVE PRACTICE EXERCISE 4.3

Time: 20 minutes
- Are you aware of your country of origin?
- Have you asked your ancestors about their history?
- Can you give examples of your enculturation?
- Can you give example of your acculturation as a result of relocating or being exposed to other cultures?

COLLECTIVISTIC AND INDIVIDUALISTIC VALUES

The degree to which a person is oriented on the collectivism versus individualism continuum is one of the least understood, yet very powerful. The continuum on worldview influences how individuals, families, and communities act, communicate, and make decisions. A person's **worldview** pertains to the lenses worn to see the world and represents beliefs, values, assumptions about people, relationships, nature, time, and activity. Multicultural counselling researchers and professionals emphasize that accurate assessment of worldview is a necessary step in understanding peoples' frame of reference for treatment options (Ibriham, et al., 2001).

Cultural competence requires professionals to understand collectivism and individualism as a guide to multiple cultures.

The collectivism versus individualism continuum of values includes orientation to self or group, decision-making, knowledge transmission, individual choice, personal responsibility, the concept of progress, competitiveness, shame and guilt, help-seeking, expression of identity, and interaction/communication styles (Hofstede, 2001; Hofstede and Hofstede, 2005; Purnell and Pontious, 2014).

KEY POINT 4.3

Collectivism is defined as a moral, political, or social outlook that stresses human interdependence. **Individualism** is defined as a moral, political, or social outlook that stresses human independence and the importance of individual self-reliance and freedom.

Elements and the degree of collectivism and individualism exist in every culture so individuality, the sense that each person has a separate and equal place in the community, must be considered (Purnell, 2013a). People from an individualist culture will more strongly identify with the values at the individualistic end of the scale. Moreover, collectivism and individualism fall along a continuum, and some people from an individualistic culture will, to some degree, align themselves towards the collectivistic end of the scale and vice versa. The degree of acculturation and assimilation and the variant characteristics of culture determine the degree of adherence to traditional collectivist and cultural individualistic values, beliefs, and practices (Hofstede, 2001; Hofstede and Hofstede, 2005; Morgan and Townsend, 2012; Purnell and Pontious, 2014).

COLLECTIVISTIC AND VALUES

In a collectivist culture the needs and wishes of the group are seen as more important than those of the individual (Hofstede, 2005; Purnell, 2013a; Purnell, 2013b). Some examples of collectivist cultures include:
➤ Traditional Arabic
➤ Amish
➤ Chinese
➤ Filipino
➤ Haitian
➤ Asian Indian
➤ Korean
➤ Japanese
➤ Mexican
➤ American Indian/Alaskan Native
➤ Taiwanese
➤ Thai
➤ Turks
➤ Vietnamese.

Far more world cultures are collectivistic than are individualistic, which can be problematic for a professional from a highly collectivist culture to communicate with other professionals from highly individualistic cultures such as the United States and Germany, or vice versa (Hofstede and Hofstede, 2005; Purnell, 2011; Purnell, 2013b). In collectivistic cultures, decisions are made in groups when consensus is attained; this is often a time-consuming, informal process with many passive or silent members who will not challenge the oldest or most senior members of the team. The collectivistic cultural members' perception is that this is a democratic, team-driven process. Rules are known; however, they are frequently bent, broken, or ignored. In addition, collectivistic members perceive they have a lower workload and less stress when working with team members who are very supportive and help each other.

In high-contexted collectivistic cultures, much of the information is implicit where fewer words are used to express a thought resulting in more of the message being in the nonverbal mode. Great emphasis is placed on personal relationships and others' perceptions of the person or family (Hofstede, 2001; Purnell, 2013b). Among collectivistic cultures, people with a mental or physical disability are *more likely* to be hidden from society to save face. The cultural norms and the values of collectivistic families mean that care of all immediate and extended family members is provided by the family at home (Purnell, 2010). In collectivist cultures, it is absolutely imperative to include the family, and sometimes the community, for effective counseling; otherwise, the treatment plan will not be followed.

For many indigenous populations (e.g., American Indians and Alaskan Natives) the fact that one member of the tribe or clan is ill means that the tribe or clan is sick, resulting in one or more members becoming ill. Thus, healing rituals and treatments or counseling should be provided to the entire tribe or clan, not just to those individuals with signs and symptoms of illness (Purnell, 2011).

Among many Middle Eastern and other collectivistic cultures, people with a mental or physical disability may be hidden from the public because 'their pollution' may mean that other children in the family will not be able to obtain a spouse if the condition is known. For other impairments, such as ones resulting from HIV, the conditions may be kept hidden, not because of confidentiality rights but for fear that news of the condition may spread to other family members and the community (Colin and Paperwalla, 2013).

In many cultures, spiritual healers (e.g., *curandero/curandera* [Hispanic folk healers], root-worker, voodoo priest/priestess, medicine man/woman) are typically consulted first for all illnesses but especially for those culture bound illnesses such as those caused by the evil-eye, curses, or bad spirits entering the person. The greater the cultural stigma the more likely will be a delay in seeking allopathic health care and counseling, resulting in the condition being more severe at the time of treatment (Purnell, 2013a).

In collectivistic cultures, people are socialized to view themselves as members of a larger group, family, school, church, educational setting, work, etc. They are bound through the expectations of loyalty and personal and familial lifetime protective ties. Children are socialized (enculturated) where priority is given to connections and interrelationships with others as the basis of psychological well-being (Bui and Turnbull, 2003; Rothstein-Fisch et al., 2001). Older people, and those in hierarchal positions, are respected, and people are less likely to openly disagree with them. Individuals are not seen as equal; those seen as not as good as others are left behind. Parents and elders may have the final say in their children's careers and life partners. The focus is not on the individual but on the needs of the group and what is best for the group as a whole (Purnell, 2013b).

Collectivism is characterized by not drawing attention to oneself and people are not encouraged to ask questions. When one fails, shame may be extended to the family; external explanations, spiritual distress, superiors, or fate, may be given as causes of the health problem with mental health concerns. To avoid offending someone, people practice smooth interpersonal communication by not openly disagreeing and may be evasive with negative issues (Ting-Toomey, 1996).

KEY POINT 4.4

In collectivistic cultures that primarily use oral history, the professional should not take copious notes in front of the individual, especially if they are refugees or undocumented. Taking notes may be perceived as the professional being stupid or rude, not being able to listen well, or not being interested enough to remember what the person is saying.

Among most collectivist cultures, to disagree or to answer the professional with a negative response is considered rude; asking questions is seen as disrespectful and causes the professional to lose face since teaching was not clear or understood. In fact, in some languages a word for 'no' does not exist. Do not ask the individual if she or he knows what you are asking, understands you, or knows how to do something, because the only option that a person would have is to answer 'yes'. Yes, could mean:

➤ I hear you but I do not understand you
➤ I understand you, but I do not agree with what has been said
➤ I agree with you but I might not necessarily follow recommendations due to cost
➤ What you are asking is culturally unacceptable.

Nodding is a sign of respect, not agreement. Repeating what is prescribed does not ensure understanding; instead ask for a demonstration, the specific times the individual will take the medication or some other response that is more likely to determine understanding (Purnell, 2013a). *See* Table 4.1.

INDIVIDUALISTIC AND VALUES

In individualistic cultures, the most important person in society is the individual. Professionals must not confuse individualism with individuality. Individuality is the sense that each person has a separate and equal place in the community and where individuals who are considered 'eccentrics or local characters' are tolerated (Purnell, 2010; Purnell and Pontious, 2014). Some highly individualistic cultures include:

Table 4.1 Ethical Considerations

Collectivistic Values **Collectivistic Cultures**	**Individualistic Values** **Individualistic Cultures**
Communication ➤ Implicit indirect communication is common. People are more likely to tell the professional what they think the professional wants to hear. ➤ More formal greeting is required by using the surname with a title. This can be a first step in gaining trust. The professional should always ask by what name the person wants to be called. ➤ Present temporality is common, although balance is sought. The person usually wants to know how the illness/condition will affect them on a short term basis. Address the individual's and family's concern before moving on. ➤ Punctuality is not valued except when absolutely necessary such as making transportation connections. If punctuality is required, explain the importance and the repercussions for tardiness such as not being seen or a charge is made for being late. ➤ Truth telling may not be valued in order to "save face". ➤ "Yes" may mean I hear you or I understand, not necessarily agreement. Do not ask questions that can easily be answered with "yes" or "no". The answer is invariably "yes". Instead of asking if the individual takes the medicine as prescribed, ask "what time do you take the medicine"? How many times have you missed taking your medicine this week/month"? ➤ Direct eye contact may be avoided with people in hierarchical positions, especially among older more traditional people but is maintained with friends and intimates. Do not assume that lack of eye contact means	*Communication* ➤ Explicit, direct, straight forward communication is the norm. ➤ More informal greeting frequently using the given name early in an encounter. Professionals should introduce themselves by the name they preferred to be addressed. Ask the individual by what name they want to be addressed. ➤ Futuristic temporality is the norm. The person wants to know how the disease/condition will affect them on a long term basis. ➤ Punctuality is valued. People are usually on time or early for formal appointments. ➤ Truth telling is expected at all times. Individuals will usually answer the professional truthfully or evade the question completely if they do not want to answer it. ➤ Questions requiring "yes" or "no" are answered truthfully. ➤ Direct eye contact is expected and is a sign of truth, respect, and trust. ➤ Sharing intimate life details is encouraged, even with non-intimates and does not carry a stigma for people or their family. ➤ Spatial distancing with non-intimates is 18 to 24 inches. Sexual harassment laws encourage a low touch culture.

that the person is being evasive or not telling the truth.

➤ Sharing intimate life details of self or family is discouraged because it can cause a stigma for the person and the family. Ask intimate questions after a modicum of trust has been developed.

➤ Spatial distancing with non-intimates may be closer than 18 inches. Do not take offense if the person stands closer to you than to which you have been accustomed.

➤ Touch is readily accepted between same sex individuals but not between people of the opposite sex. Always ask permission and explain the necessity of touch.

➤ A diagnosis of depression is usually not acceptable. Do not use this diagnosis until a modicum of trust has been established.

Family Roles and Organization

➤ Decision making is a responsibility of the male or most respected family member. The male is the spokesperson for the family, even though he may not be the decision maker.

➤ Individual autonomy is not usually the norm.

➤ Older people's opinions are sought but not necessarily followed.

➤ Young adults and children are not expected to have a high degree of dependence until they leave the parent's home.

➤ Children are not encouraged to express themselves; they are expected to be seen, not heard.

➤ A stigma may result when a family member is placed in long-term care. Home care with the extended family is the norm.

➤ Alternative lifestyles are not readily accepted and may be hidden from the public and even within the extended family. Do not disclose same-sex relationship to family or outsiders.

➤ Extended family living is common with collective input from all members.

Explain the necessity and ask permission before touching.

➤ A diagnosis of depression does not carry a stigma and can be shared with individuals and their families (if necessary) without a stigma.

Family Roles and Organization

➤ Egalitarian decision making is the norm, although there are variations. Ask who is the primary decision-maker for health-related concerns.

➤ Individual autonomy is the norm.

➤ Younger people are expected to become responsible and independent at a young age. Determine responsibilities for children and teenagers.

➤ Children are encouraged to express themselves. Allow children to have a voice in decision-making.

➤ Each person in a group has an equal right to express an opinion.

➤ No stigma is attached for placing a family member in long term-care or substance misuse rehab.

Table 4.1 continued

Collectivistic Values Collectivistic Cultures	Individualistic Values Individualistic Cultures
➤ Beneficence, a normative statement to act for the others' benefit, may mean that the health-care professional should not reveal a grave diagnoses or outcome directly because it may cause them to give up hope. Therefore, the professional should disclose this information to the family who makes the decision to disclose the diagnosis to the individual. An alternative is to tell a story about someone else who has the condition.	➤ Alternative lifestyles are gaining more acceptance than in the past. Ask about same-sex relationships after a modicum of trust has been established. ➤ Nuclear family living is the norm. However, the professional must still ask who else lives in the household and what are their responsibilities. ➤ Beneficence, a normative statement to act for the others' benefit, requires the health-care professional to reveal a grave diagnoses or outcome directly to the individual in order to make informed decisions regarding the future.
High-Risk Health Behaviors ➤ Accountability is a family affair or some hierarchal authority. ➤ High-risk health behaviors are less likely to be revealed to health-care professionals. Do not disclose substance misuse to family members.	*High-Risk Health Behaviors* ➤ People are accountable for their own actions. ➤ High-risk health behaviors are revealed to health-care professionals. However, it is still best to ask about substance misuse after a modicum of trust has been established.
Health-care Practices ➤ Traditional practices are common as a first line of defense for minor illnesses. Specifically ask about traditional practices, including herbs. ➤ Complementary and alternative therapies are frequently preferred over allopathic practices. Specifically ask about complementary and alternative practices. ➤ Preventive practices are stressed.	*Health-care Practices* ➤ Traditional practices are common as a first line of defense for minor illnesses. Ask about over-the-counter medications and herbs. ➤ Complementary and alternative therapies are gaining acceptance because they are less invasive. Specifically ask the

➤ Rehabilitation is frequently a family responsibility. Great stigma can occur by placing a family member in a long-term or rehab facility.

➤ Self-medication is common and extends to prescription medicines that may be obtained from overseas pharmacies and friends. Specifically ask what medicines the person is taking.

➤ Pain may be seen as atonement for past sins. Take every opportunity to dispel this myth.

➤ Mental health issues may be hidden because they carry a stigma for the family. Disclose mental health and substance misuse only to professionals who "need to know".

➤ Advance directives that convey how the individual wants medical decisions made in the future may not be acceptable to some because this is a family, not individual responsibility.

Health-care Practitioners

➤ Allopathic professionals may be seen as a first resource for major health problems, although traditional healers may be seen simultaneously. Professionals should partner with traditional healers.

➤ Spiritual leaders frequently serve as alternative practitioners for emotional concerns and substance misuse.

➤ Age of professional may be a concern. Ask the individual if they prefer an older professional.

➤ Opposite sex health-care provider may not be acceptable with devout Jewish and Muslim individuals. Ask the individual if a same-sex professional is required for non-life threatening conditions.

individual about their complementary and alternative practices.

➤ Curative health-care practices have been the norm but preventive practices and healthy living are gaining acceptance.

➤ Rehabilitation is well-integrated into allopathic care.

➤ Liberal pain medication is expected.

➤ Mental health issues do not carry a stigma for the family. However, ask the person about disclosure of substance misuse and reveal it only to those who need to know.

➤ Advance directives that convey how the individual wants medical decisions made in the future is compatible with individualism.

Health-care Practitioners

➤ Age of professional health-care providers are usually not a concern.

➤ Same sex health-care providers are usually not required except for traditional Muslims and orthodox Jews. Specifically ask if a same-sex professional is required for non-emergent conditions.

- Traditional European American (USA)
- British
- Canadian
- German
- Norwegian
- Swedish.

In individualistic cultures, a person's identity is based mainly on the individual's personal accomplishments, career, and challenges. A high standard of living supports self-efficiency, self-direction, self-advocacy, and independent living. Decisions made by elders and people in hierarchal positions may be questioned or not followed because the ideal is that all people are equal and expect, and are expected, to make their own decisions about their lives. Moreover, people are personally responsible and held accountable for their decisions and even for their own health and wellbeing. For example, those who are obese or misuse tobacco are held responsible for losing weight or cease tobacco use to improve their health and to minimize the cost of their health care to society. Improving self, doing 'better' than others (frequently focused on material gains), and making progress on a community or national level are expected. If one fails, the blame and shame are on 'self' (Purnell, 2013a).

Consistent with individualism, self-expression is encouraged. Adherents to individualism freely express personal opinions, share many personal issues, and ask personal questions of others to a degree that may be seen as offensive to those who come from a collectivistic culture. Direct, straight-forward questioning with the expectation that answers will be direct is usually appreciated with individualism; however, small talk before getting down to business may not be appreciated. The professional should take cues from the individual before this immediate, direct, and intrusive approach is initiated. Individualistic cultures usually tend to be more informal and frequently use first names upon first encounter. Ask the person by what name she or he prefers to be called. Questions that require a yes or no answer are usually answered truthfully from the individual's perspective. In individualistic cultures with values on autonomy and productivity, the person is expected to be a productive member of society and responsible and accountable for one's actions (Purnell, 2013a).

Individualistic cultures expect all to follow the rules and hierarchical protocols, and people are expected to do their own work and to work until the job is completed. Younger people are often expected to become responsible at an early age and have independence and self-expression. Decisions are made by those with the highest status or position in the family or group. In situations where the group makes decisions, each member has an equal right to express an opinion. Opinions can differ greatly, enhancing the chance that the final decision is better than what one person's decision would be. The expectation is that all will follow the decisions made. In low-context individualistic cultures, great emphasis is placed on the verbal mode and many words are used to express a thought (Hofstede, 2001; Purnell, 2013a).

SELF-ASSESSMENT EXERCISE 4.1 – *SEE* P. 53 FOR ANSWERS TO THIS EXERCISE

Time: 40 minutes

Case Study 4.1

The Chameau family is well respected in the Haitian community because they are religious with great moral values. They moved to Birmingham, England because of political issues in Haiti. Jean Daniel, the youngest son of this family, is 27 years old and lives at home with his parents. For the last year, he has been using alcohol to the point that he stumbles frequently. His family has been trying to get him to seek help from a local clinic. However, he refuses because many of the professionals at the clinic live in the community and they might reveal his problem to others. Recently, he began having fevers and his parents took him to the clinic where he was diagnosed with pneumonia. Laboratory tests revealed that he had elevated liver enzymes and was HIV positive. Jean Daniel was in shock when the doctor informed him that he was HIV positive. He confessed to the doctor that he was using recreational drugs, drinking alcohol to forget 'his problems', and was gay. He said he could not tell his family about his substance use or that he was gay because he did not want to bring shame to them.

1   Is the Haitian culture primarily collectivistic or individualistic?
2   What are Haitians' traditional views of homosexuality and substance misuse?
3   If Jean Daniel's parents were to learn of his positive HIV status, how might they react if they are religious and traditional?
4   Identify three culturally congruent strategies specific to Haitians in a collectivistic culture.

COLLECTIVISTIC VERSUS INDIVIDUALISTIC CULTURAL VALUES

Individuals within collectivistic and individualistic cultures change over time according to individuality and the variant characteristics of culture that includes the following (Purnell, 2013):

➤ Sex and gender: sex refers to biology; gender refers to roles
➤ Age: younger people *usually* acculturate easier and more rapidly than do older people

➤ Religious affiliation: religion, especially for the devout, may dictate what is acceptable in health-care practices

➤ Educational status: individuals with low educational levels have more difficulty with health literacy than do more educated individuals, requiring the use of more simplified language

➤ Enclave identity: people who live most of their lives in an ethnic enclave where they can get their needs met without going outside the community may not see the need to acculturate

➤ Marital status: marital status may change one's worldview and affect social support systems

➤ Parental status: when a person becomes a parent, they become more futuristic and change their worldview

➤ Sexual orientation: being gay, lesbian, or transgender may still cause a stigma for some

➤ Gender issues: decision making and family spokesperson should not be confused. However, more traditional groups may still see the male in the family having more power and decision making authority than females

➤ Length of time away from the country of origin: usually the longer one is away from his/her country of origin, the greater the acculturation. An exception might be those who live in an ethnic enclave and who might be more traditional and who do not have the desire or need to acculturate

➤ Reason for migration (sojourner, immigrant, refugee, or undocumented status): sojourners come to a new country for a short period of time for business or some other reason and do not have the need or desire to acculturate. Immigrants who come to a new country willingly usually have the desire to acculturate. Refugees migrate for fear of reprisal, including possible death, in their home county. For people who are undocumented, they may stay hidden, follow all the rules, and do not have the opportunity to acculturate.

Cultures change over time as do individuals within a culture. Table 4.1 depicts the dominant values of collectivistic and individualistic cultures from an ethical perspective that may affect decision-making. People will vary within the culture depending on the variant characteristic of culture, life circumstances, and position in the family or organization. For example, professionals who are in leadership positions require them to take on individualistic characteristics even though they come from a collectivistic cultural worldview. The position in the family where a teenager/young adult takes on a position of authority with other siblings may display individualistic traits even though he/she comes from a collectivistic culture. A scale of 1 to 10 with 1 being highly collectivistic and 10 being individualistic can be a rating system; not all cultures are at the extremes. Some cultures may be a 5 on the 1 to 10 scale; thus, an individual assessment is required before interventions are recommended.

SELF-ASSESSMENT EXERCISE 4.2

> **Time: 15 minutes**
> On a scale of 1 to 10 with 1 being highly collectivistic and 10 being highly individualistic, how do you rate yourself? Why?
>
> 1   2   3   4   5   6   7   8   9   10
>
> - Can you give examples of when you are more collectivistic?
> - Can you give examples of when you are more individualistic? Provide a variety of examples from home and work.
> - How have you changed over time within the last five years, last 10 years?
> - Have you changed significantly in the collectivism versus individualism scale from your parents?

REFERENCES

Bui Y and A Turnbull. 2003. "East Meets West: Analysis of Person-centered Planning in the Context of Asian American Values". *Education and Training and Mental Retardation and Developmental Disabilities*, 38: 18–31.

Colin J and G Paperwalla. 2013. "People of Haitian Heritage". Edited by L Purnell. *Transcultural Healthcare: A Culturally Competent Approach*, 4th ed. 269–87. Philadelphia, PA: F.A. Davis.

Giger J, R Davidhizar, L Purnell, JT Harden, J Phillips and O Strickland. 2007. "American Academy of Nursing Expert Panel Report: Developing Cultural Competence to Eliminate Health Disparities in Ethnic Minorities and Other Vulnerable Populations". *Journal of Transcultural Nursing*, 18: 95–102.

Greenfield P, E Trumbull and C Rothstein-Fisch. 2003. "Bridging Cultures." *Culture Psychology Bulletin*, 37: 6–16.

Hofstede G. 2001. *Culture's consequences: Comparing Values, Behaviors, Institutions, and Organizations Across Nations* (2nd ed.). Thousand Oaks, CA: Sage.

Hofstede G and J Hofstede. 2005. *Cultures and Organizations: Software of the Mind* (2nd ed.). New York, NY: McGraw-Hill.

Human Genome Project. (2012). National Human Genome Research Project. www.genome.gov/12011238.

Ibriham F, G Roys-Sodowsky and H Ohnishi. 2001. "Worldview". Edited by J Pontero, M Casas, L Suzuki and C Alexander. *Handbook of Multicultural Counselling*, 2nd ed. 425–56. Thousand Oaks, CA: Sage.

Markus HR and S Kitayama. 1991. "Culture and the Self: Implications for Cognition, Emotion, and Motivation". *Psychological Review*, 98: 224–53.

Morgan K and M Townsend. 2012. "Cultural and Spiritual Concepts Relevant to Psychiatric/Mental Health Nursing". Edited by M Townsend. *Psychiatric Mental Health Nursing: Concepts of Care in Evidence-based Practice*, 95–120. Philadelphia, PA: F.A. Davis.

Purnell L. 2010. "Cultural Rituals in Health and Nursing Care". Edited by P Esterhuizen and A Kuchert. *Diversiteit in de Verpleeg-kunde [Diversity in Nursing]*. 130–96. The Netherlands: Springer Utigeverij.

Purnell L. 2011. "Application of Transcultural Theory to Mental Health-substance Use in an International Context". Edited by DB Cooper. *Intervention in Mental Health-substance Use*. 52–68. Boca Raton, FL: CRC Press.

Purnell L. 2013a. "The Purnell Model for cultural competence". Edited by L Purnell, *Transcultural Health Care. A Culturally Competent Approach,* 4th ed. 15–44. Philadelphia, PA: F.A. Davis.

Purnell L. 2013b. "Application of Transcultural Theory to Practice: The Purnell Model. Edited by DB Cooper and J Cooper. *Palliative Care within Mental Health: Principles and Philosophy*. 22–44. Boca Raton, FL: CRC Press.

Purnell L, R Davidhizar, J Giger, O Strickland, D Fishman and D Allison. 2011. "A Guide to Developing a Culturally Competent Organization". *Journal of Transcultural Nursing*, 22: 7–14.

Purnell L and S Pontious. (2014). "Collectivist and Individualistic Approaches to Cultural Health Care". Edited by R Gurung. *Multicultural Approaches to Health and Wellness in America* (volume 1). Santa Barbara, CA: ABC-CLIO-LLC.

Rothstein-Fisch C, P Greenfield, and B Quiroz. 2001. "Continuum of 'Individualistic' and 'Collectivistic' Values. National Center on Secondary Education". Retrieved from www.ncset.org/publications/essentialtools/diversity/partIII.asp.

Ting-Toomey S. 1996. "Managing Intercultural Conflicts Effectively". Edited by LA Samovar and RE Porter. *Managing Intercultural Conflicts Effectively*, 8th ed. Boston, MA: Wadsworth.

TO LEARN MORE

American Nurses Association. *Code of Ethics*. www.nursingworld.org/EthicsStandards/CodeofEthicsforNurses.aspx

Douglas M, M Rosenkoetter, D Pacquiao, LC Clark, M Hattar Pollara, J Lauderdale, J Milsted, D Nardi and L Purnell. 2014. Guidelines for implementing culturally competent nursing care. *Journal of Transcultural Nursing*, 25: 109–221.
  These guidelines have been endorsed by the International Council of Nurses and the World Health Organization.

Gurung AR. Editor. 2014. *Multicultural Approaches to Health and Wellness in America. Volume 2: Mental Health and Mind-Body Connections*. Oxford, UK: Praeger.

International Council of Nurses. Code of Ethics. www.icn.ch/who-we-are/code-of-ethics-for-nurses

National Association for Addiction Counselors. 2011. Ethical Standards of Alcoholism and Drug Abuse Counselors. www.naadac.org

Nurse.com. (October 19, 2015). Tips for making patient-centered ethical decisions. https://news.nurse.com/2015/10/19/tips-for-making-patient-centered-ethical-decisions/

Royal College of Nursing Great Britain. Has standards of conduct for specialty groups. www.rcn.org.uk/

ANSWERS TO SELF-ASSESSMENT EXERCISE 4.1 HAITIAN CASE STUDY – *SEE* P. 49

---

1 Is the Haitian culture primarily collectivistic or individualistic?
a The Haitian culture is collectivistic with values of interdependence, adherence to traditional values, shame and guilt, and living with family.

2 What are Haitians' traditional views of homosexuality and substance misuse?
a Homosexuality is taboo in Haitian culture so gay and lesbian individuals remain closeted. If a family member discloses that he or she is gay, everyone keeps it quiet; there is total denial.

3 If Jean Daniel's parents were to learn of his positive HIV status, how might they react if they are religious and traditional?
a Gay and lesbian relationships are not talked about, even within the family because of the stigma they carry.

4 Identify three culturally congruent strategies specific to Haitians in a collectivistic culture.
● Do not disclose Jean Daniels's HIV status to his parents. The decision to disclose his status remains totally with him.
● Explain the universal precautions of HIV/AIDS care to Jean Daniel. For this reason alone, encourage him to disclose his status to his parents.
● Assist Jean Daniel to find a mental health professional who is unknown to the community where he lives.

CHAPTER 5

Mental health–substance use

Alyna Turner, Nola M Ries, and Amanda L Baker

INTRODUCTION

Mental ill health and substance misuse frequently occur concurrently and can negatively interact with one another. Mental ill health can range from mild, transient symptoms through to severe and persistent conditions including psychoses, such as schizophrenia and bipolar affective disorder; and severe depression or anxiety disorders. Substance misuse can also vary in severity, persistence, and significance. Use exceeding national health guidelines may be defined as 'problematic' and may place the person at longer-term health risks but may not be currently associated with any obvious functional or psychological difficulties. At the other end of the spectrum, the level of substance use may be such that it is having more immediate and obvious impacts on physical and mental health, role and identity, as well as potential social, financial, and legal consequences (Turner and Baker, 2011). Case studies presented in this chapter run as a continuing theme throughout.

With regard to substance use, although the use of tobacco and alcohol is legal and often viewed as normal and even encouraged, these substances are associated with the greatest burden of illness of all psychoactive substances. Other substances may be medically supported or controlled, in that medical prescriptions are required, however they may be misused by some people, or diverted for supply to other people. The drug types most commonly misused include opiates for pain relief, stimulants such as amphetamines for attention deficit hyperactivity disorder, or sedative medications prescribed to help manage anxiety or help with sleep (e.g. benzodiazepine). Other psychoactive substances are more easily available for use in everyday life, such as inhalants including glue, paint, and petrol (Turner and Baker, 2011). Finally, illegal drugs include opiates such as heroin, cocaine, cannabis, and synthetic drugs including amphetamine-type stimulants (e.g. amphetamine, methamphetamine, and MDMA) and new psychoactive substances (e.g. synthetic cannabinoids, phenethylamines, and cathinones).

Living with mental health challenges can result in a greater likelihood of using psychoactive substances at harmful levels (Glantz et al., 2009), while in some people substance use can trigger mental health symptoms or conditions (e.g. drug-induced psychosis or schizophrenia). Among those with first episode psychosis, around half have a history of cannabis use and a third have a current use disorder, with similar rates for alcohol use (Wisdom et al., 2011).

KEY POINT 5.1

Mental health conditions and substance use commonly co-occur and can negatively impact outcomes.

REFLECTIVE PRACTICE EXERCISE 5.1

> **Time: 15 minutes**
> What may be some of the reasons why substance use and mental ill health commonly co-occur? Consider biological, psychological, and social factors.

In addition to diagnostic and treatment complexities, people experiencing mental health–substance use problems (MHSU), their family and health professionals, as well as researchers, policy and law makers and law enforcement workers and agencies are frequently faced with dilemmas involving competing beliefs, values, priorities, policies, and laws. While many of these ethical dilemmas are relatively easily navigated by a trained individual following professional and service guidelines, others are more complex, with the 'best' option either not obvious or rendered unachievable by circumstance. Significant cultural, legal, and philosophical differences exist across countries, states, and even services and individuals.

Case Study 5.1.1

Melanie (28) presented at a drug and alcohol service following referral from her probation officer. She has reduced her heavy use of cocaine but continues to use it occasionally, despite panic attacks that have been with her since high school. She reveals she has just found out that she is pregnant.

Case Study 5.2.1

Peter (40) experiences problems with depression. He finds it difficult to socialise with people and presents to a community mental health centre with thoughts of harming himself. He drinks every night and smokes cannabis most nights.

Case Study 5.3.1

Rick (19) is brought into hospital by ambulance following an episode where he was shouting loudly on the street and threatening passers-by. He thinks people are trying to harm him and he is scared. He uses methamphetamine regularly and began to inject it a few months ago.

Case Study 5.4.1

Judy (50) has lived with a diagnosis of schizophrenia for 30 years. She started smoking when she was admitted to hospital at the age of 19. She is overweight, rarely goes out and smokes 30 cigarettes a day. Her health is deteriorating.

THE IMPACT OF MHSU ON THE INDIVIDUAL AND FAMILY

A person's experience of mental ill health and their choice of substance, as well as the social and legal consequences of these conditions, will depend on larger influences, including family, culture, religion, generational influences, and multiple systems (legal, medical, and government). These influences will impact on the individual's or family's beliefs around whether there is an issue to address, whether and how assistance should be sought, what that assistance may look like, and their experience of stigma from internal, external and institutional sources.

Stigma experienced by people experiencing MHSU is a significant issue. In a study spanning 14 countries, drug addiction was identified as the most stigmatised of 18 conditions, alcoholism the fourth, and chronic mental disorder the eighth (Room et al., 2001). Internal, or self-stigma, may result in the person seeing themselves as unworthy of help, respect, and social inclusion, often precipitated or worsened by the experience of intentional or unintentional marginalisation, prejudice, and discrimination by others and the broader society. They may experience feelings of shame, self-blame, distress, and hopelessness. They may cope with stigma by secrecy or withdrawal, to protect themselves from rejection, but resulting in further isolation (Link et al., 1997) and reluctance to seek or accept help. Self-stigma arises from the internalisation of stigmatised views held by others, which can also be represented socially by structural discrimination, including representations by the media and laws, policies and societal practices which negatively position people with MHSU problems, and/or intentionally or unintentionally restrict their opportunities (Corrigan et al., 2004).

KEY POINT 5.2

Stigma, including from internal, social, and structural sources, can have a negative impact on a person's mental health in addition to producing social and occupational discrimination and loss of opportunities.

REFLECTIVE PRACTICE EXERCISE 5.2

Time: 10 minutes
What impact would 'tough on drugs/anti-smoking/just say no' campaigns and policies have on the stigma directed at individuals who continue to use?

Case Study 5.4.2

Judy receives a pension and the cost of cigarettes is taking up most of her income. She is finding it increasingly difficult to cover household expenses, and is buying less and less food. Her brother, who often helps her out, has refused this time, telling her she needs to stop smoking first. Judy is feeling increasingly stressed, and copes by smoking.

For many people experiencing MHSU, family may be their only means of financial, emotional and/or functional support. This support can be protective, for example, in people experiencing schizophrenia in substance use treatment, support was associated with greater reductions in use (Clark, 2001). Furthermore, in contrast to the notion that money will be spent on drugs, financial support had a greater impact than quantity of informal care given on reducing substance use, and as such may help avoid the spiral into poverty and its consequences. Once basic economic needs are met, people experiencing severe mental health conditions can then better address substance use (Clark, 2001).

While family are an important source of support, as with any illness, living with MHSU is stressful for the support network as well as the individual, with carers at increased risk of burnout, and their own mental health challenges, particularly depression. They may experience stigma, judgment or 'helpful advice' from others around the situation with the individual, including expressed and implied opinions that they have some responsibility for the problem(s). In some cases, support networks may marginalise the individual experiencing MHSU problems due to differences and challenges, or attempts to push the person into treatment. Studies have found that, compared to people experiencing severe mental health conditions alone, relatives of people experiencing mental health–substance use problems perceive those individuals to have more control over the cause of their mental health symptoms (Niv et al., 2007) while the individuals themselves express lower family satisfaction and greater desire for family treatment (Dixon et al., 1995).

KEY POINT 5.3

For people experiencing MHSU, family and close networks are an important source of financial, emotional, and practical support, however they are not immune to stigma.

Case Study 5.2.2

Peter's workmates are annoyed that he keeps taking days off work. They know he uses cannabis and he often joins them for a drink after work, but does not stay long. They feel he is bringing problems on himself by smoking so much and are becoming increasingly hostile towards him on the job.

Finally, there are a number of safety issues relevant to people experiencing MHSU, including both personal safety and safety of others, such as:

➤ Increased risk of death: in people experiencing severe mental illness (schizophrenia, bipolar disorder, and unipolar depression), mortality risk is significantly higher in those with substance use disorders than those without. A large prospective Danish register study found an increased risk of death due to accidents (primarily accidental poisonings and poisonings with undetermined intent in people with alcohol, cannabis, 'hard' drug, and polydrug use disorders) and increased rates of suicide for those experiencing depression and combined alcohol and 'hard' drug use (Hjorthøj et al., 2015).

➤ Increased risk of being a victim of violence: people experiencing severe mental health conditions are up to 11 times more likely to be victims of violent crime (Teplin et al., 2005), with the risk increasing with co-occurring substance use (Hiday et al., 1999).

➤ Risk of being a perpetrator of violence: one review found that, when compared with the general population, the odds of violence by people experiencing severe mental illness with substance use disorders increased 8–10 fold (Pickard and Fazel, 2013).

➤ Safety of children: for example, children exposed to parental mental health problems, substance use, and domestic violence were more likely to have behavioural problems when young (Whitaker et al., 2006), and depression, and substance use (alcohol, smoking, and drug abuse) in adulthood (Felitti et al., 1998) when compared with children of parents with one of the issues in isolation.

KEY POINT 5.4

While stereotyped views of people with MHSU label them as violent and unpredictable, research suggests they are at greater risk of being a victim of violence or experiencing significant ill health and fatal accidents.

Case Study 5.1.2

Melanie's panic attacks have become more frequent lately, and while escalating her cocaine use, she begins to drink alcohol to help her calm down. She does not want to continue with the pregnancy. She has started sex work again to support her drug use. She is worried she might have to move back in with her parents but wonders if they will allow her back.

Case Study 5.3.2

Rick has been falling out with friends and his girlfriend has broken off their relationship because he was 'getting too jealous'. He realises he feels more paranoid the more he uses methamphetamine but he loves the initial 'high'. Last week he shared injecting equipment at a party.

REFLECTIVE PRACTICE EXERCISE 5.3

> **Time: 30 minutes**
> Of the presentations in the Case Studies above, which aspects are challenging?
> - The idea that someone took up smoking in hospital?
> - Continued drug use in pregnancy?
> - Abusive behaviour to others related to injecting methamphetamine?
> - Lack of understanding by workmates feeling the person was bringing his problems on himself?
> - Family members withdrawing support because of the behaviour?
> - Why is one (or more) of these scenarios more challenging for you than others?
> - How would you deal with this if faced with a similar presentation?
> - Where are the ethical challenges?

MENTAL HEALTH–SUBSTANCE USE AND CLINICAL SETTINGS

People experiencing MHSU problems who have contact with clinical and treatment settings may do so for treatment, rehabilitation or support for mental health issues, substance use treatment, or physical ill health, injury or chronic disease. Treatment settings may include mental health and substance use inpatient, residential and outpatient facilities, general medical inpatient, outpatient and general practice facilities, holistic health settings, and prison based facilities. The nature of the treatment settings, policies, and practices will vary across services, regions, and countries.

Informed consent (*see* Chapters 10 and 13)

Any healthcare or research activity requires valid and voluntary informed consent. This is directly related to the right of all people, including those with 'disabilities' as mandated by the United Nations as well as all major research guidelines, to make their own decisions around whether they wish to accept or decline the offer of healthcare/research. Valid informed consent requires capacity to make the decision about the specific issue at that specific time; provision of voluntary consent, free from manipulation or undue influence from others; provision of all required information specific to the healthcare or research to be carried out, in an appropriate language (or other means) that the person understands; a two way, balanced, transparent discussion; and sufficient time for the person to consider and clarify information prior to making a decision (Queensland Health, 2012). The process of informed consent may be compromised by a range of factors, for example, mental or cognitive status of the individual (e.g. influenced by mental health symptoms, or substances or withdrawal symptoms); power imbalances or other relationship factors between individuals and healthcare providers (e.g. agreeing to please, or refusing due to a poor relationship); inappropriate presentation of study information (verbal and/or written material that is too lengthy and/or technical or too short or not read or attended to); or misconceptions regarding the person's understanding or ability to understand the information to be provided. In mental health–substance use problems, the issue of involuntary treatment (treatment without consent) is significant. The degree of social acceptance for involuntary treatment of people experiencing MHSU problems varies depending on the condition/s, for example in an Australian survey, there was greater support for coercive treatment for heroin rather than alcohol (Meurk et al., 2014).

Diagnosis

For many health professionals and services, diagnosis is an integral part of the process of assessment with the view to treatment. Diagnoses are useful for treatment planning, goal setting, research, guiding treatment choice from an evidence-based perspective, communication, and determining prognosis. However, the diagnostic process raises a number of ethical issues around risk versus benefit. An accurate diagnosis requires assessment by a professional with appropriate skills, training, knowledge, and supervision, whereas this is not always the case, leading to inappropriate diagnoses, labeling and treatment. It may be that there is no access to professionals with the expertise to resolve diagnostic dilemmas (e.g. limited access to psychiatrists in rural areas), but there is an external push to 'tick a box' for service, prescribing or insurance reasons. Providing a diagnosis may cause harm, for example increased self-stigma, anxiety, stress or guilt; and risk of discrimination (e.g. within different treatment settings; employment settings and professional licensing). In some treatment situations, it may not even be necessary, for example, many psychological approaches have been shown to work for a range of different diagnoses or clusters of symptoms, e.g. CBT for depression and/or anxiety symptoms.

KEY POINT 5.5

The process of diagnosis has both benefits and risks to the individual, with risks increased should there be a lack of appropriate clinical skills, training, knowledge, and supervision.

Privacy and confidentiality

The confidentiality of personal medical information is well accepted and seemingly well protected by international guidelines, national laws, and service and professional guidelines and operating procedures. However, concerns about confidentiality are a major barrier to treatment identified by people experiencing mental health issues, and the right to confidentiality of the individuals' information does have clear limits (for example, in the case of risk of harm to self or others), as well as more subtle ones. For example, the increasing modernization of health data storage (e.g. electronic health records) results in different opportunities to access that data illegally from outside the service or by health professionals not directly involved in the person's care. For this reason, organisations have legal obligations to implement security measures for electronic systems. Such measures may be technical (e.g., firewalls, encryption, passwords) and administrative/organisational (role-based access so, e.g., a financial officer does not have access to detailed clinical notes but only the fee codes associated with a service; organisational policies about taking laptops off-site, and so on). Audits are also important to check who is accessing electronic records to ensure they have a legitimate reason for doing so.

In smaller, rural communities, the opportunities for confidentiality breaches are increased (e.g. people observing visitors to a mental health clinic, or listening more carefully to clinic staff conversations). This may lead to people not seeking or complying with treatment due to stigma concerns or health professionals acting against legal and ethical guidelines to protect privacy (e.g. by not disclosing private information despite risk of violence or reportable ill health, or omitting information from insurance forms or medical records) (Roberts et al., 1999).

KEY POINT 5.6

While confidentiality is a key feature of ethical, service, national, and international guidelines, concerns about confidentiality breaches are a significant barrier to treatment.

Role, boundaries, and dual relationships

Dual relationships between the individual and professional may range from unintended and inadvertent (e.g. a person who happens to work in the professional's local supermarket), through to deliberate exploitations (e.g. initiation of a sexual relationship). Overlapping relationships can impact on treatment boundaries, which are designed to respect and protect the individual's wellbeing and best interest, and are particularly important in the care of people experiencing MHSU problems. 'Boundary violations' (as opposed to 'boundary crossings' which are not seen to be coercive, exploitative or harmful) have negative consequences for the individual, and are exploitative and harmful to the person and their care. As with privacy and confidentiality, rural communities hold particular challenges for professionals who will experience 'everyday' dual relationships. People experiencing MHSU problems may be providers of essential services within the town, fellow parents, or even within their wider social or kin network and no other options for their care may exist in the town. Professionals may lack opportunities for consultation around these concerns, or their opportunities for supervision/consultation in their area may be impacted on by dual relationships (e.g. if the individual is in some way connected to the consultant).

KEY POINT 5.7

Treatment boundaries are important in the care of people with MHSU, with violations resulting from exploitative dual relationships having the potential to cause significant harm.

MHSU IN HEALTH PROFESSIONALS

Professionals are not immune to MHSU problems. Indeed, studies suggest rates of MHSU are higher among medical practitioners, particularly psychiatrists, than the general population (Wilson et al., 1999). In some, but certainly not all, cases these issues may result in impairment. Definitions of 'impairment' generally refer to a mental, behavioural or physical condition (including substance use) that detrimentally affects the person's capacity to safely engage in professional activities. Ethical, licensing, and registration guidelines generally direct the professional (or their colleague) to access appropriate treatment to prevent and deal with the impairment, and to report to licensing boards if the professional is practicing while intoxicated by alcohol or drugs, or the impairment places the public at risk of substantial harm (Australian Health Practitioners Regulator Agency, 2016). However, professionals experiencing MHSU problems face the same treatment barriers as others, including stigma and confidentiality concerns, as well as fear of discrimination by colleagues, licensing boards, and professional institutions (Hassan et al., 2013). These concerns can then result in reduced disclosure and help seeking behaviours. The creation and use of employee assistance programs that are contracted out to private mental health professionals otherwise unconnected to the employing organisation is one way to address confidentiality concerns (particularly with the advent of electronic medical records that can be more widely and easily accessed).

KEY POINT 5.8

Health professionals are not immune to MHSU problems, nor the stigma associated with those issues.

Case Study 5.1.3

Melanie continues to attend counselling with you for a while as it's required by her probation officer. She stops attending when her probation is up. When she last saw you she was polite but disinterested in discussing continued treatment. She continued with her pregnancy.

Case Study 5.2.3

Peter decides to leave his job and travel overseas. He thinks it may improve his mood and he might get away from his drinking and drug habits. But in the USA he starts drinking heavily again and also smoking cannabis. He takes an overdose and finds himself in hospital. The psychiatrist advises he needs to abstain from alcohol and drugs for the rest of his life because he has a disease.

Case Study 5.3.3

Rick has been throwing things around his apartment and yelling abusively at night. The neighbours call the police, who give Rick a warning. 'Can't you just lock him up?' pleads a neighbour.

Case Study 5.4.3

Judy is admitted to hospital with a transient ischaemic attack, a mini-stroke. She is strongly advised to give up smoking and is administered nicotine replacement therapy during her short hospital stay. She is a given a few days' supply upon leaving hospital and thinks she would really like to quit this time. Once NRT is finished, Judy orders herself an electronic cigarette over the internet as they are not sold in Australia. She's heard they might really help her to stay off smoking.

SELF-ASSESSMENT EXERCISE 5.1

Time: 45 minutes

1 What are some of the key requirements of valid, informed consent?
2 What are some of the pros and cons of giving a diagnosis? In what situations would the risks be increased?
3 In your professional practice (clinical and/or research), what are the guiding documents re: confidentiality (consider professional ethical guidelines, service guidelines, and state and national privacy legislation)? What are the limits to confidentiality in your service and profession, and what behaviours may result in risks to confidentiality?
4 What could you do if you were requested to assess an individual who was dating a friend of yours? What about if they were referred to your multidisciplinary team that discussed all persons as a team at each meeting?
5 What are the requirements of your ethical guidelines if you suspect a colleague is experiencing difficulties with MHSU? Where could you find support to help handle this situation?

MHSU AND RESEARCH

REFLECTIVE PRACTICE EXERCISE 5.4

Time: 15 minutes

While the principles of the requirement of voluntary informed consent are clearly laid out in ethical guidelines, translation into real life procedures can be challenging. What are some approaches that may improve or worsen the informed consent process?

Case Study 5.3.4

Rick enters a study on blood-borne viruses, partly because he will be reimbursed $40 for the interview. When he arrives he finds out he will actually receive a voucher that cannot be spent on tobacco or alcohol.

Risk/benefit assessment of research

Research into MHSU has the potential to have both significant benefits and risks of harm. Harms may be psychological (boredom, distress, embarrassment, exacerbation of an existing condition); physical (high blood pressure, death, exacerbation of an existing condition); legal (fines or imprisonment); economic (e.g. lost time at work, medical bills); or social (e.g. stigmatization, harm to reputation or relationships (Iltis et al., 2013).

The risks and benefits of a study can vary widely and need to be assessed by the researcher, the institution, ethics committees, and participants. At one end of the spectrum, the study may provide a greater understanding of the population of interest with little personal benefit to the participant but where risks may be minimal (for example, an anonymous survey asking questions around substance use in the wider community, where the risks may be limited to inconvenience, or for some, feelings of discomfort or distress at answering some of the questions). At the other end, there may be greater potential benefits to the individual participant, but greater potential for harm, which they are willing to accept (for example, a clinical trial of a promising new medication that carries risks of adverse events, and utilizes assessments with highly sensitive and detailed questions). Ethical review boards need to determine whether risks have been minimised and whether benefits justify the risks, and may halt or delay studies if concerns exist. Further, investigators may be less willing to conduct necessary research studies due to concerns about real and perceived risks (for example, suicidal ideation is commonly an exclusion criterion in research, as such there is little evidence regarding treatments with varying degrees of suicidality) (Iltis et al., 2013).

KEY POINT 5.9

The risks and benefits of a research project must be carefully considered prior to project commencement by all parties (researchers, participants, institutions, and ethics committees) with continual monitoring during project duration.

Case Study 5.2.4

Peter has been invited to take part in a clinical trial investigating whether a medication can help with reducing or ceasing cannabis use. While he is very keen to find something to help him with cutting out his cannabis use, he is concerned about possible side effects.

Case Study 5.4.4

Judy is admitted to a mental health hospital six months later. University researchers are interested in a qualitative study of ex-smokers and would like to recruit her into the study.

Confidentiality and its limits

As with clinical services, should confidentiality not be protected, risk of harm to participants is significant (e.g. risks to employment, insurance, and reputation). There are potential limits to confidentiality in research studies, particularly with regard to risk of harm to self or others (e.g. the specifics of a violent crime; children experiencing abuse or neglect; or the presence of reportable communicable diseases). Research participants, researchers, and ethics committees may need to make decisions about the disclosure, collection, and storage of sensitive information, for example criminal activities or illicit drug use and its consequences. There have been situations where researchers have been compelled through court processes to release research data when sought for law enforcement purposes. As such, the importance of information gathered in the study (and keeping information collected to the minimum required to meet the study aims) needs to be balanced against potential risks of disclosure.

KEY POINT 5.10

The necessity of the information collected, the measures taken to protect the privacy of that information, and participant explanations of the limits of that privacy, must be addressed in all research protocols.

Case Study 5.1.4

Melanie re-enters counselling some time later and is reticent to admit to drug use in case custody of her baby is questioned. Via this service, she is approached to participate in a study about sex workers. The researchers are not allowed to ask any questions about crimes she may have committed.

MHSU AND SOCIETY: LEGAL AND POLICY PERSPECTIVES

Legal and ethical issues centre on the rights of people with disabilities and the tension between personal autonomy and protection from harm. Adults should generally be free to make their own choices, take risks, and live the life that accords with their own values and preferences. Respect for this personal freedom has limits, however, as there is a social imperative to protect people from harms perpetrated against them by others. In some circumstances, individuals ought to be restrained from self-harming behaviours, but ideological differences of opinion exist on the justifiable extent of such restraints. Likewise, there is a persistent debate on the use of punitive/criminal and restrictive approaches to deal with social problems of MHSU problems, often contrasted with harm reduction and supportive approaches.

This chapter views these issues through a public health lens: 'Public health is what we, as a society, do collectively to assure the conditions for people to be healthy' (Institute of Medicine, 2003).

In regard to MHSU, any existing or proposed intervention – including legislation, funding allocations to programs, treatment options – can be scrutinised to ask whether it does or is likely to produce healthier outcomes. Answers to this question depend on the evidence base available to support choices at macro (society/governmental), meso (organisational/sectoral) and micro (client/practitioner) levels.

These moral imperatives and philosophical debates take practical form in laws and practices concerning the rights and treatment of people experiencing MHSU problems. Legal frameworks and professional practices vary across countries, but international instruments set out common principles and goals in relation to the rights of people with disabilities, including specific guidance for mental illness.

SELF-ASSESSMENT EXERCISE 5.5

> **Time: 10 minutes**
> - Does this happen in your area of practice?
> - How do you, as a professional, ensure that individual autonomy is upheld?

DECISION MAKING AND CAPACITY

Respect for autonomous decision making capacity is a hallmark of person-hood. The law in many areas – for example, in relation to older adults, adolescents, and people with various types of cognitive impairments – is slowly shifting away from assumptions or stereotypes of incapacity to recognise the importance of individualised assessments of capacity, particularly for individuals who experience fluctuations in their cognitive abilities. Research stresses the importance of individualised assessment for people experiencing MHSU problems, as different substances may affect cognition in different ways (Potvin et al., 2012). Capacity assessment must be even more nuanced in situations of triple diagnosis, the intersection of mental health and substance use with other conditions that affect cognition, such as intellectual disability (Lougheed and Farrell, 2013).

Bright line distinctions between having and not having capacity are increasingly criticised. As soon as a person is judged to lack capacity, important decision making rights are stripped from the individual and given over to third parties in formal and informal ways. Quasi-judicial tribunals or courts may make orders concerning treatment and/or detention. Vague principles of the 'best interests' of the person who lacks capacity due to mental impairment are malleable and can be used to justify a range of measures that may not accord with the person's own values and wishes.

A paradigm shift in law and policy focuses on replacing the model of substituted decision making to one of supported decision making, by which people who experience periods of reduced capacity receive the supports they need to make decisions about matters that affect them (*see* Chapter 10 and 13). Supported decision making is advocated in the United Nations Convention on the Rights of Persons with Disabilities and taking shape in domestic legal frameworks (for discussion, see Australian Law Reform Commission, 2014; Richardson, 2012). For example, new legislation in the state of Victoria, Australia, establishes a new legally recognised support person, a 'supportive attorney' (Office of the Public Advocate, 2016). A person, especially someone with a condition that causes fluctuations in cognition, may appoint a trusted individual to act as a supportive attorney to assist in and help give effect to the person's decisions. Areas of supported decision making may include financial, health, and other personal matters, including healthcare/treatment decisions, access to community support services, and housing/accommodation matters. The supportive attorney can be given the authority to obtain information from service providers such as healthcare facilities, to communicate decisions on behalf of the person, and take steps to implement the person's choices. Even if a person is judged to lack capacity to make a particular decision at a specific time, decision makers and service providers should take into consideration the person's prior expressed wishes and they should have the opportunity, to the extent possible, to contribute to current treatment planning.

The move to supported decision making is consistent with other shifts toward less restrictive approaches to the treatment of people experiencing MHSU problems. For example, treatment in community rather than institutional care or detention promotes individual autonomy and social inclusion and participation for people with disabilities. Yet, the high representation of people with MHSU histories in prisons, especially in younger incarcerated offenders, indicates that criminal justice systems may lag behind health systems (Tolou-Shams et al., 2014), and this problem is highlighted in the popular press (*New York Times*: Opinion, 2016).

Evidence-informed law, policy and practice

Rigorous research is needed to develop the evidence base for laws, policies and practices:

> Ideally, public health practitioners should always incorporate scientific evidence in selecting and implementing programs, developing policies, and evaluating progress. Society pays a high opportunity cost when interventions that yield the highest health return on an investment

are not implemented. In practice, intervention decisions are often based on perceived short-term opportunities, lacking systematic planning and review of the best evidence regarding effective approaches.

(Brownson et al., 2009)

Political ideologies drive decisions that, at times, fly in the face of available evidence. For example, politicians in some jurisdictions oppose harm reducing measures like supervised injection facilities and challenge the evidence of public health benefits (Hathaway and Tousaw, 2008); policy-making can never be value free (Hawkins and Parkhurst, 2015). Some federations have varying laws across their states/provinces that establish different models for dealing with mental health and substance use issues. These differences reflect the politics of the governments in power and evaluation research is important to determine the advantages and disadvantages of different laws. In Australia, alcohol mandatory treatment laws vary significantly in the period of legally permissible involuntary detention, with modernised laws in two states removing extended detention periods and strengthening protection for patient rights in line with public health evidence and international guidance (Lander et al., 2015).

SELF-ASSESSMENT EXERCISE 5.3

> **Time: 45 minutes**
> Judy has a moderately severe stroke. The stroke, in combination with existing cognitive changes resulting from schizophrenia, mean that Judy now has cognitive deficits which affect her attention, memory, speech, and executive functioning, making some decisions much more difficult for her than previously. Her brother, Ken, has been legally identified as her supportive attorney.
>
> Consider practical measures for supported decision making that are designed to help maximise decision-making capacity in a situation such as Judy's. Which of the options from the list below are likely to enhance supported decision making?
>
> a The doctors make the choices that they think are best for Judy as they know her case and situation well
> b Ken attends appointments with health professionals without Judy
> c Ken books double appointments where possible, to allow for extra time in appointments/conversations to discuss the choices Judy has
> d Ken takes notes during appointments to help Judy remember what was discussed
> e Ken is given standard written information that is given to all patients to read to help him make the best decision for Judy
> f Judy is provided with plain language materials written to aphasia guidelines
> g Judy is provided with audio-visual aids for explaining information

h The care provider helps Judy and Ken create a list of pros and cons of different options

i Judy, Ken, and the care provider do some role playing activities of how Judy may handle particular situations

SUMMARY AND CONCLUSIONS

People living experiencing MHSU problems are a vulnerable group, facing significant stigma, real and potential opportunity loss, and barriers to seeking and receiving appropriate care. These barriers may conflict with ethical principles of equity (including having the same access to care and research as received by people experiencing other health issues), duty of care (including receiving the same quality of care as others), and trust (including being confident that their personal information will be kept private and confidential and that professionals will develop and maintain respectful relationships that help rather than hinder treatment). People experiencing MHSU problems hold the right to personal autonomy. However, this may be limited by the social imperative to protect them from harms perpetrated against them by others or themselves. Use of punitive/criminal and restrictive approaches stand in contrast with harm reduction and supportive approaches; while the notion of surrogate decision making for those with decision making impairments is beginning to shift to a supported decision making paradigm.

REFERENCES

Australian Health Practitioner Regulation Agency. 2016. Mandatory notifications. www.ahpra.gov.au/Notifications/Who-can-make-a-notification/Mandatorynotifications.aspx.

Australian Law Reform Commission. 2014. *Equality, Capacity and Disability in Commonwealth Laws* (ALRC Report 124). Sydney: Australian Law Reform Commission.

Brownson RC, JE Fielding and CM Maylahn. 2009. "Evidence-based public health: A fundamental concept for public health practice". *Annual Review of Public Health.* 30: 175–201.

Clark RE. 2001. "Family support and substance use outcomes for persons with mental illness and substance use disorders". *Schizophrenia Bulletin.* 27: 93–101.

Corrigan PW, FE Markowitz and AC Watson. 2004. "Structural levels of mental illness stigma and discrimination". *Schizophrenia Bulletin.* 30: 481–91.

Dixon L, S McNary and A Lehman. 1995. "Substance abuse and family relationships of persons with severe mental illness". *American Journal of Psychiatry.* 152: 456–8.

Felitti VJ, R Anda, D Nordenberg, DF Williamson, AM Spitz, V Edwards, MP Koss and JS Marks. 1998. "Relationship of childhood abuse and household dysfunction to many of the leading causes of death in adults: the Adverse Childhood Experiences (ACE) Study". *American Journal of Preventative Medicine.* 12: 245–58.

Glantz MD, JC Anthony, PA Berglund, L Degenhardt, L Dierker, A Kalaydjian, KR Merikangas, AM Ruscio, J Swendsen and RC Kessler. 2009. "Mental disorders as risk factors for later substance dependence: estimates of optimal prevention and treatment benefits". *Psychological Medicine*. 39: 1365–77.

Hassan TM, S Sikander, N Mazhar, T Munshi, N Galbraith and D Groll. 2013. "Canadian psychiatrists' attitudes to becoming mentally ill". *British Journal of Medical Practitioners*. 6: a619.

Hathaway AD and KI Tousaw. 2008. "Harm reduction headway and continuing resistance: Insights from safe injection in the city of Vancouver". *International Journal of Drug Policy*. 19: 11–16.

Hawkins B and J Parkhurst. 2015. "The 'good governance' of evidence in health policy. Evidence and Policy". DOI: http://dx.doi.org/10.1332/174426415X14430058455412

Hiday VA, MS Swartz, JW Swanson, R Borum and HR Wagner. 1999. "Criminal victimization of persons with severe mental illness". *Psychiatric Services*. 50: 62–8.

Hjorthøj C, MLD Østergaard, ME Benros, NG Toftdahl, A Erlangsen, JT Anderson and M Nordentoft. 2015. "Association between alcohol and substance use disorders and all-cause and cause-specific mortality in schizophrenia, bipolar disorder, and unipolar depression: a nationwide, prospective, register-based study". *The Lancet Psychiatry*. 2: 801–8.

Iltis AS, S Misra, LB Dunn, GK Brown, A Campbell, SA Earll, A Glowinski, WB Hadley, R Pies and JM DuBois. 2013. "Addressing risks to advance mental health research". *Journal of the American Medical Association Psychiatry*. 70: 1363–71.

Institute of Medicine. 2003. *The Future of the Public's Health in the 21st Century*. Washington, DC: National Academy Press.

Lander F, D Gray and E Wilkes. 2015. "The Alcohol Mandatory Treatment Act: evidence, ethics and the law". *Medical Journal of Australia*. 203: 47–9.

Link BG, EL Struening, M Rahav, JC Phelan and L Nuttbrock. 1997. "On stigma and its consequences: Evidence from a longitudinal study on men with dual diagnoses of mental illness and substance abuse". *Journal of Health and Social Behavior*. 38: 177–90.

Lougheed DC and S Farrell. 2013. "The challenge of a 'Triple Diagnosis': Identifying and serving homeless Canadian adults with a dual diagnosis". *Journal of Policy and Practice in Intellectual Disabilities*. 10: 230–5.

Meurk C, A Carter, B Partridge, J Lucke and W Hall. 2014. "How is acceptance of the brain disease model of addiction related to Australians' attitudes towards addicted individuals and treatments for addiction?" *BMC Psychiatry*. 14: 1.

New York Times. 2016. "Opinion. Getting the mentally ill out of jail and off the streets". *The New York Times*. 9 May. www.nytimes.com/roomfordebate/2016/05/09/getting-the-mentally-ill-out-of-jail-and-off-the-streets.

Niv N, SR Lopez, SM Glynn and K Mueser. 2007. "The role of substance use in families' attributions and affective reactions to their relative with severe mental illness". *Journal of Nervous and Mental Disorders*. 195: 307–14.

Office of the Public Advocate. 2016. *Supportive Attorney Appointments*. Carlton, Victoria: Office of the Public Advocate. www.publicadvocate.vic.gov.au/power-of-attorney/supportive-attorney-appointments.

Pickard H and S Fazel. 2013. "Substance abuse as a risk factor for violence in mental illness: some implications for forensic psychiatric practice and clinical ethics". *Current Opinion in Psychiatry*. 26: 349–54.

Potvin S, K Stavro and J Pelletier. 2012. "Paradoxical cognitive capacities in dual diagnosis schizophrenia: the quest for explanatory factors". *Journal of Dual Diagnosis*. 8: 35–47.

Queensland Health. 2012. "Guide to Informed Decision-making in Healthcare". www. health.qld.gov.au/consent/documents/ic-guide.pdf.

Richardson G. 2012. "Mental disabilities and the law: from substitute to supported decision-making?" *Current Legal Problems.* 65: 333–54.

Roberts LW, J Battaglia and RS Epstein. 1999. "Frontier ethics: mental health care needs and ethical dilemmas in rural communities". *Psychiatric Services.* 50: 497–503.

Room R, J Rehm, RT Trotter II and A Paglia. 2001. "Cross-cultural views on stigma, valuation, parity and societal values towards disability". Edited by TB Üstün, S Chatterji, JE Bickenback, RT Trotter II, R Room, J Rehm and S Saxena. *Disability and Culture: Universalism and Diversity.* Seattle: Hogrefe & Huber.

Teplin LA, GM McClelland, KM Abram and DA Weiner. 2005. "Crime victimization in adults with severe mental illness: comparison with the National Crime Victimization Survey". *Archives of General Psychiatry.* 62: 911–21.

Tolou-Shams M, CJ Rizzo, SM Conrad, S Johnson, C Oliveira and LK Brown. 2014. "Predictors of detention among juveniles referred for a court clinic forensic evaluation". *Journal of the American Academy of Psychiatry and the Law.* 42: 56–65.

Turner A and AL Baker. 2011. "The psychological impact of serious illness". Edited by DB Cooper. *Introduction to Mental Health-substance Use.* Boca Raton, FL: CRC Press. pp. 94–106.

Whitaker RC, SM Orzol and RS Kahn. 2006. "Maternal mental health, substance use, and domestic violence in the year after delivery and subsequent behaviour problems in children at age 3 years". *Archives of General Psychiatry.* 63: 551–60.

Wilson A, A Rosen, P Randal, A Pethebridge, D Codyre, D Barton, P Norrie, P McGeorge and L Rose. 2009. "Psychiatrically impaired medical practitioners: an overview with special reference to impaired psychiatrists". *Australasian Psychiatry.* 17: 6–10.

Wisdom JP, JI Manuel and RE Drake. 2011. "Substance use disorder among people with first-episode psychosis: a systematic review of course and treatment". *Psychiatric Services.* 62: 1007–12.

TO LEARN MORE

Baker A and R Velleman. (Eds.). 2007. *Clinical Handbook of Co-existing Mental Health and Drug and Alcohol Problems.* London: Routledge.

Clement S, et al. 2014. "What is the impact of mental health-related stigma on help-seeking? A systematic review of quantitative and qualitative studies." *Psychological Medicine* 45: 11–27.

Mistral W (Ed.). 2013. *Emerging Perspectives on Substance Misuse.* West Sussex, UK: Wiley Blackwell. pp. 152–69.

Tamariz L., et al. 2013. "Improving the informed consent process for research subjects with low literacy: A systematic review." *Journal of General Internal Medicine* 28(1): 121–6.

United Nations Convention of Psychotropic Substances: www.unodc.org/unodc/en/treaties/psychotropics.html

United Nations Office on Drugs and Crime, World Drug Report 2015 (United Nations publication, Sales No. E.15.XI.6).

CHAPTER 6

Compassion, respect and dignity

Cynthia MA Geppert

The purpose of human life is to serve, and to show compassion and the will to help others.

Albert Schweitzer

PRE-READING EXERCISE

Time: 15 minutes

A group of medical students were asked to name two types of persons they found difficult to treat. The most frequent choices were individuals with chronic pain, addiction, psychiatric ill health, and those that were non-adherent or had social problems. They were then asked to describe two strategies they could use to have better relationships with the people experiencing illnesses they found difficult to treat. Formulate your own answers to the same two questions before you read the chapter and then after you have had some time to think about the chapter's content, respond again, then compare your answers. What have you learned? How will you apply it in your own practice?

INTRODUCTION

In February of 2013 the 'Francis Report', a public inquiry into the NHS Foundation Trust, was released (Francis, 2013). The report chronicled a culture of neglect and abuse of elderly and disabled persons in national health care institutions in Stafford, England and the surrounding area. The scandal which began in the late 2000s rocked the British nursing and medical establishment with revelations that profit and efficiency had been placed above the needs and welfare of vulnerable people, many experiencing dementia or other mental health conditions. Similar shocking revelations of abysmal treatment especially in the care of persons experiencing dementia, mental health, and substance use problems have occurred all over the developed world.

The Francis Report as well as the responses of leading nursing and medical associations in England identified three ethical values to guide the reformation of the NHS standards: dignity, respect, and compassion (Mumford, 2013; Welikala, 2014). This chapter explores the ethical implications of identifying these values as foundational to high quality health care practice and the concerns and dilemmas that face professionals who strive to integrate these values into their care of persons experiencing mental health–substance use problems.

KEY POINT 6.1

Dignity, respect, and compassion are the key virtues of the professional in health care.

REFLECTIVE PRACTICE EXERCISE 6.1

Time: 20 minutes

Prior to reading further, try and define the three values of compassion, respect, and dignity for yourself.

- How do you try to live out these values in your own professional practice?
- In your own position have you encountered pressures similar to those operating in Stafford that presented obstacles to your ability to practice according to these values?
- If so how did you try and overcome them and what was the result?

These three values have historically been a primary focus especially of nursing education and practice, yet being essential components of 'caring' they are at the heart of all the health care professions. Although almost every person has an intuitive sense of what these concepts mean, they are technically difficult to define. The three values are all interrelated, indeed inseparable conceptually and practically.

COMPASSION

Compassion is the quintessential virtue of healers. Jane Reid drawing on a large body of social science research on the value of compassion describes the practice of compassion in health care setting thus,

Compassion is also more than just doing for others, or giving technical clinical interventions of high quality; compassionate care involves creating a space to listen, giving voice to the expression of emotion, and providing opportunity for discussion of feelings.

(Reid, 2012)

Compassion is nearly synonymous with empathy, 'feeling with' in which one person through kindness and consideration, identifies with the suffering of another individual and is to be distinguished from sympathy 'feeling for' in which the person helping is set apart, and often above, the distressed individual.

KEY POINT 6.2

Compassion is empathy with the suffering of another individual.

RESPECT

Respect is the fundamental regard, even reverence, we have for the intrinsic dignity of the human being. 'To treat another person with consideration (particularly concerning that persons' values and goals) regardless of age, gender, ethnicity and class would be a general ethical requirement' (Boyd et al., 1997).

Respect in health care is expressed through taking time with individuals in care, communicating kindly, promoting their essential dignity to be clean, comfortable, and cared for.

KEY POINT 6.3

Respect is regard and consideration for the dignity of the human person.

DIGNITY

The Policy Research Institute on Aging and Ethnicity offers the following definition:

A state quality or manner worthy of esteem or respect; and 'by extension' self-respect. Dignity in care, therefore, means the kind of care, in any setting, which supports and promotes, and does not undermine, a person's self-respect regardless of any difference.

(Help the Aged, 2001)

Unethical attitudes and behaviour occur in health care when dignity is predicated on any characteristic other than essential humanity. A person by virtue deserves respect and compassion not on the basis of what they have or do not have, or what they can or cannot do, but simply by **being**. Dignity research has analysed the value into several aspects with ethical valence for health care professionals including autonomy, privacy, empowerment, and respect (Social Care Institute for Excellence, 2013).

KEY POINT 6.4

Dignity refers to the intrinsic worth of the human being.

Case study 6.1 – Alex

Alex is a 68-year-old Native American individual with alcohol induced persisting dementia and a history of schizophrenia. He was found wandering the streets of the city having been sent from a homeless program in another town on a bus. With no other options, the homeless workers take Alex to the general hospital. There the psychiatrist determines Alex to lack capacity and social workers after an exhaustive search can find no family or friends to serve as a surrogate decision maker.

As an unbefriended, incapable elder Alex becomes the responsibility of the overburdened and underfunded state protective services. Alex languishes in the hospital while the state seeks a guardian in order to place him in a nursing home if one will accept him given his remote history of conviction as a sex-offender. Such a history often prevents a person from residing in a group home as owners fear they must protect their residents from victimization.

For days he will not allow nursing staff to bathe him or change his clothes until one night, nursing staff with the assistance of hospital security hold Alex down and forcibly wash him and incinerate his clothes. From then on Alex becomes paranoid and at times sticks razor blades in his socks to defend himself from staff he believes are trying to harm him. He is considered a flight risk and so is not allowed to leave the ward without an attendant. The house officers are often overheard protesting having to care for Alex saying, 'we went into medicine to treat sick people, not babysit drunk Indians.' Nursing staff are now afraid of Alex and believe he should be either in jail or a psychiatric unit because 'we don't know how to handle these people.' Even the kindest of nursing staff are so harried caring for other ill people that they give up trying to get Alex to eat or keep up his hygiene. For days at a time no one even goes into Alex's room to change the bedding and social workers suggest letting him elope because, 'then it won't be our problem anymore.' The director of the hospital agrees saying 'he made his bed by wasting his life drinking and now he should have to lie in it.'

SELF-ASSESSMENT EXERCISE 6.1

> **Time: 40 minutes**
> Read case study 6.1 and make note of those aspects of Alex's case that could be the source of bias. Then turn to Box 6.1 and compare your list to those identified. What is the origin of these biases? Are they social, cultural, historical, psychological?

BOX 6.1

- Alex has a mental health disorder (schizophrenia) the public fears and associates with violence
- Alex has a history of sexual offense which is stigmatized in our society
- Alex has a criminal record (registered sex offender) that makes him a member of an underclass
- Alex is a member of an ethnic minority (Native American) that like many indigenous peoples has been historically exploited and politically disenfranchised
- Alex is an elder in a youth-oriented culture
- Alex is poor and powerless in a society that values wealth and power
- Alex has no family or friends to advocate for or assist him
- Alex has dementia and cannot defend or fend for himself
- Alex is an 'alcoholic' and so responsible for his behaviour and socially rejected. (*See* Chapters 4 and 7.)

Stigmatization

Alex's case reflects many of the psychosocial conditions stigmatized in Western culture. The philology of stigma is as a 'mark of disgrace'. The Canadian Mental Health Association defines stigma and differentiates it from the allied construct of discrimination. 'Discrimination is unfair treatment due to a persons' identity . . . Stigma is the negative stereotype and discrimination is the behaviour that results from this negative stereotype' (Canadian Mental Health Association, 2016).

Individuals experiencing mental health–substance use problems often live within overlapping domains of discrimination. For example, an immigrant African trans-gender sex worker experiencing bipolar and opioid use problems would be stigmatized as a prostitute with a psychiatric 'patient', and 'addict' and hence might be discriminated against on the basis of race, ethnicity, and sexual origin.

KEY POINT 6.5

Stigma is the negative stereotype of, and discrimination of, the behaviour that follows it.

Dignity and discrimination

Research has found that the combination of mental health–substance use problems is more stigmatized than either condition alone (Crisp et al., 2000). So devastating and pervasive is stigma in these areas that major governmental and advocacy organizations around the world have launched anti-stigma campaigns. Stigma has a deleterious effect on an individual's mental, physical, and spiritual health especially in light of the reality that these individuals frequently have less access to quality medical, psychological, and pastoral care.

Seeing and treating each and every person with dignity worthy of respect and compassion is the strongest safeguard for professionals and hence those they care for. Professional codes of ethics prohibit discrimination against persons on the basis of non-material, immutable characteristics such as race and gender. For example, the American Nurses Association Code of Ethics provision 2 states: 'The nurse practices with compassion and respect for the inherent dignity, worth, and unique attributes of every person' (Winland-Brown et al., 2015).

KEY POINT 6.6

Health Care Professional's Codes of Ethics prohibit discrimination and stigmatization.

Respect and stigma

Health care professionals are people who inherit the prejudices of their family of origin; who despite their education often share the ignorance of the public toward mental health–substance use problems. As members of cultural groups and segments of society, professionals share the fears and resentments of their peers, the blind spots and biases of their time and place. The ethical difference is that professionals have a higher duty to develop awareness of these limitations and how they may ethically impede or erode their ability to respect each and every person in their care. When a professional's bias or beliefs interfere with or prevent them from providing care with dignity, respect, and compassion as they are ethically mandated to do, then a conflict of interest is generated.

Conflicts of interest

Avoiding all conflicts between one's beliefs and even values as a private person and one's duty and principles as a professional is impossible. Professionalism is the commitment to identify and manage, minimize, and ameliorate any and all conflicts of interest that either potentially or in actuality harm an individual or hinder the professional from doing all the good he or she can to a person under her or his care. The obligation of the professional is to be transparent in communicating these conflicts, fair and consistent in managing them, and courageous in standing up to any forces or entities that would compromise their integrity.

KEY POINT 6.7

Professionals cannot avoid all conflicts of interest but must develop awareness of them and resolve them in the best interest of the person under care.

Ethical erosion

Empirical research has demonstrated that the erosion of ethical principles is a slippery slope trajectory in which each unethical action lowers the bar of professionalism while at the same time numbing ethical awareness and creating a sense of shame and guilt that further degrade self-respect, leading to repeated unethical conduct (Feudtner et al., 1994).

Ethical erosion occurs when conflicts of interest are not resolved in accordance with professional standards and principles. Erosion and the accompanying moral distress is more likely to be experienced when the conflict of interest involves core values of professional identity such as altruism, respect, and compassion. The last decades have seen an acceleration of ethical erosion under the corrosive pressures of the commercialization of health care and the widespread utilization of managed care methods of utilization review (Churchill, 2007). Where 25 years ago, the honour and appreciation of a community was more than sufficient reward to become and remain a health care professional, today, the professions have lost social prestige, a consumer model has replaced the traditional 'professional-patient' relationship and its fiduciary fulfilment (Starr, 1982).

KEY POINT 6.8

Ethical erosion occurs when witnessing or performing unethical actions makes it easier to continue unethical conduct.

Conscience clauses

In the months before this chapter was written, a number of states in the American South and Midwest passed laws discriminating against lesbian, gay, bisexual, and transgender individuals (LGBT). Among the most offensive of these is a North Carolina statute that allows counsellors to refuse to see individuals on the basis of 'moral principles' (Wagner, 2016). Health care institutions and the legal apparatus generally accommodate the conscientious objection of professionals unless doing so would impede the ability and right of an individual to obtain needed treatment. So called, 'conscience clauses' require the professional to refer the person in a timely manner to an equally competent professional who is willing to provide the service (Wicclair, 2014). Increasingly ethicists have questioned the traditional formulation of conscience clauses as legitimizing or concealing discrimination and violating human rights as well as the fundamental dictum of the professions that the interests of the person under care must take precedence over all other priorities (Cantor, 2009).

KEY POINT 6.9

The conscientious objection of professionals is generally upheld unless it interferes with the right of the individual to access care.

Transcendent compassion

When reflecting on the case of Alex the most glaring ethical lapse on the part of almost all the staff is a lack of compassion. Compassion is a metavirtue, a crux of most spiritual systems, and a quality that can transcend almost any conflict of interest. The forces and entities in modern health care that would contravene and enervate compassion are legion. Many of these conflicts of interest figure prominently in the Stafford crisis with which this chapter opens and other health care scandals. Table 6.1 inventories some of the most corrupting stressors as they bear on the treatment of persons experiencing mental health–substance use problems.

Compassion fatigue

Of all the forces enumerated in Table 6.1, the most insidious and pervasive is 'burn out' or more properly compassion fatigue. Burn out has reached such epidemic proportions in the United States, that American medical ethicist Arthur Caplan declared it a public health crisis (Caplan, 2016). While an exploration of the topic is outside this chapter, the important ethical implications are twofold. First, studies have found an association between burn-out and unethical behaviour and attitudes (Dyrbye et al., 2010). Second, professionals thus have an ethical obligation to take reasonable care of

Table 6.1 Forces of Ethical Erosion and Professional Prevention

Forces of Ethical Erosion	Professional Prevention
➤ Profit over people: bottom line is budgetary efficiency.	➤ Reward high quality care with appropriate incentives and privileges.
➤ Inadequate training in the care of persons with mental ill health and substance use.	➤ Increase exposure at all stages of health care professional school to supervised care of persons experiencing mental ill health and substance use problems and role-models of ethical conduct.
➤ Lack of education about persons regarding the strengths and coping skills of persons experiencing mental health-substance use problems leads to negative attitudes, beliefs, and actions.	➤ Facilitate interactions with persons in recovery who engage in shared decision-making with professionals.
➤ Absence of techniques to handle psychiatric distress or threatening behaviors.	➤ Hands-on instruction in de-escalation techniques, talking down, motivational interviewing and crises management.
➤ Over-work and under staffed due to labor shortages, greater demand, and over emphasis on bottom line leading to lower trained professionals doing higher complexity jobs.	➤ Take political and professional action to lobby governments and institutions to fund the training of critical need professionals. Ensure adequate supervision and management of line staff so that all professionals work within their scope of practice and reasonable tours of duty.
➤ Leaders who are not held accountable for their own mismanagement and unethical conduct or who do not consider professionalism a priority.	➤ Choose and promote leaders and managers on basis of integrity, fairness, and transparency and hold those who fail these tests of character publicly responsible.

themselves; following a healthy lifestyle, engaging in restorative activities, and taking well-deserved time for self and enjoying friends and family.

These are steps the individual can take to prevent compassion fatigue that is ethically eroding but there are systems that generate the conditions that lead to burn-out. Unless these are addressed proactively and positively the epidemic of compassion fatigue and unprofessional actions it breeds will not be ameliorated.

KEY POINT 6.10

Compassion fatigue contributes to unprofessional behaviour and so reasonable attention to professional wellness is an ethical obligation.

Case Study 6.2 – Mary

Mary is a 20-year old individual with recurrent major depression. Three years ago she was seriously injured in a motor vehicle accident that left her with chronic neck and back pain. During a long recuperation she became dependent on prescription pain medications. When she could no longer obtain these legally, she switched to heroin and often traded sex for drugs. Her family disowned her and she was eventually arrested for prostitution but given the option of entering residential treatment rather than incarceration. She reluctantly agreed, fearful of the withdrawing. Professionals provided a comfortable detoxification with buprenorphine and then maintained her on medication assisted therapy to minimize cravings. Mary was given an anti-depressant medication. At first Mary was sullen with professionals and rude to her peers but the staff consistently met this behaviour with gentle but firm limit setting, insisting upon zero tolerance for disrespectful conduct. When Mary relapsed while on a weekend pass, the program compassionately accepted her back although with closer monitoring. Treated with dignity, Mary began to regain her own self-esteem and her respect for others. Efforts to reconcile with her family over a weekend at the program failed and Mary became more depressed, attempting suicide several days later. She was hospitalized in an acute psychiatric unit where program staff visited her regularly until she could be discharged back to the program.

REFLECTIVE PRACTICE EXERCISE 6.2

Time: 30 minutes
Using this chapter as a lens, examine your own practice with a critical eye looking for pressures, conflicts, entities, circumstances that threaten your ability to act with compassion. Describe two instances in which these defeated your aspirations to be a compassionate professional. Can you in retrospect see two alternative means of responding compassionately?

CONCLUSION

The case study of Mary purposefully contrasts with the Alex scenario to illustrate that delivery of health care with dignity, respect, and compassion, is good work but is hard work. These efforts of dedicated professionals caring for persons experiencing mental health–substance use problems must be measured not in dollars, not in length of stay, not in meeting performance or regulatory measures – all of which are utilitarian goals. Outcomes will not always be satisfying, recovery is often halting, and every professional no matter how they strive to be ethical will from time to time fail. Success for a professional living in accordance with an ethics of virtue and value can only be gauged in the ability of professionals in, and systems of, health care to embrace the unique suffering of each person with compassion, to counter the stigmatisation of society with respectful acceptance, and to hold each discarded individual with infinite dignity.

REFERENCES

Boyd KM, R Higgs and AJ Pinching. 1997. *The New Dictionary of Medical Ethics*. London: British Medical Journal Publishing.

Canadian Mental Health Association. 2016. *Stigma and Discrimination*. Ontario, Canada. http://ontario.cmha.ca/mental-health/mental-health-conditions/stigma-and-discrimination/.

Cantor JD. 2009. "Conscientious objection gone awry–restoring selfless professionalism in medicine". *New England Journal of Medicine*, 360: 1484–5.

Caplan AA. 2016. Physician Burnout is a Public Health Crises, Ethicist Says. *Medscape*. www.medscape.com/viewarticle/859300.

Churchill LR. 2007. "The hegemony of money: commercialism and professionalism in American medicine". *Cambridge Quarterly Healthcare Ethics*, 16: 407–14; discussion 439–42.

Crisp AH, MG Gelder, S Rix, HI Meltzer and OJ Rowlands. 2000. "Stigmatisation of people with mental illnesses". *British Journal of Psychiatry*, 177: 4–7.

Dyrbye LN, FS Massie Jr., A Eacker, W Harper, D Power, SJ Durning, MR Thomas, C Moutier, D Satele, J Sloan and TD Shanafelt. 2010. "Relationship between burnout and professional conduct and attitudes among US medical students". *Journal of the American Medical Association*, 304: 1173–80.

Feudtner C, DA Christakis and NA Christakis. 1994. "Do clinical clerks suffer ethical erosion? Students' perceptions of their ethical environment and personal development". *Academic Medicine*, 69: 670–9.

Francis R. 2013. Report of the Mid Staffordshire NHS Foundation Trust and Public Inquiry. London.

Help The Aged. 2001. "Towards Dignity: Acting on the Lessons from Hospital Experiences of Black and Minority Ethnic Older People". In *Policy Research*, edited by Institute on Ageing and Ethnicity/Help The Aged: London.

Mumford B. 2013. "Compassion, respect and dignity must be at the heart of social care practice". *The Guardian*, 10 July.

Reid J. 2012. "Respect, compassion and dignity: the foundations of ethical and professional caring". *Journal of Perioperative Practice*, 22: 216–19.

Schweitzer A. *Humanity Healing: 12 Keys for Ethical Living*. http://humanityhealing.org/who-we-are/12-keys-for-ethical-living/

Singh I. *Compassion, Care, Dignity and Respect – Fundamental Principles In The Care Of Older People*. General Medical Council Viewpoint. www.gmc-uk.org/guidance/25070.asp.

Social Care Institute For Excellence. 2013. *Overview of selected research: What dignity means.* London. www.scie.org.uk/publications/guides/guide15/selectedresearch/whatdignity means.asp.

Starr P. 1982. *The Social Transformation of American Medicine.* New York: Basic Books.

Wagner L. 2016. "Tennessee Enacts Law Letting Therapists Refuse Patients on Religious Grounds". USA: National Public Radio.

Welikala J. 2014. "Respect, dignity and compassion to be 'mandatory' for NHS training posts". *Nursing Times,* 2 May. www.nursingtimes.net/roles/nurse-educators/respect-dignity-and-compassion-to-be-mandatory-for-nhs-training-posts/5070484.fullarticle

Wicclair MR. 2014. "Managing conscientious objection in health care institutions". *HEC Forum,* 26: 267–83.

Winland-Brown J, VD Lachman and EO Swanson. 2015. "The New 'Code of Ethics for Nurses With Interpretive Statements' (2015): Practical Clinical Application, Part I". *Medsurg Nursing: The Jounal of Adult Health,* 24: 268–71.

TO LEARN MORE/USEFUL CONTACT

Compassionate Care in the NHS. www.gov.uk/government/policies/compassionate-care-in-the-nhs

Meyer J. "Promoting dignity, respect, and compassionate care". *Journal of Research in Nursing,* 2010 15: 69–73.

Substance Abuse and Mental Health Services Administration. Developing a Stigma Reduction Initiative. SAMHSA Pub No. SMA-4176. Rockville, MD: Center for Mental Health Services, Substance Abuse and Mental Health Services Administration, 2006.

World Health Organization, Mental Health Day 2015, Dignity and Mental Health. www.who.int/mental_health/world-mental-health-day/2015_infosheet/en/

CHAPTER 7

Culture and cultural dilemmas

Geraldine S. Pearson

INTRODUCTION

This chapter will discuss the cultural influences and ethical implications, concerns, and dilemmas that arise when providing care to individuals with mental health–substance use issues. The age of technology has altered the ways different cultures are viewed and understood. It has increased world-wide communication and information transfer (Whelton, 2015). It has necessitated the need for even more cultural awareness when providing mental health–substance use care.

REFLECTIVE PRACTICE EXERCISE 7.1

> **Time: 10 minutes**
> Consider the effect of technology on an individual's cultural presentation.

Ethical issues emerge in all aspects of health care but particularly when providing care to populations afflicted with mental health and substance use disorders. In order to address an ethical issue, one must be able to describe it; similarly understanding how this influences culture, requires a rudimentary understanding on how those cultural issues are influencing the ethical dilemma (Geppert, 2014). These issues are intermingled.

DEFINITION OF TERMS

Definition of ethics and its relationship to culture

Culture is a social and anthropological construct defined by Purnell as: 'The totality of socially transmitted behavioural patterns, arts, beliefs, values, customs, lifeways, and all other products of human work and thought characteristics of a population of people that guide their worldview and decision making' (Purnell, 2012, 24).

Each person involved in an interaction consciously or unconsciously brings their culture to the process. This is made up of their gender, ethnicity, professional affiliation, and the sum total of their childhood and adult experiences. Culture is both anthropological and social with three primary levels. These include:

1 A primary level that represents the deepest level in which rules are known by all, observed by all, implicit, and taken for granted (Koffman, 2006)
2 A secondary level, in which only members know the rules of behavior and can articulate them
3 A tertiary level that is visible to outsiders, such as things that can be seen, worn, or otherwise observed

---

KEY POINT 7.1

Individuals bring conscious and unconscious cultural influences to all interactions

---

Ethics defined

Health care professionals have a moral compass for their practice. At the center of this is the code of ethics that contains concrete principles to guide and determine ethical behavior between healthcare professionals and the individuals within their practice (Lachman, 2009).

General ethical principles that have guided health care for centuries are:

➤ **Beneficence**: the obligation to provide benefit and to balance benefits against risks
  Beneficence implies that the individual providing care will do good and will not harm the individual receiving care. Risks to this ethical principal might occur when the health care professional believes their recommendations supersede the choice of the individual who is seeking care. One of the risks of beneficence is paternalism which assumes that the individual is not able to grasp or understand the health care situation.
➤ **Non-maleficence**: the obligation to avoid causation of harm
  Non-maleficence is related to the general principal of doing no harm but implies that the health care professional must honestly present the benefits and burdens of treatment to the individual and offer truthful explanations about risks and benefits. It requires that confidentiality be maintained.
➤ **Respect for autonomy**: the obligation to respect the decision-making capacities of autonomous persons
  Individuals have a right to privacy and self-determination. They must make an informed consent that respects the boundaries of their culture and belief systems.
➤ **Justice**: the obligations of fairness in the distribution of benefits and risks
  Justice involves treating people with fairness and making sure there is just

distribution of risks and benefits (Indiana State Nurses Association, 2011; Stanley, 1998, 45).

SCOPE OF THE PROBLEM

World populations have become more mobile and communicative and there is even more need for understanding the complexities of ethical issues that are interpreted differently by different cultures. This increasing mobility and potential complexity has created even more risk for cultural dilemmas that overlap with ethical principles.

KEY POINT 7.2

Populations are no longer homogenous in their culture and heterogeneity is commonly faced by caregivers as they provide treatment and by individuals seeking care.

It is important to note that cultural beliefs, values and practices, while they have a powerful influence on health and ill health, are generally unconscious (Purnell, 2012). Purnell notes a number of issues that will influence ethics in care provision. They include the following:

➤ **Cultural awareness:** has more to do with an appreciation of the external presentation or material signs of diversity such as the arts, music, dress, or physical characteristics. It is expressing respect for another person's manner of communicating and coping with health related issues while realizing the individual is motivated from a perspective that the health care provider may not know or understand.

➤ **Cultural sensitivity:** has more to do with personal attitudes and avoiding statements that might be perceived as offensive. Self-reflection and understanding allows the health care provider to examine and understand their own upbringing and cultural origins and how they bring these into interactions with others.

➤ **Cultural competence:** is defined as having the knowledge, abilities and skills to deliver care congruent with the person's cultural beliefs and practices in a conscious manner. This acknowledges that other cultures exist in the world and may require self-education to understand and appreciate how this is influencing current functioning.

➤ **Cultural relativism:** is the belief that behaviours and practices should be judged only from the context of their cultural system. This concept requires particular assessment and evaluation from health care providers given that behaviours and actions may be emerging from the psychiatric problem contributing to the behavior. The challenge is in understanding the role that culture might play in the presentation of psychiatric symptoms.

> **Cultural imposition:** is the intrusive application of the majority groups' cultural view upon individuals and families. This is a particular risk when individuals are seeking care in a setting where the dominant culture differs from their own.

> **Cultural imperialism:** is the practice of extending policies and procedure of one organization to disenfranchised and minority groups. Similarly, imposing rules and boundaries of the dominant culture on a less powerful group of a different culture is a behavior that might occur with the view that this is what the population needs to maintain health. It is much more complex than this and must be carefully explored and understood (Purnell 2012, 25).

Developing cultural awareness is a process of self-identification and reflection about the populations engaged in treatment and the environment where care is delivered. It is essential to understand the cultural nuances of the individuals and their collective groups. While impossible to know all of this information, the basic knowledge about an individual's cultural practices and beliefs and the way this influences their health behaviors is essential. This begins with acknowledging the various populations that seek care in a particular treatment environment. Providers must understand their own cultural biases and the ways these translate into care models with others. At the same time the provider must understand the cultural stance of the institution where care is being provided. How does this influence the risk of cultural imposition or cultural imperialism?

Cultural relativism is more difficult to implement since it requires the caregiver to suspend judgment of a particular group that differs from self. Cultural imposition is most likely to occur when individuals from a differing culture are seeking care in an environment where the majority culture is different.

REFLECTIVE PRACTICE EXERCISE 7.2

Time: 10 minutes

How are cultural nuances of professionals and individuals seeking care influencing the interactions between them?

COLLECTIVIST AND INDIVIDUALISTIC CULTURES AND THEIR INFLUENCE ON PROVISION OF TREATMENT FOR MENTAL HEALTH–SUBSTANCE USE ISSUES

Purnell (2012, 30) defines the differences between collectivist and individualistic cultures (*see* Chapter 4). Elements of both exist in all cultures and individualistic cultures are viewed as low-context while collectivist cultures tend to have high contexts. This can include areas such as:

➤ orientation to self or group
➤ decision making
➤ autonomy
➤ knowledge transmission
➤ individual choice and personal responsibility
➤ competitiveness
➤ stigma
➤ gender roles
➤ help seeking
➤ identity
➤ communication style.

This can translate into trust issues for the individual entering into a care relationship. Van Hoorn (2015) hypothesized that individualism is associated with a broader trust radius while collectivism is related to a narrower trust radius. They hypothesize that the cultural influences experienced in the individual or group will influence the level of trust.

Trust is an essential component of fostering productive societal exchanges or communications (Fukuyama, 1995). If trust is built, at least partially on the cultural norm experienced by the individual, it is essential for the health care provider to understand the tendency toward individualism and collectivism that might be influenced by culture of origin. Purnell (2012) notes that examples of highly individualistic cultures include traditional American, British, Canadian, German, Norwegian, and Swedish. Examples of highly collectivistic cultures include traditional Arab, Asian, Latin American, Native American Indians, and Turkish. Collectivistic cultures are more dominant in the world (Purnell, 2012).

| KEY POINT 7.3 |

Understand the key origins of the culture of the individuals seeking care.

REFLECTIVE PRACTICE EXERCISE 7.3

Time: 15 minutes
Why is this important?
Consider the elements that you may encounter or have encountered in a person whose culture is different from yours.

IDENTIFYING ETHICAL ISSUES IN TREATMENT THAT INTERSECT WITH CULTURE

All mental health systems that provide care to individuals are culturally complex from the perspective of the professionals providing care and the individuals seeking services. Phinney (1996) noted that values, norms, attitudes, and behaviors that characterize a particular ethnic group generally come from a common culture of origin. In the process of integration these aspects of culture change and alter, with subsequent generations taking on the values of the culture around them. This creates particular dilemmas for the mental health professional providing care as they try to understand what is operative and interactive with presenting symptoms and disorders. 'This has far reaching influences on issues such as perception of mental health, adherence to treatment recommendations, and overcoming barriers to care' (Pearson, 2014, 32).

These issues have an influence, conscious and unconscious, on the individual providing care. They bring their cultural background to the interaction, apart from the professional position taken as caregiver or mental health provider.

SELF-ASSESSMENT EXERCISE 7.1

Time: 10 minutes

How are these issues identified and understood in the context of culturally sensitive care?

Self-knowing

Certainly education about the importance of being self-aware and knowing is required in all professional schools training to provide care for others. This involves having an identified belief system about health, ill health, life, and death. It involves a personal identification and awareness of attitudes towards stigma in mental health–substance use issues on an interpersonal level and on a broader culture of origin level. This means identifying core beliefs emerging from childhood, country or place of origin, ethnic background, race, and socioeconomic group (Cooper and Cooper, 2014).

SELF-ASSESSMENT EXERCISE 7.2

Time: 30 minutes

- How have these historical characteristics, inherently part of every person, interacted with professional training to create the gestalt of the professional caring for individuals experiencing mental health problems?
- How do our own belief systems influence the ways we interpret the stories of those around us seeking care?

Role of supervision

REFLECTIVE PRACTICE EXERCISE 7.4

Time: 15 minutes

It is impossible for all mental health–substance use professionals to know all the nuances of each culture represented by the individuals they treat.

What can we do to ensure that we are not violating cultural norms?

Stevenson (2015) notes that supervising mental health clinicians is a complex process which must consider the needs of the individual seeking care, and what the supervisee and supervisor bring to the process. He notes that the dynamics between the individual and the provider are influenced by and may reflect the organizational dynamics of the agency where care is being provided.

Stevenson (2015) argues for an inter-subjective approach that allows the supervisor to be part of the experience between the provider and individual seeking care. This then allows the supervisor to have a potentially positive impact on the developing helping relationship and to better understand the organizational influences on care.

This concept has great applicability to understanding the cultural overlay that exists in all relationships between providers, those seeking care, and the organizations where care is provided. An essential aspect of understanding the sensitive cultural issues that influence care is trust.

Trust is essential for the provider acknowledging their cultural origins and the way this influences the care they are delivering. The supervisor has to foster the trust in the relationship with professionals so they can reveal and open up their interactions to scrutiny.

KEY POINT 7.4

Cultural issues are some of the most difficult aspects of care to identify.

SELF-ASSESSMENT EXERCISE 7.3

Time: 10 minutes

What factors might have direct influence on the supervisory relationship?

Influencing factors include the culture of the provider, the individual seeking care, the dominant culture of the organization, and the subsequent care values that influence all relationships.

Engagement is the overarching concept that influences all relationships. This is strongly influenced by cultural competence, which is a fluid process, necessitating constant awareness and understanding of the cultural influences on the care relationships, the supervisory relationship, and the institutional norms and values.

Risk of ethnocentrism

Ethnocentrism is defined as the belief that a culture of origin or belief system is superior or correct compared to others that differ. It involves risks of prejudice, stereotyping, discrimination, and stigmatization (Huggins, 2009). Countries in which there are high numbers of immigrants, who infuse a different culture into the dominant, prevailing one, struggle with embracing concepts of cultural awareness and competence. It is easier to require the less dominant culture to adjust to that which prevails. This does not acknowledge or embrace cultural diversity or enhance care models.

KEY POINT 7.5

Supervision for the professionals of care is essential when examining the cross cultural issues influencing the interactions.

INTERVENTION IN ETHICAL ISSUES IN TREATMENT

SELF-ASSESSMENT EXERCISE 7.4

Time: 30 minutes
What does an ideal treatment setting look like that maintains an awareness of the influence of culture when treating mental health–substance use problems?

It is characterized by cultural competence in which providers have the skills (academic and interpersonal) to 'understand and appreciate cultural differences and similarities within, between, and among groups to meet the social, cultural, and linguistic needs of an individual' (Huggins, 2009, 96).

The message received by those seeking care is one of cultural congruence, conveyed both verbally and nonverbally, that validates the individual's cultural presentation. Value system, life history, and current situation are integrated to facilitate healing and health based on the individuals' cultural reality (Huggins, 2009).

For the professional an ideal treatment setting values self-reflection and understanding that is aimed at helping identify biases and influences of personal culture. This is best done in a supportive, trusting supervisory relationship that occurs over time and builds the process of trust and engagement.

Trust and engagement are hallmarks of developing a treatment environment that is respectful, aware, and acknowledges different cultural backgrounds, norms, and influences on health and illness.

Case Study 7.1 – Fadyaa

Fadyaa is a newly trained child psychiatrist of traditional Muslim faith. She is working in a community health clinic with an underserved population of children and adolescents in order to satisfy her visa requirements for remaining in the USA. At a group supervision, which she is conducting with counselors and social workers in the clinic, she begins speaking about her difficulties with a particularly complex individual in her caseload. Another professional, a social worker, is providing psychotherapy services. Fadyaa speaks of the symptoms presented by the young man, who presents as wishing to transition his gender to female. Struggling with depression and mood symptoms, Fadyaa seems particularly focused on this person's psychiatric status and dismisses the psychosocial difficulties faced by a transgender teen. During the supervision she seems to dismiss the dilemmas he is facing with his community and family.

SELF-ASSESSMENT EXERCISE 7.5 – FADYAA – ANSWERS ON P. 97

Time: 30 minutes
1 What are the cultural issues that could be influencing the perception that others have of Fadyaa as she works with this transgender teen?
2 How do the other professionals who work on her team plan to handle their concerns about this situation?
3 What are the nuances of supervision versus consultation that might influence the actions of the other team members?

Case Study 7.2 – Anne

Anne is a 55-year-old nurse who has worked for many years on an inpatient psychiatric unit in a busy urban hospital. In the last two years the unit has seen more and more individuals with severe mental health–substance use problems. Anne, who had previously been skilled and adept at providing care for individuals with predominant psychiatric problems, is struggling with those abusing substances. She is finding young people especially difficult. When her supervisor, in her annual performance review, gently points this out, Anne bursts into tears and talks about her 23-year-old daughter, who is heroin addicted and has abandoned her own child to her parents.

SELF-ASSESSMENT EXERCISE 7.6 – ANNE – ANSWERS ON PP. 97–98

Time: 30 minutes

1 What changed in Anne's life that coincided with changes in the treatment environment?
2 What actions should the supervisor take to support Anne with this dilemma?
3 How much information should Anne share about her life situation and at what point should she consider changing positions?

Case Study 7.3 – Irfan

Irfan is a 70-year-old Pakistani man who is living with his family in Great Britain. He is suffering from Alzheimer's and is frequently confused. His impulsivity is frequently unsafe and he has managed numerous times to unlock the door to the family home and leave the neighborhood. The first time the police were called he had taken his clothes off in the Tube and was trying to get on the subway. He was taken to the emergency room and his family took him home with promises of managing him with a one-to-one sitter. The second time he was found wandering in the neighborhood he had unlocked the dead bolt on the door and managed to walk into a neighbor's home. She came home to him sitting in her kitchen eating an apple. The police were called this time and he was taken to the emergency room.

SELF-ASSESSMENT EXERCISE 7.7 – IRFAN – ANSWERS ON P. 98

Time: 30 minutes

1 What actions can be taken with his family to help them understand his need for constant supervision?
2 Are there any medical interventions that would help his family care for him?
3 What cultural issues are influencing the family's management of him as his mental status deteriorates?

Case Study 7.4 – Daiki

Daiki is a 17-year-old Japanese male who is taking his final exams for entrance into university. When he finds out that his exam scores were not good enough to gain entrance into a top university, he commits suicide by jumping off a bridge. His mother and father, while grief stricken, seem to believe that he did the most honorable action that would avoid shame in their family. Daiki's sister, who is more Westernized than her brother or parents, is upset with her parents and their acceptance of her brother's suicide.

SELF-ASSESSMENT EXERCISE 7.8 – DAIKI – ANSWERS ON P. 98

Time: 30 minutes

1 Daiki's sister is quietly asking for help, since seeking mental health intervention is frowned upon in her family. She is over 16 and can ask for assistance. What would be most helpful to her?

2 How can providers best understand the role of honor and shame in the Japanese culture, especially with older generations?

3 Are there community interventions that need to be considered with Daiki's school or friends?

CONCLUSION

It is essential that culture be considered when providing care to populations seeking services for mental health–substance use problems. Cultural influences are bi-directional in interactions between those seeking care and the professionals offering that care. The changing mobility of the world population necessitates that even more awareness of differing cultures be operative when providing care.

REFERENCES

Cooper J, and DB Cooper. 2014. "Palliative care within mental health: the need." In *Palliative Care Within Mental Health: Care and Practice*, edited by DB Cooper and J Cooper, 1–10. Boca Raton, FL: CRC Press.

Fukuyama F. 1995. *Trust: The Social Virtues and the Creation of Prosperity.* London: Hamish Hamilton.

Geppert CMA. 2014. "Overcoming ethical dilemmas." In *Palliative Care Within Mental Health: Care and Practice*, edited by DB Cooper and J Cooper, 19–29. Boca Raton, FL: CRC Press.

Huggins M. 2009. "Culture." In *Psychiatric-Mental Health Nursing: Evidence Based Concepts, Skills, and Practices*, 7th ed., edited by WK Mohr, 93–116. Philadelphia, PA: Lippincott Williams & Wilkins.

Indiana State Nurses Association. 2011. *Ethics: Independent Study.* Indianapolis, IN: ISNA.

Koffman J. 2006. "Transcultural and Ethical Issues at the End of Life." In *Stepping into Palliative Care*, edited by J Cooper, 171–186. Oxon: Radcliffe Medical Press.

Lachman VD. 2009. *Ethical Challenges in Health Care: Developing Your Moral Compass.* New York, NY: Springer Publishing.

Pearson GS. 2014. "Overcoming cultural dilemmas." In *Palliative Care Within Mental Health: Care and Practice*, edited by DB Cooper and J Cooper, 30–46. Boca Raton, FL: CRC Press.

Phinney J. 1996. "When We Talk About American Ethnic Groups, What Do We Mean?" *American Psychologist 51*: 918–927.

Purnell LD. 2012. "Application of transcultural theory to practice: the Purnell Model." In *Palliative Care Within Mental Health: Principles and Philosophy*, edited by DB Cooper and J Cooper, 22–44. London: Radcliffe.

Stanley R. 1998. "Applying the Four Principles of Ethics to Continence Care." *British Journal of Nursing 7*: 33–51.

Stevenson S. 2015. "Supervising mental health clinicians in the context of complex organisational dynamics." *Journal of Social Work Practice 29*(4): 445–456.

Van Hoorn A. 2015. "Individualist-Collectivist Culture and Trust Radius: A Multilevel Approach." *Journal of Cross-Cultural Psychology 46*: 269–276.

Whelton BJB. 2015. "Being human in a global age of technology." *Nursing Philosophy 17*: 28–35.

TO LEARN MORE

Bonder B and LE Martin. 2013. *Culture in Clinical Care: Strategies for Competence*, 2nd ed. Thorofare, NJ: Slack.

Galanti GA. 2014. *Caring for Patients from Different Cultures*, 5th ed. Philadelphia, PA: University of Pennsylvania Press.

Giger J, R Davidhizar and L Purnell. 2007. "American Academy of Nursing Expert Panel Report: Developing Cultural Competence to Eliminate Health Disparities in Ethnic Minorities and Other Vulnerable Populations." *Journal of Transcultural Nursing 18*: 95–102.

ANSWERS TO SELF-ASSESSMENT EXERCISE 7.5 – P. 94

1 Fadyaa comes from a culture that does not support homosexuality or transgender issues. It is considered a punishable crime or sin in traditional Muslim cultures. Her attitudes about the current care with the individual may be unconsciously influenced by her past. This needs clarification.

2 In an ideal clinical environment, the team members would have enough trust and understanding to self-monitor and identify problematic issues such as this. Staying silent about the concerns is not acceptable but speaking and confronting/identifying this requires sensitivity and respect for Fadyaa's culture.

3 Supervision implies a power differential between supervisor and supervisee. In contrast, a consultation is conducted on a more level plane. One suggestion for this clinical team might include bringing in a consultant who helps identify and educate any of the cultural biases any member of the team might have. This could be done as a quality improvement project.

ANSWERS TO SELF-ASSESSMENT EXERCISE 7.6 – P. 95

1 Anne's difficulties with her daughter are undoubtedly weighing heavily on her day-to-day functioning on a unit with increasingly large numbers of individuals who are using substances. Is Anne aware of her countertransference? Is her supervisor aware of the dilemmas she is facing in her personal life with her daughter? Can she use an employee assistance program to help her understand how her personal life is adversely affecting her professional work?

2 The supervisor should be honest with concerns and observed changes in behavior. Directing to other resources might be helpful. Creating a supportive atmosphere of work with altered assignments might assist in the short term.

3 Anne must decide how much of her personal life to share with her supervisor or any of her work colleagues. Many individuals choose to keep a sharp boundary between these two worlds. However, if Anne wishes to handle this, she will need an aware and supportive supervisor to help her manage the feelings that come up over treating a substance using population.

ANSWERS TO SELF-ASSESSMENT EXERCISE 7.7 – P. 95

1 Depending on the family's spiritual beliefs and affiliations with a place of worship, this might be a source of support. It is not clear how much the family understands Alzheimer's and subsequent behavior changes. A psychoeducational model followed by practical planning for care will be most helpful.

2 It is not clear if Irfan has been medically evaluated for any physical conditions affecting his mental status. This should occur with a clinic or family physician.

3 In Pakistani culture the family foundation is essential and this unit manages all the issues that emerge in its members. This includes medical illness, psychiatric issues, behavior problems, and difficulties with others. Solutions are sought within the family unit.

ANSWERS TO SELF-ASSESSMENT EXERCISE 7.8 – P. 96

1 This depends on the venue within which she is asking for assistance. Depending on whether this is at her school, in her community, or with her same age peers, the response will need to consider her role in her family and her parents' response to the suicide.

2 Honor and shame are hallmarks of an Asian culture and this young woman seems caught between her parents' views about honor and her feelings of loss about her brother. This might be difficult to understand for non-Asian professionals. The task will involve helping her grieve her brother's death, gain understanding and acceptance of her parents' response.

3 The assumption could be made that Daiki's friends may have been shared with his sister. She is likely not alone in her grief and can look to peers for understanding and support. Other community interventions can include school based mental health interventions or community based services.

CHAPTER 8

Service provision

Ethics in everyday practices of mental health–substance use work

Barbara J Russell and WJ Wayne Skinner

INTRODUCTION

George Santayana, Spanish philosopher and novelist (1863–1952), memorably pointed out that 'Those who cannot remember the past are condemned to repeat it' (1906, 284).

His insight is still relevant today for those working in substance use and mental health treatment programs. Herring et al. (2013) describe how the moral acceptability or unacceptability of substance use and the legal or illegal status of psychoactive substances – natural and human made – have varied greatly among and within different communities as well as over the decades and even centuries (see also Room 2001). Kleinig recommends 'seeing drugs (and other social practices that, if unconstrained, might be sufficiently deleterious socially to warrant intervention) historically and cumulatively and not merely discreetly and comparatively' (2004, 379).

Accordingly, this chapter includes aspects of the historical and contemporary socio-politics of substance use. The same socio-historical context must be included in order to 'see' mental ill health fully. Today, what we consider mental ill health and its standard of care are not based solely on clinicians' cases, researchers' study findings, and academics' unifying theories. The evolution of psychiatry's Diagnostic and Statistical Manual (American Psychiatric Association 2016) from 1 to 5 and medicine's International Classification of Diseases (World Health Organization 2016a) from 1–10, for instance, has been impacted substantively by various societal, political, and judicial norms and interests (Fulford & Sartorius 2009; Paris 2008).

Healthcare ethics, as a field of activity and scholarship, emerged in a particular context and time: expensive, technologically advanced, acute care 'Western' medicine of the 1960s and 1970s. Organ transplantation, reproductive technologies, and intensive care units created new and urgent ethical dilemmas for the individual, service providers, healthcare organiza-tions, and funders. Seminars, lectures, and articles tackling these dilemmas have favoured a case-based approach wherein an actual or prototypical case is described. Then the question 'Ethically, what should the healthcare worker do?' is answered using a discrete set of principles and concepts.

We are 'breaking free' of this familiar approach in this chapter in three ways. First, our approach does not focus solely on the professional's decisions and perspectives. Nor does it begin with the individual experiencing ill health. Instead we begin with a person: a person with complex problems related to mental health and substance use. The chapter examines this person's responsibilities – some shared, some not – as well as the responsibilities and responses of those with whom he or she has a relationship. Some of these people are healthcare professionals; most of them are not.

Second, people's stories, rather than clinical cases, are engaged below. As sociologist Arthur Frank persuasively argues, stories capture more ethically important subtleties and interpretations of living with serious illnesses or disabilities. For instance, stories usually have no obvious beginning or ending. Instead, the 'here and now' is the result of innumerable prior individual and collective interactions and decisions as well as luck and 'unchosen choices' (Frank 2004; Frank 2010, 25). And looking ahead, stories unfold over time, in ways that are neither straightforward nor certain. Frank often uses the word 'drama' to underscore the meaningful impact of those who become involved:

> Medical workers—physicians, nurses, technicians, and adminis-trators—need to be reminded that they are playing parts in the drama of the ill person's plight, and that how they play their parts shapes this drama just as consequentially as the disease—the cellular [or neurological] pathology—shapes it.
>
> (2007, 380)

Third, clinical cases in ethics-related articles and chapters tend not to have an explicit or particular context, setting, and time. As noted in the opening paragraph, these features matter ethically in terms of when and why mental health and substance use are problematized and when and why healthcare workers are ascribed professional duties to intervene. Accordingly, the time, setting and context of all the dramas that follow are: 2016; Ontario, Canada; existent and diverse provincial and federal legislation[1]; 26 health professions are regulated[2] (many of which have codes of ethics); and a healthcare system that is 'mixed' (i.e., a combination of public and privately funded and delivered services).

Case Study 8.1

Abdiel and Rosa's[3] drama

Abdiel scrolls through recent texts on his phone while waiting for his appointment at the local health clinic. Although he texts and emails regularly, he now uses social media much less, given how public they actually are. Abdiel's worries are multi-faceted: increased alcohol and marijuana use, the temptation of injectable drugs, a possible sexually transmitted disease, and deteriorating interpersonal connections.

As he sits waiting, he is much more than a clinic patient. When he walked in, he entered as Abdiel, Canadian citizen, Ontario resident, 22 years of age, and financial services company employee. If there was a device that could read people's ethical 'density' – some type of ethics Geiger counter or sonograph – his reading would be strong. Membership in the Canadian community means he has various freedoms and rights protected by the country's foundational Charter. The community democratically and legally protects these freedoms and rights because they connect to valued ways of life, human abilities, belongingness, interpersonal reciprocity, and human diversity. Given certain qualities that contribute to the person Abdiel is, stigmatization, discrimination and harassment by other community members and institutions are prohibited by national and provincial human rights codes. Furthermore, his preferences about the privacy of his health and medical treatment are safeguarded by provincial legislation. This privacy right means healthcare organizations and workers have correlative duties to keep all individually-identifiable details as confidential as possible and to collect, use, and disclose it only with his consent.

While this conceptual structure is a preventive measure and these pathways are remedial options for him, Abdiel's lived actual experiences are heavily determined by his interactions with other people and vice versa. This begins with those he meets at the clinic, from receptionist and support staff to waiting co-patients. This extends to the professionals responsible for helping him within their defined scope of practice and clinic routine. In the background will be the local community's views about substance use, mental ill health, individual responsibilities, and shared obligations. Abdiel is not a solipsistic or sole creator or interpreter of his health: these other people and groups all contribute to his 'here and now' experiences and their meaning.

After 20 minutes, Abdiel is invited into a clinic room and the nurse practitioner (NP) greets him, 'Hello Abdiel, I'm Rosa. Sit here please. The note says you want to talk about nausea you've had recently . . .'

'Well, not really,' he replies. 'I was too embarrassed to tell the receptionist what I really want to talk about. I've partied way too much these past months and worry I might have a sexually transmitted disease.' When asked what 'partying' means, he says: wine, hard liquor, beer, marijuana, either at friends' apartments or clubs. Asked if he had problems with substances in the past, Abdiel admits 'alcohol has really messed up my life at times. And marijuana is everywhere'. He says nothing about a phase of injection drug use (IUD) eight years ago when he lived elsewhere in the province.

Questions race through Rosa's mind:

1   Has he been sexually active since thinking he has a sexually transmitted disease (STD)? Is he sharing intravenous (IV) drugs such that he could be infected and be infecting others? What if it's human immunodeficiency virus (HIV)? Who do I and/or he have to notify?

2   Is he driving impaired? Must I notify the Ministry of Transport? Or is it my 'call'?

Rosa worries that if she notifies others, Abdiel may never return for needed treatment and support. As Weddle and Kokotailo (2002) notes, many jurisdictions support privacy rights about mental health, substance use and STDs because adolescents and young adults are more likely to seek out medical treatment and support.

A long-standing ethical defense of non-interference with individual decisions in liberal democracies such as Canada comes from *On Liberty* (1859) by British philosopher, John Stuart Mill (1806–1873). Liberty or freedom means we can choose to put ourselves at risk. But freedom is limited, notes Mill, when other people's well-being is at risk (1947). This helps justify public health legislation and agencies' paternalistic protection of non-consenting community members as well as of the community as a whole. Mill constrains individual liberty and supports others' interference for another ethical reason, one routinely overlooked in published analyses. He holds that

> there are also many positive acts for the benefit of others which [the individual] may rightfully be compelled to perform, such as give evidence in a court of justice, bear his fair share in the common defensive, or in any joint work necessary to the interest of the society of which he enjoys protection.
>
> (Kleinig 2004, 373)

British philosopher and political activist, TH Green (1836–1882) also conceptualized of individuals as inescapably and necessarily communal members (1888). Accordingly, privacy's value rested on one's 'society [as] the crucible of a freedom worth having' (Kleinig 2004, 375). Appelbaum (2013) suggests that mental health and substance use therapists' goals go beyond preventing or mitigating illness. They include 'a concomitant increase in treated persons' abilities to fulfill their social roles, whether as worker, parent, or friend' (71).

Just as Abdiel is relationally situated, so too is Rosa. Plambeck holds that all too frequently [healthcare workers] are considered 'neutral arbitrator[s]' of patients' ethical dilemmas, when in fact they are 'part[ies] to these conflicts' (2002, 27). Rosa's immediate thoughts recognize that divided commitments and loyalties are part of Abdiel and her drama. Mental health and substance use problems are connected with the judicial system in ways that expand these dramas because various authoritative, powerful social institutions will have a role (Buchanan et al. 2002; Kremer & Arora 2015; Quinn & Barton 2000). Yet her client and her community's justice system each have very different expectations of Rosa. In this drama, could a 'duty to warn' justify breaching confidentiality duties owed to Abdiel (Karol et al. 2007)? If 'yes,' who is justified in doing so?

Membership in a community is based on the expectation that members can and will decide to 'do the right thing'. Rosa should avoid presuming that Abdiel is not prepared to notify partners if an STD is diagnosed. But if Abdiel does not accept this responsibility, Rosa should let him know of her communally-supported responsibility to safeguard identifiable innocent parties. That said, information conveyed should be only what is necessary to effect such protection. The community has other agencies with responsibilities for its members' safety. Professionals should be clear as to which public duties rest on their shoulders and which rest on those of other public institutions and agents.

When Rosa's attention moves back to Abdiel, it will also be for reasons beyond his physiological symptoms. It is important for her to ascertain the degree that Abdiel himself is both disabled and made vulnerable by his mental health and substance use problems. Is he at imminent risk of serious self-harm? Or, perhaps less of a crisis, but just as damaging, has the gradual accumulation of negative symptoms and compromised functioning resulted in Abdiel being terribly disconnected, confused, uncertain, and depleted?

In terms of Abdiel being possibly driving impaired, Ontario's Ministry of Transport guidelines stipulate that physicians have a legal duty to report individuals with medical conditions likely to impair their driving abilities (Government of Ontario 1990c). This guideline specifies physicians only. But could an argument be made that, while not legally obligated to report, Rosa has an ethical obligation to notify someone . . . perhaps the Ministry or the local police? Since all community members have shared responsibilities for co-members' safety, she should act only if her chosen action is the best option for preventing imminent, clear harms to identifiable persons. Here, too, she should not assume that Abdiel is unconcerned either about other people or about the impact of not driving on his other-regarding roles. Healthcare professionals' proactive and early discussions with the individual about limits to their legal and ethical duties of confidentiality can demonstrate honesty, respect, acceptance and empowerment (Geppert & Bogenschutz 2009).

Case Study 8.2

Amelie, Rene, and Zane's drama

Amelie gazes at the ceiling of the critical care unit. She has mixed feelings being in the hospital: glad for some 'down time' but worried that, in her absence, her girlfriend, Keri, may relapse to increased drug use. Amelie is the 'head' of her household made up of two children (Mathieu and Madeleine ages six and eight; she has been separated for 12 years from their father) and her ailing, elderly mother, Thérèse. She is also concerned that her part-time job will be in jeopardy if she is absent too long. She helps organize inventory and clean the facility. She had persuaded the manager to pay in cash to avoid significant reductions to her provincial disability benefits.

Amelie was rushed to the hospital after collapsing en route to work. Acute cardiac myopathy was diagnosed and her hospitalization journey has been from intensive care to critical care to general medicine (GM), and back to critical care. A few times, Keri brought in narcotics which Amelie ingested and twice injected in her upper thigh. When discarded needles were found in the morning bedside trash and subsequently tested positive for narcotics, Amelie was moved to a bed nearest to the nursing station. She disavowed all knowledge of the needles and drug use. When challenged by the medical resident, Rene, Amelie declined urine screening.

Today, the new attending physician says to Rene, 'This cycle of transfers hasn't accomplished what was expected. And we can't just stand by while a patient takes illegal, unsafe drugs. What are you thinking about doing next?' The resident replies, 'I'll give her two options. One: I'll explain one last time how narcotics have caused her cardiac problems, the pros and cons of medications versus surgery for her to think about at home and then discharge her after we remove the catheter. Two: she signs a contract to not take any narcotics here and have random urine screens and room searches. Then transfer her back to GM to get her in better shape for cardiovascular surgery; that's best medically. Either way, it's up to her.' The assigned nurse, Zane, interrupts, 'But knowing Amelie's using, it's wrong for us to consider discharging her back to the kids. Children's Services needs to be involved right now.'

Better interpersonal communications and being empathic would be common recommendations for healthcare professionals facing this clinical drama (Gillett 2004). However, if the ethics Geiger counter scanned typical patient charts, its reading would be low. These charts are repositories of test results, diagnoses, reported symptoms, treatment outcomes, and clinician judgments. As Gillett notes, 'It is common in clinical medicine ... for patients to be disempowered and silenced by the lack of any discourse in which their subjectivity can be conveyed' (25).

Therefore, it is unsurprising that Rene and Zane do not see Amelie as the person she is nor her life within a particular socio-political context. Three years ago, she was financially able to move from community housing to a small apartment, albeit still in a deteriorating downtown area. She augments her part-time income with flea market sales of items she finds in recycling bins.

The concept of place is ethically relevant here:

> transforming spaces into places is existential activity, as through the creation of places people visualise, memorise and thus stabilise constitutive human goods such as the sense of belonging, social integration, purposes that give meaning to life (values) and the sense of self.
>
> (Hunziker et al. 2007, 51)

Having a 'place' means having a specific space wherein one controls who enters and what happens, one is missed if absent, valued memories are tied to it, and one feels pride in it as well as safe. 'Housing' is a physical, human-made, bounded entity for human life. 'Place' entails meaning and psycho-emotional elements in addition to spatial, physical elements. Amelie has created a place for her children, mother and herself, the ethically-relevant richness of which no city address alone can convey.

Anthropologist Nila Hofman's study (2003) of inner city, injection drug use (IDU) women, highlights two pivotal ethical values: respectability and responsibility. The women fulfilled their ongoing responsibilities for dependent family and community members' welfare in various ways, some of which involved minor criminal activities. Understanding such dependency as unending meant the women's commitment was unending and for which they knowingly sacrificed their own health. Being respected by others and themselves was equally difficult. Discriminatory gender ideology resulted in harsher moral judgment of them compared to their male partners who also used injectable drugs. Efforts to protect or boost their respectability were twofold. The women's own drug use tended to be secretive and alone. They also accepted risky, but admired, community roles such as 'nursing' wherein they cared for other users, even helping those users with HIV/AIDs (acquired immune deficiency syndrome) to inject safely. Bogren's 2008 study has similar findings of a community's disparate moral judgments of women versus men substances users.

Substance users' actions and decisions often are labelled 'anti-social'. Yet the above narrative reveals highly social, other-regarding motivations. Marginalization of families like Amelie's means the range of legal options and opportunities is smaller and a 'last resort' range of illegal options and opportunities becomes more reasonable. The label of 'anti-social' can result in it being interpreted as indicative of certain personality disorder symptoms or conditions. This can discline health professionals to be empathic and respectful and consign people, such as Amelie, to enduring negative identities.

In response to the clinical team's conversation, an expected ethical response would rely on the principle of individual autonomy and the process of informed consent. Zane's suggestion to contact the Children's Aid Society reflects his belief that Amelie's decisional ambit is too narrow and her decisional authority is excessive. His concern stems from a common formulation of individual autonomy. This formulation considers people to be independent, self-sufficient, and self-governing individuals. As such, they are the most knowledgeable about their own values and preferences and so their healthcare decisions are to be accepted. Supportive of individual autonomy, legislated informed consent processes operationalize health professionals' correlative responsibilities of honestly disclosing diagnosis and prognosis, answering questions, avoiding pressure and undue influence, involving interpreters, and using appropriate substitute decision making procedures if the individual is incapable (Government of Ontario 1996). This formulation grounds the stereotypic belief that mental health–substance use problems significantly, often irreversibly, diminish rationality and self-determination. This belief, in turn, will change the individual from being seen as an authoritative agent to being seen as a vulnerable victim. In response, the focus of professionals' obligations can shift from empowerment, opportunities and respect to protection, safety, and empathy.

In the past decade, many people within the bioethics community have challenged this standard formulation of autonomy. For instance, William Gaylin and Bruce Jennings, two prominent American bioethicists, wrote *The Perversion of Autonomy* (2003). Moreover, philosopher Susan Sherwin (1998) points out that

> focusing only on the moment of medical decision making . . .fail[s] to examine how specific decisions are embedded within a complex set of relations and policies that constrain (or, ideally, promote) an individual's ability to exercise autonomy with respect to any particular choice.
>
> (32)

For this drama involving Amelie, her children and mother, Zane, and Rene, relational autonomy is a more realistic and ethical formulation in the context of mental health–substance use (McLeod & Sherwin 2000).

Sherwin describes relational autonomy's special strengths. First, informed consent procedures cannot be tied to time-limited acceptance or refusal of recommended treatments. Instead, most person's decisions evolve over time as they make sense of their illness or injury for their lives and relationships.

Second, one person may have several health-related options but another person with the same illness has few options, simply because of different social status and circumstances. Discriminatory societal norms may create and perpetuate such injustices in health outcomes and recovery. Third, relationality also means professionals are 'sensitive to their own biases and assumptions . . . and listen carefully to the concerns and priorities of patients who belong to groups that are systematically oppressed' (1998, 44).

Case Study 8.3

Ardash and Rashod's drama

Ardash retired last year, a bit too early for his liking, when work became physically too demanding. He has smoked since age 26 with intermittent, albeit unsuccessful, attempts to quit. He has been recently diagnosed with COPD (chronic obstructive pulmonary disease). His geriatrician of 10 years refers him for a full cardiac work-up at the local hospital. The vascular surgeon's recommendation is for surgery as soon as possible, preceded by at least six weeks of pre-surgical smoking cessation to reduce possible complications. She adds that her report will be sent to his geriatrician who can help him prepare for surgery.

He meets with his geriatrician, Rashod, two weeks later. Rashod summarizes the report, noting that the wait will be two months. Ardash says, 'I remember her talking about stopping smoking first. That's going to be impossible. If I don't quit, I can still have the surgery, right?' To which Rashod replies, 'I think the surgery will be re-scheduled until you can stop for at least six weeks.' 'What? You mean smokers don't get needed medical treatment just because they smoke? I've never heard of such a thing! I have a right to smoke if I want to! You've got to convince that surgeon to schedule me now.' Rashod replies, 'I think she's right; this is what the medical evidence shows. Stopping is smart, and improves your surgical chances. It's just six weeks. And you can decide whether or not to re-start afterwards, but I'll bet you won't want to.' Ardash responds angrily, 'Easy for you to say. I need the surgery now!' Rashod shakes his head, 'As your physician, I am thinking about your best interests.'

Individuals who smoke would have an extremely high reading on the ethics Geiger counter. This is another substance and another group subject to much variability in moral scrutiny. In the 1950s and 60s, commercial marketing portrayed cigarettes as part of a socially-desirable lifestyle and physicians deemed them safe. Retail taxation provided large, increasing, and reliable funds for governmental priorities. Eventually cigarettes' health hazards prompted sustained public health initiatives to persuade smokers to quit and adolescents to not start. Today, about 18 percent of the Canadian population smoke despite these initiatives (Government of Canada 2014). Renewed efforts to reduce this percentage have included stigma promoting measures; in other words, intentionally blaming and shaming users (Berger et al. 2011; Courtwright 2013; Brown-Johnson & Prochaska 2015). This constitutes communal coercion which is ethically problematic because it ignores other community members who share responsibility for the harmful consequences of this extremely unsafe, but legal, commercial product.

With that said, it is ethically appropriate to help smokers to stop and convince non-smokers not to start. There is no safe cigarette. If tobacco products are used as designed, serious morbidities leading to premature suffering and death are likely. Tobacco (and alcohol, another legal substance) causes far more health problems than illegal substances nationally and worldwide (Degenhardt & Hall 2012; World Health Organization 2015a,b & 2016b).

As Ardash and Rashod's drama becomes oppositional, Rashod turns to the 'best interests' standard, common in many healthcare professions' code of ethics, to try to persuade Ardash of the ethical defensibility of the pre-surgery smoking cessation requirement. Kleinig thoughtfully questions these codes' adequacy relative to the ethical density of the professional-client relationship and interactions:

> It may be right to do what the code requires, but it is not right to do it *just* because the code requires it. What is done ought to be done for the reasons that make it appropriate to codify it, not because it is codified. And minimalism occurs when people treat the code of ethics as exhaustive of their ethical obligations to others. Codes generally specify minimum requirements, and not all or the whole extent of the ethical obligations that hold between the various relevant parties in treatments for substance use. Indeed, to the extent that codes are rule driven rather than value-driven, they tend to concentrate on behaviors that have proven particularly problematic.
>
> One of the reasons for the susceptibility of codes to the dangers I have noted is that, despite occasional hints in preambles, they have been severed from their ethical roots. They focus on ethical outcomes rather than ethical values and their underpinnings. They speak of the need for informed consent, confidentiality, and so on, without indicating or articulating the deeper sources of such expectations in notions of human dignity, respect, justice, and so on.
>
> (2004, 385)

Professional-person . . . a simple hyphen marks an ethically complex inter-relationship (Gillett 2004). This complexity deepens when the individual lives with mental ill health or substance use problems and the professional practices within contemporary medical organizations. Both the life and the practice are influenced by their context: societal, political, and professional beliefs about the person's as well as the professional's responsibility for recovery or lack thereof. Compared to traditional paternalism and expertise, empowerment and openness are ethically stronger 'investments' in Rashod's clinician–patient relationship with Ardash.

CONCLUSIONS

Since mental health and substance use practice involves people helping other people, the work is always ethically dense. Historically, mental ill health and psychoactive substance use and their personal and communal impact have been associated with ethically honorable versus dishonorable human aspirations, qualities and behaviours. Despite contemporary scientific inquiry into biopsychosocial causes of mental health and substance use problems and clinical development of more effective treatments, firmly-held and prejudiced ethical judgements endure. Explicit or implicit assumptions about users' irresponsibility, irrationality, weakness of will, and pitiable quality of life can strongly influence professionals' responses to and professional relationships with those who have substance use and mental health problems. As a result, healthcare work in this area is, all things considered, ethically more conflicted than, say, dermatological or gastroenterological work.

The dramas in substance use and mental health work can be especially serious. People can experience moral uncertainty: e.g., 'Is my therapist being completely honest with me or trying to keep me hopeful?' They can feel morally ambivalent (Dale et al. 1997): e.g., 'I think the patient, her family, and the case worker all have good ethical reasons for their different positions.' They can also suffer significant moral distress: i.e., 'Things that I cannot change are preventing me from doing what I should.' This chapter has presented a different approach for healthcare professionals tackling these ethical complexities. Drama, rather than the clinical case, is a recommended conceptualization of the professional-person encounter. Dramas accept that healthcare professionals themselves impact the immediate and unfolding situation. This chapter presented dramas wherein each section deliberately began with the person, not with the patient, diagnosis, prognosis, and treatment history. Similarly, focus moved from recommended next steps for the professional to take. Instead the focus was on next steps for both the individual and professional.

This chapter closes with two further recommendations. First, Barry Schwartz, an American professor of philosophy, presents Aristotle's virtue theory in a way that persuasively illuminates uncommon subtleties and depths of our ethical engagement of one another in the context of healthcare. This is not about ethical theories, abstract concepts, or academic debates. In 'Loss of Wisdom', a compelling 2009 TED talk, he explains that Aristotle's practical wisdom comes from two human qualities: moral skill and moral will (see also Schwartz & Sharpe 2010). Moral skill is different from moral knowledge. Skill requires attentiveness to the situation at hand, lots of experience, understanding others' perspectives, and reflection. Moral will includes self-motivation and doing what is right for the right reasons. Schwartz cautions against excessive reliance on externalized rules and incentives to motivate people to do what is right. Frank's incisive comment echoes Schwartz's insight, 'being ethical (possessing a greater measure of practical wisdom) is never anything that one *has . . .*' (2004, 335).

Whether Rosa, Rene, and Rashod 'see' their 'patients' as situated persons, 'hear' their subjective experiences of substance use or mental illness, and 'welcome them' in their health system journey will reveal much about Rosa, Rene, and Rashod's ethical 'being.'

Second, accepting and working with the history, chronicity, and complexity of mental health and substance use lend themselves to a type of engagement that may, at first blush, seem opposed to critical thinking, clinical reliability, professional consensus, and ethical principlism.[4] In 1959, Charles Lindblom, professor of political science at Yale, coined the term 'muddling through' as a more realistic and useful metaphor for tackling important socio-political policies and commitments. More recently, various published articles have extolled its practicality for certain endeavors (Mechanic 1997; Robertson 2007; Landry et al. 2009; Hoeyer & Jensen 2011; Strumberg 2012; Murray 2015). For instance, 'We contend that the kind of dialogue that health professionals need is better facilitated by an ethics of muddling through – which does not presume clarity where there is none – than by a set of principles that they rarely get the chance to apply' (Hoeyer & Jensen, 109).

As formally explained by Landry et al. (2009), muddling through is:

> the informal gathering and triangulation of information to arrive at a solution, based on the premise that a rational (or evidence-based) approach is not always possible or appropriate in solving complex socio-political problems and that less formal approaches to decision making are equally effective.
>
> (61)

This concept is not the usual connotation of 'muddling' as described by Forrest: 'when faced with an insoluble problem you should forget it and press on regardless. The more you think about it the worse it gets' (2009, 164).

Instead, Lindblom (1959) held that some problems are so complex and dynamic that it is unreasonable – perhaps even naïve – to expect we can identify all their components, connections, and interactions. His insight is pertinent to substance use programs and professionals today in 2016 and in Ontario's advantaged health system.

> A wise decision maker [therefore] uses a successive limited comparisons approach, being aware that one only ever can achieve part of one's goals, and hopeful to avoid as many unanticipated consequences as possible.
>
> (Strumberg 2012, 1223)

Wisdom, perseverance, labour (i.e., 'doing the work'), and affiliation are essential and ethical aspects of substance use and mental health professionals' responsibilities and accomplishments in their daily work with and on behalf of the individual and families.

Harkening back to the ethically robust concept of 'place', what kind of a place does a health care setting need to be to responsively, insightfully work with and empower people experiencing mental health–substance use concerns? To help 'see' and 'work with' the inescapable complexities in people's daily lives and professional's daily practices, integrative and practical approaches are needed by busy and caring healthcare professionals. We recommend the CLEOS (clinical/scientific, legal/regulatory, ethical, organizational, and systemic) approach because it works with realistic aspects or 'spheres' relevant to a specific question or clinical drama and it works towards responses honouring the people involved and their interrelationships (Russell 2008). The 'place' that is created when healthcare activities are based on enduring and deliberate co-creation among workers, clients, and significant others, as collaborating actors or dramatis personae, is itself an ethical accomplishment – albeit never finished – with a luminous narrative.

NOTES

1   Federal: Canadian Constitution Act/Charter of Rights and Freedoms (Government of Canada 1985), Canadian Human Rights Act (Government of Canada 1985). Provincial: Ontario Human Rights Code (Government of Ontario 1990a), Health Care Consent Act (Government of Ontario 1996), Mental Health Act (Government of Ontario 1990b), Personal Health Information Protection Act (Government of Ontario 2004), Patient Restraints Minimization Act (Government of Ontario 2001), Highway Traffic Act (Government of Ontario 1990c).
2   Examples: psychologists, psychotherapists, occupational therapists, nurses, physicians, dentists, homeopaths, chiropodists (Government of Ontario 1991).
3   All names are fictitious.
4   In contemporary healthcare and bioethics, the most well-known principlist theory is Tom Beauchamp and James Childress's (2012) four principles: beneficence, nonmaleficence, autonomy, and justice.

REFERENCES

American Psychiatric Association. 2016. DSMs I–5. www.psychiatry.org.

Appelbaum PS. 2013. "Let Therapists Be Therapists, Not Police". *American Journal of Bioethics.* 13: 71–72.

Beauchamp TL and JF Childress. 2012. *The Principles of Biomedical Ethics,* 7th ed. Oxford, UK: Oxford University Press.

Berger BE, MC Kapella and JL Larson. 2011. "The Experience of Stigma in Chronic Obstructive Pulmonary Disease". *Western Journal of Nursing Research.* 33: 916–932.

Bogren A. 2008. "Women's Intoxication as 'Dual Licentiousness': an exploration of gendered images of drinking and intoxication in Sweden". *Addiction Research & Theory.* 12: 95–106.

Brown-Johnson CG and J Prochaska. 2015. "Shame-Based Appeals in a Tobacco Control Public Health Campaign: potential harms and benefits". *Tobacco Control.* 24: 419–420.

Buchanan D, K Khoshnood, T Stopka, S Shaw, C Santelices and M Singer. 2002. "Ethical Dilemmas Created by the Criminalization of Status Behaviors: case examples from ethnographic field research with injection drug users". *Health Education and Behavior.* 29: 30–42.

Courtwright A. 2013. "Stigmatization and Public Health Ethics". *Bioethics.* 27: 74–80.

Dale R, R Barton, J Shepherd, A Burrows, D Brooke and G Adshead. 1997. "Why Are Doctors Ambivalent about Patients Who Misuse Alcohol?" *British Medical Journal.* 315: 1297–1300.

Degenhardt L and W Hall. 2012. "Extent of Illicit Drug Use and Dependence, and Their Contribution to the Global Burden of Disease". *Lancet.* 379: 55–70.

Forrest P. 2009. "The Philosophical Scandal of the Wrong Kind of Religious Disagreement". *Sophia.* 48: 151–166.

Frank AW. 2010. *Letting Stories Breathe: a socio-narratololgy.* Chicago: University of Chicago Press.

Frank AW. 2007. "Five Dramas of Illness". *Perspectives in Biology and Medicine.* 50: 379–394.

Frank AW. 2004. "Ethics as Process and Practice". *Internal Medicine Journal.* 34: 355–357.

Fulford KWM and N Sartorius. 2009. A Secret History of ICD and the Hidden Future of DSM. In *Psychiatry as Cognitive Neuroscience: Philosophical Perspectives,* edited by Broome M and L Bortolotti. Oxford, UK: Oxford University Press.

Gaylin W and B Jennings. 2003. *The Perversion of Autonomy: coercion and constraints in a liberal society.* Washington, DC: Georgetown University Press.

Geppert CM and MP Bogenschutz. 2009. "Ethics in Substance Use Disorder Treatment". *Psychiatric Clinics of North America.* 32: 283–297.

Gillett GR. 2004. *Bioethics in the Clinic: Hippocratic reflections.* Baltimore, MA: Johns Hopkins University Press.

Government of Canada. 2014. Canadian Community Health Survey. www.statcan.gc.ca/daily-quotidien/150617/dq150617b-eng.htm.

Government of Canada. 1985. Canadian Human Rights Act (R.S.C. 1985, c. H-6). laws-lois.justice.gc.ca/eng/acts/h-6.

Government of Canada. 1982. Constitution Act, 1982. Charter of Rights and Freedoms. laws-lois.justice.gc.ca/eng/Const/page-15.html.

Government of Ontario. 2004. Personal Health Information Protection Act, 2004, S.O. 2004, c. 3, Sched. A. www.ontario.ca/laws/statute/04p03.

Government of Ontario. 2001. Patient Restraints Minimization Act, 2001, S.O. 2001, c. 16 – Bill 85. www.ontario.ca/laws/statute/s01016.

Government of Ontario. 1996. Health Care Consent Act, 1996. S.O. 1996, c. 2, Sched. A. www.ontario.ca/laws/statute/96h02.

Government of Ontario. 1991. Regulated Health Professions Act, 1991, S.O. 1991, c. 18. www.ontario.ca/laws/statute/91r18

Government of Ontario. 1990a. Human Rights Code, R.S.O. 1990, c. H.19. www.ontario. ca/laws/statute/90h19.

Government of Ontario. 1990b. Mental Health Act, R.S.O. 1990, c. M.7. www.ontario. ca/laws/statute/90m07.

Government of Ontario. 1990c. Highway Traffic Act, R.S.O. 1990, c. H.8. www.ontario. ca/laws/statute/90h08#BK304.

Green TH. 1888. Lecture on Liberal Legislation and Freedom of Contract. In *Works,* volume III, edited by R Nettleship. London: Longmans, Green, 365–386.

Herring J, C Regan, D Weinber and P Withington. 2013. Starting the Conversation. In *Intoxication and Society: problematic pleasures of drugs and alcohol*, edited by J Herring, C Regan, D Weinberg and P Withington. London: Palgrave Macmillan, 1–30.

Hoeyer K and AMB Jensen. 2011. "Organ Donation and the Ethics of Muddling Through". *Critical Care.* 15: 109.

Hofman NG. 2003. "Maintaining Respectability and Responsibility: gendered labor patterns among women injection drug users". *Health Care for Women International.* 24: 794–807.

Hunziker M, M Buchecker and T Hartig. 2007. Space and Place – two aspects of the Human-landscape relationship. In *A Changing World; challenges for landscape research*, edited by F Kienast, O Wildi and S Ghosh. Dordrecht: Springer, 47–62.

Karol DE, IN Schuermeyer and CA Brooker. 2007. "The Case of H.S.: the ethics of reporting alcohol dependence in a bus driver". *International Journal of Psychiatry in Medicine.* 37: 267–273.

Kleinig J. 2004. "Ethical Issues in Substance Use Intervention". *Substance Use and Misuse.* 39: 369–398.

Kremer ME and KS Arora. 2015. "Clinical, Ethical and Legal Considerations in Pregnant Women with Opioid Abuse". *Obstetrics & Gynecology.* 126: 474–478.

Landry MD, J Tepper and MC Verrier. 2009. "Moving from 'Muddling Through' to Careful Planning: physical therapy human resources in Canada". *Physiotherapy Canada.* 61: 60–62.

Lindblom CE. 1959. "The Science of 'Muddling Through'". *Public Administration Review.* 19: 79–88.

McLeod C and S Sherwin. 2000. Relational Autonomy, Self-Trust, and Health Care for Patients Who are Oppressed. In R*elational Autonomy: feminist perspectives on autonomy, agency, and the social self*, edited by C Mackenzie and N Stoljar. New York: Oxford University Press, 259–279.

Mechanic D. 1997. "Muddling Through Elegantly: finding the proper balance in rationing". *Health Affairs.* 16: 83–92.

Mill JS. 1947. *On Liberty.* New York: F.S. Crofts.

Murray G. 2015. "You Say You Want a Revolution: recovery, biomedicine and muddling through". *Australian & New Zealand Journal of Psychiatry.* 49: 1085–1086.

Paris J. 2008. *Prescriptions for the Mind: a critical view of contemporary psychiatry.* Oxford, UK: Oxford University Press.

Plambeck CM. 2002. "Divided Loyalties. Legal and bioethical considerations of physician-pregnant patient confidentiality and prenatal drug abuse". *Journal of Legal Medicine.* 23: 1–35.

Quinn C and A Barton. 2000. "The Implications of Drug Treatment and Testing Orders". *Nursing Standard.* 14: 38–41.

Robertson JA. 2007. "The Virtues of Muddling Through". *Hastings Center Report.* 37: 26–28.

Room R. 2001. "Intoxication and Bad Behaviour: understanding cultural differences in the link". *Social Science and Medicine.* 53: 189–198.

Russell BJ. 2008. "An Integrative and Practical Approach to Ethics in Everyday Health Care". *Risk Management in Canadian Health Care.* 10: 9–13.

Santayana G. 1906. *The Life of Reason: or the phases of human progress.* London: Archibald Constable & Co.

Schwartz B. 2009. "The Loss of Wisdom". *TED talk.* www.ted.com/talks/barry_schwartz_on_our_loss_of_wisdom?language=en.

Schwartz B and K Sharpe. 2010. *The Loss of Wisdom: the right way to do the right thing.* New York: Riverhead Books.

Sherwin S. 1998. A Relational Approach to Autonomy in Health Care. In *The Politics of Women's Health: exploring agency and autonomy,* edited by S Sherwin. Philadelphia, PA: Temple University Press, 19–47.

Strumberg JP. 2012. "Caring for People with Chronic Disease: is 'muddling through' the best way to handle the multiple complexities?" *Journal of Evaluation in Clinical Practice.* 18: 1220–1225.

Weddle M and P Kokotailo. 2002. "Adolescent Substance Abuse. Confidentiality and consent". *Pediatric Clinics of North America.* 49: 301–315.

World Health Organization. 2016a. International Classification of Disease (ICD). www.who.int/classifications/icd/en/.

World Health Organization. 2016b. Tobacco Fact Sheet. www.who.int/mediacentre/factsheets/fs339/en/.

World Health Organization. 2015a. Other Psychoactive Substances Fact Sheet. www.who.int/substance_abuse/facts/psychoactives/en/.

World Health Organization. 2015b. Alcohol Fact Sheet. www.who.int/mediacentre/factsheets/fs349/en/.

CHAPTER 9

Policy

Louise Nadeau

INTRODUCTION

During the decade of the 1980s, I was the Chairperson of a treatment center for addictions. Since the center had opened in the 60s the treatment plan was abstinence, from time of admission to time of discharge. Furthermore, being free of substance use was the primary criteria to assess treatment effectiveness. Women and men desiring help for an addiction, both alcohol and/or drugs, had to be abstinent at admission and were dismissed if they used substances during treatment. The rules and regulations of our center were no different than those of many other treatment centers at the time, in North America and Europe.

In that same decade, the human immunodeficiency virus and acquired immune deficiency syndrome (HIV/AIDS) epidemic occurred. Those were the days when all who were infected died for lack of known medication to prolong life. Persons who had unprotected sex and/or used intravenous (IV) drugs were at high risk of being contaminated, which included persons that were served in our center. For many community workers involved with active users of substances and for public health clinicians and scientists examining surveillance data, it had become clear that the requirements for abstinence of addiction treatment centers were not helping to fight the dissemination of the virus; quite the contrary. Their position was clear, and forceful: a harm reduction strategy had to be put in place. The entire population needed information about safe sex and safe drug practices; all those at risk required a distribution of free condoms and intravenous (IV) users, an access to free sterile injection kits (Pates and Riley, 2012). Faced with a lethal virus, the priority was to save lives, not aim at a hypothetical abstinence, a mirage for many persons struggling with an addiction. The course of action supported by treatment centers was viewed as dangerous, destructive, and devastating.

During a conference on substance use at the time, a speaker advocating for harm reduction accused those responsible for compulsory abstinence in treatment centers of being serial killers. The statement on the inequity of abstinence was a direct attack on the integrity of our board. If our center was in fact betraying its mission, i.e., helping persons with an addiction, then the board had to re-examine the principles on which abstinence was founded. The request made by the harm reduction pressure groups involved a radical change in the course of action of our treatment agency. It meant changing from an abstinence prescription aiming at the prevention/eradication of substance use to a procedure of preventing the deleterious consequences that arise while persons continue to use substances. I could hear beforehand the issues that would/could be raised by members of the board:

➤ Isn't it wrong to 'encourage' drug use?
➤ Would harm reduction discourage abstinence for those who desired that legitimate goal?
➤ Are the data presented before us sound or are they modulated to favor harm reduction?
➤ Would professionals accept working within such a diametrically opposed framework?
➤ Would police and, ultimately, the Law cause trouble?

The controversy opposing abstinence and harm reduction in treatment centers for addictions constitutes a telling example of the process that takes place when a board of concerned citizens must decide on a given course of action as part of its management mandate. Such a debate illustrates the development and setting of policy.

OBJECTIVE

This chapter examines policy in treatment centers for substance use problems. A short definition of policy will be given. Then, using abstinence vs. harm reduction as a case study, the key elements involved in policy development and setting will be described.

POLICY

A policy is the system of principles, or a set of ideas, selected by a group of persons responsible for deciding on a given course of action. A policy is ela-borated in a given field of intervention or a sector of activity. In this chapter a center responsible for the treatment of substance use problems and other dependencies.

Different contexts command policy. Professional, legal, economical, organizational, social, ethical, political situations may require boards to make statements about a course of action. Policies can also originate from beliefs and values shared by the stakeholders – the board, the staff, the persons served, stakeholders from other agencies, including governments. Consequently, the nature of policy is quite diverse.

Treatment agencies, as other organizations, have a mission statement. The mission sets the goal towards which of the activities of the establishment thrive. Generally, it is a short, constructive and positive declaration. The mission can be the guiding star when an unpredicted event takes place and the board needs to set a policy that could modify the entire organization, such as the HIV/AIDS epidemic that put into question the existing policy of abstinence in treatment agencies for substance use problems in the 1980's and the following years (Pates and Riley, 2012). For instance, the mission of Alcoholics Anonymous did not changed with the HIV/AIDS epidemic: the recovery program in the Fellowship has not modified its objective of abstinence from alcohol (Alcoholics Anonymous, 2016).

Policy is more detailed than the mission because it gives specific attention to the desired outcomes of the organization and, in some cases, provides procedures. Policy in a treatment center can serve as a guideline to help clinicians and persons in treatment make decisions. For instance, in the example of an abstinence policy, professionals and persons in treatment know that the use of substances during treatment leads to treatment termination: it was an authoritative procedure that was not put into question in the centers.

The abstinence/harm reduction quandary raised new and taught questions:
➤ How much should be dictated to staff?
➤ Could an abstinence model co-exist with a harm reduction model in the same setting?
➤ Were those decisions within the policy or the clinical realm?

Policy should not be so prescriptive that it dictates the entire repertoire of what can or cannot be done by personnel/professionals. In such cases, professionals cannot use their own competence, judgment, and experience to examine a problem, find a solution and apply it. It seems preferable that space be left for individual judgment and use of initiative. Striking a balance, it is also preferable that decisions in an organization not be taken at the fantasy of each professional without some form of internal coherence. Furthermore, many professionals are bound by the code of ethics imposed by their professional corporations that determine what is appropriate and acceptable in their dealings with the persons they are helping and outside agencies. This adds an additional layer to the policy of the organization.

In the years following the HIV epidemic, health authorities tackled differently the dilemma of abstinence vs. harm reduction: certain boards used stringent policy settling for one or the other treatment strategies while others left to clinicians and persons in their care the decision to choose the most appropriate treatment plan. In many large jurisdictions, certain units of care within the centers maintained their substance free goals while others adopted risk reduction and harm mitigating strategies, thus allowing professionals and individuals experiencing substance use problems to make choices. In setting policy, a board will attempt, or at least should attempt, to find the happy medium that will allow the recognition of the professional competence of the staff and a reference to the common denominator that links a team together and provides secure boundaries for those using services.

SELF-ASSESSMENT EXERCISE 9.1

Time: 30 minutes

You sit on a board of an agency responsible for the care of homeless persons in a city of one million people. The priority of the board is getting the homeless persons off the streets and providing permanent supervised dwellings for at least one year.

● Could you formulate the mission of the agency, on the one hand, and two policy statements, on the other?

GOAL SETTING

Policy generally stems from a problem that requires attention. The first choice that confronts a board is to assess if voting on a new policy is an adequate answer to the problem situation. Policies are norms that generally apply to the entire organization and are difficult to change. A specific problem does not always require a response that commands such a universal response. However, if it is deemed necessary to solve the problem, boards first need to identify what goal is pursued by the new policy.

Goals are not an easy decision to agree upon. The discussion between deciders should involve true reciprocity, i.e., mutual respect, openness to other member's points of view, and a willingness to change perspective if other members bring forth points of view that enrich the discussion (Gutman and Thomson, 1990). The mission statement in a treatment center is to keep heading for increased wellness among those that are served.

The impact of policy is not always predictable, and lack of control over future events may lead to multiple predictions that hinder decision-making. For instance:

➤ Would the distribution of syringes unintentionally increase drug use or simply protect intravenous (IV) users?

➤ Could a treatment center encourage promiscuity by free distribution of condoms?

➤ Would harm reduction constitute an obstruction to abstinence-centered treatment?

Furthermore, there are always unique challenges in health care that implicitly affect goals. Is it preferable to select a policy that saves a few lives at a very high cost or to improve the quality of life of a large group of individuals, but at a relatively low cost per person? To state the issue differently, can an organization support the entire continuum of care, with a large number of individuals at the base of the pyramid that need short but competent interventions and a small but costly group of persons that need long-term care at the top of the pyramid? The issues at stake generally have a common denominator: is the policy under study a move in the right direction? As we will see in the next section, scientific evidence supports rational decision making in policy setting, but even the soundest data do not erase the fundamental questions that are frequently dissimulated in policy, i.e., what will this policy really achieve? In fact, the reasons to select a policy are manifold, implicit and explicit, from a strategic statement to increase funding, passing into improved quality of service to moral/religious reasons. Sometimes, private interests are favored and at other times public good interests predominate.

In our case study here, the confrontation between the abstinence and the harm reduction proponents was inseparable from the different goals pursued by the two unalike policies: the former adhered to a recovery/remission objective and the latter aimed at harm minimization and risk mitigation strategies that did not necessarily imply remission. Each choice carried specific deleterious consequences and significant improvement of quality of life. Certain centers decided to reject the harm reduction strategy, those very close to the Alcoholics Anonymous fellowship for instance, while others introduced harm reduction. In many cases there are no good or bad answers to a challenge, there are different goals pursued by an organization. Organizations are entitled to pursue goals that are consequent with their established mission.

The choice of policy is inseparable from the goal pursued by a board. For integrity purposes, goals of a selected policy should be explicit, not implicit, and state the strengths and limitations that are expected with its implementation. Integrity also requires consistency of speech from one policy to another, and performance consistency (Gutmann and Thompson, 1990, 82). In addition, it is highly preferable that the goal pursued reflects as closely as possible the contingencies that constraint the organization: a policy is not an impossible dream à la Don Quixote lead by a chivalric romance concerning a given organization or its mission. It is an attainable and concrete project that solves a current difficulty or improves existing conditions. For instance, there may be a policy forbidding sexual misconduct and harassment of the staff and the persons in treatment, such as verbal or physical unwanted advances. However, if there is no confidential and trustworthy center to report inappropriate and harmful sexual behavior that will provide protection, support, information, and referrals if needed, to victims, and if the perpetrator is allowed to continue his or her aggressive behavior in all impunity within or outwith the organization, then the policy forbidding sexual misconduct is what one could call a 'feel good policy' that reassures the board but is, in fact, ineffective, and hypocritical. In short, the board should ensure that the organization can and will provide the means to allow the effective implementation of a selected policy. The agendas of a board should include periodic points that report on the overall effectiveness of the policies that have been voted. This commands the need for an on-going monitoring system.

If policy makers take to heart the goals they are pursuing, goals that are operationalized in their selected policies, it is therefore necessary to assemble valid and sufficient information to examine if the decisions are working in the desired direction. This evaluation procedure is named a 'monitoring system'. Monitoring is defined as a systematic, on-going process to collect, analyse, and interpret accurate and relevant information – selected indicators – with a view to describing and examining changes in a specific phenomenon over time. The monitoring plan in a treatment center for substance use problems aims at assessing the situation in the center. It is an essential tool for deciders, including management, to check if the situation in the center is improving in the expected direction and if adjustments need to be made. Monitoring allows periodically taking the pulse of the wellness of all involved in the organization, from management to the persons served and the partners in other agencies (Nadeau et al., 2014, 20).

SELF-ASSESSMENT EXERCISE 9.2

> **Time: 20 minutes**
> Many countries are currently struggling with the legalization of cannabis and its use for medical purposes.
> - What are the similarities between the current debate about cannabis and that associated to abstinence and harm reduction?
> - What are the differences between the two debates?

SELF-ASSESSMENT EXERCISE 9.3

> **Time: 15 minutes**
> Effective policy needs to be validated by an on-going monitoring system. Choose a policy in your field that you consider important.
> - What could be the indicators that need to be measured over time if you want to ensure that the policy is attained?

SCIENTIFIC EVIDENCE

Most boards pursue the objective of evidence-based decision-making in policy setting. There is a will in most boards to have reliable scientific data guide, if not instruct, decision makers (Massé, 2003, 282). Is it the main objective of decision makers to make policy more accountable, rational and objective, and, ultimately, to produce the best possible health outcomes?

Evidence-based decision-making has become the buzzword in health and health care since the decade of the 1990s (National Forum on Health, 1997a,

16–17). Sackett et al. (2000; Stratford, 2015) coined the term 'evidence-based decision-making' when Sackett was at McMaster University, Canada. There are scientific journals carrying that title, encyclopedias, and nearly 10,000 titles in PubMed in 2016. The concept is dated around mid-nineteenth century Paris or earlier (British Medical Journal, 1996) however, Howick inquires 'what on earth was medicine based on before evidence-based medicine?' (2011, 4), signifying that empirical facts have been a concern to evaluate treatment effectiveness throughout the history of medicine. Today that is still true in all realms of health care, including social services (Institut national d'excellence sur la santé et les services sociaux, 2015).

Some board members may be scientists, and others not. It is not, and should not be, a pre-requisite for any board member to be an expert on all the policy matters that are brought forth for discussion. On the contrary, health boards are made of a diversity of competencies that are intended to facilitate balanced decision-making. In the instance of policy development, it is not the responsibility of boards to collect, analyze, and synthetize research results. However, board members need to be informed of the state of the art on a given topic by reliable experts, or by valid syntheses, or both to inform policy development. The quality of the data that is shared with a board is a key component to policy setting based on facts. In the ideal situation, experts and/or written materials describe the strengths and limitations of the data presented and the gaps in knowledge or lack of scientific research focusing specifically on the area under study. Experts should make full disclosure of their conflicts of interest when personal concerns could undermine their impartiality in the assessment of a situation. A board should fear being presented with erroneous information as if these data were exact leading to the sabotage of the decision-making process.

In the health care world, the 'gold standard' of evidence is the randomized clinical trial. Even they, however, have their limitations (National Forum on Health, 1997b, 6). If a constellation of such studies confer in the same direction, policy development is made easier. Nevertheless, other types of information are needed for policy setting. Reliable epidemiological data are generally available on the prevalence rates in the field of addictions and various studies on treatment effectiveness have been done, with or without a control group, and their limitations are now well known (Miller and Moyers, 2015).

In the case of the social care sector, in which addiction services are parts in many jurisdictions, it is preferable that data presented to the decision makers include randomized clinical trials when available, proven clinical practices such as treatment effectiveness studies, qualitative studies, case studies, and expert opinions (Institut national d'excellence sur la santé et les services sociaux, 2015, 25; National Forum on Health, 1997b, 16–17). Furthermore, policy development, at least in the social care sector, should take into account contextual information that describes the circumstances in which the policy will be applied as well as the knowledge, working conditions, and preferences of staff and those being served by the organization (Institut national d'excellence sur la santé et les services sociaux, 2015, 25). The data associated to a prospective policy is assessed by the triangulation of the different data sources taking into account strengths and limitations of each source of information in an attempt to strike the balance between the two. However, reliable data do not guarantee that the decision made or the results will be perfect, but it does increase the probability.

In the abstinence/harm reduction dilemma, the inquiry of many boards pertained to the quality of the data brought before them:

➤ Was the evidence sound?

➤ Does evidence justify that such a turnabout be taken?

➤ Was there a causal link between compulsory abstinence required in treatment centers on the one hand and increased mortality among persons that the centers served on the other?

In the 1980s and early 1990s, when the dramatic loss of persons living with HIV/AIDS took place, even if the mode of transmission was understood, considerations other than scientific evidence had to be included in the algorithm in policy development.

SELF-ASSESSMENT EXERCISE 9.4

Time: 20 minutes

Policy should rely on multiple sources of evidence.

- What kind of data would need a board or staff working within an institution for sex-offenders to develop policy about visits with family members including children and adolescents?
- What kind of data would need a board or staff working within an agency that attends the needs of parents experiencing severe substance use problems and legal issues to develop policy about visits with family members including children and adolescents?

VALUES AND MORAL CONSIDERATIONS

When the quest for evidence has been fulfilled, with or without entire scientific satisfaction, a second but more challenging query arises in policy setting: does the evidence justify a policy? This is the time when values and moral considerations, inseparable from policy development, come into play. Many decisions related to health care, including mental health–substance use (MHSU), rest on values.

Values are the principles on which people choose and assess behaviors, events or states (Rokeach, 1973). Values are processes 'running deep, rarely surfacing and revealed only indirectly and imperfectly through the political process' (National Forum on Health, 1997a, 10).

When a policy is voted by a board of governors, the beliefs and opinions (or values) underlying may be evident, or opaque. Furthermore, in certain circumstances there may be a dissonance between the values that are affirmed in the policy and the known future effects of that same policy. The example of a policy forbidding sexual misconduct in the organization but providing no confidential and trustworthy center for victims could be re-stated here. In extensive consultations that were conducted in 1994 and 1995, the Canadians that were surveyed stated that equality of access to health care was a priority for them. Health care was seen as totally different from housing or automobiles or vacation: egalitarianism was the dominating value for the Canadian health care system. Being as healthy as possible was defined as being part of the national trademark, the Canadian identification. The investment in the health care system was considered as a smart investment for the country and universal Medicare was an essential part of the Canadian identity (National Forum on Health, 1997c, 10–11). However, at that time and in the past 20 years, policies in most jurisdictions have indented the egalitarianism principle supported in the Canadian population, albeit the acknowledgment that equality of access is a fundamental and persisting value in the constituencies that are being served. This discrepancy between an enunciated value and the predictable impact of a given policy commands vigilance on the part of deciders concerned with the integrity of policy setting. To state it differently, boards should attempt to have coherence between goals, evidence, values, and the foreseen effects of a policy. However, some groups in the population are more susceptible to being the target of the contradictions between avowed goals, evidence, and the predictable deleterious effects of a policy.

SELF-ASSESSMENT EXERCISE 9.5

Time: 20 minutes

You are a counsellor in an agency serving adults experiencing mental health problems. An individual presents describing to you that her immediate superior has made unwanted verbal advances towards her. There is a policy forbidding sexual misconduct in the organization but provides no confidential and trustworthy center for victims.

- What are the options that are offered to you as a counsellor in this instance?
- Which one will you choose and why?

SELF-ASSESSMENT EXERCISE 9.6

Time: 20 minutes

There is evidence that alcohol consumption in pregnancy can cause harm. Foetal alcohol spectrum disorder impacts on individuals, their families, and society. Binge drinking occurs frequently among women during adolescence as well as unprotected sex. You are a member of a board responsible for adolescent health that includes 100 staff of diverse religious affiliation.

- Would you vote for a policy that includes compulsory information on pregnancy termination for all young people that have reported alcohol consumption?

Your answer should take into account the value and the unintended consequences of such a policy.

This risk of being treated unjustly by a health care policy is particularly acute for vulnerable groups. In many parts of the world, there are still disorders that are considered as 'real' and those that are seen as less genuine. A 'real' disorder is one in which the ill person is seen as being the victim of biological fate in comparison to a person seen as suffering from problems in an undertaking of his or her own. Consequently, societies have perceived causes of certain physical and mental disorders as moral: those who have become disturbed were seen, and still are in many instances, as having violated moral principles. The given explanations comprehend what is understood within a specific cultural context as fair or unfair, good or bad, taking into account the level at which a person is considered accountable or irresponsible for his or her behavior. The determining factor in this instance is the notion of personal responsibility. When a choice is judged as wrong or bad, it is considered a manifestation of personal weakness, i.e., of moral failure (Massé, 2003, 363). Another consequence of this disease stratification is that there are more research funds, more complex and valid studies, as well as more exceptional scientists and specialized clinicians involved in the treatment of disorders considered as purely organic than in mental health–substance use increasing the probability that more resources be allotted to the former.

Presently in the Western world, those who are considered irresponsible are the sub-groups of the population involved in risk taking behaviors because they have been oblivious to the public health injunctions informing them of the danger of such practices. Stigma is related to the perception that a condition is self-inflicted. These sub-groups are seen as delinquents not obeying the prescriptions that are good for them, which would make them more competent citizens (Massé, 2003, 246–247). Substance use problems, as well as excessive gambling have been an on-going key disqualifier in many societies. This legacy of stigma was a key factor in the predicament that confronted decision makers when the HIV/AIDS epidemic broke out affecting those individuals using substances.

Drugs, alcohol, and gambling have been known in societies for a long time and there is evidence that regulation of non-problematic consumption – public drug or alcohol policies as we would call them today – have been in place historically in many societies (Angel et al., 2005, 5–11). There has been historical recognition that such dependent behaviors are no ordinary commodity (Babor et al., 2003). Greek philosophy was concerned with the idea of keeping control over devouring desires provided by food, sex, money, and alcohol (Valleur, 2005, 1). Self-control was also required of Roman citizens, i.e., free males only, whatever the abuse inflicted on women or slaves (Dupont, 2013). Self-control was congenial to being a competent citizen. In corollary, transgressing that code was immoral. During the early Renaissance in the extremely popular *Narrenschiff* (*The Ship of Fools*), Sebastian Brant (1494) defined all gambling behavior in the realm of sin, the crime of gamblers being attempting to steal from God, His prerogatives on chance, and the final statement in the book affirming that gamblers are all creatures of Satan. The religious references in this more recent text set the emphasis on the sacrilege committed by gamblers. The locus of the immorality was changed but the stigma remained.

Substance use problems are not a recent discovery either. A text from Seneca established in year 42 of this era the distinction between 'a man who is drunk' and one 'who has no control over himself . . . who is accustomed to get drunk and is a slave to his habit' (Seneca, 1942). This enslavement was considered a form of insanity. The quotation indicates that alcohol use problems were known to the Romans and were perceived as a lessening of the person. Physician and philosopher Pâquier Joostens d'Eeklo (1561) published a monograph that provides extensive and vivid descriptions of gambling disorder. Gambling is described as a medical disease but also as an immoral activity: it is wrong to want someone else's money and wrong to become rich without effort or merit, without any other legitimacy than pure chance. It is unacceptable that vulnerable individuals are targeted as prey by excessive gamblers. In short, there are reliable sources that indicate that addictions were a significant social issue that engendered moral, if not religious disapproval: stigma, i.e., shame and discredit, associated to addictions, with or without substances, is not recent. One can speculate if these ideas about the value of self-control and the stigma associated with loss of control in substance use problems have or have not been transmitted from one generation to another in the Western tradition since their contents still have contemporary resonance. This question leads to plausible conjectures. In short, we don't know. However, to quote again Babor et al. (2003), there is agreement, historically, that alcohol, drugs, and gambling are no ordinary commodities.

For those responsible for policy development in treatment centers for substance use, the ambient values and moral considerations about substance use problems, that are more often than not implicit than explicit, need to be acknowledged. The awareness of the hierarchy in diseases may help decision makers in policy development so that the effects of the double standard do not permeate decisions. With the HIV-AIDS epidemic, this stigma related to personal responsibility became extremely explicit. There were those who had been infected through a blood transfusion, such as persons suffering from hemophilia – the 'good people' – and those who had been infected by sexual contact or by syringe exchange – the 'bad people'. The double standard between those perceived as 'real victims' and those alleged as being personally responsible was striking. It was in this controversial context, in which moral considerations were upfront, that harm reduction policies were taken: adopting risk reduction and harm mitigating strategies was perceived by certain groups of citizens as reinforcing behaviors that were conceptualized as irresponsible, and contrary to good citizenship and the public good.

Most of the time values, moral considerations, and clinical vulnerability interplay with each other blurring the picture for decision makers. This is particularly true of persons heavily dependent on substances. The case of women struggling with an alcohol addiction is a telling example. Women admitted to treatment for alcohol related problems, as a group, present more severe and more numerous signs of psychological distress and co-occurring disorders than their male counterparts. These individuals have experienced more frequent antecedents of child abuse and neglect, including sexual abuse during childhood, adolescence, and adulthood. The prevalence of post-traumatic stress disorder is high as is the rate of suicide attempts. These psychosocial characteristics have not changed significantly (Poole and Greaves, 2007) since attention has been given to women dependent on alcohol during the 1970s (Beckman, 1976; Gomberg, 1974; Schuckit and Morissey, 1976). Concurrently, as several pioneer authors have stated (Gomberg, 1974; Knupfer, 1982), drunkenness precludes the accomplishment of the working tasks traditionally allocated to women: taking care of husband and children, cooking, and cleaning the home. Drinking women also stopped being sensitive to the needs of others. Blume (1991) offers evidence that the loss of sexual restraints and inhibitions is a cause of concern. This perceived moral failure is associated to the greater social stigma associated to female intoxication. Such moral considerations and stigma in turn consolidate psychological distress of women experiencing substance use problems in the form of the low self-esteem, the MHSU problems, the lack of constructive social support and limited affirmative skills that are reported in the literature. These factors are obstacles to recovery, and, paradoxically, reinforce the ambient stigma.

Decision makers should be aware of this spiral at play in stigmatized populations – the LGBT (*see* Chapter 14) community, offenders, homeless persons, and persons living with HIV. These individuals struggle in a maelstrom of disapproval of others albeit a frequent history of poverty, childhood abuse and neglect, of social rejection and an inhibiting lack of trust in oneself. Decision makers need to think of policies concerning those they serve as if they were salmon moving upstream against strong currents: it is their moral responsibility to create conditions in their centers that defy the ambient stigma.

SELF-ASSESSMENT EXERCISE 9.7

Time: 30 minutes
There are countries in which the LGBT population is more accepted than in others.
● What are the national policies that have contributed to more acceptance of this population?
● What are the prevention policies that have contributed to more acceptance of this population?
● What are the treatment policies that have contributed to more acceptance of this population?

CONCLUSION

There is no right or wrong answer to the abstinence/harm reduction quandary. There are only policies that are selected in a context in which goals are explicit and the expected results are measured, strengths and limitations of evidence have been weighted with experts that have declared conflicts of interest. The wellness of people being served should be the dominating value. Alcoholics Anonymous rejected harm minimization and risk mitigation strategies to maintain the focus on abstinence and, in doing so, respected their mission. Countless persons are in recovery because of this fellowship that has maintained it cohesiveness, integrity, and effectiveness while rejecting harm reduction. On the other hand, for many persons dependent on substances, particularly individuals using IV drugs, information about safe sex and safe drug practices, free condoms and free sterile injection kits, protected injection sites coupled to the unconditional positive regard and empathic understanding of counsellors have saved lives, and given dignity to individuals who were seen as degenerate.

Decision makers in treatment centers should be concerned with best practices to maximize treatment effectiveness and by the application of a code of ethics that determines what is appropriate and acceptable in dealings within and outwith the organization. Moreover, policy makers should keep the focus on vulnerable populations and ensure that their decisions contribute best to the wellbeing of those they serve.

REFERENCES

Alcoholics Anonymous. 2016. Web site. www.aa.org/pages/en_US/what-is-aa.
Angel P, S Angel and M Valleur. 2005. "Contexte: drogues et société". Edited by P Angel, D Richard, M Valleur and É Chagnard. *Toxicomanies*. Paris: Masson. pp. 5–14.

Babor T, R Caetano, S Casswell, G Edwards, N Giesbrecht, K Graham, J Grube, P Gruenwald, L Hill, H Hoder, R Homel, E Österberg, J Rehm, R Room, I Rossow. 2003. *Alcohol: no Ordinary Commodity. Research and Public Policy.* New York: Oxford University Press.

Beckman LJ. 1976. "Alcoholism problems and women: an overview". Edited by M Greenblatt and MA Schuckit. *Alcoholism Problems in Women and Children.* New York: Grune and Stratton. pp. 65–97.

Blume S. 1991. "Women, alcohol, and drugs". Edited by NS Miller. *Comprehensive Handbook of Drug and Alcohol Addiction.* New York: Marcel Dekker. pp. 147–77.

Brant S. 1494. "La nef des fous". In *La Nef des Fous et les Songes du Seigneur Sebastian Brant.* Trad. et présentation par Nicole Taubes. Paris: J. Corti; 1997.

British Medical Journal. 1996. "Evidence based medicine: what it is and what it isn't". *British Medical Journal,* 312: 7023.71

Dupont F. 2013. *L'Antiquité, Territoire des Écarts.* Paris: Albin Michel.

Gomberg E. 1974. "Women and alcoholism". Edited by V Franks and V Burtle. *Women in Therapy.* New York: Brunner and Mazel. pp. 169–91.

Gutman A and D Thomson. 1990. "Moral conflict and political consensus". *Ethics.* 101: 64–88.

Howick J. 2011. *The Philosophy of Evidence-based Medicine.* Foreword by P Glasziou. Chichester, West Sussex: Wiley-Blackwell, BMJ Books.

Institut national d'excellence sur la santé et les services sociaux (INESSS). 2015. *Cadre d'élaboration des guides de pratique dans le secteur des services sociaux.* Document rédigé par S Beauchamp, M Drapeau, C Dionne and J-P Duplantie. Québec: Institut national d'excellence sur la santé et les services sociaux.

Knupfer G. 1982. "Problems associated with drunkenness in women: some research issues". *Alcohol and Health Monograph no 4: Special Population Issues.* Rockville, MA: National Institute on Alcohol Abuse and Alcoholism. pp. 3–39.

Massé R (en collaboration avec J Saint-Arnaud). 2003. *Éthique et Santé Publique: Enjeux, Valeurs et Normativité.* Québec: Presses de l'Université Laval.

Miller WR and TB Moyers. 2015. "The Forest and the trees: relational and specific factors in addiction treatment". *Addiction,* 110: 401–13.

Nadeau L, M Dufour, R Guay, S Kairouz, JM Ménard and C Paradis. 2014. *Le jeu en ligne: Quand la réalité du virtuel nous rattrape /Online Gambling: When Reality Catches Up with Us.* Montréal: Groupe de travail sur le jeu en ligne. www.groupes.finances. gouv.qc.ca/jeu/index_en.asp

National Forum on Health. 1997a. *Canada Health Action: Building on the Legacy. The Final Report of the National Forum on Health.* Ottawa: Ministry of Public Works and Government Services.

National Forum on Health. 1997b. Creating a culture of evidence-based decision making in health. In *Canada Health Action: Building on the Legacy. Synthesis Reports and Issues Papers.* Ottawa: Ministry of Public Works and Government Services.

National Forum on Health. 1997c. Values working group: synthesis report. In *Canada Health Action: Building on the Legacy. Synthesis Reports and Issues Papers.* Ottawa: Ministry of Public Works and Government Services.

Pates R and D Riley. 2012. *Harm Reduction in Substance use and High-Risk Behaviour. International Policy and Practices.* Toronto: Wiley-Blackwell.

Pâquier Joostens d'Eeklo. 1561. Le jeu de hasard, ou comment soigner le désir de jouer pour de l'argent. Trad. et présentation par Jean-François Cottier. In L Nadeau and

M Valleur (Eds.). 2014. *Pascasius ou comment comprendre les addictions.* Montréal: Presses de l'Université de Montréal. pp. 84–179. www.pum.umontreal.ca.

Poole N and L Greaves, (Eds.). 2007. *Highs and Lows: Canadian Perspectives on Women and Substance Use.* British Colombia Centre of Excellence for Women's Health and Centre for Addiction and Mental Health.

Rokeach M. 1973. *The Nature of Human Values.* New York: The Free Press.

Sackett D, S Straus, E Richardson, WS Rosenberg, WHR Brian. 2000. *Evidence-based Medicine: How to Practice and Teach EBM.* 2nd ed. Toronto, Ontario, Canada: Churchill Livingstone.

Schuckit MA and ER Morissey. 1976. "Alcoholism in women: some clinical and social perspectives with an emphasis on possible subtypes". Edited by M Greenblatt and MA Schuckit. *Alcoholism Problems in Women and Children.* New York: Grune et Stratton. pp. 5–37.

Seneca. 1942. "Classics in Alcohol Literature: Seneca's Epistle LXXXIII: On Drunkenness". *Quarterly Journal of Studies on Alcohol.* 3: 302–7.

Stratford P. 2015. "In Tribute" DL Sackett. *Physical Therapy.* 95: 1084–6.

Valleur M. 2005. "Introduction drogues: plaisir, jeu, transgression". Edited by P Angel, D Richard, M Valleur and É Chagnard. *Toxicomanies.* Paris: Masson. pp. 1–4.

CHAPTER 10

Informed consent

Jacqueline Talmet

INTRODUCTION

Upholding human rights to access treatment and for self-determination has four major considerations, these are the right to:

1 access and receive services
2 to give, withhold or withdraw informed consent
3 receive treatment without consent when capacity for self-determination is diminished or absent or when the individual poses a risk to themselves or others or are vulnerable and at risk from others
4 receive treatment and the right to live is accepted as the predominant right.

KEY POINT 10.1

Human rights place obligations on professionals to act in a person's best interests and to fulfil their responsibilities.

However, professionals, despite being members of 'ethical professions', often stigmatise and discriminate against people experiencing mental health–substance use problems and do not afford the same rights or access to services that are made available to people in other treatment populations. This is an issue continually needing to be remediated by professionals seeking to advocate for these vulnerable individuals. Denial of access to evidence based treatment and exposure to unsafe or negligent practices and unethical professional behaviour, such as denying a competent person the right to refuse treatment, may cause the person harm and at times harm to their families.

This chapter explores informed consent and what it means for clinical practice in the presence and impact of the severity and complexity of mental health–substance use problems and other health and social issues on a person's capacity for self-determination. How this relates to a person's right to informed consent and to receive treatment when there is diminished capacity for self-determination is identified. Two case studies highlight the possible positive and negative outcomes when a person's right to self-determination is upheld or refused.

INFORMED CONSENT

No assessment, minor or invasive treatment or care process can occur without a person's implied, verbal or formalised consent. In a person experiencing mental health–substance use problems, the capacity for informed consent is made transient due to the nature of the mental ill health, substance use and/or subsequent intoxication or withdrawal. Capacity may be further complicated by the presence of comorbidities related to physical illness, AOD related brain injury, intellectual disability and/or social issues such as family violence, poverty and homelessness. These all add to the person's burden of vulnerability and further complexity to the person's needs for assistance and in obtaining informed consent.

> Informed consent is a person's agreement to allow something to happen to them based on a full disclosure of the risks, benefits, alternatives and consequences of refusal. Consent can be verbal, implied or written and is an agreement to undertake a specific treatment or intervention.
>
> (Australian Commission on Safety and Quality in Health Care – ACSQHC 2012, p. 6)

Voluntary treatment is associated with the use of informed consent that is given voluntarily and freely (ACSQHC 2012, p. 9). 'Consent cannot be lawful if accompanied by a threat or implied threat of compulsion, or if alternatives are not offered for consideration' (World Health Organization – WHO 2003a, p. 1).

Consent is valid for a specific treatment and/or intervention and is obtained prior to its commencement (ACSQHC 2012, p. 9).

PROFESSIONAL RESPONSIBILITIES WITH INFORMED CONSENT

KEY POINT 10.2

Professionals have responsibilities to act in accordance with accepted practices to ensure a valid and informed consent is obtained.

This includes:
➤ Creating an unhurried environment where the person has the opportunity for the presence of a supportive family and friends, and that adequate time

is made available for the discussion, to answer questions, address concerns and make a decision.

➤ Utilising the discussion as the primary component of the consent process. The act of signing the consent form is a minor part and is only proof that the discussion occurred, that the person understood the information and agreed to treatment.

➤ Information being provided in language the person understands and that considers the persons' circumstances, beliefs, priorities, culture, communication and/or cognitive difficulties and allows for the use of interpreters. Providing full information and repeating information if necessary about:
  ➤ The diagnosis and its significance
  ➤ Treatment and/or intervention options and their effectiveness including the option for no treatment
  ➤ Who would provide the service?
  ➤ The benefits, alternatives and risks and expected outcomes or consequences for each option and their likely significance. This includes medication use, unwanted side effects, length of treatment and/or recovery time, effectiveness adherence requirements, and any associated costs.
  ➤ The time period the consent will remain valid e.g. for a course of treatment, current episode of care, until it is withdrawn or a change in circumstances

➤ Documenting a full summary of the discussion, information provided, questions asked and concerns raised and the responses given. (Australian Capital Territory (ACT) Government, pp. 1–7).

REQUIREMENTS FOR INFORMED CONSENT

The expectations for enabling informed consent and upholding a person's right to access services are ensconced in international conventions, legislation, health department policy, organisational operational procedures and professional standards of practice, codes of ethics and conduct. These usually articulate the same principles and establish the responsibility to incorporate requirements in practice and to address practice deficits when they occur. The approach that might be taken in this is determined by the reason underpinning the deficit.

When a country is a signatory to an international convention through the World Health Organization (WHO 2003a, p. 3), it demonstrates its commitment to uphold its principles and practices and to meet its obligations. The WHO (2003a) principles around mental health service provision are found in the following statement:

> 'All people with mental disorders have the right to receive high quality treatment and care delivered through responsive health care services.

They should be protected against any form of inhuman treatment and discrimination'

(WHO 2003a, p. 1)

Finally, and most importantly, service provision is impacted on by the professional's personal attitudes and beliefs towards the individual experiencing substance use problems such as being viewed as a moral rather than a health issue. The care provided is underpinned by the extent to which they believe in and uphold professional standards and the obligation to act in accordance with requirements. Other issues impacting on the approach taken to people experiencing mental health–substance use problems may include:

➤ Willingness to engage
➤ Knowledge, skills and feelings of competence to respond
➤ Perception of self responsibility and deservingness of care
➤ Beliefs about their role and what they should and should not have to do
➤ Personal agreement with societal or negative workplace beliefs and culture
➤ Negative experiences with people experiencing mental health–substance use problems in their professional role or private life.

Informed consent is more than about obeying the law. It is about being ethical, considering and valuing how one should act, about being moral, doing no harm and having the moral courage to act to create change to prevent harm.

Professionals seeking to act ethically demonstrate knowledge of all requirements related to their practice. They enact the principles of safety and respect for the person's experience and its meaning to them which is evident in the manner care is provided.

KEY POINT 10.3

There is a belief that everyone has the right to receive quality, evidence based, humane care that upholds their rights, culture and dignity, and maintains their safety and the safety of others.

Ethical professionals hold a sense of personal responsibility for the standards of care provided, decisions made and their conduct. Most importantly, these professionals act with compassion, empathy and care about the best interests of people they work alongside and seek to work in partnership to empower, providing support ensuring the right to participate in decisions is upheld, and wishes are granted.

How an individual professional acts is also determined by the principles used when working in accordance with accepted practice when there is no formal guidance available, and, the individual professional's agreement with and willingness to consider and address complex ethical issues (Horsfall et al. 1999, p. 3).

ASSESSMENT OF CAPACITY

Due to the changing nature and relapse potential of mental health–substance use problems, comprehensive clinical assessment should be continuous and inclusive of all issues relevant to the person's situation. For people new to a service, the initial assessment, issue identification and intervention planning process is the first step to engagement in a therapeutic person-professional partnership.

Individuals experiencing mental health–substance use problems often, but not always, encounter a range of other issues relating to their physical health, workplace, criminality, family and intimate relationships, unstable housing or homelessness that may impact on their capacity to provide informed consent and/or willingness to participate in assessment and treatment (Treloar and Holt 2008, pp. 84–88).

Assessing capacity for informed consent can be disconcerting in the presence of complex issues to observe and assess for its impact on cognitive ability (intellect, memory and judgment). What these cognitions are will depend on the nature and severity of a person's mental ill health, their dependence and drug interactions between the substance used; prescribed medications to treat mental health–substance use problems. This may result in ineffective treatment, poor outcomes, cross tolerance and intoxication or drug toxicity which may not be evident but create risk for a medical emergency and/or impact on cognitive ability. These factors interact to create transience in cognitive abilities and affect capacity for informed consent and may negate a consent already obtained.

However, components of mental health–substance use assessment can indicate a person's capacity for informed consent, which when considered in tandem with other corroborative evidence, assists in an accurate determination. The findings of a well-considered assessment provide this through enabling the professional to get to know the person's world, what it means to her or him; the extent that a person is able to participate in his or her world, manage her or his affairs and make the decisions surrounding care.

KEY POINT 10.4

Other factors impacting on a person's willingness to consent to treatment relate to feeling afraid and/or vulnerable when they have been exposed to discriminatory, negative and/or judgemental professional behaviours.

Following this, people acknowledge feelings of shame, anger and resentment and report being fearful of further sanction. This results in non-engagement or not listening during contact with professionals to reduce exposure to censure and further hurt. In addition, there is a reluctance to disclose their mental health–substance use problems and the avoidance of health care by opting out or refusing services. This creates difficulties for the professional when encouraging a person to access and consent to receive services. In these circumstances, the person is exercising a right to refuse care which places them at further risk of preventable health morbidity and premature mortality, when unmanaged conditions deteriorate.

The capacity for informed consent is evident where the person is able to:

➤ Understand the options, believes and retains the information provided
➤ Able to consider the benefits and risks of each option
➤ Can articulate the treatment, the nature of the treatment, why it is required and the associated benefits and risks
➤ Choose an option and communicate the decision (ACT 2015, p. 5).

Case Study 10.1 – John

John, in his mid-thirties living in a country town has a history of depressive illness with high lethality suicides and alcohol and opioid dependence. John was a university graduate specialising in pharmacological drug actions prior to becoming unwell and unemployed. John was admitted for withdrawal that completed without incident. During the admission, John was linked with mental health services and a general practitioner (GP) who with the substance use nurse became his professional team. The team undertook a comprehensive mental health–substance use assessment, negotiated an intervention plan including additional support from a non-government organisation.

Following discharge, John's relationship ended, he became homeless and experienced a relapse of his depressive illness. John rang the substance use professional to say goodbye as he was going to the city to see his son and would not be returning. The substance use professional, concerned that John was depressed and may be at risk of self-harm sought to see him. John refused. He was on his way to the city, with no money and nowhere to stay, which meant he would be 'sleeping rough' and therefore increasingly vulnerable. John was encouraged to return and when he refused, permission was sought to provide a homelessness service with his mobile number and to arrange for someone to contact him to ensure he was safe. John agreed to keep himself safe until he had spoken with the homelessness professional in person. The homelessness service was advised of John's imminent arrival, risk status based on history and an intervention response was planned.

John's team continued to contact him as did the homeless worker to encourage him to present to hospital or to return to the country town. Following three days of living out of his car, John agreed to attend the accident and emergency (A&E) and admission was offered. John refused and as he was assessed as having capacity for self-determination . . . he left.

Six days later, John agreed to return and be admitted to the local hospital. Three days into the admission, he handed the substance use professional a syringe and vial of medication saying 'thank you for caring – if you had not all been there I would have used this'. The suicide would have been successful.

The team undertook additional case planning and ensured John had stable housing before discharge. John moved into new accommodation and implementation of his care plan recommenced.

SELF-ASSESSMENT EXERCISE 10.1

Time: 30 minutes
Consider the following:
- What ethics underpinned the crisis response to John?
- How was his right to self-determination upheld?
- What was the result?
- What contributed to John's return and subsequent provision of consent to receive treatment?
- What actions contributed to maintaining John's safety and contributed to the positive outcome?

INDIVIDUAL'S RIGHTS

The right to access treatment

As mentioned earlier, the assumption underlying the right to informed consent includes that services are available and treatment is accessible. This implies that a person who has a health issue has the right to access services needed and for services to respond and make recommendations that are in the person's interest.

The right to receive treatment

When a person has diminished capacity for self-determination and/or poses a risk to themselves or others, mental health legislation identifies when society will intervene. This provision of mandated care ensures that a person's right to receive treatment is upheld, and that other human rights remain protected. Decisions are made in the person's best interests and to ensure his or her safety, protection, survival and treatment aimed at restoring the capacity for self-determination, i.e. to decide whether or not to accept interventions/treatment. This right to treatment includes emergency situations where consent cannot be obtained, non-intervention would endanger life or cause significant harm (*see* Chapter 11).

However, is there an end to upholding a person's right to receive treatment? Trueman (2016, p. 21) states in these situations a person could be discharged even where 'the decision may well have fatal consequences'. The same author (2016, p. 21), raised the rare situation when continuing mandated care may not be in the person's best interests through presenting a court scenario of a young woman who had experienced severe mental illness (anorexia nervosa and obsessive compulsive disorder) from childhood. The treating team sought to discharge the person from mandated care to ongoing community based care. This person had received many years of mandated care during which:

➤ All treatment options and goals had been tried and exhausted without benefit

➤ There were no other treatments presently available nor possible gains to be made from further mandated treatment in a restricted environment

➤ Continuing treatment was 'futile', 'unduly burdensome' and 'not in the person's best interests'.

The recommendation made to the court was to continue to provide community based care. Care was not withdrawn but was made more humane and provided in the least restrictive environment. In this, health professionals were acting humanely and in the client's best interests.

People who do not meet the criteria for informed consent can have a say regarding their treatment when they have previously nominated a person to hold an enduring power of medical attorney or developed advanced care directives. In jurisdictions with these legislated provisions, an individual can prepare for future diminished capacity and therefore, maintains the right to consent to or refuse treatment by communicating his or her wishes to a nominated person or documenting them in a care directive. These often relate to not being kept alive by highly technological means; for palliative care to be the aim of intervention; for non-resuscitation or for treatment or life support to be terminated when there is no possibility of recovery.

KEY POINT 10.5

It is the responsibility of the health professional to know when and how to use the mechanisms for obtaining informed consent from advanced care directives or others where a person has diminished capacity (ACT 2015, pp. 1–7).

When a person is to receive mandated treatment, they should be advised of:

➤ What will occur
➤ Who will be the person making the final decision
➤ Care arrangements and reassurance, that the individual will be cared for and involved in making decisions about what happens to them to the extent that she or he is able
➤ Being included in meetings with a person who has enduring power of attorney or the authority to confirm their wishes documented in advanced care directives
➤ Whether a request for guardianship will occur, the supports available to assist and advocate for what they want to occur and/or to appeal decisions made on their behalf (CPSO 2007, p. 35).

The right to refuse treatment

KEY POINT 10.6

People who have capacity for informed consent have the right to refuse treatment.

Professionals have a duty to uphold the right to self-determination including when the refusal or withdrawal of consent may not be in the interest of the individual. This supports the right of a person to die with dignity rather than prolonging life at all costs or being kept alive by technological means following incidents that usually lead to end of life. Palliative care is usually considered when treatment is refused (or covered in advanced care directives) as it allows for timely care consent and planning processes to ensure dignity is preserved throughout the end-of life-process.

Case Study 10.2 – Florence

Florence (86) lived with her daughter and family, had an alcohol problem, early signs of dementia, type two diabetes and glaucoma with significantly impaired vision. Florence was admitted to hospital unable to stand. A large blood clot in her right leg quickly developed into gangrene in three toes and consent was sought for amputation. Florence fearfully gave consent 'but only to the toes, not the leg', stating she would not have her leg removed. The surgery was performed. The wound did not heal, leaving an open, infected surgical area and Florence was transferred to a rural aged care facility near where she lived. Unable to manage the deteriorating wound, after two weeks, the facility with the consent of Florence and her daughter transferred Florence back to the acute hospital. There was no change in Florence's mental state or capacity for informed consent.

During the admission, ulceration developed in both lower legs which became gangrenous. Consent was sought from Florence for amputation of both legs above the knee. Florence refused. The professional declared she had dementia and an order under the Mental Health Act was sought to perform the surgery despite advocacy from Florence's daughter and other members of the family. The family were religious and while they did not want Florence to have a 'horrible gangrene death' recognised what was occurring as an end-of-life event. A nurse member of the family asked Florence about her understanding of what would occur and if she did not have surgery. Florence was aware she would die and accepted that consequence which indicated she understood the consequences of her decision. This family member advised the professional of Florence's knowledge of the consequences of her decision and was ignored. When advocating for her mother, the professional accused Florence's daughter of wanting her death to get the inheritance. Florence had no personal assets.

The order was granted. Neither Florence or her family were advised they could appeal the order. Mental health legislation designed to protect vulnerable people was used to deny Florence her right to refuse treatment.

The surgery was performed under local anaesthetic. Florence's legs were carried out of theatre within her sight with no cover and were seen by her. For the remaining seven months of her life Florence remained cognitively aware, in bed at the aged care facility having nightmares and every night calling out one of the following in distress "no", "stop them", "they are chopping off my legs", and "they are taking them out", "I can see them". Florence was denied her right to refuse treatment and die in a way that she saw as dying with dignity.

SELF-ASSESSMENT EXERCISE 10.2

Time: 45 minutes

Consider the actions of the professional in this scenario.
- What ethical considerations were taken into account?
- Do you consider this as ethical practice?
- What would you do in this circumstance?
- What were the consequences for Florence and her family?

Consider the consequences for Florence. If you were involved in Florence's care what could you have done to ensure her wishes were upheld?
- What is your own understanding of 'palliative care'?
- How would this have helped Florence and her family initially?

Upholding the right to die when a person is experiencing a significant depressive illness and/or suicidal ideation poses ethical dilemmas relating to whether the person would want this if they did not have the ill health, which may be clarified by the person's family and friends. This is complex and confounding in jurisdictions which have provisions for assisted euthanasia and the criteria includes time frames for terminal ill health and mental health–substance use assessment, which could result in a person wishing to end her or his life being overturned because of concomitant comorbidity.

CONCLUSION

The capacity of a person experiencing mental health–substance use may be impacted on by a number of variables. These create complexity in assessing their capacity for self-determination. Through careful clinical assessment by a professional who knows the individual and the use of processes aimed at upholding an individual's rights to self-determination wherever possible, a partnership can be formed with people and the family and friends to obtain informed consent ensuring access to treatment, therefore maximising care and protection.

In relation to this vulnerable population it is our personal values and beliefs that will determine what we do. This will determine what we would do when a person is discriminated against, stigmatised and denied their rights to access services, and/or to consent or refuse treatment. The case scenarios demonstrate that while ethical decisions are not always easy, better and/or more humane desired outcomes occur when rights are upheld. This is the goal of all human rights statements and responses (*see* Chapter 13).

REFERENCES

Australian Capital Territory Government. 2015. "Policy: Consent and Treatment". October. www.search.act.gov.au/s/cache?collection=act-gov-healthpolicyConsentand Treatment.

Australian Commission on Safety and Quality in Health Care (ACSQHC). 2012. "Informed Consent: Safety and Quality Improvement Guide Standard 1: Governance of Safety and Quality in Health Service Organisations". Sydney: Australian Commission on Safety and Quality in Health Care (ACSQHC).

College of Physicians and Surgeons of Ontario (CPSO). 2007. Determining capacity to consent. Consent law, Dialogue, July. www.cpso.on.ca/uploadedFiles/policies/policies/policyitems/capacity_consent_july07dialogue.pdf.

Horsfall J, M Cleary and J Raighne. 1999. *Towards Ethical Mental Health Nursing Practice*, Monograph 3. Deakin West ACT 2600: The Australian College of Mental Health Workers, September.

Treloar C and M Holt. 2008. "Complex vulnerabilities as barriers to treatment for illicit drug users with high prevalence mental health comorbidities." *Mental Health and Substance Use: Dual Diagnosis*, Vol. 1, No. 1 pp. 84–95 February.

Trueman S. 2016. Australian College of Mental Health Nurses "*News.*" Winter June–August 2016.

World Health Organization. 2003a. "Mental Health Legislation & Human Rights: Mental Health Policy and Service Guidelines Package". Geneva. www.who.int/entity/mental_health/policy/essentialpackage1/en/index1.html

TO LEARN MORE

Department of Constitutional Affairs, Mental Health Act, 2005 – Code of practice. www.gov.uk/government/uploads/system/uploads/attachment_data/file/497253/Mental-capacity-act-code-of-practice.pdf.

World Health Organization. 2003a. "Mental Health Legislation & Human Rights: Mental Health Policy and Service Guidelines Package". Geneva. www.who.int/entity/mental_health/policy/essentialpackage1/en/index1.html.

World Health Organization. 2003b. "Mental Health Legislation & Human Rights: Mental Health Policy and Service Guidelines Package, Policy Checklist". Geneva. www.who.int/mental_health/policy/WHOPolicyChecklist_forwebsite.pdf?ua=1.

CHAPTER 11

Practice

John Richard Ashcroft and Siân Bensa

INTRODUCTION

Mental health professionals are faced with ethical issues on a daily basis throughout their working life. The present chapter aims to raise awareness of such dilemmas rather than conduct a detailed analysis of any single problem. The ethical issues raised by the use of Electro-Convulsive Therapy (ECT – *see* Chapter 12) will be discussed in a separate chapter although a number of cross references have been made where appropriate to reinforce a number of similar discussion points.

BRAIN AND MIND

Arguably no other subject has raised greater discussion than the nature of mind versus brain. Are the brain and mind discrete entities or is the mind an inseparable function of the brain? Such questions have major philosophical, ethical, moral, humanistic, religious, and scientific implications. The issues raised are so diverse as to cause some to avoid asking such questions in the first instance. Yet, such questions need to be considered, if not fully answered, when addressing subjective emotional distress whether from a neurochemical or psychological perspective.

If one subscribes knowingly or otherwise to the notion of dualism, the separability of mind and brain, what would be the purpose and mechanism of action of pharmacological intervention? Similarly, if our behaviour is simply the product of a complex interplay between neurons, nuclei, and other such neural structures, all of which may become dysfunctional by disease, are we fully accountable for our actions? Are all men or women truly made equal? Macroscopically there is much consistency between one brain and the next, albeit some variation between the sexes (Ruigrok et al., 2014). However, on a microscopic level, at the level of neuronal connectivity, the variation between one person and the next is 'robust and reliable' and functional connectivity profiles may act as a 'fingerprint' accurately identifying subjects from a large group (Finn et al., 2015).

Our brains represent a rainforest of reciprocal interconnections between neurons cultivated through experience from an early age, and the nature of such interconnection is greatly affected by the quality and intensity of experiences over time (Ratey, 2001). As our understanding of the brain has evolved in the last twenty years or so, as has our understanding of the complex interplay between environmental experience and brain structure on a macroscopic and inter-neuronal level.

Armstrong (2015) asks whether there is such a thing as a 'normal brain'. Similarly, as there is no such thing as a normal flower or culture should we accept the fact that there is no such thing as a normal mind? Of course, arguments become redundant with the presence of clear structural damage caused by physical trauma, infection, neoplasia etc. Such brains are evidently abnormal. However, in such cases an individual's brain acts as its own comparator. The brain is different to how it was; it has become abnormal. However, the minds of individuals deemed to suffer with mental disorders are regarded as abnormal despite the absence or lack of evidence for brain disease or structural abnormality. There is a presumption that such individuals have brains that are functioning abnormally. The 'norm' in this sense, however, refers to the majority and clearly this can change over time.

DIAGNOSIS

Mental health services continue to use classification systems of mental disorder such as Diagnostic Statistical Manual, Volume 5 (American Psychiatric Association, 2012) and the International Classification of Diseases, Volume 10 (WHO, 1992). Are such descriptive systems, whereby disease is classified on the basis of reported symptoms and syndromes, truly reflective of and in step with the major improvements in neuroscience? Certainly the main criticism of the DSM-V is that more than any of its previous editions it appears to medicalise human distress.

Is it appropriate to cluster all individuals experiencing a set of symptoms or syndromes into a single homogenous group and assume a commonality of cause, as yet to be discovered? Most certainly there are considerable doubts as to the validity of research by doing so. It could be argued that using such methods to determine appropriate pharmacological treatments may be a particularly flawed approach.

With such means of classification, as symptoms change over time, it would be expected for diagnosis to similarly change. Are mental disorders classified in this way as stable as entities as we are often led to believe? This question has major implications in terms of prognosis and treatment.

SCHIZOPHRENIA

Schizophrenia remains a controversial, potentially stigmatising diagnosis and many argue that the term should be abandoned (Henderson and Malhi, 2014; Moncrieff and Middleton, 2015). Despite occasional media announcements of major breakthroughs in determining its cause, 'schizophrenia' remains poorly understood both by the layperson and professionals alike. There is evidence of huge variation of diagnosis and treatment of schizophrenia both between countries and between individual psychiatrists within a given country (Banerjee, 2012).

Despite a general agreement that bipolar affective disorder and schizophrenia represent separate disease entities some researchers suggest that many people diagnosed with schizophrenia would be more appropriately diagnosed as suffering with a psychotic mood disorder and there appears evidence to suggest that the ability to distinguish the conditions using current classification systems is poor (Lake and Hurwitz, 2006). Most researchers now agree that schizophrenia is most certainly not a single homogenous disease although many individuals continue to receive a diagnosis of paranoid schizophrenia as if it was such.

Given that the medication used to treat major psychiatric disorder has major physical health side effects both in the short, intermediate, and long term, the potential implications for inaccurate, misleading, and potentially stigmatising 'diagnoses' cannot be overstated. Prescribers should be aware of the limitations of the psychiatric diagnostic system and conduct risk–benefit analyses before initiating medication. Rarely do mental health professionals look at and assess the organ that we treat. Regardless of our personal view of the nature of brain versus mind, the fact remains that the targeted organ of psychopharmacological intervention is the brain.

KEY POINT 11.1

A desire to ameliorate the distress of an individual in the short term needs to be balanced against the long-term consequences of such intervention to both body and brain.

We need to ensure that efforts to treat an individual presenting with symptoms suggestive of a mental disorder are not an effort to reduce our own anxiety.

The option of not intervening pharmacologically and managing an individual's distress through psychological and social supportive measures alone should be a carefully considered but yet viable approach. Professionals ought to remain mindful of the adage 'do no harm'. This is of particular importance where the idiosyncratic consequences of medical treatment are not immediately evident or difficult to establish with certainty, albeit strongly suspected.

DISTRESS

The common feature of all individuals described as suffering from a mental disorder is distress.

When a classification system uses symptoms alone as a means of diagnosing mental disorder there will inevitably be a tendency to identify symptoms (anxiety, depression, mania, psychosis) as disease itself. Such an approach may be fundamentally flawed if we consider the possibility that the various means by which mental disorders present may simply reflect the multiple means by which individuals may express distress knowingly or otherwise. Psychological defense mechanisms serve to protect the conscious mind from painful subconscious thoughts, emotions, and memories.

An analogy could be made between the psychological consequences of environmental stressors and swelling. Swelling occurs in response to physical trauma and serves a purpose to protect the site of injury although itself may cause pain and secondary problems. Although efforts are certainly made to treat and reduce swelling this is not carried out without, at the very least, an acknowledgement of the cause of swelling.

It could be argued that anxiety, depression, and psychosis may serve to indicate psychological trauma, whether in the present or from the past. By treating the 'swelling' alone and deeming the presence of such symptoms as evidence of disease (indeed regarding the symptoms as disease) are we at risk of overlooking psychological trauma?

Such an alternative approach in no way negates a medical or neuroscientific approach to understanding subjective psychological experiences, whether psychotic or otherwise. All pain whether physical or psychological is mediated through neurotransmitters.

PSYCHIATRY AND RELIGION

The church has seen a decline in attendance over recent years. The 2014 annual Statistics for Mission returns provided by churches in the United Kingdom (Archbishop's Council, 2016) highlighted a 1 percent reduction in church attendance per year over the last decade with 10 percent of the population regularly attending church services. This trend appears to be evident in other Western countries.

Is it a coincidence that as there has been a decline in church attendance there has been an increase in the prescription for psychotropic drugs and diagnosis of mental disorder in Western countries (Hafner, 1985; Kessler et al., 2005; Wittchen and Jacobi, 2005)? Karl Marx is famously reported to have said

> Religious suffering is, at one and the same time, the expression of real suffering and a protest against real suffering. Religion is the sign of the oppressed creature, the heart of a heartless world, and the soul of soulless conditions. It is the opium of the people.
>
> (McLellan, 2006)

However, the subtlety of Marx' quote is sometimes overlooked. Marx is evidently describing the analgesic effects of religion but he is also critical of it. He acknowledges an opioid's ability to ease pain and suffering although he also refers to the ineffectual nature of an opioid to address the **cause** of suffering and for its dependence potential. But what is the source of the suffering for which an opioid is required? Marx is referring to the human condition, the subjective sense of one's own vulnerability and ultimately mortality, and the hardships of life.

The human condition remains and the approach to suffering has moved from the clergy to the professional. Has human suffering been redefined and repackaged as 'mental illness'? Is Psychiatry simply the new religion within this context, the latest opium for the people? As we in the West turn away from the church have we simply recreated another church, another religion (Whitley, 2008)?

Rather than represent an increase in brain disorder, the seeming increase in mental illness and the increased prevalence of diagnosed mental disorder, may reflect a lowering of the diagnostic threshold and an eagerness of 'Big Pharma' to support the ring fencing of 'symptoms,' as diagnosable disorders in order for drugs to be prescribed to an increasingly wide number of the population. If this is the case, it is extremely alarming as in addition to failing to accurately identify potential causes of mental distress, namely adverse experiences and poor lifestyle choices, there may be a financial incentive for drug companies to promote the diagnosis of mental disorder.

Moncrieff (2010) makes a strong argument for psychiatric diagnosis having the potential to be used as a political device through legitimising a particular social response (medicalisation) to aberrant behaviour, yet protecting that response from democratic challenge. In this way, social problems can be regarded as medical issues and means by which unwanted behaviours are modulated, can be conceptualized as medical treatments.

LEGISLATION (*SEE* CHAPTER 13)

The Human Rights Act and the European Convention on Human Rights (The Convention)

The Human Rights Act (1998) served to bring into UK domestic law the 18 articles of the Convention for the Protection of Human Rights and Fundamental Freedoms, also referred to as the European Convention on Human

Rights (ECHR, 1950). Article 3, the prohibition of torture, inhuman or degrading treatment or punishment, Article 5, the right to liberty and security, and Article 8, the right to privacy are of particular relevance when considering ethical issues relating to the Mental Health Act 1983, as amended in 2007.

In response to the proposition of the conservative government suggestion to repeal the Human Rights Act, in the penultimate paragraph of his Liberty speech in 2009, Lord Bingham (2009) stated:

> Human rights are not, however, protected for the likes of people like me – or most of you. They are protected for the benefit above all of society's outcasts, those who need legal protection because they have no other voice – the prisoners, the mentally ill, the gipsies, the homosexuals, the immigrants, the asylum-seekers, those who are at any time the subject of public obloquy.

However, Bindman et al. (2003) describe how the ECHR 'harbours old prejudices against those with mental illness'. Note how this is apparent in the language of Article 5. They argue how the Human Rights Act perpetuates such prejudice that allows for an individual's capacity to make treatment decisions to be essentially ignored providing they are deemed to have a mental disorder.

Article 5 of ECHR (1950) states that: 'Everyone has the right to liberty and security of person. No one shall be deprived of his liberty save in the following cases and in accordance with a procedure prescribed by law.' The article goes on to list six such cases; of particular relevance are cases 'A' and 'E' as outlined below:

> A: the lawful detention of a person after conviction by a competent court;
> E: the lawful detention of persons for the prevention of the spreading of infectious diseases, of persons of unsound mind, alcoholics or drug addicts or vagrants;

The obvious subsequent question, therefore, would be what constitutes a person of unsound mind and how are they identified? Few could dispute the words of Lord Bingham (2009) in that human rights are necessary to protect the most vulnerable in society against **public obloquy** a term which implies unfairness and excessive harshness.

However, does current legislation truly protect the rights of those deemed of unsound mind or allow society or government to firstly determine who meets such criteria and secondly to refuse such individuals the same rights allowed other individuals deemed to be of sound mind?

The ethical implications are enormous. In the absence of clinical measures of soundness of mind, assessment invariably involves the interpretation of speech and other aspects of behaviour to determine thought process, mood, and cognition. Can such assessments ever be truly objective? How far must an individual's behavior and mode of communication drift from the accepted social and cultural norm before it is deemed to be, at first eccentric, and then possibly representative of an individual with unsound mind?

Although it can be accepted that mental illness may be as likely to be affected by culture as other illnesses (Bhugra, 2006) how can we explain the observation of an individual's behaviour being accepted in one cultural domain but not in another? Similarly, within a single society or culture over time certain behaviours have become more socially acceptable and consequently those previously deemed to be of unsound mind are no longer thought to be so (e.g. homosexuality).

THE MENTAL HEALTH ACT (1983 AS AMENDED 2007)

Compulsory detention

Although safeguards have been put in place to avoid arbitrary use of the Act, several situations remain whereby it may be used in an arbitrary fashion. Between 2011 and 2014 it was reported that there was a 7 percent reduction in the number of psychiatric inpatient beds (Gilbert, 2015). With major bed pressures, there may be a temptation to bend the rules increasing the risk of the arbitrary use of the Mental Health Act to meet service demands, and concerns have been raised with Members of Parliament that the Mental Health Act may be being misused to detain patients in order to obtain beds (Cooper, 2013). Baroness Hale has described how the Mental Health Act relies on the right to challenge an admission 'ex post facto' and regularly thereafter rather than on prior authorisation, leading to many compulsory admissions going unchallenged (2007).

Enforced treatment

There are major ethical issues when considering the long-term side effects of drugs for diseases of uncertain cause of which we have, at best, a hypothetic understanding of their mode of action. Are we truly treating a known disorder or disease or rather modifying behaviours to ensure that an individual's actions are less risky or socially acceptable?

KEY POINT 11.3

To be deemed to have capacity a person needs to be able to understand and retain information sufficiently to then weigh up, balance, and use such information in order to communicate a decision.

What if the outcome of the decision to be made is both influenced by and subsequently influences the mental state (in short and long term) of the person for whom the decision is being made? (*See* Case Study 11.1 and 11.2.)

There does appear to be a considerable issue whereby decisions are made to treat the mental health of individuals with extremely sedating and cognitively impairing medication when the consequence of 'improving' a person's mental state (treating a diagnosed 'mental disorder') is a potential diminution of capacity. Who has the right to decide in such instances? If we removed 'risk' and 'accountability' of such risk, would 'watchful waiting' become more palatable as an approach?

Individuals deemed to be suffering with mental disorder (and of *unsound mind* as per The Convention) might be forcibly administered treatment under the Mental Heath Act regardless of their capacity to weigh up the benefits versus risks of such treatment.

Conversely, it could be argued that should an individual consent to treatment and appear superficially to have capacity to consent to medical treatment, this overlooks the fact that the mental state itself of an individual in distress has an impact on the decision-making process. Could any individual truly be deemed to have consented to Electro-Convulsive Therapy (ECT – *see* Chapter 12)? If we accept that the level of distress needed to be present before ECT is considered is significantly severe it seems counterintuitive at best (ridiculous at worst) to conclude that an individual is able to consent without the targeted problem itself influencing the decision.

Non- refusal, lack of resistance, willingness to do anything to feel better, is not synonymous with consent. An individual may superficially satisfy the capacity test and it is the duty of the assessor to ensure that the degree of impact of mental state on any decision made has been considered. In all likelihood the first occasion an individual would have to discuss issues about ECT would be the time somebody else is considering prescribing it for them. How often has the following question been posed? If you had been provided with all the evidence for and against ECT before you were deemed to require it would you have consented to its use?

KEY POINT 11.4

An individual either has capacity to consent to treatment or does not. However, which category an individual finds him- or her-self in is not always as straight forward as a capacity assessment would lead us to believe.

---

1   If an individual **lacks capacity,** they can be given treatment for a mental health condition under the MHA, albeit with a second opinion after a specified period (SOAD).

2 If an individual **has capacity**, they can be given treatment for a mental disorder under the MHA if refusing such treatment (although not ECT under the 2007 MHA amendments).
3 An individual can be treated informally if accepting of treatment.

The first possibility is a contentious area in its own right. However, there certainly appears to be an ethical dilemma in the decision to treat an individual with full capacity against their will and following such treatment deem a person to be 'well', should they now be accepting of the treatment which they initially refused. Given that antipsychotic drugs (major tranquilisers) affect cognition, volition and perception, could this sudden change of heart be explained other than by 'improved insight'?

It appears that should an individual be deemed to require administration of psychotropic medication under the Mental Health Act, such an individual would be hard pressed to avoid receiving it on the basis of reasoning alone. However, how do we define individuals who are only accepting of treatment *because* of their mental state? Such individuals are willing to do *anything* to alleviate their suffering. Superficially such individuals may appear to have full capacity to make decisions about treatment suggested by experts.

Such treatment is accepted based on an assumption that experts have evidence of its success, and evidence that the benefits outweigh the risks. This aspect is fundamental in the individual's capacity to weigh up the decision. It could be argued that where the decision-making process itself is influenced by mental state and the sole purpose of intervention is to reverse/alter/improve/modulate a mental state (whichever term is preferable) an individual's capacity to consent to such intervention is questionable, and this may be particularly so in the case of ECT.

In addition, an individual may consent to a variety of offered interventions at this stage (even euthanasia, which is one of the arguments against legislation for it) and be deemed to have capacity to accept it.

KEY POINT 11.5

Their 'weighing up' is based not on their understanding of the intervention per se but their trust in the professional who is offering the intervention.

The United Nations Convention on the Rights of Persons with Disabilities (CRPD, 2006)

The CRPD is a less familiar piece of international legislation than the ECHR adopted by the General Assembly in 2006, ratified by the UK Government in 2009, and ratified by the European Union in 2010. Jones (2015, p. 18) describes how although it does not have a direct effect in UK law it is a legally binding international treaty and provides a framework for member states to address the rights of people with disabilities. Article 14 of the CRPD describes how the existence of a disability should in no way justify detention whether additional grounds for such detention (such as risks to the public) are present or not. The Mental Health Act and CRPD are consequently incompatible in this regard.

It is particularly concerning that individuals identified as posing a risk to self or others may be diagnosed as having a mental disorder, not by the presence of clinical signs or organic pathology but by the observation of behaviour and the interpretation of reported 'symptoms' as illness, having come into contact with a member of the mental health profession.

This ethical stance forces us to ask the question whether individuals deemed to be of unsound mind and of risk to the public should be treated any differently from those of sound mind but potentially equally as risky? It raises the uncomfortable fact that the MHA allows us to treat individuals deemed risky in a different way on the basis of the additional presence of 'unsoundness of mind'. According to the CRPD this is discriminatory and contravenes article 14 of this convention. That is to say, all individuals deemed at risk to their self and others should be treated the same regardless of the presence or absence of mental disorder.

The logic of having two legal schemes, namely the Mental Capacity and Mental Health Acts, with capacity alone being central to one piece of legislation alone, has been disputed. A fusion of the two acts, whereby an individual may be involuntarily detained or treated if lacking capacity regardless of the presence of mental disorder or risk, has been proposed (Dawson and Szmukler, 2006; Szmukler et al., 2010).

Case Study 11.1 – Mike

Mike is a 39-year-old man who has a diagnosis of paranoid schizophrenia. He is currently detained in hospital under Section 3 of the Mental Health Act and prescribed depot antipsychotic medication (Haldol). He regularly hears voices that tell him that he has a special purpose in life to become a film star. He believes the voice is that of his father who died when he was aged three. His stepfather sexually abused Mike as a child. He has been involved with mental health services since his early teenage years and has received a number of diagnoses including schizophrenia, schizoaffective disorder, borderline personality disorder, and simply attention-seeking behaviour. He is not particularly distressed by the voices although his behaviour becomes rather disinhibited on occasion particularly when under the influence of alcohol or illicit substances, namely cannabis which he has used on and off since the age of 17. Such behaviour has led to three hospital admissions. He has been prescribed oral antipsychotic medication previously although due to non-concordance. At the time of his most recent admission to hospital he was prescribed a depot antipsychotic. Mike does not want to take medication, as he is fearful of the side-effects both in the short- and long-term. The risks of diabetes, raised cholesterol, and weight gain have been discussed with him and he would prefer to continue to experience voices than have an increased risk of cardiovascular disease. His father died of a Myocardial Infarction.

REFLECTIVE PRACTICE EXERCISE 11.1

Time: 30 minutes
- Mike has received several diagnoses and mental health professionals have mixed opinions of the cause of his symptoms. Article 5 makes reference to 'unsoundness of mind'.
  - Has this been established?
  - What are the ethical implications?
- Despite Mike having capacity to weigh up the risks versus benefits of receiving antipsychotic medication, an antipsychotic depot may still be forcibly administered under the Mental Health Act.
  - Does this constitute a violation of his human rights?
  - Should it be viewed as such?
- In the above case history:
  - is there an argument to suggest that Mike has experienced potential violations of his human rights under Articles 3 and 8?
- What is the purpose of the Mental Health Act?
  - Has the focus of the 2007 amendments shifted to address public risk at the expense of the rights of the individual?

INPATIENT MENTAL HEALTH UNITS

There are a number of ethical dilemmas of practical significance, which are arguably unique to individuals within an inpatient setting.

Smoking in inpatient mental health units

> ### Case Study 11.2 – Bob
>
> Bob is a 54-year-old gentleman admitted to an inpatient psychiatric unit who is believed to have set fire to his bedroom in protest at the decision for him to remain in hospital. The fire brigade was required to attend and Bob was subsequently arrested by police for questioning and transferred to the Psychiatric Intensive Care Unit for further assessment of risk. A professionals meeting was subsequently arranged at which point the inpatient smoking policy was reviewed in addition to means by which fire safety could be improved on the ward. All staff members were invited to comment and express their opinion as to how the current situation could be improved. Discussions raised a number of issues and developed from the initial discussion of fire safety to the question of whether smoking should be allowed on inpatients wards, albeit in a designated outside smoking area.

There are clearly a number of ethical dilemmas and questions that should be considered above and beyond simply whether smoking should be banned or not.

REFLECTIVE PRACTICE EXERCISE 11.2

> **Time: 30 minutes**
> - Should we be aggressively promoting smoking cessation during acute inpatient admission, a time when people are likely to be suffering most distress?
>   - Is this the right time to do so?
> - Should we allow people experiencing symptoms of depression and psychosis to put themselves at physical risk of their often-increased cigarette use, often associated with a desire to alleviate boredom or modulate the effect of prescribed medication?
> - People who are acutely unwell often have a lack of concern or seeming disregard for their physical well-being.
>   - Does this constitute a lack of capacity?
>   - Do we have a duty to intervene?

People on leave

People experiencing mental health problems detained under the MHA are granted leave (Section 17 leave) following an assessment of risk and progress since admission. The Responsible Clinician, usually a psychiatrist, grants such leave, although typically following discussion with members of the inter-disciplinary team. However, before being granted periods of unescorted leave, these individuals are often required to be accompanied by members of staff to further assess risk and progress in the community.

The ability to facilitate such leave appears to be related to a number of factors. These include:

➤ The number of detained individuals on the ward at any one time.
➤ Staff availability.
➤ The level of disruption on the ward, which may directly or indirectly affect the focus of the ward staff.
➤ The amount of time granted by the responsible clinician/consultant psychiatrist each week.

In addition, there are a finite number of hours of escorted leave that staff are able to facilitate and rarely is there a formal analysis of this. Clearly, to indiscriminately grant section 17 leave without consideration of whether this can be facilitated in practice is both unfair to people experiencing mental health problems, unreasonable for staff, and given the frustration that the decision to decline leave may invoke, is a potential source of risk and untoward events.

Although the rationale for being unable to grant escorted leave maybe justified logistically from a service perspective, does this negate an individual's right to access such leave? Is this a potential contravention of an individual's human rights? To be kept locked inside an inpatient psychiatric unit having been initially granted or denied escorted leave, solely on the basis of a lack of staff recourses seems, at best, counterintuitive.

SUBSTANCE USE

Ethical dilemmas arise and need to be considered in individuals who use illicit substances regularly. Relapse rates are high (Witkiewitz and Marlatt, 2004) and the prevalence of personality disorder and other mental health problems has been described as common enough to be considered to be the expectation more than the exception (Grant et al., 2004; Buckley and Brown, 2006).

However, although there have been improvements in drug and alcohol service delivery, many providers are non-National Health Service (UK – NHS) and remain separate from NHS services. Stigma remains an obstacle for many individuals.

KEY POINT 11.6

Clearly any treatment for drug or alcohol dependence requires combined access with improved co-ordination with mainstream mental health, physical health, and social services.

Individuals with opioid dependence may be prescribed methadone or buprenorphine as a substitute for heroin, which is typically smoked or injected. Despite the prescription of opioid substitute medication, the ongoing use of heroin remains high and this has led to some advocating the prescription of heroin in the treatment of individuals with opioid dependence who have not profited from other forms of treatment (Haasen et al., 2007).

CONCLUSION

Each of the topics discussed above are huge subjects in their own right. We aimed to provide a brief overview of some of the ethical dilemmas and areas of consideration within the practice of mental health. Efforts should be made by all practitioners to remain aware that the principle aim of any intervention is not to promote a particular model or professional approach or to influence behaviours deemed abnormal or unacceptable. Although more recently with the 2007 amendments to the Mental Health Act there has been a focus on risk, both to the public and the individual, many areas of dispute may be resolved if professionals have a common goal of reducing subjective distress in individuals deemed to be suffering with mental disorder.

If we acknowledge the limitations of the concept of mental disorder, and indeed psychiatric classification itself, this forces us to ask the question whether there could ever be justification to treat individuals deemed to be of unsound mind any differently to those of sound mind regardless of the presence of risk.

REFERENCES

American Psychiatric Association. 2013. *Diagnostic and Statistical Manual of Mental Disorders*, 5th ed. DSM-5. APA.

Archbishops Council. 2016. Statistics for Mission 2014. Research and Statistics Department Archbishop's Council. www.churchofengland.org/about-us/facts-stats/research-statistics.aspx.

Armstrong T. 2015. "The myth of the normal brain: embracing neurodiversity." *American Medical Association Journal of Ethics* 17: 348–352.

Banerjee A. 2012. "Cross-cultural variance of schizophrenia in symptoms, diagnosis, and treatment." *Georgetown University Journal of Health Sciences* 6: 18–24.

Bhugra D. 2006. "Severe mental illness across cultures." *Acta Psychiatrica Scandinavica* 112: 17–23.

Bindman J, S Maingay and G Szmulker. 2003. "The Human Rights Act and mental health legislation." *The British Journal of Psychiatry* 182: 91–94.

Bingham T. 2009. Liberty conference final speech. www.liberty-human-rights.org.uk/sites/default/files/lord-bingham-speech-final.pdf.

Buckley PF and ES Brown. 2006. "Prevalence and consequences of dual diagnosis." *Journal of Clinical Psychiatry* 67: 5–9.

Cooper C. 2013. Mentally ill patients sectioned unnecessarily as 'only way' to a hospital bed. www.independent.co.uk/news/ukpolitics/mentally-ill-patients-sectioned-unneccessarily-as-only-way-to-a-hospital-bed-87060166.html.

Dawson J and G Szmukler. 2006. "Fusion of mental health and incapacity legislation." *British Journal of Psychiatry* 188: 504–509.

European Convention for the Protection of Human Rights and Fundamental Freedoms. 1950. www.echr.coe.int/Documents/Convention_ENG.pdf

Finn ES, X Shen, D Scheinost, MD Rosenberg, J Huang, MM Chun, X Papademetris and RT Constable. 2015. "Functional connectome fingerprinting: identifying individuals using patterns of brain activity." *Nature Neuroscience* 18: 1664–1671.

Gilburt H. 2015. *Mental health under pressure.* Kings Fund Briefing. www.kingsfund.org.uk/sites/files/kf/field/field_publication_file/mental-health-under-pressure-nov15.pdf.

Grant BF, DS Hassin, FS Stinson, DA Dawson, S Patricia Chou, W June Ruan and B Huang. 2004. "A co-occurrence of 12-month alcohol and drug use disorders and personality disorders in the United States: results from the National Epidemiologic Survey on Alcohol and Related Conditions." *Archives of General Psychiatry* 61: 361–368.

Haasen C, P Verthein, P Degkwitz and J Berger. 2007. "Heroin-assisted treatment for opioid dependence. Randomised controlled trial." *The British Journal of Psychiatry* 191: 55–62.

Hafner H. 1985. "Are mental disorders increasing over time?" *Psychopathology* 18: 66–81.

Hale B. 2007. "The Human Rights Act and Mental Health Law: Has it helped?" *The Journal of Mental Health Law* May: 7–18.

Henderson S and GS Malhi. 2014. "Swan song for schizophrenia?" *Australian and New Zealand Journal of Psychiatry* 48: 302–305.

Human Rights Act. 1998. www.legislation.gov.uk/ukpga/1998/42/data.pdf.

Jones R. 2015. *Mental Health Act Manual.* 18th ed. Hebden Bridge: Sweet and Maxwell.

Kessler RC, P Berglund, O Demler, R Jin, KR Merikangas and EE Walters. 2005. "Lifetime prevalence and age-of onset distributions of DSM-IV disorders in the National Comorbidity Survey Replication." *Archives of General Psychiatry* 62: 617–627.

Lake CR and Hurwitz, N. 2006. "Does schizophrenia = psychotic bipolar disorder?" *Current Psychiatry* 5: 43–60.

Liégeois A and C Van Audenhove. 2005. "Ethical dilemmas in community mental health." *Journal of Medical Ethics* 31: 452–456.

McLellan D. 2006. *Karl Marx. A Biography.* 4th ed. Palgrave: Macmillan.

Mental Health Act 1983 as amended 2007. www.legislation.gov.uk/ukpga/2007/12/contents.

Moncrieff J. 2010. "Psychiatric diagnosis as a political device." *Social Theory & Health* 8: 370–382.

Moncrieff J and H Middleton. 2015. "Schizophrenia: a critical psychiatry perspective." *Current Opinions in Psychiatry* 28: 264–268.

Pilgrim D. 2007. "The survival of the psychiatric diagnosis." *Social Science & Medicine* 65: 536–547.

Porter R. 2002. *Madness. A Brief History.* Oxford University Press: Oxford.

Ratey J. 2001. *A User's Guide to the Brain.* London: Abacus.

Ruigrok ANV, G Salimi-Khorshidi, L Meng Chuan, S Baron-Cohen, MV Lombardo, RJ Tait and J Suckling. 2014. "A meta-analysis of sex differences in human brain structure." *Neuroscience & Behavioural Reviews* 39: 34–50.

Sidley GL. 2015. *Tales from the madhouse. An insider critique of psychiatric services.* Monmouth: PCC Books.

Szmukler G, R Daw and J Dawson. 2010. "A model law fusing incapacity and mental health legislation." *Journal of Mental Health Law* 20: 1–40.

United Nations Convention on the Rights of Persons with Disabilities. 2006. www.un.org/disabilities/convention/conventionfull.shtml.

Whitley R. 2008. "Is Psychiatry a religion?" *Journal of the Royal Society of Medicine* 101: 579–582.

Wittchen HU and F Jacobi. 2005. "Size and burden of mental disorders in Europe: a critical review and appraisal of 27 studies." *European Neuropsychopharmacology* 15: 357–376.

Witkiewitz K and GA Marlatt. 2004. "Relapse prevention for alcohol and drug problems: that was Zen, this is Tao." *American Psychology* 59: 224–235.

World Health Organisation. 1992. *The ICD-10 Classification of Mental and Behavioural Disorders.* World Health Organisation.

CHAPTER 12

Electroconvulsive therapy

Siân Bensa and John Richard Ashcroft

BACKGROUND

It is vital that medical ethics has a large role to play in the role of protecting people from themselves and from others during times of difficulty. In such situations it may be useful to remind ourselves of the four principles of medical bioethics:

➤ autonomy (respect individual freedom, opinion)
➤ justice (equality of opportunity)
➤ beneficence (doing good)
➤ non-maleficence (not doing harm – Beauchamp and Childress, 2001).

The following discussion will focus on some of the ethical issues surrounding the use of Electroconvulsive Therapy (ECT) used in the UK for the treatment of depression.

ECT in the UK is generally indicated for 'severe, life-threatening depression and when a rapid response is required, or when other treatments have failed' (NICE Pathways, 2015).

The procedure involves the application of electrodes to the head and the passing of electrical current through the brain, enough to induce a convulsion. It is carried out under general anaesthetic and usually within designated ECT suites. Policymakers and psychiatrists regard ECT as an effective intervention (Singhal, 2011). However; ECT is one of the most controversial interventions within mental health services (Read and Bentall, 2010) due to uncertainties regarding how it works, whether it is effective, side-effects, issues around consent, as well as related psychological issues.

DEMOGRAPHICS OF ECT ADMINISTRATION

According to Electroconvulsive Therapy Accreditation Service (ECTAS, 2015) between April 2014 and March 2015 there were 119 clinics in England and Wales providing ECT. Data from 81 (68 percent) of these reported that 2,022 acute courses of ECT (i.e. given twice a week for a period of a few weeks) were given to 1,856 people, totalling 18,057 individual treatments. Of these people, 65 percent were female and 35 percent were male, with nearly half aged between 60 and 79 years of age, indicating clear age and gender differences in its use. Such discrepancies may indicate that depression is more common in older and female people. However, a greater percentage of women experiencing depression are more likely to be treated with ECT compared to men (Bloch et al., 2005). The majority of people who underwent ECT were diagnosed with depression (84.4 percent): the rest experiencing bipolar disorders in a depression phase (5.4 percent), catatonia (2.4 percent) and schizophrenia (1.2 percent).

HOW DOES ECT 'WORK'?

SELF-ASSESSMENT EXERCISE 12.1

> **Time: 10 minutes**
> What is your current understanding of how ECT works?

It is not clear how ECT works. The Royal College of Psychiatrists (2015) stated that 'it has been suggested that ECT works not because of the fit, but because of all the other things – like the extra attention, support and the anaesthetic – that happen to someone who has it'.

Some theories suggest ECT changes blood flow to parts of the brain associated with low mood (Takano et al., 2007). Others propose that it interferes with the retrieval of information, thereby possibly breaking automatic negative thinking bias loops (Kroes et al., 2014). Others state that ECT works by reducing 'frontal cortical connectivity . . . in the dorsolateral prefrontal cortical region' (Perrin et al., 2012), which happens to be the same area of the brain targeted in surgical lobotomy. This area contains reciprocal neuronal connections between the frontal lobes (the area of the brain which is thought to control our capacity to be thoughtful, insightful, loving, and creative) and the rest of the brain. Research by Fosse and Read (2013, p. 333) stated that

> temporarily improved scores on depression instruments following ECT reflect the combination of frontal and temporal frontal lobe functional impairments and activation of the hypothalamic–pituitary–adrenal axis and mesocorticolimbic dopamine system . . . similar to those typically seen after severe stress exposure and/or brain trauma.

Hence, the implication is that the mode by which ECT works relates to damage to certain areas of the brain. It might be that if connections to the prefrontal cortex and/or memory are damaged as a result of administrating electricity, then people may be less able to recall or feel the depression, making it seem as though their mood has improved. From this perspective it suggests that some degree of brain damage is useful for perceived recovery.

DOES ECT 'WORK'?

There is a mixed picture of how effective ECT is. Some contend that ECT has little or no benefits in the treatment of depression (Lamborne and Gill, 1978; Read and Bentall, 2010). Others have said it is no more effective than sham ECT during the treatment period (Sackheim et al., 2001) yet some state that it is superior (Carney et al., 2003, UK ECT Review Group). Read and Bentall (2010) systematically evaluated all the ECT research they could find that had previously been used to justify the use of ECT by claiming efficacy and found little or no evidence for the effectiveness of ECT in the treatment of depression. In clinical practice there also seems to be discrepancies between clinician and recipient views regarding the effectiveness of ECT. A fact sheet on ECT from the Royal College of Psychiatrists (2015) states that between 30 percent and 80 percent of ECT recipients found it helpful. However, Fosse and Read (2013) point out that relapse rates for ECT are high: 15–20 percent one week after treatment and 50–80 percent after six months (e.g. Bourgon and Keller, 2000; Sackheim et al., 2001).

Studies reporting higher satisfaction tended to be carried out by doctors while studies reporting lower satisfaction tended to have been conducted by those who had undergone the intervention. So why such discrepancy? One reason may be in the measurement of effectiveness. The Clinical Global Impressions Scale (Guy, 1976) is proposed by ECTAS as a quick and easy to use assessment tool for measuring severity and clinical improvement following ECT. Clinicians rate severity of mental health at baseline (not at all ill to extremely ill) and then after intervention (very much improved to very much worse) on a seven-point scale. The individual is not involved in the assessment of improvement and there is no measure of risk–benefit ratio of side-effects to symptom relief. The ECTAS Minimum Dataset (2015) makes use of this tool alone as an outcome measure without considering possible side-effects, which is somewhat unusual. If pharmaceutical companies were to use this outcome assessment tool to assess the response to analgesics, for example, there would be uproar if side-effects were ignored or not looked for. Is such an outcome measure fit for purpose given the concerns for the use of ECT in terms of informed consent and long term side-effects primarily by those who have undergone ECT?

There are other methodological issues which may influence findings from efficacy studies of ECT. For example, Rose et al. (2003) reported that certain variables may exert a powerful effect on expressed satisfaction with ECT: interviews with people immediately after ECT, especially within a medical setting, using brief interview and conducted by the treating physician, may lead people to considerably over-estimate the extent to which they express their satisfaction with ECT. Issues revealed by people who had undergone ECT from the Service User Research Enterprise (SURE; Rose et al., 2003), which are not routinely explored or reported in clinical research studies, included:

➤ expressions of extreme trauma
➤ lying about improvement in order to stop treatment
➤ becoming 'manic'
➤ feeling more suicidal following treatment
➤ the desire to take legal action
➤ the need to seek support and validation from other individuals and organisations.

Chakrabarti et al. (2010) also acknowledge differences between recipients and physician perceptions regarding the usefulness and experience of ECT. However, they conclude that consumer-led research reflects a strong antagonistic and negative bias against the use of ECT but did recognise certain themes that emerged from ECT recipient perception studies. Examples of acknowledged themes included:

➤ that most people who had ECT felt they were not given adequate knowledge about the potential side-effects and risk of ECT
➤ many felt that they were coerced into having ECT
➤ many persons were anxious or fearful about ECT
➤ that memory loss was a relatively common, persistent and distressing side-effect of ECT.

SELF-ASSESSMENT EXERCISE 12.2

Time: 20 minutes
Look at the themes above.
● Using the four principles of medical ethics, which principles were used and which were breeched?
● What would you aim to do, in order to maintain the ethical values?

COGNITIVE SIDE-EFFECTS

There is no doubt that ECT does something to the brain, but is not without damage and therefore potential risk to cognitive functioning (e.g. Greenhalgh et al., 2005). However, the reported nature and degree of cognitive deficits following ECT administration in the literature is also conflicting. Some suggest fairly high incidences of persistent memory loss. Rose et al., (2003) stated that the rates of reported persistent memory loss experienced by those who had undergone ECT varied between 29 percent and 55 percent, with relatively high levels reported by both clinician led and patient led studies. Complaints of memory problems have also been reported to continue long after ECT treatment (Sienaert et al., 2005) and Sackeim et al. (2007) concluded from a follow-up study of 347 people who had undergone ECT that it causes permanent brain damage and dysfunction. In the summary they stated that their study

> 'provides the first evidence in a large, prospective sample that adverse cognitive effects can persist for an extended period, and that they characterize routine treatment with ECT in community settings'
>
> (p. 253)

Therefore, it seems that by trying to do good, mental health professionals may actually be doing a degree of harm. Indeed, guidance on the use of ECT issued by the National Institute for Clinical Excellence (NICE) recommended sharp restrictions on its use until more information becomes available about its effects on memory, quality of life and other pertinent health outcomes (NICE, 2009, paras. 4.1.2, 5.5).

Regarding possible cognitive effects of ECT, ECTAS (Royal College of Psychiatrists, 2013) standards recommend that an assessment of memory is performed using a standardised cognitive assessment tool and subjective questioning, and that the person's orientation and memory is assessed before and after the first one or two months following ECT and re-assessed at intervals throughout the treatment course (M7.12). It would be interesting to explore what routine and standardised assessment processes are included and conducted in clinical practise within the UK, and it could be questioned whether one to two months for follow-up to assess for cognitive side-effects is sufficient. It is somewhat ironic that brain damage and cognitive disturbance seem to be the premise upon which ECT works. Read and Bentall (2010, p. 333) state that:

> Given the strong evidence [summarised in their paper] of persistent and, for some, permanent brain dysfunction, primarily evidenced in the form of retrograde and anterograde amnesia, and the evidence of a slight but significant increased risk of death, the cost-benefit analysis for ECT is so poor that its use cannot be scientifically justified.

This discussion is not to say whether ECT is helpful or not, but that clinicians in mental health need to be more explicit and open about the uncertainties of its effectiveness, possible modes of action and side-effects. Thereby enabling people and their relatives to be as well-versed as possible, so that they may provide 'informed' consent to such treatment.

KEY POINT 12.1

Healthcare professionals have an ethical duty to provide as much unbiased information as possible . . .

. . . if healthcare clinicians are 'misleading' individuals and relatives by not stating the uncertainties in mechanism and effectiveness and side-effects, this could potentially lead to legal action, aside from ethical obligations to do the best thing with the least harm.

PROFESSIONALS' PERSPECTIVES

Despite some of the research outlined above it seems that psychiatry continues to focus on poor evidence, which may be subject to personal biases. This may lead mental health professional to persist in claims that ECT is effective and that the cognitive side-effects are a risk worth taking for those with severe depression. In mental health settings, discussions about whether people should undergo ECT frequently include comments such as 'I've seen it work . . . it changes their lives . . . don't know how it works but it does' (from the author's experience). If we assume that people who work in mental health systems are primarily there because they want to help people, it might be awkward to challenge its use, discuss the potential risks associated with its administration and that seemingly initial positive changes might be due to something else, for example post concussive brain damage (particularly in psychiatric led services)? If professionals work for the overall good of people (i.e. with beneficence), then there may be difficulties and significant barriers to 'objectively' reviewing practises that take place. What would the implications be for professionals that believe in ECT's therapeutic effectiveness, actively promote it, and even administer it? Could professionals be willing and able to consider that ECT could be anything other than a positive intervention due to its nature? Mental health professionals may struggle to adequately acknowledge the different aspects of dissatisfaction arising from discussion with those who have undergone ECT compared to their and other mental health professionals' views, as this may subject professionals to cognitive discomfort and dissonance.

Medical models of health are encouraged by both public expectations and the medical profession itself to do something to help the 'ill'. Underlying these expectations are implicit assumptions that something can and should be done by a clinician, in order to make a person better. Because of such assumptions, it may be difficult for the public, medical and other mental health professionals to tolerate doing 'nothing' in terms of intervening. Doing nothing may not be valued or considered very useful: after all where is the research base for doing 'nothing' (if such a thing exists)? However, in mental health one could argue that seemingly doing nothing (e.g. wait and see) could actually be a very powerful intervention, and may be the best and least harmful option, which may allow individuals time to be distressed and process what has been going on.

KEY POINT 12.2

In this day and age, it seems that distress is not tolerated and that people who react badly to bad things run the risk of being diagnosed as having a mental illness (American Psychiatric Association – DSM 5's 2015 exclusion of bereavement in the diagnosis of major depression).

Could it be that people may benefit from having time to process distress, with care and support, without being told there is something wrong with them and administered a fundamentally biomedical intervention? When referring individuals for ECT, NICE guidance is clear that its use should be limited to those with severe depression, which is thought to be intractable and/or life threatening to an individual. To sit with someone who is in the midst of dark depression where avenues for recovery seem blocked can be difficult, so to have ECT as an option for professionals (a last hope) could seem an attractive option and valuable for bystanders, practitioners and those people who have faith in medical interventions to do the best thing.

SELF-ASSESSMENT EXERCISE 12.3

Time: 15 minutes
This presents a challenge in attitudinal behaviour. In your own environment . . .
- What could **you** do?
- What would it need?

AUTONOMY AND CONSENT

Another ethical factor to consider in relation to ECT is how mental health professionals perceive individuals' ability to be involved in decisions about their treatment (i.e. their autonomy). At times, depressed individuals may be regarded as less able to demonstrate autonomy because of difficulties with their cognition and mental health at that time, which might lead to their contribution being minimised and/or to being excluded from the discussion about treatment options altogether. As Reiter-Theil (1992) states, a challenging conflict that clinicians have in providing ECT involves balancing autonomy (i.e. respect for the individual), and the principle of beneficence (i.e. doing good). This is particularly problematic with regard to ECT since the autonomy and ability of people experiencing severe depression to have the capacity to consent may be compromised by their cognition and future outlook (e.g. hopeless). If a person with severe depression refuses ECT, should this be respected or overridden? Some may argue that the 'mentally ill' must be regarded as fully autonomous in all circumstances, and consequently that all their wishes regarding treatment must be respected, but in the case of severe depression, are people able to have capacity to consent?

REFLECTIVE PRACTICE EXERCISE 12.1

Time: 45 minutes
Reflect on the above statement. From experience, consider and write down your views. Discuss this with a colleague. Is there a consensus?

To be deemed to have 'capacity' a person needs to be able to retain, weigh up, and relay information, and then subsequently instruct a decision. However, there appears to be a potential and significant issue for making capacity assessments where ECT is considered: the consequence of 'improving' mental state via ECT may inadvertently result in a diminution of their capacity (e.g. cognitive impairment) in both the short and longer term. But could anybody really be deemed to have consented to ECT? If we accept that the level of distress needed to be present before ECT is considered must be significantly severe, as per NICE guidelines, it seems counterintuitive at best (ridiculous at worst) to conclude that an individual is able to consent without the targeted problem itself influencing the decision making process. Non-refusal, lack of resistance, willingness to do anything to feel better, are not the same as consent. Additionally, as discussed above, the mechanisms of action of ECT are unclear and side-effects uncertain hence, there is insufficient time and scope for individuals and their relatives to be given sufficient information to consent and make an informed decision.

The issue of consenting to ECT seems complex but also quite unique. Compare this to a decision to assist an individual to manage their money. The latter has little or no direct adverse impact on the person's mental state, mood, or cognition hence, their capacity isn't improved or diminished by the decision to intervene. This may not be said in relation to ECT: this is likely to affect such things as their ability to retain, weigh up, relay information, and instruct a decision. Even if an individual does consent to ECT and appears to have capacity, this overlooks the fact that the mental state itself will impact on the decision making process. In addition, compare the decision to consent to ECT with the decision to consent to a physical health intervention. Severely depressed people who are deemed to have capacity can be forcibly administered treatment (including ECT) under the auspices of the Mental

Health Act (1983, amended 2007, chapter 20, section 62(1)) regardless of their view and even Advanced Directives: those with a physical health condition cannot. Assuming the principle of autonomy is an ethical priority, it should be questioned as to whether the person's refusal is arrived at competently and if it is, then it should be respected: if it is not, it should be overridden (according to the prevalent autonomy-oriented bioethics). The ECT Minimum Dataset Activity Data Report (Royal College of Psychiatrists, 2013) reported that in 2012–2013, 84 percent of those who received ECT while detained under the Mental Health Act (1983) did not consent to treatment when it was commenced, and of those who were informal, 92 percent were reported to have consented to treatment hence, approximately 8 percent of informal people did not consent (who apparently later consented while undergoing the course). Is this ethically acceptable? Recently, in the Republic of Ireland, there has been a legal move to ensure that ECT can only be administered to those who are consenting (Tracey, 2016) as, according to the MHA, if a person is 'capable of understanding the nature, purpose and likely effects of treatment' then ECT cannot be given without his or her consent. This would indicate that mental health professionals in the UK may not be following best practice guidance. Further exploration of how the decision making process is conducted and informed consent acquired may be required for the safety of individuals, professionals and organisations within the UK.

OPINIONS OF ECT FROM THOSE EXPERIENCING IT

ECT literature appears to be characterised by considerable disagreement about the benefits and risks, which could reflect potential author and/or journal bias (Van Daalen-Smith and Gallagher, 2011). Some people who have undergone ECT report positive benefits, which should be validated and not undermined. Historical physician reviews on attitudes to electroconvulsive therapy in the 1980s concluded that people found ECT beneficial and that they were satisfied with it (Freeman, 1986; Goodman et al., 1999). However, involving people who have undergone ECT is possibly the most valid population to use when exploring whether ECT is effective, beneficial and tolerable. In 2001, the Service User Research Enterprise (SURE) at the Institute of Psychiatry was commissioned to conduct a review of people who had undergone ECT and Professionals perspectives on ECT (Rose et al., 2003). The testimony data displayed a continuum of opinion about perceived benefits. However, 61 percent of those who had undergone ECT provided accounts and said they would not have ECT again, and 43 percent describe their experience of ECT in extremely negative terms. Some stated great concern with the manner in which the treatment was given: whether or not it helped was not the major issue. In addition, there was evidence that individuals who would have ECT again tended to trade-off benefits and risks. For example, some participants said that they were willing to suffer a degree of permanent memory loss in exchange for some relief from depression. Hence, it seems, there is not a unidimensional attitude towards ECT from those who have experienced it, not even on the question of whether it is helpful or not.

A possible reason for people opting to undergo ECT might be that they feel so awful, or unable to refuse treatment that is presented and viewed as their last chance for recovery, perhaps believing that there are no more treatment options (Johnstone, 1999), they have reached the 'end of the road' and that ECT is the only hope remaining. Maintaining individual autonomy is relevant here and it is suggested a greater notion of autonomy is required for people experiencing severe depression to bring about improvement in their care and treatment at such a vulnerable point in their lives. When severely depressed, at a level it needs to be before ECT is considered, a person's decision to undergo ECT may not be based on their understanding of the intervention per se, but their trust in the professional who is offering the intervention. To superficially agree with the view of the professional does not infer capacity to consent: an individual might consent to a variety of offered interventions at this stage (even euthanasia, which is one of the arguments against legislation for it). The potential power of the relationship between individuals and mental health services at a time of despair may be a significant influential factor on outcome. People have also reported feeling that they had been coerced into receiving ECT (Rose et al., 2003), felt powerless during the consent process and felt poorly informed about the risks and the actual procedure of ECT (Fisher et al., 2011).

PLACEBO VERSUS POSITIVE CARE EFFECTS OF ECT

It is well known that people given a placebo, or 'inactive' treatment, may have an improvement in their condition, a phenomenon commonly called the placebo effect. If placebos are assumed to be influential to recovery in some way, perhaps the way in which individuals are involved in the decision making process, providing informed consent and the process of receiving ECT itself might be significant in influencing perceived outcome or recovery. The placebo effect might account to some degree for the positive effects seen after sham ECT (Sackheim et al., 2001). Friedberg (1976) stated that the 'influence of ECT was on the minds of the psychiatrists, producing optimism and earlier discharges' (cited Read and Bentall, 2010, 334), suggesting that the attitude and expectations provided by 'experts' in the field (e.g. the psychiatrist or other mental health professionals) might produce placebo or positive care effects on those individuals and relatives leading to better perceived outcomes.

Louhiala and Puustinen (2008) state that there is always a care effect in every therapeutic context. They argue against the notion of a placebo being 'inert', as this implies that there is no action through its administration (unless the person is unconscious), and that care effects cannot be excluded from any form of therapeutic encounter. In the literature surrounding placebo treatments, many factors regarding the mode of treatment have been proposed that might bring about perceived recovery over the years. For example, individuals seem to fare better to larger pills than smaller ones due to response expectancy (Montgomery and Kirsch, 1997); people respond better if told to take pills four times a day compared to twice a day (De Craen et al., 2000); and people do better as a result of participating in clinical trials, whether they receive 'active' treatment or not (Howick, 2009). The mechanism for positive care effects is thought to be via classical conditioning: cues within the therapeutic encounter which induce an expectation of recovery on the part of the individual (Kirsch et al., 2004). Whatever any ECT effect is, there may be positive care effect processes operating (Rasmussen, 2009). The process of receiving ECT involves many 'expectancy for improvement' elements that might influence perceived outcome. For example, ECT is a significant intervention, of long duration, involving multi-professionals, and with a large expectation for recovery.

In addition, the actual process surrounding ECT administration may provide people with greater opportunities for positive care experiences, which could be therapeutic. People may view engagement on an ECT pathway as validating: they are being listened to, their difficulties are being taken seriously, people care, people believe that their distress is 'great enough' to warrant such an intrusive procedure, they have more time and contact with mental health personnel etc. Furthermore, Blease (2012) hypothesises that positive effects of sham ECT may be due to the 'theatre' of the intervention, which include side-effects of headaches and memory loss, as well as the belief in the effectiveness of treatment. If positive care effects are influential, could it be possible that services should attend to some of the 'ingredients' associated with the process of undergoing ECT, which seem to positively affect individuals' mental health, rather than people risking memory loss and looking to external interventions in the form of ECT to feel better? Could people who undergo ECT be informed that it may work as a placebo in addition to the effects it may have on the brain itself (e.g. Placebos without Deception; Kaptchuk et al., 2010)? Ethically it could be argued that if other forms of intervention received the similar positive expectations, validation of distress, investment of time and expenditure, then these too could be perceived as beneficial for people experiencing depression, influencing perceived outcomes, for example, psychosocial interventions. Hence, is there an equality of opportunity for people to access other interventions, for example, justice?

EXTERNAL ATTRIBUTION, HELPLESSNESS AND HOPELESSNESS

Aside from positive care effects, ECT can be considered as an external therapy to alleviate the distress of depression, that is, it is an intervention that is done to a person. Although most people will struggle with motivation when feeling depressed, an external treatment such as ECT may inadvertently reinforce the notion of helplessness within an individual and potentially foster a belief for the need or desire for ECT should they experience depression in the future. Many people who receive ECT may think it was a last resort and by doing so implicitly assume that their mental health recovery was not of their own volition (aside from perhaps agreeing to treatment). Fisher et al. (2011, p. 350) suggest that the idea of ECT being a last resort is inadvertently reinforced by the NICE guidance (2003), which states that ECT should only be used in 'life threatening situations or when medication and other interventions have failed'.

If someone perceives that they did not recover after undergoing ECT, this may lead them to feel even more helpless and hopeless, as well as possibly extending the period of depression, making it worse, and even result in suicide (e.g. Beck et al., 1989).

Potential suicide is an argument which has been used to advocate the use of ECT in severely depressed individuals, with an assumption that it can prevent suicide because it is not safe to wait for other interventions to have beneficial effects (Kellner et al., 2005). However, a study reported that while suicide attempts were less frequent after ECT compared to antidepressants alone, ironically there were significantly more severe suicide attempts following ECT than following antidepressants (Brådvik and Berglund, 2006), meaning that ECT may potentially increase the risk of suicide.

CONCLUSION

This chapter has introduced some of the ethical issues surrounding the use of ECT in clinical practice. It appears clear that ECT does something to help people experiencing low mood. However, the precise mechanisms of action are unknown and change may be attributed to factors that may or may not be viewed as favorable. In addition, the effectiveness and acceptability of ECT is not clear, and there are specific ethical issues around consent in this area. Consideration of such issues may lead to the promotion of greater autonomy, justice, beneficence and non-maleficence in the use of ECT, which remains one of the most ethically controversial interventions in mental health. Ethically it is probably time to rethink and examine the processes, outcomes and side-effects involved in administering ECT as a treatment to promote safer practices. Identifying causes of improvement and influential positive care effects and applying these to a broader range of interventions may be worthy of exploration.

REFERENCES

American Psychiatric Association. 2015. DSM-5 Development: G 04 Adjustment Disorders. American Psychiatric Association. www.psychiatry.org/psychiatrists/practice/dsm/dsm-5.

Beauchamp TL and JF Childress. 2001. *Principles of Biomedical Ethics.* 5th ed. Oxford: Oxford University Press.

Beck AT, G Brown and RA Steer. 1989. "Prediction of eventual suicide in psychiatric inpatients by clinical ratings of hopelessness." *Journal of Consulting and Clinical Psychology* 57: 309–310.

Blease C. 2012. "The principle of parity: the 'placebo effect' and physician communication." *Journal of Medical Ethics* 38: 199–203.

Bloch Y, G Ratzoni, D Sobol, S Mendlovic, G Gal and Y Levkovitz. 2005. "Gender differences in electroconvulsive therapy: a retrospective chart review." *Journal of Affective Disorders* 84: 99–102.

Bourgon LN and CH Kellner. 2000. "Relapse of depression after ECT: a review." *Journal of ECT* 16: 19–31.

Bråsdvik L and M Berglund. 2006. "Long-term treatment and suicidal behaviour in severe depression: ECT and antidepressant pharmacotherapy may have different effects on the occurrence and seriousness of suicide attempts." *Depression and Anxiety* 23: 34–41.

Breggin PR. 2011. "Psychiatric drug-induced Chronic Brain Impairment (CBI): Implications for long term treatment with psychiatric medication." *International Journal of Risk & Safety in Medicine* 23: 193–200.

Carney S, P Cowen, J Geddes, G Goodwin, R Rogers, K Dearness, A Tomlin, J Eastaugh, N Freemantle, H Lester, A Harvey and A Scott, The UK ECT Review Group. 2003. "Efficacy and safety of electroconvulsive therapy in depressive disorders: A systematic review and meta-analysis." *Lancet* 361, 9360: 799–808.

Chakrabarti S, S Grover and R Rajagopal. 2010. "Electroconvulsive therapy: A review of knowledge, experience and attitudes of patients concerning the treatment." *World Journal of Biological Psychiatry* 11: 162–174.

De Craen AJ, JG Tijssen, J de Gans and J Kleijnen. 2000. "Placebo effect in the acute treatment of migraine: subcutaneous placebos are better than oral placebos." *Journal of Neurology* 247: 183–188.

ECT Accreditation Service. 2015. *Standards for ECT Accreditation service*, 15th ed., edited by S Hodge and N Buley. www.ectas.org.uk.

Fisher P, L Johnstone and K Williamson. 2011. "Patients' perceptions of the process of consenting to electroconvulsive therapy." *Journal of Mental Health* 20: 347–354.

Fosse R and J Reed. 2013. "Electroconvulsive treatment: hypothesis about mechanisms of action." *Frontiers in Psychiatry* 4: 1–10.

Freeman C. 1986. "Patients' attitudes towards ECT." *Psychopharmacologica Bulletin* 22: 487–490.

Goodman JA, LE Krahn, GE Smith, TA Rummans and TS Pileggi. 1999. "Patient satisfaction with electroconvulsive therapy." *Mayo Clinic Proceedings* 74: 967–971.

Greenhalgh J, C Knight, D Hind, C Beverley and S Walters. 2005. "Clinical and cost-effectiveness of electroconvulsive therapy for depressive illness, schizophrenia, catatonia and mania: systematic reviews and economic modelling studies." *Health Technology and Assessment* 9: 1–156, iii–iv.

Guy W. 1976. "The Clinical Global Impression Scale." Edited by Guy W, *ECDEU Assessment Manual for Psychopharmacology.* 125–126. Rockville, MD.

Howick J. 2009. "Escaping from placebo prison." *British Medical Journal* 338: b1898.

Johnstone L. 1999. "Adverse psychological effects of ECT." *Journal of Mental Health* 8: 69–85.

Kaptchuk TJ, E Friedlander, JM Kelley, MN Sanchez, E Kokkotou, JP Singer, M Kowalczykowski, FG Miller, I Kirsch and AJ Lembo. 2010. "Placebos without Deception: A Randomized Controlled Trial in Irritable Bowel Syndrome." *PloS ONE* 22;5(12): e15591.

Kellner C, M Fink, R Knapp, M Husain and T Rasmussen. 2005. "Relief of expressed suicidal intent by ECT." *American Journal of Psychiatry* 162: 977–982.

Kirsch I, SJ Lynn, M Vigorito and RR Miller. 2004. "The role of cognition in classical and operant conditioning." *Journal of Clinical Psychology* 60: 369–392.

Kroes MCW, I Tendolkar, GA van Wingen, JA van Waarde, BA Strange and G Fernández. 2014. "An electroconvulsive therapy procedure impairs reconsolidation of episodic memories in humans." *Nature Neuroscience* 17: 204–206.

Lamborne J and D Gill. 1978. "A controlled comparison of simulated and real ECT." *British Journal of Psychiatry* 133: 514–519.

Louhiala P and R Puustinen. 2008. "Rethinking the placebo effect." *Medical Humanities* 35: 407–409.

Mental Health Act. 1983 and 2007. Department of Health. London, HMSO. www.legislation.gov.uk/ukpga/2007/12/contents.

Montgomery GH and I Kirsch. 1997. "Classical conditioning and the placebo effect." *Pain* 72: 107–113.

National Institute of Clinical Excellence. 2003/2009. *Guidance on the use of Electroconvulsive Therapy (Technology Appraisal Guidance 59).* London: NICE.

National Institute for Clinical Excellence Pathways. 2015. Step 4: Complex & severe depression in adults, NICE. www.pathways.nice.org.uk/pathways/depression.

Perrin JS, S Merz, DM Benett, J Curriea, DJ Steele, IC Reid and C Schwarzbauer. 2012. Electroconvulsive therapy reduces frontal cortical connectivity in severe depressive disorder. www.pnas.org/content/109/14/5464.long.

Rasmussen KG. 2009. "Sham electroconvulsive therapy studies in depressive illness: a review of the literature and consideration of the placebo phenomenon in electro-convulsive therapy practice." *Journal of ECT* 25(1): 54–59.

Read J and R Bentall. 2010. "The effectiveness of electroconvulsive therapy: A literature review." *Epidemiol Psychiatry S* 9: 333–347.

Reiter-Theil S. 1992 "Autonomy and beneficence: Ethical issues in electroconvulsive therapy." *Convulsive Therapy* 8: 237–244.

Rose D, P Fleischmann, T Wilks, M Leese and J Bindman. 2003. "Patients' perspectives on electroconvulsive therapy: systematic review." *British Medical Journal* 21, 326: 1363.

Royal College of Psychiatrists. 2013. ECT minimum dataset activity report – England and Wales. www.rcpsych.ac.uk/pdf/ectas%20Minimum%20Dataset%20Report%202012-13.pdf.

Royal College of Psychiatrists. 2015. Information about ECT (Electro-convulsive therapy). Royal College of Psychiatry. www.rcpsych.ac.uk/healthadvice/treatmentswellbeing/ect.aspx.

Sackeim HA, RF Haskett, BH Mulsant, ME Thase, JJ Mann, HM Pettinati, RM Greenberg, RR Crowe, TB Cooper and J Prudic. 2001. "Continuation pharmacotherapy in the prevention of relapse following electroconvulsive therapy: a randomized controlled trial." *Journal of the American Medical Association* 14, 285: 1299–1307.

Sackeim HA, J Prudic, R Fuller, J Keilp, PW Lavori and M Olfson. 2007. "The cognitive effects of electroconvulsive therapy in community settings." *Neuropsychopharmacology* 32: 244–254.

Sienaert P, T De Becker, K Vansteelandt, K Demyttenaere and J Peuskens. 2005. "Patient satisfaction after electroconvulsive therapy." *Journal of ECT* 21: 227–231.

Singhal A. 2011. "Electroconvulsive therapy and its place in the management of depression." *Progress in Neurology & Psychiatry* 15: 19–26.

Takano H, N Motohashi, T Uema, K Ogawa, T Ohnishi, M Nishikawa, H Kashima and H Matsuda. 2007. "Changes in regional cerebral blood flow during acute electroconvulsive therapy in patients with depression: positron emission tomographic study." *British Journal of Psychiatry* 190: 63–68.

Tracey C. 2016. British Broadcasting Corporation: New laws to limit use of Electro Convulsive Treatment in Ireland. www.bbc.co.uk/news/uk-35609166.

Van Daalen-Smith CL and J Gallagher. 2011. "Electroshock: A discerning review of the nursing literature." *Issues in Mental Health Nursing* 32: 203–213.

CHAPTER 13

Human rights in mental health

Scott Macpherson and Dan Warrender

All human beings are born free and equal in dignity and rights. They are endowed with reason and conscience and should act towards one another in a spirit of brotherhood.

(Article 1 of the Universal Declaration of Human Rights [UDHR], United Nations 1948, p. 2).

INTRODUCTION

Human rights can be understood as entitlements inherent to all humans simply because they are born human and irrespective of race, creed, gender, ethnicity, nationality or any other subdivision of their humanity. Human rights are secured in law and include civil and political rights as well as economic and social rights (*see* Table 13.1).

Throughout human history there are documented examples of what we now understand as attempts to define and protect peoples' 'rights'. As far back as the first century AD the Roman Stoic philosopher Seneca delivered teachings on the importance of beneficence, connectedness and fellowship of human beings (Seneca 1968). Indeed, even further back in history in Ancient Greece while Plato and Aristotle mused about justice and the common good, the term 'cosmopolitan' meaning 'world citizen' was coined (Nascimento 2016). From these early works came the concept of natural rights which were considered the basic inalienable rights of all humans, bestowed by nature rather than by man-made laws. The philosopher John Locke considered these rights to include life, liberty and estate (property) and these rights were prominent in discussions during the French and American Revolutions of the late eighteenth century, eventually leading to the French Declaration of the Rights of Man and of the Citizen and the American Declaration of Independence (Donnelly 2013).

It is fair to say that, until recently, ethics and human rights have rarely been an important consideration in the field of mental health. During the French

Table 13.1 Examples of Civil, Political, Economic and Social Rights

Examples of Civil and Political Rights	Examples of Economic and Social Rights
Right to freedom of assembly	Right to adequate food, housing, water and sanitation
Right to freedom of expression	Right to an adequate standard of living
Right to freedom of religion or conscience	Right to education
Right to privacy	Right to health
Right to property	Right to science and culture
Right to vote	Right to work and fair working conditions

*Adapted from Scottish Human Rights Commission, 2010. *Care about Rights?* Glasgow: Scottish Human Rights Commission.

Revolution the psychiatrist Phillipe Pinel introduced the notion of treating patients with human dignity through 'moral therapy' which involved having staff interact with patients in as normal a way as possible and involving patients in discussions about their treatment (Pinel 1806). This was entirely at odds with common practice up to that point which had involved patients being held in iron shackles for their entire lives and displayed to members of the public for an admission fee, as people feared that mental disorder was a sign of demonic possession (Osborn 2009). Pinel's work led to a move towards the humanitarian treatment of individuals experiencing mental health problems both in his home country and overseas, including in the UK by the early nineteenth century. Things had changed by the end of the nineteenth century with people literally being dumped in asylums for spurious reasons and neglected and ill-treated for decades to come (Musto 1991).

The history of human rights as we understand them today however, is a relatively short one. In the wake of the atrocities committed during World War II and the creation of the United Nations, world leaders collaborated to develop the Universal Declaration of Human Rights – a guidance document designed to guarantee the rights of everyone, everywhere and thus protect against such atrocities occurring again (Donnelly 2013). This declaration is not a legally binding document in itself but has inspired in excess of 60 human rights instruments addressing rights in relation to a variety of issues including war crimes, marriage, social welfare, health and many more (Office of the United Nations High Commissioner for Human Rights (OHCHR) 2016). These tools together set out a universal standard of human rights.

The application of human rights creates obligations through international law for states to respect, protect and fulfil human rights for all. This means they must not interfere with or remove human rights (respect), they must protect both individuals and groups from human rights abuses (protect) and they must be pro-active in enabling the enjoyment of human rights (fulfil). While everyone is entitled to have their human rights respected, protected and fulfilled there is also a universal obligation to ensure that our actions or inaction do not infringe the human rights of others.

Human rights are interdependent and interrelated i.e. if one right is fulfilled it aids the achievement of others and, conversely, if one right is denied it makes the fulfilment of others more challenging.

MENTAL HEALTH ACT

While mental health legislation differs across the UK each of the Acts is built around similar ethical principles. In Scotland the Millan Committee (2001) was commissioned by Parliament to make recommendations for a new Mental Health Act including consideration of an ethical underpinning for the compulsory treatment of people experiencing mental disorders. The committee developed a set of principles on which they recommended mental health law should be based. These are now known as the 'Millan Principles':

BOX 13.1 Millan Principles

  1 Non-discrimination
  2 Equality
  3 Respect for diversity
  4 Reciprocity
  5 Informal care
  6 Participation
  7 Respect for carers
  8 Least restrictive alternative
  9 Benefit
 10 Child welfare (Millan Committee 2001)

HUMAN RIGHTS LAW

There are a number of core United Nations (UN) human rights treaties (or conventions) setting international standards for particular human rights issues such as the elimination of racial discrimination and the rights of persons with disabilities. Each member state is obliged to implement these standards within their own legal and policy processes. Some states simply integrate the conventions into their legal systems, however the UK does not do this as standard. The UK has its own Human Rights legislation: in Scotland there is the Scotland Act (1998) and the Human Rights Act (1998) in the rest of the UK. These laws make the rights contained in the Convention for the Protection of Human Rights and Fundamental Freedoms (European Human Rights Convention) (1950) enforceable in law in the UK.

REFLECTIVE PRACTICE EXERCISE 13.1

> **Time: 15 minutes**
> It has been said that nurses are caught between two moral imperatives:
> 1 To protect the individual from harm
> 2 To uphold the principle of self-choice
> - Think about a time when you have found yourself in a situation like this . . . what does it feel like?
> - Which imperative won out in the end?
> - Does this mean that particular imperative carries more weight? Why?

CAPACITY AND THE LAW

While each of the constituent countries of the UK has its own legislation in place around mental capacity they are all based on the principles of justice, autonomy, beneficence and non-maleficence. In Scotland the Adults with Incapacity (Scotland) Act 2000 provides a system for protecting the welfare, finances and property of adults (age 16 and over) who lack capacity to make decisions for themselves due to mental disorder or an inability to communicate due to physical impairment.

The Act authorises other relevant and appropriate people to make decisions on behalf of people who are deemed to lack capacity. However, there are a number of safeguards in place that are intended to prevent abuse of these decision making powers. These protections include the prevention of certain decisions being made on the person's behalf such as giving consent to marriage or the drawing up of a will. Additionally, persons acting on behalf of someone who is deemed to lack capacity are prevented from having the person admitted to a mental health hospital against their will or consenting to certain medical treatments on their behalf.

One of the underpinning principles of the Act is that peoples' autonomy should be respected by allowing (and enabling) them to make any and all decisions for themselves that they are capable of making. This means that the person may not have the capacity to make certain decisions, while retaining the capacity to make others.

The Act requires that those who are making decisions on behalf of another person follow the following principles:
- Act in the benefit of the person
- Take the least restrictive option
- Consult with relevant others
- Encourage, in the person, the use of existing skills and development of new skills
- Act in fitting with the present and past wishes of the person

It is easy to see how these principles are grounded in the aforementioned underpinnings of beneficence, non-maleficence, autonomy and justice. It would be comforting to think that everyone acting on behalf of someone with impaired capacity would always follow these principles, however, this is not always the case. In order to protect the interests of people who lack capacity the Act tasks four public bodies with the supervision and regulation of the people who are authorised to make decisions for them: the Mental Welfare Commission for Scotland, the Office of the Public Guardian (Scotland), local authorities and the courts. These bodies variously offer support and advice, supervise financial decisions made on behalf of people with impaired capacity, investigate complaints and reduce or remove any decision making powers previously granted.

LIVING WILLS

A Living Will is, as the name suggests, a statement of wishes during a person's life, rather than following their death. Known as advance directives in Scotland and advance decisions in the rest of the UK they allow a person to communicate their decision to refuse specified medical treatments in the future should they be unable to communicate their preference at that time, or lack the capacity to make such a decision. Again, this is autonomy in practice, allowing people to refuse ahead of time any medical treatment, including treatment that is life-sustaining. Of course, advance directives are not valid while the person has capacity to make decisions and can communicate their wishes. In England and Wales advance decisions are legally binding, while in Scotland advance directives are not. If a medical decision were ever to be challenged in court however, it is highly unlikely a judge would rule against respecting the person's advance directive.

If a decision is taken or treatment given which conflicts with a person's advance directive this must be reported to a number of parties. The Mental Health (Care and Treatment) (Scotland) Act 2003 requires that the person (or tribunal) authorising or giving the treatment must make a written record of why the decision was taken, including the context and circumstances around the decision. This must be recorded in the person's medical notes and a copy sent to:

➤ The person who made the advance directive
➤ The person's named person
➤ Any welfare guardian or welfare attorney of the person
➤ The Mental Welfare Commission

In addition to advance directives a person can set out their personal wishes in relation to treatment for a mental disorder in a personal statement. This is a written document which details the person's wishes for what they would like to happen and how they would like to be treated if, for instance, they have to be admitted to hospital. A personal statement may include preferences relating to, for example, how the person wishes to be addressed, any dietary preferences, wishes regarding who should visit or have contact with the person. Personal statements do not require to be witnessed by another person and can be attached to a person's advance directive but they do not carry the same weight in law.

While people are free to refuse medical treatment there is no legal provision for requesting or demanding a particular treatment, though people are entitled to have the reasons for not providing a particular treatment to them or request a second opinion.

REFLECTIVE PRACTICE EXERCISE 13.2

Time: 20 minutes
- Should people have the right to demand particular medical treatments?
- What would this mean for the health professions?

MENTAL HEALTH TRIBUNALS

Mental Health Tribunals (MHTs) are independent judicial organizations that deal with one of the fundamental human rights: the right to liberty. These tribunals are tasked with making certain decisions about the compulsory care and treatment of people experiencing mental disorder. The Mental Health Tribunal for Scotland was established by the Mental Health (Care and Treatment) (Scotland Act, 2003) and similarly the tribunals in England, Northern Ireland and Wales were set up by their respective pieces of mental health legislation. These tribunals serve very similar functions and the focus here is on the Mental Health Tribunal for Scotland. The tribunal aims to provide an independent and impartial service for those who are subject to the 2003 Act (and for those who have had an application made to subject them to the Act). The tribunal is overseen by a President and each tribunal panel must consist of three members: one legal (a lawyer), one medical (a psychiatrist) and one general (a layperson with some mental health experience – this is sometimes a person experiencing mental health problems, or a carer).

What does the tribunal do?

The tribunal's main tasks are to make decisions on applications for compulsory treatment orders (CTOs) and to consider and adjudicate on appeals made against CTOs imposed under the 2003 Act. The tribunal plays an important role in reviewing existing CTOs and deciding whether these should continue or be discharged if no longer required.

The person whose situation is being considered by the tribunal is invited to attend and can bring a supporting person with them. The person themselves, as well as anyone else who has an interest that the tribunal thinks should be allowed to speak will be allowed to do so.

CONFLICT

While on an individual basis, and from an objective point of view, we can look at human rights and agree what appears to concord with our professional ethical framework, it is when rights come into conflict that we swim into muddy waters. Ethics is not science, and when two rights come into conflict, there must be a detailed discussion between professionals as to which should become the clinical priority.

> *Man is born free, and everywhere he is in chains.*
>
> (Rousseau 1913)

The UDHR refers to human rights as inalienable, meaning that they cannot be removed, however there is a caveat to this . . . they can be removed in certain situations as provided for by part 2 of Article 29:

> In the exercise of his rights and freedoms, everyone shall be subject only to such limitations as are determined by law solely for the purpose of securing due recognition and respect for the rights and freedoms of others and of meeting the just requirements of morality, public order and the general welfare in a democratic society.
>
> (UDHR 1948)

It is here that subjectivity plays an important role and this can lead to discord and frustration.

Particularly challenging in mental health care, with reference to the use of detentions under the mental health act, is the conflict between any perceived clinical need for intervention, versus a person's right to liberty. The mental health act, while differing in terminology across the British Isles, has the consistent aim of protecting the rights of people experiencing mental health issues. However, this protection extends to granting professionals legally sanctioned powers to remove liberty, administer medication (knowingly and covertly) and contain risk through detention within hospital settings. These measures are taken if there is a justification based on risk, and a person's perceived lack of capacity as a result of their mental health. However, these actions can be taken in the name of risk not only if a person *cannot* consent to treatment, but also if they *will not* consent (Richardson 2002). This is entirely at odds with the treatment of people who are physically ill and refuse treatment, for instance Jehovah's Witnesses who refuse blood products despite the fact that this may present serious risk to them. Those working in the field can often find themselves in a difficult situation where under-estimation of risk may lead to disastrous consequences and potential trial by media, an overestimation of risk jeopardizes both therapeutic relationships and the professional's position of providing beneficent care. Certainly, to the person involved while professional intentions may be pure and beneficent, intervention may not always feel like protection and instead may be perceived as paternalistic, maleficent and bereft of justice.

REMOVING AUTONOMY AND ITS JUSTIFICATION

A useful question to ask is; 'just what is being protected by a person's detention?' While clinical reasoning would perhaps cite a risk to self and a risk to others (with risk covering multiple physical, environmental and psychosocial factors), if there is no obstacle to any person's right to life, through no risk of harm to themselves or the general public, can detention ever be justified? This echoes the sentiment of Thomas Szasz (2010), who argued that any person who was not in breach of criminal law should be left in peace, with any coercion deemed a breach of that person's human rights. This idea would allow a person to be 'pleasantly mad', being mentally ill as per our working definitions, yet living their own life in their own way. It could be argued that intervention and coercion with this person is an attempt to correct social deviance, with a societal pressure to make people 'more like us' and closer to our social norms and expected patterns of behaviour (*see* Case Study 13.1, p. 183).

INTERPRETATIONS OF RISK AND SOCIAL NORMS

It is here we perhaps see an interpretation of risk which presupposes that mental health which differs from social norms harms a person's social dignity. Foreseeable Risk as a concept aims to 'anticipate the likelihood of injury or damage associated with a given set of circumstances' (Fisher and Scott 2013, p. 21).

This perceived injury or damage appears in an all-encompassing array of categories that extend to risk which is; material or psychological, immediate or delayed, arising from our own actions or that of others, and resulting in us paying a price in many different ways (Fischhoff and Kadvany 2011). With the concept of risk allowing such subjectivity of interpretation, it is vague enough to accommodate a risk to social dignity which could justify professional intervention. Ethics, like all philosophy, often sees an infinite wall of questions surrounding an answer. To further our discussion, two rhetorical bricks in this wall would be; what is the level of good mental health necessary for sufficient social dignity, and who decides on its definition?

If good mental health is linked to social norms, we should reflect on our not too distant (and it could be argued shameful) past, where homosexuality was classified as a mental illness (Bayer 1981). Using this example to highlight the obvious; social norms change. Therefore, mental health could be bound to the culture and time in which it presents. In this way mental health can be viewed as a wholly social construct, in which deviance (illness) is contained and corrected (treated), with the societal need being expressed as clinical need. The use of coercion to correct difference could be viewed as a 'militant goodness' to give people the social dignity of a life **we think** is worth living, while any attempt to define a true and objective 'life worth living' has been described as absurd (Glover 1990).

Moving on, we can explore the experience of the person meeting current criteria of mental ill health, and ask whether or not they are in distress. Beyond the idea of risk to self and others, and whether or not risk also includes a social dignity, exploring the person's level of distress could see any intervention based on compassion. More questions arise when we examine whether the person expresses this distress, or whether it is subjectively inferred through the assessment of professionals (Szasz 1997). Again there is dispute about whether the priorities are based on the individual experiencing the mental health issue or the expectation that anyone outside social norms must be distressed and 'corrected' for their own good.

A HUMAN RIGHT TO GOOD MENTAL HEALTH?

Mental ill health 'comprise[s] a broad range of problems, with different symptoms. However, they are generally characterized by some combination of abnormal thoughts, emotions, behaviour and relationships with others' (World Health Organisation [WHO] 2016).

However, consider a person with 'abnormal' thoughts, emotions and behaviours, who presents no risk to themselves or the public, and who does not voice any psychological distress (see Case Study 13.1, p. 183). The Human Rights Act (1998) cites a right to freedom of thought, conscience and religion, with a right to freedom of expression. Could freedom of thought extend to include a right to unusual (being out-with social norms) ideas, and could freedom of expression extend to the expression of these ideas in an unusual way? These human rights are in tension with the right to liberty, when there is a perceived professional need to intervene. Have we subconsciously created a new and unwritten human right, that of a right to a standard of good mental health, and has meeting this standard become a perceived clinical need? If so, there must be an acute awareness that the social expectations of others which form our ethical, legal and professional frameworks are only objective within their own context and subjective across time and culture.

CONFLICTS IN THE MENTAL HEALTH TRIBUNAL PROCESS

Vitally the human right to liberty and autonomy, if removed by mental health legislative frameworks, allows an appeals process through that of a mental health tribunal. Here the person experiencing a mental health issue has their right to autonomy weighed up against the clinical need for coercive intervention. Tribunals open up individual cases to a more detailed scrutiny, examining the subjective view of mental health professionals, ensuring justice on behalf of the person involved. Nonetheless, this process is not bereft of moral tension, as there may be instances which involve more than the individual, and that of carers and families. While we previously discussed the concept of the 'pleasantly mad' person, if there are families involved this becomes more complex.

It could be argued from a utilitarian and consequentialist standpoint that to ensure the greatest happiness for the greatest number of people, families need to be taken into account. If the mental health condition of the person has an inevitable spill into the lives of the ones closest to them, the person may not meet the criteria for continued detention, but may return to a family environment, where the 'mad' is experienced as anything but pleasant. Here we could see justice through a person's autonomy being returned, while what may seem the beneficent act of returning an individual's freedom indirectly breaches the concept on non-maleficence through the impact to family. While the tribunal aids the human rights of the person experiencing the mental health condition, there may be unseen consequences.

The mental health professional, while championing the concept of care which is beneficent, often does so through a deontological and Kantian concept of duty (Kant 2005). This is where morality is neither rooted in intention nor consequence, but a strict duty to do what is right. One difficulty the professional may face would be to see a person with a mental illness walk away from treatment, feeling they have a duty to intervene, with a tribunal overriding this duty with a respect for autonomy and justice. Reflecting on the loose definition of risk, the failure to act in the moment may result in the delayed risk of a condition worsening, and more challenging circumstances for the person experiencing the condition, and more difficulty for the professionals in providing effective treatment.

MORAL TRIAGE: INTENTIONS, DUTIES AND CONSEQUENCES

Much of our moral sensibilities can be captured through the triage of intentions, duties and consequences, and reflecting on these can be useful when examining any tension. Mental health professionals it would be hoped would carry an innate virtue, being a caring profession, and their intentions to fulfil care which respects principles of beneficence, non-maleficence, justice and autonomy should be expected. However, when it comes to duties and consequences, the clarity ends. As regards duties, we may ask whether or not these duties are to the profession e.g. nursing, medicine etc, whether they are to the person receiving treatment, or whether they can extend to others beyond this. Certainly with a view to containing risk, there is often a duty to protect the person, and protect others. Nevertheless, how risk is defined is sufficiently vague to allow a variety of consequences and it is here that the confusion reaches its peak. How can professionals potentially predict consequences sufficiently to inform care?

Case Study 13.1

Mrs O was detained in an acute mental health ward under the mental health act on a short term detention. She had made contact with several health boards over a three-year period, travelling frequently and presenting as eccentric with unusual beliefs regarding snakes in the water pipes. She did not voice any internal distress, had never been in breach of clinical law, and was not deemed a risk to herself or others.

In her time on the ward she was entirely pleasant in manner, yet clearly meeting professional criteria of a psychotic episode without insight. The pleasantry of her manner was pushed however by the coercion involved in her hospital stay. She was pleasant in all interactions, besides the conversations with professionals regarding their perceived clinical need for her to receive treatment for a mental health condition.

Mrs O challenged her detention, and after a mental health tribunal ruled in her favour, she was allowed to leave the ward.

SELF-ASSESSMENT EXERCISE 13.1

Time: 30 minutes

Consider the following questions:

a   What was the clinical need for Mrs O's detention?
b   What, if any, risks do you think were perceived by the professionals involved in Mrs O's care?
c   Would you agree with the mental health tribunals decision? Why?
d   Which moral principles were involved in the decision making process?

REFLECTIVE PRACTICE EXERCISE 13.3

Time: 15 minutes

People receiving methadone maintenance treatment for opioid dependence are often asked to attend pharmacies only during limited hours or to enter via a separate door to the general public. Is this a breach or protection of their human rights? Do these practices protect their right to privacy or breach their right to be treated equally?

REVIEW QUESTIONS 13.1 – ANSWERS ON P. 186

---

1 The guidance document 'The Universal Declaration of Human Rights' was designed to protect the rights of:
   a Everyone everywhere
   b Everyone everywhere, except prisoners
   c People who are subject to mental health legislation
   d Victims of war crimes
2 The Adults with Incapacity (Scotland) Act 2000 is not based on which of the following principles?:
   a Act in the benefit of the person
   b Take the least restrictive option
   c Consult with relevant others
   d Control financial decisions
3 Which of the following statements is true in the UK?:
   a People have a legal right to request specific medical treatments
   b Personal statements are legally binding
   c Advance statements are legally binding in Scotland but not in England and Wales
   d Advance statements are legally binding in England and Wales but not in Scotland
4 The main tasks of a Mental Health Tribunal include which of the following?:
   a Making decisions on applications for compulsory treatment orders (CTOs)
   b Deciding the appropriate medication to be given to a person subject to a CTO
   c Considering and adjudicating on appeals made against CTOs imposed under mental health legislation
   d Considering and adjudicating on conflicts between treatment and wishes set out in personal statements

---

REFERENCES

Adults with Incapacity (Scotland) Act 2000. a.s.p 4. www.legislation.gov.uk/asp/2000/4/contents.

Bayer R. 1981. *Homosexuality and American Psychiatry: The Politics of Diagnosis*. New York: Basic Books.

Convention for the Protection of Human Rights and Fundamental Freedoms (European Human Rights Convention) (Rome, 4 November 1950; T.S. 71(1953)); Cmd. 8969. www.echr.coe.int/Documents/Convention_ENG.pdf.

Donnelly J. 2013. *Universal Human Rights in Theory and Practice*. 3rd ed. Ithaca, NY: Cornell University Press.

Fischhoff B and J Kadvany. 2011. *Risk: A Very Short Introduction*. Oxford: Oxford University Press.

Fisher M and M Scott. 2013. *Patient Safety and Managing Risk in Nursing.* London: Sage.

Glover J. 1990. *Causing Death and Saving Lives.* London: Penguin.

Human Rights Act 1998. C. 42. www.legislation.gov.uk/ukpga/1998/42/contents

Kant I. 2005. *The Moral Law: Groundwork of the metaphysics of morals,* Translated and analysed by H.J Paton. London: Routledge.

Mental Health (Care and Treatment) (Scotland) Act 2003. A.s.p 13. www.legislation. gov.uk/asp/2003/13/contents.

Millan Committee. 2001. *New Directions: Report on the Review of the Mental Health (Scotland) Act 1984.* (Chairman: Rt. Hon Bruce Millan). Edinburgh: Scottish Executive.

Musto D. 1991. "A Historical Perspective". Edited by S Bloch and P Chodoff. *Psychiatric Ethics* (2nd ed.). Oxford: Oxford University Press.

Nascimento A. 2016. "Human Rights and the Paradigms of Cosmopolitanism: From Rights to Humanity". Edited by M Lutz-Bachmann and A Nascimento. *Human Rights, Human Dignity, and Cosmopolitan Ideals. Essays on Critical Theory and Human Rights.* New York, NY: Routledge.

Office of The United Nations High Commissioner for Human Rights (OHCHR). 2016. Universal Human Rights Instruments. [online]. Geneva: United Nations. www.ohchr. org/EN/ProfessionalInterest/Pages/UniversalHumanRightsInstruments.aspx.

Osborn LA. 2009. "From Beauty to Despair: The Rise and Fall of the American State Mental Hospital". *Psychiatric Quarterly,* 80: 219–31.

Pinel P. 1806. *A treatise on insanity, in which are contained the principles of a new and more practical nosology of maniacal disorders than has yet been offered to the public.* Translated from the French by D.D. Davis. London: W. Todd.

Richardson G. 2002. "Autonomy, guardianship and mental disorder: one problem, two solutions". *The Modern Law Review,* 65: 702–22.

Rousseau J-J. 1913. *Social Contract and Discourses.* Translated with introduction by GDH Cole. New York: E.P. Dutton.

Scotland Act 1998. c. 46. www.legislation.gov.uk/ukpga/1998/46/contents.

Scottish Human Rights Commission. 2010. *Care about Rights?* Glasgow: Scottish Human Rights Commission.

Seneca LA. 1968. *The Stoic Philosophy of Seneca: Essays and Letters.* Translated and with an introduction by M. Hadas. New York: W.W. Norton.

Szasz TS. 1997. *Insanity: The Idea and its Consequences.* New York: Syracuse University Press.

Szasz TS. 2010. *The Myth of Mental Illness.* Revisited paper presented at the Annual Conference of the Royal College of Psychiatrists, Edinburgh.

United Nations. 1948. *Universal Declaration of Human Rights.* New York: United Nations.

World Health Organisation. 2016. *Health Topics: Mental Disorders.* [online]. Geneva: World Health Organisation. www.who.int/topics/mental_disorders/en/.

TO LEARN MORE

Mental Welfare Commission for Scotland. 2011. *The Right to Treat.* Edinburgh: Mental Welfare Commission for Scotland.

Mental Welfare Commission for Scotland. 2013. *Good Practice Guide: Deprivation of Liberty.* Edinburgh: Mental Welfare Commission for Scotland.

Mental Welfare Commission Scotland: www.mwcscot.org.uk.

Mental Health Tribunal for Scotland: www.mhtscotland.gov.uk.

Principles into Practice: www.principlesintopractice.net.

ANSWERS TO REVIEW QUESTIONS 13.1 P. 184

1 The guidance document 'The Universal Declaration of Human Rights' was designed to protect the rights of:

a Everyone everywhere

2 The Adults with Incapacity (Scotland) Act 2000 is not based on which of the following principles?:

d Control financial decisions

3 Which of the following statements is true in the UK?:

d Advance statements are legally binding in England and Wales but not in Scotland

4 The main tasks of a Mental Health Tribunal include which of the following?:

a Making decisions on applications for compulsory treatment orders (CTOs)

c Considering and adjudicating on appeals made against CTOs imposed under mental health legislation

CHAPTER 14

Gender

Sensitive practice beyond binary divisions

Agnes Higgins and Ailish Gill

KEY POINTS 14.1

Gender goes beyond the binary division of male and female, and includes people who identify as transgender or gender fluid.

Gender difference in relation to substance misuse is not confined to biological difference but includes social and cultural influences.

Gender impacts on the person's journey into substance misuse, their willingness to access support and help, as well as influencing the way society and professionals interpret and respond to the person's needs.

Gender sensitive services means that professionals are knowledgeable of existing gender differences and are competent to incorporate these differences into care.

A failure to systematically take gender differences into account results in existing inequities being perpetuated and reinforced.

INTRODUCTION

Substance misuse and dependence are major public health issues that have significant impact on the person, family and community. The importance of gender in the context of all aspects of health is becoming increasingly recognised at an international level (World Health Organisation 2002). In the context of substance misuse gender identity is a critical issue, as it influences people's socioeconomic positions, roles, relationships, as well as societal expectations. Gender identity also impacts on people's journey into substance misuse, their willingness to access support and help, as well as influencing the way professionals interpret and respond to the person's needs.

This chapter explores gender identity and substance misuse, beyond the traditional binary division of male and female, with a view to highlighting the importance of understanding the life world of the person seeking help, as well as creating a culture where all gender identities and sexual orientations are considered important factors in the provision of person-centred and gender sensitive services. It is also important that practitioners recognise the often subtle, hidden and unexpected ways gender infiltrates to shape personal beliefs and values, and influence interactions in the therapeutic context.

LANGUAGE, IDENTITIES AND CATEGORISATION

Before we consider the complex interface between substance misuse, gender identity and sexual orientation, there is a need to examine the meaning of concepts such as sex, gender, gender identity, gender expression and sexual orientation.

REFLECTIVE PRACTICE EXERCISE 14.1

Time: 20 minutes

Samir is attending a substance misuse support group for men that you are facilitating. During the discussion Samir says that he was born as a girl in Nairobi but from the age of four he knew that nature and biology did not get it right. On leaving his home country and coming to Europe at the age of 16 years, he started a transition process and now lives his life as a man, even though he has not undergone gender reassignment surgery. He is the CEO of his own advertising company which he started seven years ago. He describes himself as a caring, emotional, assertive person with a love of rugby, cooking and the violin. Samir is not in a relationship and is attracted to men, and has only ever had sexual relationships with men.

- How would you describe Samir's sex, gender, gender identity, gender expression and sexual orientation?
- Do you think Samir should be permitted to continue in a therapy group designed for men?
- How would you respond to a member of the group who insists Samir is a woman and continually uses female pronouns when talking to or about Samir?

Language is not a neutral vehicle for expressing thoughts and emotions in everyday interactions, but has the potential to shape thinking and behaviour, and can restrict or expand our conceptualisation of the world. Thus, understanding language is not just about political correctness, but about developing an ethical sensitivity to how labels and categories frame identities, exclude or include, respect or disrespect difference, and frame thought, actions and the production of knowledge. This section examines some key concepts and categories that are not only taken for granted but are often confused or conflated.

The term 'sex' is used in everyday language in two ways: it is used to describe the 'sexual' or physical 'sexual act' (Beasley 2005), and used to identify a person's designation at birth as either male or female, based on biological and morphological differences, such as differences in anatomy (genitalia/reproductive organs) or biology (sex chromosomes and/or hormones). Within this biological perspective xy chromosome pairing denotes 'male' and xx chromosomes 'female'. However, 2 percent of the population are born intersex with sex characteristics (chromosomes, genitals, and/or hormonal structure) that fall outside the accepted norms of male or female. This very fact clearly indicates that sex is a spectrum and that people with variations of sex characteristics other than male or female do exist, thus challenging the simple binary division of male and female.

The term 'gender' is an invention of the twentieth century, replacing sex as a denominator of difference (Nye 1999). Like 'sex', 'gender' has traditionally been linked to the physical body, the person's genitals and the belief in the existence of only two mutually exclusive sex typologies (male and female). Today, the alignment of gender exclusively to biology is also challenged by people who identify as gender non-binary, gender fluid or transgender. Gender non-binary is an umbrella term for gender identities that fall outside the gender binary of male and female. This includes individuals whose gender identity is neither exclusively male nor female, a combination of male and female, or between or beyond genders. Similarly, gender fluid is a term used by people who do not feel confined by the binary division of male and female, and whose gender varies over time. Transgender (T) is an umbrella term referring to people whose gender identity and/or gender expression differs from the sex they were assigned at birth. A trans boy/man is a person who was assigned female at birth but who identifies as male or lives as a boy/man. Similarly, a trans girl/woman is a person who was assigned male at birth but who identifies as female or lives as a girl/woman. Some trans men and women make physical changes through hormones or surgery; others do not (Higgins et al. 2016).

Related to the term 'gender' are the terms gender identity, gender role and gender expression. Gender identity refers to a person's deeply-felt identification as male or female, which may or may not correspond to the sex they were assigned at birth. The term gender role, describes the behaviours that are viewed as masculine or feminine by a particular culture. In other words, society's expectations of what it means to be male or female and what is considered appropriate for men and women. While ideologies of masculinity and femininity change over time, traditionally, normative masculinity positions men as self-reliant, tough, competitive, emotionally in control if not emotionally inexpressive, and dominant. By contrast, western feminine ideologies view women as emotional, caring, compassionate, and more passive and maternal than men. Thus, gender as Ettorre (2004:329) suggests is 'a normative and moralising system that exerts social control' on men and women.

The term gender expression refers to the way in which a person acts to communicate gender within a given culture, which includes mannerisms, grooming, physical characteristics, social interactions and speech patterns (Higgins et al. 2016). A person's gender expression may or may not be consistent with socially prescribed gender roles, and may or may not reflect gender identity (American Psychological Association 2009).

The term 'sexual orientation' refers to a person's physical, emotional or romantic attraction to another person. Categories of sexual orientation include people attracted to the opposite sex (heterosexual), same sex (lesbian (L) or gay (G)), both sexes (bisexual (B)), or neither. However, research indicates that sexual orientation does not always appear in such definable categories or fixed positioning and can be fluid for some people, so like gender it is best to think of sexual orientation on a continuum as opposed to some binary positioning of attraction.

REFLECTIVE PRACTICE EXERCISE 14.2

Time: 20 minutes

Now that you have read this section, please return to the exercise and reconsider your response. If you have changed your response spend a few moments considering why that might be.

GENDERED DISCOURSE OF SUBSTANCE MISUSE

Research clearly reveals that the prevalence of substance use differs greatly depending on gender. Although the prevalence of substance misuse (both alcohol and illicit drugs) among women is on the increase in some countries (United Nations 2012), due to the changing social position and status of women, substance misuse continues to be male dominated. The lifetime prevalence rates of alcohol and drug dependence are much higher in men than women (Substance Abuse and Mental Health Services Administration (SAMHSA) 2011, WHO 2001), with the WHO (2001) estimating that in developed countries, approximately 1 in 5 men and 1 in 12 women develop alcohol dependence during their lives. There is also a pronounced gender gap in relation to illicit drug consumption. In nearly all countries where solid gender-disaggregated data are available illicit drug use levels among women are significantly lower than that found among men (Degenhardt and Hall 2012). While female drug use is about two thirds that of males in countries such as the USA, in contrast for example, the gender gap is much more pronounced in countries such as India and Indonesia, where female drug use is as low as one tenth that of males (United Nations 2012). While illicit drug use among males greatly exceeds that of females, with the 'typical' substance misuser profiled in the research being young males, a notable exception to this is the misuse of prescription drugs such as tranquillisers, sedatives and anti-depressants, which is much higher among women in countries where data are available (United Nations 2012).

The simple gender binary division which has guided the majority of research in the area, does not give the complete picture, as it ignores those who identify as transgender and gender fluid. Despite awareness of health disparities experienced by transgender people in other aspects of life (Maguen and Shipherd 2010, Higgins et al. 2016), as a group they are largely invisible within the larger studies on substance misuse, hence, robust information on the pattern of prevalence among this group is rather patchy. What is available estimates rates of substance misuse to be about 30 percent (SAMHSA 2011), with higher rates of substance misuse being reported among transgender identified young adults (Coulter et al. 2015) and transgender women involved in the sex industry (Hoffman 2014, Nadal et al. 2014).

As neither those categorised as male, female or transgender are homogenous groups, a deeper analysis, especially in relation to sexual orientation, reveals a more nuanced picture. Numerous studies over the years indicate that in comparison to heterosexual cohorts, lesbian, gay and bisexual (LGB) people are more likely to use alcohol and drugs, have higher rates of substance abuse, are less likely to abstain from use, and are more likely to continue heavy drinking into later life (SAMHSA 2001, Cochran and Cauce 2006, McCabe et al. 2010), with studies indicating that drug and alcohol misuse (Tucker et al. 2008, Corliss et al. 2008, 2010), including prescription drugs (Kecojevic et al. 2012) are also much higher among young LGB people than their heterosexual peers.

A further within-group analysis also reveals other variations. From a male perspective gay and bisexual men have higher rates of alcohol and drug dependency than heterosexual men (Ford and Jasinski 2006, Tucker et al. 2008, McCabe et al. 2009, Hughes et al. 2010), with drug use being more problematic than alcohol for gay men (Green and Feinstein 2012). Studies have found that gay men and men who have sex with men (MSM) are significantly more likely than heterosexual men to have used marijuana, psychedelics, hallucinogens, stimulants, sedatives, cocaine, 'poppers' and party drugs (SAMHSA 2001). Although there is a difference in rates of substance misuse between heterosexual and gay men, the difference between lesbian and heterosexual women appears to be much larger, which may be due to the high baseline substance misuse among all men. Indeed, in McCabe et al.'s (2009) study substance misuse by sexual minority women exceeded those of sexual minority men.

From a female perspective although there is little difference with respect to the misuse of medically prescribed drugs among women who identify as lesbian and their heterosexual peers (McCabe et al. 2004), there is consistent evidence that lesbian and bisexual women have much higher rates of alcohol, marijuana and cocaine problems and dependency than heterosexual women (Scheer et al. 2002, McCabe et al. 2004, Ford and Jasinski 2006). This is particularly the case for younger lesbian and bisexual women (Drabble et al.

2005, Ziyadeh et al. 2007, Tucker et al. 2008), as female gender does not appear to be a strong protective factor against substance misuse within the LBT female community.

JOURNEYS INTO SUBSTANCE MISUSE

The journey into substance misuse is influenced by a myriad of factors involving personal, social and environmental factors, with gender and sexual orientation also influencing people's journey.

REFLECTIVE PRACTICE EXERCISE 14.3

Time: 10 minutes
- How might the different positioning of men and women influence their substance use and misuse?
- What personal, societal and subcultural factors do you consider leave the LGBT community at risk of substance misuse?

A considerable number of men and women accessing treatment for substance misuse have experienced different forms of trauma, including childhood trauma, and sexual and physical abuse (Kendler et al. 2000, Dube et al. 2006, Begle et al. 2011). In addition, women report high rates of domestic violence, including intimate partner violence, with Kecojevic et al. (2012) reporting that young adults exposed to various forms of child abuse were at risk of early initiation into prescription drug misuse. Having a partner who is a substance misuser can also be integral to women's initiation into substance misuse, their continuing use and relapse (O'Mahony-Carey 2009), with research over the years indicating that women are more likely to report social network pressure from friends, family and sexual partners as the cause of initiation, including first time injecting (Crofts et al. 1996, Day et al. 2005, Frajzyngier et al. 2007). In addition, women experience more adverse medical, psychological and social consequences of substance use and misuse, including heightened risk of sexual exploitation (Greenfield 2007), with problematic drug and alcohol use being identified as one of a number of risk factors for women engaging in sex work, as well as a barrier to them ceasing selling sex (Sanders 2007, Balfour and Allen 2014).

Those that explore differences in people's journeys into substance misuse at the level of sexual orientation highlight that gay men are more likely than heterosexual men to report childhood sexual abuse, childhood neglect, partner violence and assault with a weapon (Hughes et al. 2010), with lesbian and bisexual women twice as likely to report life-time victimisation in comparison to heterosexual women (Hughes et al. 2010). Others focus on the minority stress model, which posits that substance misuse is a direct result of multiple forms of stigma, prejudice, discrimination and exclusion that people within the LGBT community experience (Meyer 1995, 2003, McCabe et al. 2009, Green and Feinstein 2012). According to this model substance misuse is viewed as a means of coping with and regulating the negative feelings associated with minority stress, with some studies reporting that LGBT youth commence using alcohol and illicit drugs to deal with negative feelings associated with their LGBT identity (Ford and Jasinski 2006), and others finding that LGBT people who experience victimisation are more likely to report lifetime substance use problems (Mereish et al. 2014). While LGB people experience many forms of discrimination and victimization, transgender people in particular experience a higher burden of discrimination in multiple settings, including within the family and LGB community, with family rejection because of gender identity being strongly associated with substance misuse in transgender and gender non-conforming individuals (Klein and Golub 2016). Family rejection also means that LGBT people lack the emotional support that other people get from their family when they encounter other challenges throughout their lives.

Writers who take a social learning theory perspective suggest that LGBT people occupy distinct social spaces, with their social life limited to bars or clubs, which increases exposure to alcohol and drugs, and normalizes engagement in activities that are alcohol and drug related (Trocki et al. 2005). For LGBT people from an ethnic or racial minority background, finding a comfortable place in society is even more complex and difficult, as they are not just coping with gender identity and sexual orientation issues amid a tangle of cultural traditions, values, and norms, but they may also have to cope with racism and discrimination within the LGBT community.

HELP SEEKING BEHAVIOUR

Similar to journeys into substance misuse, pathways to support and barriers to accessing support may also be gendered. While women are traditionally considered more likely than men to seek help for problems, including mental health problems, and are no longer invisible in substance misuse research, women are underrepresented in substance misuse treatment programmes relative to the prevalence of their substance abuse problems (Greenfield et al. 2007, United Nations 2012).

Case Study 14.1 – Help seeking behaviour

You are concerned about a 28-year-old underweight woman Fran, mother of two young children who presented to the emergency department with a broken arm following a fall down the stairs two days ago. Fran was noticeably uncomfortable and anxious when asked about her alcohol intake. Although she denied usage, you strongly suspect from your assessment that intoxication contributed to her fall and delay in seeking help. She is reluctant to make contact with her partner who is away traveling on work business.

SELF-ASSESSMENT EXERCISE 14.1

> **Time: 15 minutes**
> - What factors might be influencing Fran's decisions to disclose and seek help?
> - How might your gender impact on the situation?

While there are many cross cultural gender variations in relation to the consumption of alcohol and other substances, with different rules and norms governing what is deemed acceptable behaviour, feminist writers note that, irrespective of culture, women who misuse substances, especially illegal drugs, are considered doubly deviant, first for their drug use, and secondly for their involvement in what has traditionally been considered a 'male domain' (Bandwell and Bammer 2006:504). In particular, women who misuse substances are more heavily stigmatised in cultural contexts where the consumption of alcohol and other substances is strongly divided along gender lines, with their substance misuse being judged much more harshly than substance misuse within the male population. Consequently, acknowledging the need for help and help seeking may be extremely difficult for many women.

For women to seek help, they first need to believe that the cost will not outweigh any potential benefit, and for some women, especially those who are mothers, fears of potential negative consequences may make help seeking a near impossibility. In all cultures, women who misuse substances and who are mothers are portrayed as the antithesis of the 'good or ideal mother', with pregnant women viewed as 'lethal foetal containers' engaging in a form of child abuse and neglect (Ettorre 2004). Consequently, women in these circumstances may avoid contact with services for fear of negative judgement around parenting ability and custody issues in relation to their children. Fears around custody loss are also heightened for lesbian or transgender parents who are already constructed by society as suspect parents (Erlandsson et al. 2010). Consequently, they may be even more reluctant to seek help for fear of further negative judgements and discrimination.

Greenfield et al. (2007) in their review highlight other barriers including lack of childcare facilities within or outwith treatment programmes or a caregiving role within the family, which may result in women prioritising the needs of family members rather than themselves. Trauma histories, including sexual and physical abuse, may make mixed gender treatment programmes less desirable to women. In addition, high rates of co-morbid mental health problems such as depression, eating disorders and post-traumatic stress disorder may make it difficult for women to initiate help seeking and obtain treatment for both problems. Many women with substance use problems may also live with a partner or other family members with a substance use problem, which makes it more difficult to obtain support to undergo treatment and remain substance free long-term.

As previously highlighted, different cultures have different rules and norms governing sexual orientation and sexual behaviour which may compound challenges in accessing appropriate help and services. For individuals who do not identify as heterosexual and live in cultures, communities or families where there is a high intolerance of LGBT identities, concerns over confidentiality, personal safety, and fear of discrimination and rejection may influence help seeking behaviour. In addition, fear of the medical system, especially the mental health–substance use system which has, in the past, pathologised LGBT identities, and attempted to modify people's behaviour, through the use of aversion therapy, psychotherapy, libido-reducing drugs and electroconvulsive therapy, may make LGBT people fearful and reluctant to seek help (Higgins 2008).

Case Study 14.2 – Yousef

You are a health professional working with Yousef, a 15-year-old bisexual male living at home with his parents, on issues related to self-harm and social anxiety for several weeks. During the session Yousef hesitantly disclosed that he uses substances to pluck up the courage to go out to bars where he meets various men and women with whom he has unprotected sex. He is worried that you will report this information to his parents.

SELF-ASSESSMENT EXERCISE 14.2

Time: 15 minutes
- What issues need to be taken into consideration when working with families with a high level of intolerance for (1) the LGBT community (2) people with mental health or substance misuse problems?
- How would you respond to Yousef's concerns? Would your response differ if Yousef was a female, and if so why?

SERVICE PROVISION: AN EQUITABLE APPROACH?

Data presented so far, in this chapter, underscores the need to provide services that are equitable and ensure that people who identify as male, female, transgender, or any other gender identity have access to the resources they need to satisfy their respective health needs.

REFLECTIVE PRACTICE EXERCISE 14.4

Time: 10 minutes

In response to a question on whether the substance abuse programme is gender sensitive and one that is LGBT inclusive your manager states that the service does not discriminate based on gender identity or sexual orientation and provides the exact same treatment and service to the men and women attending.

In terms of equality, equity, and respect for individuality what concerns might you have about this response?

Unfortunately, research indicates that substance abuse services, for a variety of reasons, are neither gender sensitive nor LGBT affirmative. First, from a gender perspective research suggests that historically male cultural norms dominate treatment programmes, with few substance misuse programmes taking into account the different needs of men and women (Claus et al. 2007; Cochran et al. 2007). Yet the limited research available suggests that, for a number of reasons, women-only programmes are perceived by women to be more beneficial than a mixed-sex programme. Women report experiencing less sexual harassment within women-only programmes, greater ease in discussing issues such as children, sexuality, prostitution and sexual/physical abuse, and greater likelihood of encountering a more empathetic and less confrontational therapy environment. In addition, retention rates appear to be higher in women-only programmes, with length of stay being positively associated with availability of childcare facilities or policies that allowed children to accompany their mothers in treatment (Sun 2006; Claus et al. 2007; Greenfield et al. 2007).

Second, despite substance misuse disproportionately impacting on the lives of the transgender community, the majority of the research into substance misuse collects data using the binary options of male and female. In addition to reinforcing the idea that binary identities are the only valid identities (Flentje et al. 2015), creating a sense of 'otherness' and exclusion, the absence of transgender identities within research leaves policy makers and service providers without robust data on the needs of transgender and gender non-conforming people to inform decision making. Similarly, despite evidence of the differing needs and challenges encountered by sexual minority groups, services designed specifically to meet the needs of LGB people are virtually non-existent (Cochran et al. 2007), with a dearth of evidence on the efficacy of available programmes for sexual minority groups (Green and Feinstein 2012). Consequently, existing inequalities within society are recreated and maintained within substance misuse programmes.

Third, whether healthcare professionals are aware of it or not, they are not immune to the discriminatory attitudes towards LGBT individuals held within society. There is evidence that when men and women access substance misuse services they encounter practitioners that sometimes respond based on gender stereotypes (DeJong et al. 1993), hold heteronormative, negative or ambivalent attitudes towards LGBT people (Eliason and Hughes 2004, Reisner et al. 2015), lack knowledge on LGBT issues or ignore the possible relationship between LGBT people's lives and substance misuse (Cochran et al. 2007), including the minority stress framework. Research also suggests that women with mental health issues, including substance misuse, who are parenting children are subjected to a greater amount of surveillance by practitioners and social services, with greater risks that children may be taken into care (Bandwell and Bammer 2006). In addition, despite claims of objectivity, research focusing on women who are mothers often uses a language of deficit, inability, and positions women as damaging to children, defective as parents, and less responsive emotionally, which in itself is a form of academic discrimination undermining dignity and equality.

GENDER SENSITIVE CARE PRACTICES

A gender sensitive approach recognises diversity as a core aspect of care and addresses gender biases in all health care practices.

REFLECTIVE PRACTICE EXERCISE 14.5

Time: 15 minutes
You have been asked to conduct an audit of a substance abuse service to identify the degree to which it is gender sensitive. What criteria might you use to devise the audit tool?

The importance of addressing gender inequalities and promoting healthcare practices that recognise, acknowledge and take into consideration the different needs of men and women and different groups of women and men is recognised internationally. By simply focusing on the binary division of male and female, and ignoring or not making explicit people who identify as transgender or gender fluid, there is a risk that those promoting gender sensitive services are themselves perpetuating inequalities. Table 14.1 provides some examples of gender sensitive criteria at an organisational and practitioner level that you might consider including.

LGBT AFFIRMATIVE PRACTICE

The LGBT community, although far from a homogenous group, has a shared history of stigmatisation, discrimination and health disparities with poor recognition of their needs by substance use services. Substance use services can perpetuate heteronormative cultures or challenge discriminatory and stigmatising LGBT practices.

Table 14.1 Examples of gender sensitive criteria

Organisational level	Gender concerns and gender equality are addressed within all organisational and clinical policies on substance misuse to create legitimacy for efforts to improve gender equity of programmes. Definition of gender within the policies moves beyond the binary division of male and female to include transgender and gender fluid identities.
	Evidence that service used gender-disaggregated data in planning and designing services, and are collecting gender-disaggregated data (including information on transgender) to inform ongoing service delivery.
	Organisation provides education to staff on gender issues and gender-sensitive care including training to detect, discuss, and refer individuals to services that address sexual orientation and gender-based violence.
	Gender sensitive care is identified as a criterion in evaluations or audits conducted within the service.
Practitioner level	Care and treatment models accommodate the realities of the differences between male, female and transgender people. Professionals take account of how and why people misuse substances from a gendered perspective.
	Professionals acknowledge gender differences in communication and adjust communication styles to accommodate differences.
	Professionals understand the experience of women's lives and the lives of people who identify as transgender and develop services that are based on trauma informed principles.
	Professionals review research evidence when planning care to consider if findings are equally applicable to those who identify as male, female and transgender. For example, does evidence support gender-specific group programmes for people who have experienced sexual trauma?
	Professionals are sensitive to the need to provide a safe space where women can discuss issues of sexual abuse, domestic and intimate partner violence, and safety and work from a trauma informed perspective.
	Professionals are respectful of people's gender identities and their requests for same sex practitioners.
	Professionals interrogate their own gender stereotypes and have the confidence to challenge gender stereotyping within the team that is exploitative or harmful.
	Professionals create therapeutic context that promotes shared power, control and decision making between all individuals irrespective of gender.
	Professionals provide health information that makes explicit gender differences and avoids gender stereotyping and discriminating language.
	Child friendly substance misuse programmes and services are available.

Case Study 14.3 – LGBT sensitive practice

Craig, a mental health professional, engages an Arabic interpreter to assist with a mental health assessment of Mustafa, a 25-year-old male with limited English, brought to services by police as a consequence of agitated behaviour on the street.

In the initial stages of the interview the interpreter becomes outraged shouting in English that Mustafa should be imprisoned or hanged for engaging in sex with another man.

SELF-ASSESSMENT EXERCISE 14.3

Time: 15 minutes
- What organisational issues arise for you in this situation?
- What issues need to be taken into consideration before undertaking clinical work with a professional with a high level of cultural intolerance for (1) the LGBT community (2) people experiencing mental health–substance use problems?

LGBT-affirmative care requires organisations and professionals that work in the area of substance misuse to understand how the historical, cultural and social context of LGBT individual's lives impact on their journey into substance misuse, their experience of health care as well as their recovery journey. LGBT-affirmative policies and practices are open, inclusive, non-discriminatory and welcoming of those that identify as LGBT. Table 14.2 provides some examples of LGBT-affirmative practices.

CONCLUSION

Ensuring the same access for everyone to substance use services assumes that everyone has similar health statuses and similar healthcare needs. When it comes to gender and substance use/dependency, differences in gender go beyond biological differences and include social and cultural influences. Research clearly indicates that gender not only shapes people's journey into use and dependency, but influences help seeking behaviour, the treatment provided, as well as society's and professionals' views of people who misuse substances. Although considered a male domain, changing patterns among women suggest that female gender is no longer a protective factor. In the context of substance misuse, the binary division of male and female has dominated research and as a result information on people who identify as transgender or gender fluid is lacking. At a time when people's rights are increasingly being emphasised, evidence suggests that substance misuse programmes, if not

Table 14.2 Examples of LGBT-affirmative practices

Policies and service planning	Service policies make a clear statement of inclusiveness of LGBT people and zero tolerance of discriminatory practices by staff and by people who use the service.
	Service planning and development informed by research evidence on LGBT issues.
Organisational culture	Services display signs that highlight inclusiveness of LGBT people.
	Substance misuse programmes are developed that address the specific needs of LGBT people.
	All staff act as advocates by challenging heterosexism, homophobia, biphobia and transphobia within the organisation, irrespective of the source.
Professional practice and interpersonal communication	Professionals acknowledge the person's sexual orientation and gender identity, and promote safe and supportive relationships that are respectful of LGBT identities.
	Professionals work within a minority stress framework and recognise the different pathways into substance misuse for LGBT people, their fears and challenges in accessing support and being open about LGBT identities.
	Professionals recognise that for some LGBT people the only safe and inclusive space available is the bar or club scene, which may make it more difficult to avoid triggers to substance misuse and impact on recovery.
	Language used is inclusive and affirming of LGBT relationships and reflects the individual's preference.
	LGBT friendly reading material, literature and resources are provided, including information on local LGBT service and supports. In addition to gender, documentation is inclusive of LGB identities, where relevant.
Education and research	Professionals are informed and educated on LGBT issues, including LGBT issues as they relate to substance misuse.
	A process to address staff attitudes and practices that may be a barrier to LGBT-affirmative care is available.
	Research into LGBT identities and substance misuse is ongoing, including the impact of various models of care on health outcomes of LGBT people.

gender-blind, are gender neutral, with the impact of gender identity and sexual orientation being ignored. Gender sensitive services means that professionals are knowledgeable of existing gender differences and are competent to incorporate these differences into their decisions and care. If gender differences are not systematically taken into account by health professionals, existing inequities are perpetuated and reinforced.

REFERENCES

American Psychological Association. 2009. *Report of the APA Task Force on Gender Identity and Gender Variance.* Washington, D.C. American Psychological Association. www.apa.org/pi/lgbt/resources/policy/gender-identity-report.pdf.

Balfour R and J Allen. 2014. A *Review of the Literature on Sex Workers and Social Exclusion.* London: UCL Institute of Health Equity for Inclusion Health, Department of Health UK.

Banwell C and G Bammer. 2006. "Maternal habits: narratives of mothering, social position and drug use." *International Journal of Drug Policy* 17: 504–513.

Beasley C. 2005. *Gender and Sexuality: Critical Theories, Critical Thinkers.* London: Sage.

Begle AM, RF Hanson, C Kmett Danielson, MR McCart, KJ Ruggiero, AB Amstadter, HS Resnick, BE Saunders and DG Kilpatrick. 2011. "Longitudinal pathways of victimization, substance use, and delinquency: findings from the National Survey of Adolescents." *Addictive Behaviors* 36: 682–689.

Claus RE, RG Orwin, W Kissin, A Krupski, K Campbell and K Stark. 2007. "Does gender-specific substance abuse treatment for women promote continuity of care?" *Journal of Substance Abuse Treatment* 32: 27–39.

Cochran BN and AM Cauce. 2006. "Characteristics of lesbian, gay, bisexual, and transgender individuals entering substance abuse treatment." *Journal of Substance Abuse Treatment* 30: 135–146.

Cochran BN, MK Peavy and JS Robohm. 2007. "Do specialized services exist for LGBT individuals seeking treatment for substance misuse? A study of available treatment programs." *Substance Use and Misuse* 42: 161–176.

Corliss HL, M Rosario, D Wypij, LB Fisher and SB Austin. 2008. "Sexual orientation disparities in longitudinal alcohol use patterns among adolescents: findings from the Growing Up Today Study." *Archives of Pediatric and Adolescent Medicine* 162: 1071–1078.

Corliss HL, M Rosario, D Wypij, SA Wylie, AL Frazier and SB Austin. 2010. "Sexual orientation and drug use in a longitudinal cohort study of U.S. adolescents." *Addictive Behaviors* 35: 517–521.

Coulter RW, JR Blosnich, LA Bukowski, AL Herrick, DE Siconolfi and RD Stall. 2015. "Differences in alcohol use and alcohol-related problems between transgender- and nontransgender-identified young adults." *Drug and Alcohol Dependence* 154: 251–259.

Crofts N, R Louie, D Rosenthal and D Jolley. 1996. "The first hit: circumstances surrounding initiation into injecting." *Addiction* 91: 1187–1196.

Day CA, J Ross, P Dietze and K Dolan. 2005. "Initiation to heroin injecting among heroin users in Sydney, Australia: cross sectional survey." *Harm Reduction Journal* 2: 1–7.

Degenhardt L and W Hall. 2012. "Extent of illicit drug use and dependence, and their contribution to the global burden of disease." *Lancet* 379: 55–70.

DeJong CAJ, W van den Brink and JAM Jansen. 1993. "Sex role stereotypes and clinical judgement: how therapists view their alcoholic patients." *Journal of Substance Abuse Treatment* 10: 383–389.

Drabble L, LT Midanik and K Trocki. 2005. "Reports of alcohol consumption and alcohol-related problems among homosexual, bisexual and heterosexual respondents: results from the 2000 National Alcohol Survey." *Journal of Studies on Alcohol* 66: 111–120.

Dube SR, JW Miller, DW Brown, WH Giles, VJ Felitti, M Dong and RF Anda. 2006. "Adverse childhood experiences and the association with ever using alcohol and initiating alcohol use during adolescence." *Journal of Adolescent Health* 38: 444 e1–10.

Eliason MJ and T Hughes. 2004. "Treatment counsellor's attitudes about lesbian, gay, bisexual, and transgendered clients: urban vs. rural settings." *Substance Use and Misuse* 39: 625–644.

Erlandsson K, H Linder and E Häggström-Nordin. 2010. "Experiences of gay women during their partner's pregnancy and childbirth." *British Journal of Midwifery* 18: 99–103.

Ettorre E. 2004. "Revisioning women and drug use: gender sensitivity, embodiment and reducing harm." *International Journal of Drug Policy* 15: 327–335.

Flentje A, CL Bacca and BN Cochran. 2015. "Missing data in substance abuse research? Researchers' reporting practices of sexual orientation and gender identity." *Drug and Alcohol Dependence* 147: 280–284.

Ford JA and JL Jasinski. 2006. "Sexual orientation and substance use among college students." *Addictive Behaviors* 31: 404–413.

Frajzyngier V, A Neaigus, AV Gyarmathy, M Miller and SR Friedman. 2007. "Gender differences in injection risk behaviors at the first injection episode." *Drug and Alcohol Dependence* 89: 145–152.

Green KE and BA Feinstein. 2012. "Substance use in lesbian, gay, and bisexual populations: an update on empirical research and implications for treatment." *Psychology of Addictive Behaviors* 26: 265–278.

Greenfield SF, AJ Brooks, SM Gordon, CA Green, F Kropp, RK McHugh, M Lincoln, D Hien and GM Miele. 2007. "Substance abuse treatment entry, retention, and outcome in women: A review of the literature." *Drug and Alcohol Dependence* 86: 1–21.

Higgins A. 2008. "Sexuality and gender." In P Barker (Ed.), P*sychiatric and Mental Health Nursing: The Craft of Caring.* 618–625. London: Hodder Arnold.

Higgins A, L Doyle, C Downes, R Murphy, D Sharek, J DeVries, T Begley, E McCann, F Sheerin and S Smyth. 2016. *The LGBT Ireland report: national study of the mental health and wellbeing of lesbian, gay, bisexual, transgender and intersex people in Ireland.* Dublin: GLEN and BeLonG To.

Hoffman BR. 2014. "The interaction of drug use, sex work, and HIV among transgender women." *Substance Use and Misuse* 49: 1049–1053.

Hughes T, SE McCabe, SC Wilsnack, BT West and CJ Boyd. 2010. "Victimization and substance use disorders in a national sample of heterosexual and sexual minority women and men." *Addiction* 105: 2130–2140.

Kecojevic A, CF Wong, SM Schrager, K Silva, JJ Bloom, E Iverson and SE Lankenau. 2012. "Initiation into prescription drug misuse: differences between lesbian, gay, bisexual, transgender (LGBT) and heterosexual high-risk young adults in Los Angeles and New York." *Addictive Behaviors* 37: 1289–1293.

Kendler KS, CM Bulik, J Silberg, JM Hettema, J Myers and CA Prescott. 2000. "Childhood sexual abuse and adult psychiatric and substance use disorders in women: an epidemiological and cotwin control analysis." *Archive of General Psychiatry* 57: 953–959.

Klein A and SA Golub. 2016. "Family rejection as a predictor of suicide attempts and substance misuse among transgender and gender nonconforming adults." *LGBT Health* 3: 193–199.

Maguen S and JC Shipherd. 2010. "Suicide risk among transgender individuals." *Psychology & Sexuality* 1: 34–43.

McCabe SE, TL Hughes and CJ Boyd. 2004. "Substance use and misuse: are bisexual women at greater risk?" *Journal of Psychoactive Drugs* 36: 217–225.

McCabe SE, TL Hughes, WB Bostwick, BT West and CJ Boyd. 2009. "Sexual orientation, substance use behaviors and substance dependence in the United States." *Addiction* 104: 1333–1345.

McCabe SE, WB Bostwick, TL Hughes, BT West and CJ Boyd. 2010. "The relationship between discrimination and substance use disorders among lesbian, gay, and bisexual adults in the United States." *American Journal of Public Health* 100: 1946–1952.

Mereish EH, C O'Cleirigh and JB Bradford. 2014. "Interrelationships between LGBT-based victimization, suicide, and substance use problems in a diverse sample of sexual and gender minorities." *Psychology, Health & Medicine* 19: 1–13.

Meyer IH. 1995. "Minority stress and mental health in gay men." *Journal of Health & Social Behavior* 36: 38–56.

Meyer IH. 2003. "Prejudice, social stress, and mental health in lesbian, gay, and bisexual populations: conceptual issues and research evidence." *Psychological Bulletin* 129: 674–697.

Nadal KL, KC Davidoff and W Fujii-Doe. 2014. "Transgender women and the sex work industry: roots in systemic, institutional, and interpersonal discrimination." *Journal of Trauma and Dissociation* 15: 169–183.

Nye R. 1999. *Sexuality: Oxford Readers*. Oxford: Oxford University Press.

O'Mahony-Carey S. 2009. "An exploratory study of the treatment needs of female drug and alcohol mis-users." *Critical Social Thinking: Policy and Practice* 1: 315–332.

Reisner SL, ST Pardo, KE Gamarel, JM White Hughto, DJ Pardee and CL Keo-Meier. 2015. "Substance use to cope with stigma in healthcare among U.S. female-to-male trans masculine adults." *LGBT Health* 2: 324–332.

Sanders T. 2007. "Protecting the health and safety of female sex workers: the responsibility of all." *BJOG* 114: 791–793.

Scheer S, CA Parks, W McFarland, K Page-Shafer, V Delgado, JD Ruiz, F Molitor and JD Klausner. 2002. "Self-reported sexual identity, sexual behaviors and health risks." *Journal of Lesbian Studies* 7: 69–83.

Substance Abuse and Mental Health Services Administration (SAMHSA). 2001. *A Providers introduction to Substance Abuse Treatment for Lesbian, Gay, Bisexual, and Transgender Individuals*. HHS Pub. No. (SMA) 12–4104 Revised 2003, 2009 and 2012. Rockville, MD: Substance Abuse and Mental Health Services Administration. http://store.samhsa.gov/shin/content//SMA12-4104/SMA12-4104.pdf.

Substance Abuse and Mental Health Services Administration (SAMHSA). 2011. *Addressing the Needs of Women and Girls: Developing Core Competencies for Mental Health and Substance Abuse Service Professionals*. HHS Pub. No. (SMA) 11–4657. Rockville, MD: Substance Abuse and Mental Health Services Administration. http://store.samhsa.gov/shin/content/SMA11–4657/SMA11–4657.pdf.

Sun A-P. 2006. "Program factors related to women's substance abuse treatment retention and other outcomes: a review and critique." *Journal of Substance Abuse Treatment* 30: 1–20.

Trocki KF, L Drabble and L Midanik. 2005. "Use of heavier drinking contexts among heterosexuals, homosexuals and bisexuals: results from a National Household Probability Survey." *Journal of Studies on Alcohol* 66: 105–110.

Tucker JS, PL Ellickson and DJ Klein. 2008. "Understanding differences in substance use among bisexual and heterosexual young women." *Womens Health Issues* 18: 387–398.

United Nations Office on Drugs and Crime. 2012. *World Drug Report 2012*. Vienna: United Nations. www.unodc.org/documents/data-and-analysis/WDR2012/WDR_2012_web_small.pdf.

World Health Organisation. 2001. Gender Disparities in Mental Health. Geneva: World Health Organisation. www.who.int/mental_health/media/en/242.pdf.

World Health Organisation. 2002. Gender and Mental Health. Geneva: World Health Organisation. http://apps.who.int/iris/bitstream/10665/68884/1/a85573.pdf.

Ziyadeh NJ, LA Prokop, LB Fisher, M Rosario, AE Field, CA Camargo, Jr. and BS Austin. 2007. "Sexual orientation, gender, and alcohol use in a cohort study of U.S. adolescent girls and boys." *Drug and Alcohol Dependence* 87: 119–130.

TO LEARN MORE

Greene ME. 2012. A practical guide for conducting and managing gender assessments in the health sector. Population Reference Bureau on behalf of the Interagency Gender Working Group: Washington DC. www.igwg.org/~/link.aspx?_id=EF882B1668CE4B208A669E7F2BD098BD&_z=z.

Greene ME and A Levack. 2010. Synchronizing gender strategies: a cooperative model for improving reproductive health and transforming gender relations. Interagency gender working group (IGWG). Washington: Population Reference Bureau; 2010. www.prb.org/igwg_media/synchronizing-gender-strategies.pdf.

Huygen C. 2006. "Understanding the needs of lesbian, gay, bisexual, and transgender people living with mental illness." *Medscape General Medicine.* 8: 29. www.ncbi.nlm.nih.gov/pmc/articles/PMC1785208/.

Institute of Medicine. 2011. The Health of Lesbian, Gay, Bisexual and Transgender People: Building a Foundation for a Better Understanding. http://nationalacademies.org/HMD/Reports/2011/The-Health-of-Lesbian-Gay-Bisexual-and-Transgender-People.aspx.

Luckstead A. 2004. Raising Issues: Lesbian, Gay, Bisexual, & Transgender People Receiving Services in the Public Mental Health System. Baltimore, MA: Center for Mental Health Services. www.tandfonline.com/doi/abs/10.1300/J236v08n03_03.

Ministry of Justice. 2013. Gender substance misuse and prisoners, Annexes. Ministry of Justice Analytical Services, UK. www.gov.uk/government/uploads/system/uploads/attachment_data/file/220061/gender-substance-misuse-mental-health-prisoners-annex.pdf.

New York City Health and Hospitals. 2015 [Vimeo]. LGBT Healthcare Training Video to Treat Me, You Have to Know Who I Am [Video file]. Retrieved from: https://vimeo.com/134039906.

Substance Abuse and Mental Health Services Administration (SAMHSA). 2015. Trauma-informed approach and trauma specific interventions. Rockville, MD; National Center for Trauma-Informed Care & alternatives to seclusion and restraint. www.samhsa.gov/ nctic/trauma-interventions.

Vanderheyden K [TEDxUHowest]. 2013, June 18th. The problem with sex and gender in health [Video file]. https://youtu.be/xnPq_MVv22c.

World Health Organisation. 2010. Gender, women and primary health care renewal: a discussion paper. Geneva: World Health Organisation: Department of Gender Women and Health. http://apps.who.int/iris/bitstream/10665/44430/1/9789241564038_eng. pdf.

World Professional Association for Transgender Health. 2011. "Standards of care for the health of transsexual, transgender, and gender nonconforming people, Version 7." *International Journal of Transgenderism* 13: 165–232. www.researchgate.net/publication/ 254366000_Standards_of_Care_for_the_Health_of_Transsexual_Transgender_and_ Gender_Non-Conforming_People.

CHAPTER 15

The family

Triadic collaboration: partners in mental health–substance use care and treatment

MJM Verhaegh and DPK Roeg

INTRODUCTION

Triadic collaboration; the individual, family and professional are partners in mental health–substance use care and treatment.

Some years ago I was walking with the chairman of the then Board in the grounds of our organization. We mused about the future of mental health-care and expressed the hope that the time would come when mental healthcare facilities would no longer be necessary. Moreover, that extraordinary persons would have a place in our society and that the area where we walked would get a new destination. Now, 25 years after this walk, I watch families outside the window and see young people from the neighborhood on a paved soccer field, where for years an old pavilion stood. In contemporary jargon this is termed 'reverse integration', and with that thought, I feel a similar euphoria that I felt during that particular walk. With only the rather important difference that the former musing thought is partly true and is nearly realized.

It is important to indicate here our focused attention, both at the individual and societal level. To be able to do it differently, creativity and courage on both levels are needed. We should be allowed to ask questions regarding the 'common sense' approach and take considered risks to explore boundaries to find alternative ways of coping. Think of professionals who tend to be, from reasons of privacy or confidentiality obligations, extremely careful in taking initiative to inform others and to engage them in counseling.

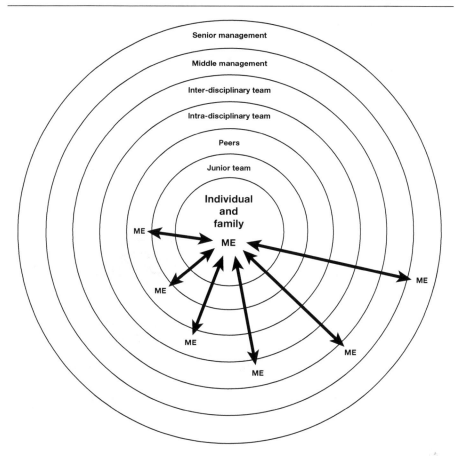

Figure 15.1 Triadic Collaboration – The Individual, Family and Professional at the Centre of Care. (Reprinted with permission of the editor from © DB Cooper and J Cooper. 2014. "The heart of care and caring". In *Palliative Care Within Mental Health: Care and Practice*, edited by DB Cooper and J Cooper. Boca Raton, Florida: CRC Press. p. 236.)

SELF-ASSESSMENT EXERCISE 15.1

Time: 10 minutes
- What do you understand by the term 'triadic collaboration'?
- Is this an active approach in your working environment?
- What could you do to improve the 'triadic relationship' in your workplace?

This chapter focuses on what is involved in realizing partnerships which widen the network of the person experiencing mental health–substance use problems and the professional from a 'dual' to a so-called 'triadic' way of work-ing. In a 'triad' relationship the individual, family and professional(s) work together. It is substantiated that this is of great importance to enhance the recovery and social participation of the individual in mental health–substance use care. Here we discuss ethical dilemmas encountered in the triadic cooperation from different perspectives. We use the knowledge and experience of peer-experts (includes the individual and family) and profes-sionals who have a broad experience in this field of cooperation. Experience-based knowledge and expertise are recorded in five training modules known in the Netherlands as 'Family as Ally' (www.familiealsbondgenoot.nl/). The objective of adding these insights to the expertise of mental health–substance use professionals is to enhance the growth of the professional understanding and awareness in order to be able to let the individual recover in his or her own environment. According to recent research and literature the triadic recovery process not only results in better and faster recovery but it is also cost-effective (Ciompi, 1997; Fadden, 1997; Falloon, 2003; Harding et al., 1987; Spaniol, 2010).

WHY INVOLVEMENT OF OTHERS

People are herd animals and are dependent on each other to survive, develop and add quality to life itself. In the 'theory of belonging' (Baumeister and Leary, 1995), the authors report that 'belonging to someone' is a very important driving force behind much human behavior. It is also shown that there is a correlation between having a social network and the incidence of psychological and/or physical health problems (Perkins and Repper, 2003; Todd et al., 2004).

At times when people for a longer or shorter time cannot live independently because their health does not allow this, family support is essential. It is a moral right, in these moments of desperation, to meet people who take their relative by the hand and get back together to find the way to recovery (Beneken genaamd Kolmer, 2007).

In particular people experiencing mental health–substance use problems have to deal with such periods in life. Major international mental health surveys show that from all diseases, people who experience serious and long-lasting mental ill health, are exposed to serious 'burden of living' (burden of disease) (Whiteford et al., 2013). People experiencing mental ill health have a far greater chance of premature (7–24 years earlier) death than people in the general population; substance use increases these risks moreover, to a very high degree (Chesney, 2014). People experiencing substance use in com-bination with psychological problems are at the greatest risk.

A relationship and definitely a familial relationship have a certain degree of reciprocity. There is a (blood) band which can never be completely disconnected (Boszormenyi-Nagy and Spark, 1984). This implies that not only the person experiencing ill health but also the stakeholders have rights and obligations. There is no permissiveness; relationships have the system characteristic that seeks for oblique homeostasis (Dillen, 2016). In nature there is no code for it; nature naturally strives for balance and assumes 'justice' rather than 'law'.

Based on this argument, they owe to each other naturally occurring rights, and the obligations of people to each other. The point here is that close relatives in principle should always be involved where possible in recovery processes of vulnerable people. This justifies the following statement: 'not more involvement than necessary and not less than needed'. It is important that there is a prioritization that initially the system itself strives to reach homeostasis and if that does not result in a solution there, in the (last) instance, we look to the law for a position to take (Crijns, 2012).

This principle is the premise on which the following themes can be discussed.

WHAT, WHO AND HOW MUCH

The acronym MICA represents the phrase: 'mentally ill chemical abusers' and is occasionally used to designate people who have Alcohol and Other Drugs (AOD) problems and markedly severe and persistent mental disorders such as schizophrenia or bipolar. A preferred description is: 'mentally ill chemically affected people', since the word 'affected' better describes their condition and is not pejorative. Other acronyms are also used: MISA (mentally ill substance abusers), CAMI (chemical abuse and mental illness) and SAMI (substance abuse and mental illness) (Ries, 1996).

According to the Alcohol, Drug Abuse, and Mental Health Administration (ADAMHA) at least 50 percent of the 1.5 to 2 million Americans experiencing severe mental ill health use illicit drugs or alcohol, compared to 15 percent of the general population (Drake et al., 1991).

Individuals experiencing schizophrenia have higher rates of alcohol, tobacco, and other drug use than the general population. Based on nationally representative survey data, 41 percent of respondents with past-month mental illnesses smoke, which is about double the rate of those with no mental illness. In clinical samples, the rate of smoking among individuals experiencing schizophrenia has ranged as high as 90 percent (National Institute on Drug Abuse, 2010).

The term dual diagnosis is a common, broad term that indicates the simultaneous presence of two independent medical disorders. Recently, within the fields of mental health–substance use problems the term has been used frequently to describe the coexistence of a mental health disorder and AOD problems. The equivalent phrase 'dual disorders' also denotes the coexistence of two independent (but invariably interactive) disorders (Ries, 1996).

People experiencing severe mental health–substance use problems experience high levels of discrimination and are far more often victims of violence and crime than people in the general population (Kamperman et al., 2014). Moreover, people experiencing serious mental health–substance use problems (dual diagnosis) have a poorer quality of life (Sibitz et al., 2011; Fawcett et al., 2012). The social network and stigma play an important role; both in a promotional and preventive way. Relatives could for example be aware of the use of vocabulary ('my sister suffers from a psychotic disorder' instead of 'my sister is a schizophrenic' and 'my father is a very nice, talented man, just look at this beautiful painting of his hand' instead of focusing on his psychotic vulnerability).

Several authors speak positively to a more dominant and influential role of the person and his or her close relatives in the process of recovering from mental health vulnerabilities, whether or not combined with substance use problems (Sibitz et al., 2011; Verhaegh, 2009). Studies prove recovering in the home environment is not just faster but demonstrates better results. The findings of the WHO (World Health Organisation) studies demonstrate better courses and treatment outcomes for people in the developing world and have been attributed to the following factors:

➤ family environment and expressed emotion
➤ social role expectations
➤ stigma and discrimination (International Society for Psychological and Social Approaches to Psychosis – iSPS, 2006).

POLITICAL AND PROFESSIONAL POINTS OF VIEW

For decades in international politics, there have been movements that advocate greater self-direction of the individual's mental health and less government interference with citizens (Minkoff and Drake, 1991; Stein and Test, 1998). It points to the importance of socialization of psychiatry, a trend that started in the 70s and which has led to a decrease in clinical capacity and an increase of outpatient mental health services 'living in the community' (Stein and Test, 1998). Initiatives arose intended to contribute to the participation (rehabilitation) of people experiencing serious mental health–substance use problems in society (Bond et al., 2001; Dixon, 2000; Drake et al., 2001; Mueser et al., 1998).

During the last decade, the Dutch politic and its correlating policy interventions in the Mental Health department show developments towards 'more self-direction for the person and less government interference with citizens' (van Yperen, 2016). Moreover, the Dutch government advocates more 'self-direction' and more 'client responsibility for recovery'. The government refers to this development using terms such as 'return psychiatry to society'. The views are consistent with the conclusions described in the context of the 'Recovering at home' (Meerjarenvisie Lister, 2015) and are also found in the study of Verhaegh (2009).

The views are not only prompted by economic motives, but international studies demonstrate that recovering in the home environment happens faster and gives better results; moreover, it is more cost-efficient (Essock et al.,

1998; Verhaegh, 2009): 'The findings of the WHO studies demonstrate, as mentioned earlier, better courses and outcomes (iSPS, 2006)'.

In addition to the previously stated premise, these findings justify reversing the common position adopted now: 'when in doubt, do not involve relatives in the recovery process of the client.' The adage changes from 'not engage unless . . .' to 'be involved, unless . . .'.

A PROMISING ROAD; FIRST AID KIT FOR ALL PROFESSIONALS WORKING IN/WITH/FOR TRIADS (ROAD WORKERS AND DRIVERS)

In general, developments and innovations take place in a dynamic environment. They take place in a natural way, but are often deliberately initiated by people, and intentionally initiated. The purpose of innovation is frequently found in external impulses of human, social or economic and financial origin. People have ideas, different needs and viewpoints or are dissatisfied with the existing possibilities and solutions to give their lives a desired level of quality of life.

In the current time span, policymakers promote an own-direction policy and advocate for bearing responsibility for your own health and well-being. It is no longer obvious to knock for every problem at the doctor's door to get a solution. The diagnosis-prescription model makes way for recovery thinking that, initially, starts with the individual responsibility and the use of resources in their own environment.

It may be that changes are made on the basis of changing social attitudes. A society responds because a group of people is excluded from participation in their environment. Finally, a driver for change can be found in low economic circumstances. Recent media frequently report about the dispute which has been about (un)affordability of health care (van der Bles, 2012). These developments are current and act as forces that stimulate triadic cooperation and recovery in the person's own environment.

RECOVERY: WHO, WHAT AND HOW?

Each person is unique and everyone's recovery is different. The panacea for a successful recovery does not exist and for that reason asks for creativity, endurance and good, open communication with the individual and family.

It is possible, on a higher level of abstraction, however, to mention more general truths that are supportive in the individual process of recovery of each individual. In the following part some of these findings will be discussed.

. . . But in our situation it is different!

Recovery processes regularly refer to the uniqueness of the human being and the personal circumstances of each individual concerned. This principle is adequate here also. However, from a professional point of view, it is impossible and unwise to react immediately in detail on the requests for help. Indeed, a professional is trained in the use of professional expertise theories, models and interventions that have been developed and examined at group level. The diagnosis takes place at group level and follows the process from general insights to the more specific circumstances; only secondarily detailed professional customized care can be given.

This deductive way of reasoning is also necessary to aspects of the whole picture. Both the living areas of the person experiencing mental health–substance use and the system (i.e. the immediate social network) should be explored and this knowledge should be included in a comprehensive recovery plan for the complete system.

The customized recovery plan, therefore, describes the circumstances and interventions tailored to the individual. These personal elements are over the course of time in close contact with family members co-added to the recovery plan. The network (*see* Figure 15.1) and the triadic communication should result in a tailored recovery plan, but also serves to build the triadic relationship to a relationship where trust and respect are essential characteristics (McLeod, 2011; Shirk and Karver, 2003).

On the road to recovery everyone involved discovers his own recovery process. It asks for daring, considered risks, expertise and close cooperation with individuals in the network.

A blessing in disguise?

The existence of a causal relationship in social science is often difficult to prove. There mostly are correlational relationships and/or multi-causal connections between certain events.

In this part of the chapter, triadic working is associated with the economic recession and is the impact on care delivery. This economic incentive has a positive impact on the realization of the already developed vision in mental health care in which concepts like 'self-direction', 'empowerment' and 'recovering at home' are dominant subjects.

The policy of 'recovering at home' gives a positive impulse to the development for people experiencing mental health–substance use disability or vulnerability to rejoin members of society. This has an integrative meaning and contributes to reducing stigma. Citizens increasingly come into contact with other vulnerable citizens and 'social contacts' appear to be the most effective remedy for individuals experiencing stigmatization (Corrigan et al., 2014).

This trend contributes positively to more realistic views about psychiatry and perspectives to recovering from/experiencing a mental health–substance use problem. Binary 'ill health thinking' makes way for a new humanity in which no one is perfect, but where everyone has competences, to a greater or lesser extent, to have a positive significant contribution to the functioning of society. The development also has a positive impact on what Nijhof (1997) in the book *Individualization and Exclusion* described and leads to more understanding, more attention and more positive development of the skills of people who experience a mental health–substance use vulnerability.

A few remarks should be made here; the case under consideration is worth taking into account but should be used with caution. It often happens that close relatives feel overwhelmed and unable to take on the additional duties and stress on their own. In many situations, the stress-level (family burden), as measured by the Family Burden Scale, is already high (Hjärthag et al., 2010; Levene et al., 1996). Usually it is not a matter of unwillingness, but a matter of family members having to deal with impotence, ignorance and inability to cope with their new roles and responsibilities. We can teach them how to deal with the new situation and demonstrate how they can contribute constructively to the recovery of the person experiencing mental health– substance use problems. It should be carefully assessed whether there is a potential of support competence and energy and that the so-called 'family burden' is not too high at the start of the recovery process. The course content of 'Family and Ally' (Bergen, 2014) is available and attracts specific attention and informs us that the close relatives go through a recovery process parallel to, but also runs integrated with, the recovery process of the individual.

If the close relative learns how he or she can participate in the individual's recovery process, it may well happen that the score on the family burden scale, despite the contribution delivered, is lower because they are given strength. In addition, family receive mental health–substance use education, and are therefore more able to give to their limits and are more responsive to the ways in which they can help.

If forming a triad system fails, then respect and patience is needed; this does not mean that the contacts with these close relatives should cease to exist. It can be beneficial to the recovery of the person when close relatives have counseling in parallel with the recovery process of the individual.

At the outset, it is imperative to establish the family network, determining the nature and quality of the relationship and to assess the future possibilities in a triadic sense.

Various cultures have different views about mental health–substance use problems. As it is recommended from the start to involve family in the process of recovery, it is also recommended from the first contact to address immediately the subject of cultural competence (*see* Chapters 4 and 7) and to take cultural aspects into account in caregiving (Leininger and McFarland, 2006).

What makes it difficult . . .

➤ There is not always expertise among all professionals about collaborate triadic, and the individual and close relatives are not always familiar with this system and lack expertise in working together in triads. This means that professionals must give priority to it maintaining respect and patience. They should not only take initiative, and inform, but also need to persuade and persevere. In practice, we hear quotes put forward by those closely involved such as 'they do not meet their commitments' or 'they are never present when you need them'. Professionals too express their prejudices: 'the people are tough and they always have something to complain about'. Professionals should be able to interpret such comments as commitment, and concerns due to accumulated frustrations and disappointments.

➤ The remedy is relatively simple. The policy basis for this transformation has to be that in the future, 'all communication is now done in triads, unless . . .' and 'we do not talk 'about' others, but 'with' the individual and close relatives'. From this authors clinical experience, it can be said that effective communication instantly changes completely.

➤ In daily practice, it has proved effective to start with the review of the daily working process on logistic points of engagement in triadic cooperation. For example, the persons' transfer can only take place in the presence of the individual and close relatives and treatment meetings would not take place if there are no family members present and are not involved in the process, unless . . .

KEY POINT 15.2

Triadical cooperation is a starting point.

➤ Knowledge in this relatively new domain is still unknown. Often a safety margin is respected and professionals fail to search for limits of the possible and legally permissible. Managers should aim to create a safe working area for professionals who naturally often choose the safe way, and thus, fail to further explore the field. Should we receive a complaint or accusation, management is responsible and must act as support in reducing the issue. Focken advocated this practice and considers that professionals are far too cautious and thus restrict themselves in their scope for action (Adema, 2006).

➤ A recent phenomenon is the fact that professionals are busy. Production, heavy workload, administrative obligations, complaints are often heard about activities that regularly take up about 40 percent of available working time. 'And then working together with close relatives, takes even more time!' It is indeed a fact that triadic cooperation from the start is more time intensive (mental health–substance use education, making appointments, sharing emotions and experiences, practicing new roles and discussing issues) but the investment pays off in the long term (Falloon, 2003). Falloon (2003) states in his research that triadic collaboration not only produces better results but is also cost-effective.

What makes transition possible?

Triadic cooperation and connected advantages will not be realized automatically. A number of conditions, that the realization of the above-mentioned advantages will accelerate, the transition:

First, the development can ride on the wave of socialization, a policy that introduced social transition that relates to outstanding triadic working. We described these developments at the beginning of this chapter.

A second development that accelerates the transition is the fact that there are now individuals and family experts who as professionals and as ambassadors fulfill the role of a gadfly (someone who fulfils the role in which he or she upsets the status quo); they pose questions about routine issues, pay attention to different perspectives and say no the moment that colleagues agree. In addition to regular tasks, they also perform a role as an ambassador and carry the triadic collaboration policy within and outwith our organization.

Experienced experts are more than people who have gained experience in mental health-substance use care. They are people who, after they themselves have gained experiences, have completed a program that represents the body of knowledge behind the profession. Finally, they reach the third stage in their development; beside experience and expertise, they are able to share their experiences and the knowledge gained to reach a level of wisdom that is characterized as 'beyond the disease' and 'control of their own vulnerability' (van Haaster, 2013).

Skills to work in triads?

Professionals working in triads are advised to meet some basic requirements. They must embrace the philosophy and its principles, possess good communication skills; cooperate on the basis of equality and respect, and have a permanent sharpness and critical reflectivity at themselves and the environment in which they work.

In addition, professionals will be more focused on specific professional knowledge and relevant skills. Knowledge must be present on systems theory, recovery processes (of close relatives), empowerment and proactive rather than reactive intention to cooperate.

Many professionals act as rescuers, solving crises and performing other necessary activities. This is not a call to dismiss the necessary things, but to provide a cry for help addressed to policy makers and funders, to no longer only mean that reactive work should be aimed at solving problems. It requires professionals to enable the process/person-centered care. It obliges professionals to think creatively and cost-consciously about how this target can be reached. An example is the deployment of peer-experts.

Ethical dilemmas and issues

The moral obligation in triadic working is advocated in this chapter. This provides certain advantages . . . but we must remember that:

➤ There are close relatives who, even with support and attention to their own recovery process, are unable to raise the capacity to be of importance to the recovery of their relative. We should not blame, but respect their choices. Family burden ranks high for some close relatives. It is ethically not 'just' to do a little extra. In these situations, it is advisable to offer people individual guidance which runs parallel to the recovery process of the individual and where possible to discuss guilt, self-blame and other emotions.

➤ In this chapter we take the position: triadic cooperation unless . . . Unless it is applied when there is suspicion or when there are impure/false intentions; if there is any (threatening) violence or physical/mental or any kind of abuse. In such situations, the professional is required to turn to an authority who is an expert in this area.

➤ We often see in practice professionals hiding behind legislation such as the protection of privacy of persons. A component here is an often-used excuse not to provide disclosure about treatment matters to close relatives. This chapter calls for professionals not to use the law as an excuse to avoid openness. The legislation is intended only to come into force if there is an interpersonal unresolved situation. Crijns (2012) speaks in this context; the law is only used as a last resort.

REFERENCES

Adema A. 2006. Nooit meer verschuilen achter privacy. Ypsilon Nederland, jrg 22, nr1.

Baumeister RF and MR Leary. 1995. "The Need to Belong, Desire for Interpersonal Attachments as a Fundamental Human Desire". *Psychological Bulletin,* 117: 497–529.

Beneken genaamd Kolmer DM. 2007. *Family care and care responsibility.* Dissertation. University of Tilburg.

Bergen AM and A van Poll. 2014. Ze begrijpen mij!, Movisie, www.woordendiespreken.nl/uploads/images/erv,%20Publicatie%20Handreiking%20EW_FC_DEF_lr.pdf.

Bles van der W. 2012. "Politiek erkent: zorg wordt onbetaalbaar". Trouw Newspaper www.trouw.nl/tr/nl/4500/Politiek/article/detail/3303603/2012/08/20/Politiek-erkent-zorg-wordt-onbetaalbaar.dhtml.

Bond GR, R Drake, K Mueser and E Latimer. 2001. "Assertive Community Treatment for People with Severe Mental Illness: Critical Ingredients and Impact on Patients". *Disease Management and Health Outcomes,* 9: 141–159.

Boszormenyi-Nagy I and GM Spark. 1984. *Invisible loyalties: reciprocity in intergenerational family therapy.* New York: Brunner/Mazel.

Chesney E. 2014. "Risks of all-cause and suicide mortality in mental disorders: a meta-review". *World Psychiatry,* 13: 153–160.

Ciompi L. 1997. "The concept of affect-logic: an integrated psycho-socio-biological approach to the understanding and treatment of schizophrenia and related disorders". *Psychiatry,* 60: 158–170. See more at: www.isps.org/index.php/learning-resources/recommended-articles#sthash.xLe7Wem4.dpuf.

Cooper DB, J Cooper. 2014. "The heart of care and caring". In *Palliative care within mental health: care and practice,* edited by DB Cooper and J Cooper. Boca Raton, FL: CRC Press. p. 236.

Corrigan PW, PJ Michaels, E Vega, M Gause, J Larson, R Krsysanowski and L Botcheva. 2014. "Key ingredients to contact-based stigma change: A cross-validation". *Psychiatric Rehabilitation Journal*, 37: 62–64.

Crijns JH. 2012. "Strafrecht als ultimum remedium. Levend leidmotief of archaïsch desideratum". *Ars Aequi*, 61: 11–18.

Dillen A. 2016. Ongehoord vertrouwen, ethische perspectieven vanuit het contextuele denken van Ivan Boszormenyi-Nagy. Uitgever: Garant Uitgevers nv.

Dixon L. 2000. "Assertive Community Treatment: Twenty-Five Years of Gold". http://ps.psychiatryonline.org/doi/abs/10.1176/appi.ps.51.6.759.

Drake R, P McLaughlin, B Pepper and K Minkoff. 1991. "Dual Diagnosis of Major Mental Illness and Substance Disorder". *New Directions for Mental Health Services*, 50: 3–13.

Drake RE, H Goldman, HS Leff, AF Lehman, L Dixon, KT Mueser and WC Torrey. 2001. "Implementing Evidence-Based Practices in Routine Mental Health Service Settings". *Psychiatric Services*, 52: 179–182.

Essock SM, LK Frisman and NJ Kontos. 1998. "Cost-effectiveness of assertive community treatment teams". *American Journal of Orthopsychiatry*, 68: 179–190.

Fadden G. 1997. "Implementation of family interventions in routine clinical practice following staff training programs: a major cause for concern". *Journal of Mental Health*, 6: 599–612. www.tandfonline.com/doi/abs/10.1080/09638239718464.

Falloon IRH. 2003. "Family interventions for mental disorders: efficacy and effectiveness". *World Psychiatry*, 2: 20–28.

Fawcett B, Z Weber and S Wilson. 2012. *International Perspectives on Mental Health: Critical Issues Across the Lifespan*. New York: Palgrave Macmillan.

Haaster van H. 2013. "Kaderdocument ervaringsdeskundigheid". *Herziene versie januari*. www.ervaringswijzer.nl/vragen/14/Kaderdocumentervaringsdeskundigheidversiejanuari2013.pdf.

Harding CM, GW Brooks, TSJS Asolaga and A Breier. 1987. "The Vermont longitudinal study of persons with severe mental illness". *American Journal of Psychiatry*, 144: 718–726.

Hjärthag F, L Helldin, U Karilampi and T Norlander. 2010. "Illness-related components for the family burden of relatives to patients with psychotic illness". *Social Psychiatry and Psychiatric Epidemiology*, 45: 275–283.

International Society for Psychological and Social Approaches to Psychosis. 2006. *Long-Term Follow-Up Studies of Schizophrenia*. www.isps-us.org/koehler/longterm_followup.htm.

Kamperman AM, J Henrichs, S Bogaerts, EM Lesaffre, AI Wierdsma, RR Ghauharali, W Swindens, Y Nijssen, M van der Gaag, JR Theunissen, PA Delespaul, J van Weeghel, JT Busschbach, H Kroon, LA Teplin, D van de Mheen and CL Mulder. 2014. "Criminal victimisation in people with severe mental illness: a multi-site prevalence and incidence survey in the Netherlands". *Plos one*, 9: e91029.

Leininger MM and MR McFarland. 2006. *Culture care diversity & universality: A worldwide nursing theory*. Boston: Jones & Bartlett Learning.

Levene JE, WJ Lancee and MV Seeman. 1996. "The perceived family burden scale: measurement and validation". *Schizophrenia Research*, 22: 151–157.

Meerjarenvisie L. 2015. 2015–2020: 'Herstellen doe je thuis'. www.lister.nl/lister/organisatie/meerjarenvisie-herstellen-doe-je-thuis/.

McLeod BD. 2011. "Relation of the alliance with outcomes in youth psychotherapy: A meta-analysis". *Clinical Psychology Review*, 31: 603–616.

Minkoff K and RK Drake. 1991. "Dual diagnosis of major mental illness and substance disorder". *New Directions for Mental Health Services*, 50: 95–107. San Francisco: Jossey-Bass.

Mueser K, G Bond, R Drake and S Resnick. 1998. "Models of community care for severe mental illness: a review of research on case management". *Schizophrenia Bulletin*, 24: 37–74.

National Institute on Drug Abuse. 2010. www.drugabuse.gov/publications/research-reports/comorbidity-addiction-other-mental-illnesses/.

Nijhof GJ. 1997. Individualisering en uitstoting; een perspectief voor een psychiatrische sociologie; Event: 7e druk; Publication Year: 1997.

Perkins R and J Repper. 2003. "Social exclusion, discrimination and social isolation." *The Handbook of Community Mental Health Nursing*: 54.

Ries R. 1996. Assessment and treatment of patients with coexisting mental illness and alcohol and other drug abuse. https://books.google.co.uk/books?id=2HebpsNa4Lg C&printsec=frontcover&dq=Ries+R.+1996.+Assessment+and+treatment+of+patient s+with+coexisting+mental+illness+and+alcohol+and+other+drug+abuse&hl=en&sa =X&ved=0ahUKEwjsgYXo7-jOAhWBJ8AKHaAcA_oQ6AEIJzAA#v=onepage& q&f=false.

Shirk SR and MS Karver. 2003. "Prediction of treatment outcome from relationship variables in child and adolescent therapy: A meta-analytic review". *Journal of Consulting and Clinical Psychology*, 71: 452–464.

Sibitz I, M Ameringa, A Ungera, ME Seyringera, A Bachmann, B Schrank, T Benesch, B Schulze and A Woppmanna. 2011. "The impact of the social network, stigma and empowerment on the quality of life in patients with schizophrenia". *European Psychiatry*, 26: 28–33.

Spaniol LJ. 2010. "The pain and the possibility: the family recovery process". *Community Mental Health*, 46: 482.

Stein LI and MA Test (Eds.). 1998. "The Training in Community Living model: A decade of experience". *New Directions for Mental Health Services*, 6. San Francisco, CA: Jossey-Bass.

Todd J, G Green, M Harrison, BA Ikuesan, C Self, DJ Pevalin and A Baldacchino. 2004. "Social exclusion in clients with comorbid mental health and substance misuse problems". *Social Psychiatry and Psychiatric Epidemiology*, 39: 581–587.

Verhaegh MJM. 2009. Effectiveness of Assertive Community Treatment in Early Psychosis, dissertation. University of Tilburg. www.narcis.nl/publication/RecordID/oai%3A tilburguniversity.edu%3Apublications%2Ff45a1c52–1578–47be-8236–10572be9 a330.

Van Yperen T. 2016. Om eigen kracht aan te spreken in de jeugdzorg heb je beroeps-krachten nodig, lecture at University of Tilburg, Tranzo department, www.social evraagstukken.nl/.

Whiteford HA, L Degenhardt, J Rehm, AJ Baxter, AJ Ferrari, HE Erskine, FJ Charlson, RE Norman, AD Flaxman, N Johns, R Burstein and CJ Murray. 2013. "Global burden of disease attributable to mental and substance use disorders: findings from the Global Burden of Disease Study 2010". *The Lancet*, 382: 1575–1586.

CHAPTER 16

The young person

Philip D. James

INTRODUCTION

Substance use problems have been a source of intense debate for decades. Unfortunately, too often those who are involved in substance use and related fields take up entrenched positions that are often based on ideology more than evidence. Here we review four common areas of debate in relation to mental health and substance use that effect young people. Examination attempts to highlight some of the difficult ethical questions raised.

DEFINING MENTAL HEALTH–SUBSTANCE USE

Various terms exist in relation to substance use including addiction, substance abuse, substance misuse and substance dependence. In my experience many young people are quite resistant to these labels and so throughout, this chapter refers to the use of substances simply as substance use. The nuanced differences between these terms is not important. Here we discuss individuals who use substances regardless of whether they meet the diagnostic criteria.

Mental health is a broad concept with many various definitions. The definition of the World Health Organisation (WHO) will be used:

> Mental health is defined as a state of well-being in which every individual realizes his or her own potential, can cope with the normal stresses of life, can work productively and fruitfully, and is able to make a contribution to her or his community.
>
> (World Health Organisation 2014)

The reason why this definition has been chosen is that it is quite broad. Some definitions of mental health are quite narrowly focused on the absence of a 'mental illness'. The definition by WHO mentions two aspects of mental health that are relevant to young people engaged in substance use. The first of these is the ability to achieve their potential. Many people who engage in substance use struggle to achieve their potential, particularly in relation to education and employment. The second relevant aspect is the ability to make a contribution to their community. Again many people engaged in substance use can have difficulties in this area. Crime and public disorder often bring the young person into conflict with their wider community but there are frequent struggles to engage with their immediate family and local community. So, while many people engaged in substance use may not meet the criteria for a mental health problem, there can still be considerable deficits in relation to their mental health.

THE ETHICAL PRINCIPLES

Ethics is a vital aspect of healthcare and draws upon classical ethical ideas such as those proposed by Kant and Bentham hundreds of years ago (Callan & Callan 2005). However, throughout the last century a number of ethical principles have been developed and applied to health care. Traditionally called medical ethics, in reality they apply equally to all healthcare professionals. The main ethical principles are as follows.

Justice

Justice requires that all people are treated equally and that no one is discriminated against. This might include having to ensure that treatments are received by those who most need them. However, there are occasions when people are not treated equally, often due to the problems they present.

Autonomy

The generally accepted rule is that professionals should respect people's autonomy. In simple terms this means that people should be allowed to make their own decisions about their healthcare, and professionals need to ensure the individual has provided consent before administering any treatment.

KEY POINT 16.1

Consent is not a straightforward concept and it is generally accepted that consent is meaningless unless the person truly understands fully what they are consenting (or refusing consent) to. This is often referred to as informed consent.

This creates a number of ethical dilemmas for young people with substance use and/or mental health problems. First, autonomy and informed consent raise the issue of at what age is someone deemed competent to make decisions, and particularly those in relation to their health. Second, for consent to be valid we need people to be able to give meaningful consent.

SELF-ASSESSMENT EXERCISE 16.1

> **Time: 10 minutes**
> - To what extent does mental health or substance use inhibit that ability to make meaningful decisions?
> - We do not let intoxicated people drive cars so should we let them make important decisions about their future?

Non-maleficence

Non-maleficence is the concept of not doing harm. This would seem a straightforward proposition but there are many cases when interventions can have undesirable or unforeseen consequences. An example would be with medications, which may have side effects. In reality we must always look at the negative effects that come with any intervention and see if the negatives outweigh the positives or not (*see* Chapter 13). Put simply, a medication may not be stopped just because it has side effects. You would have to look at the severity of the side effects in conjunction with the benefits of the medication before you could decide on balance whether it should be stopped or not.

Beneficence

Beneficence is the idea that treatments or interventions by professionals should bring about some benefit to people. This is naturally linked with the idea of evidence based practice where there is an onus on professionals not just to do what they think is right but to carry out interventions that they can demonstrate are useful. To use the example of medication again, it is not ethical to use a medication simply because it does not do harm (non-maleficence). There is an onus to ensure the medication provides some tangible benefits.

Ethical dilemmas typically arise when these ethical principles come into conflict with one another and one must choose which is more important. For example, within mental health care the situation sometimes arises where a person is at risk from suicide but refuses treatment. The professionals then have to make a choice between either respecting autonomy or respecting the principle of beneficence . . . to do good. In these scenarios you may be able to help the person or respect their autonomy; not both.

ETHICAL ISSUE 16.1: THE RIGHT TO USE DRUGS

The idea that we have a right to use drugs might seem like a strange one but it is growing in popularity. There are several organisations who now view the status quo of criminalising drug use as out-dated, unfair and ineffective. The National Association for the Reform of Marijuana Laws (NORML) was originally a US based group who advocated for the changing of laws regarding marijuana. Effectively they are asking for cannabis to be legalised and treated like any other product. In particular, they state that they want:

> the right of individuals to grow their own cannabis as an alternative to purchasing it from licensed commercial producers [recognised (NORML 2015)]. [Their rationale for this is their claim that] Responsible marijuana use causes no harm to society and should be of no interest to state and federal governments. Today, far more harm is caused by marijuana prohibition than by the use of marijuana itself.
>
> (NORML 2016)

This statement seems to have a significant harm reduction message that by making cannabis illegal we are possibly doing more harm. The Students for Sensible Drug Policy (SSDP) state that they have a neutral stance on drug use but rather that they respect individuals' rights to make their own decision in relation to health matters (SSDP 2016).

Some research and scientific literature supports these claims. For example, the study by Professor David Nutt classified a variety of drugs based on a combination of their harms to the individual who uses them and others in society (Nutt et al. 2010). They found that alcohol was the most harmful drug overall but particularly in relation to the harm that it causes to others. Cannabis, by comparison has a much lower score, less than a third of the score of alcohol. Such findings have been interpreted as a justification for legalisation of cannabis as it is less harmful than other legal drugs such as alcohol and tobacco.

This raises a number of ethical dilemmas. The fact that users of one substance (and when compared to alcohol and tobacco probably a less harmful one) are criminalised and legally forbidden from using it raises the question of autonomy. Respect of autonomy is a major ethical principle and should the autonomy of people to use a substance like cannabis not be respected? Organisations, such as NORML and SSDP, argue that the real harm comes from the criminalising of otherwise law abiding citizens for their drug use. As a consequence of a conviction for cannabis use, many individuals may find their ability to travel to foreign countries or obtain employment greatly curtailed. This further suggests that the current situation breaches the ethical principle of non-maleficence . . . do no harm. These arguments seem quite credible. The status quo impinges on individual rights to self-determination and secondly impinges to such an extent that it actually causes social harm to an individual.

However, like most ethical issues, this one is not so black and white and if we view it from other angles more complicated ethical issues arise.

SELF-ASSESSMENT EXERCISE 16.2

> **Time: 15 minutes**
>
> Consider this from a child's perspective and see what may happen if countries
> such as Ireland or the UK were to recognise the right to use or grow cannabis
> and adopt a more liberal approach to legalisation.

NORML in particular is clear that cannabis use is not for children and so
have enshrined adult use only as one of their five principles for responsible
cannabis use (NORML 2015). This suggests good practice as there is growing research that starting cannabis use before the age of 18 seems to be
associated with increased harm in the long-term, such as negative effects on
intelligence quotient (IQ – Meier et al. 2012). While some debate continues
about allowing adults the right to use cannabis or other drugs, there does
not seem to be any significant lobby group claiming that children should be
allowed to do so.

The Health Behaviour in School-Aged Children is another large study
repeated every few years in 38 countries across Europe and North America.
A recent study pooled together the data from 172,894 children who were
surveyed in three iterations of the study from 2001 to 2010. They found
that more liberal policies within a country was associated with higher rates
of regular cannabis use among their adolescents (Shi et al. 2015). A study
in the USA found the passing of medical marijuana laws within a state
appeared to amplify adolescent cannabis use within that state possibly by:
'allaying the social stigma associated with recreational cannabis use and
by placating the fear that cannabis use could potentially result in a negative
health outcome' (Stolzenberg et al. 2015).

This makes sense, if drugs are perceived to be less harmful and more
available more people will use them. In Ireland the number of young people
requiring treatment for use of the so called novel psychoactive substances sold
through shops on high streets, was greatly reduced by the introduction of
a legislative ban (Smyth et al. 2015).

KEY POINT 16.2

Across Europe use of the legal drug alcohol is much more prevalent than use
of the most common illegal drug cannabis (Hibell et al. 2012).

A clear ethical dilemma exists for policy makers.

SELF-ASSESSMENT EXERCISE 16.3

> **Time: 15 minutes**
> - Do we construct laws that recognise an individual's right to self-determination and use substances as they see fit in order to avoid the harm potentially caused by criminalising them?
> - If we do accept these rights, are we prepared to accept the likely increases in drug use among our adolescents?

This would seem to fly in the face of the ethical principle of non-malefi-cence, or do no harm. If we do decide that an increase in adolescent use is preferable, how much of an increase is tolerable? Interestingly we do not allow motorcyclists to ride without helmets even though it is only their own health that is at risk. Therefore, is there really a right to self-determination?

ETHICAL ISSUE 16.2: THE DUTY TO TREAT

It is not unreasonable to suggest that we owe a duty of care to all, and that this duty of care is larger for those aged under 18 than the one owed to adults. As discussed in the first ethical issue, some people claim they have a right to use drugs but even pro-drugs groups such as NORML clearly state that this does not apply to minors. If a 26-year-old is using drugs they are generally not compelled into treatment. Undoubtedly family, loved ones and even the state through its criminal justice services might bring considerable pressure to bear on them. However, in general these powers do not extend to treatment against their will. Should the same rules be applied to a 16-year-old with a significant drug problem? A recent review of the research suggests that about 1 in 10 cannabis users will become dependent, but this rises to 1 in 6 among those who commence use in adolescence (Hall 2015), suggesting that we should not treat teenagers the same as adults.

In Ireland, a clear difference between a mental disorder and a substance use problem is enshrined in our mental health act which declares that a mental disorder (for the purposes of compulsory treatment) does not include 'addictions', 'personality disorders' or 'social deviancy' (Government of Ireland 2001). The rationale for this may be unclear but the result **is** clear ... a person experiencing a substance use problem cannot be made to receive treatment in the same way as someone experiencing mental ill health. Such a stance could be seen to emanate from the ethical principle of respect for autonomy. However, there is a body of research that suggests more stig-matising and negative views exist towards those with a substance use problem than those experiencing mental health problems, particularly when the person is not currently abstinent (Rao et al. 2009). Individuals experiencing substance use problems are frequently seen as not having a 'genuine' mental ill health and not seen by staff in mental health services as requiring psychiatric treatment. It appears that this conceptual split between mental health and substance use problems has led to the development of services that operate parallel to each other. The scientific basis for such a stance seems scarce as many of the causes of and treatment for substance use problems overlap with other psychiatric disorders. For example, there is evidence for biological processes in the development of substance use problems (Goldstein & Volkow 2002, Kalivas & Volkow 2005). In addition, many teenagers experiencing substance use problems have a mental health problem (James, Smyth & Apantaku-Olajide 2013).

Most substance use problems seem to start in childhood and early onset of drug use tends to be associated with more problematic substance use. For example, a recently published study of injecting drug users found that most of them had commenced use of illicit drugs by age 13, and by age 16 had already started using heroin (Barry, Syed & Smyth 2012). Perhaps if we were to treat adolescent substance use problems more aggressively we could avoid the escalation to more harmful problems.

KEY POINT 16.3

One of the biggest challenges in treating young people is the reality that frequently they do not see themselves as having a problem. Therefore, they do not want treatment, even when their parents, school or probation officer might disagree.

Thus, we come back to the same ethical dilemma . . . should we treat adolescent substance use aggressively and sometimes compel them to receive treatment? This naturally conflicts with the ethical principle of autonomy.

Coercive treatment is a commonly used option within mental health services. Most countries have laws that allow people, particularly those who pose a risk to themselves or others, be treated against their will. Usually this involves the person being committed to inpatient care for assessment and treatment. In some countries, including the UK, Community Treatment Orders exist that can compel people to take treatment in the community (Richardson 2008). As mentioned earlier, because substance use is not classified as mental health problems this means that such mechanisms for enforced treatment are often not available to these individuals or their family. However, in reality many individuals enter substance use treatment only after a third party has exerted pressure on them. Spouses threaten to end relationships, parents threaten to throw children out of the house, employers threaten being fired and courts threaten stiffer penalties if treatment is not taken. For this reason, many who enter treatment without being legally mandated are still there under duress.

An obvious retort to the concept of enforced treatment is that people have to want to change for treatment to work.

However, is this really the case? A study in California of 350 adults attending both inpatient and outpatient treatment for methamphetamine use found that those under pressure to enter were not significantly different from those that were not. Moreover, while they were more likely to relapse there were still positive outcomes such as prolonged periods of abstinence that were not vastly different from those not under pressure (Brecht, Anglin & Dylan 2005). Another US study found that pregnant or postpartum mothers mandated to treatment for substance use actually did well, particularly when the treatment approach was more intensive and structured and they continued to have custody of their child (Nishimoto & Roberts 2001). Yet another study found that those who were legally coerced into treatment were more likely to be abstinent at six month follow-ups than those who were not coerced and that 'readiness to change' on admission showed no relationship to treatment outcomes (Burke & Gregoire 2007). A review of 11 studies on legal coercion of individuals into substance use treatment found that in general there is empirical support for the concept of legally mandating people to treatment (Farabee, Prendergast & Anglin 1998). However, the general consensus seems to be that more research is needed into what kind of mandated treatment works for different individuals before conclusive evidence is available (Farabee, Prendergast & Anglin 1998, Hall et al. 2014).

None of the studies outlined above assessed coerced treatment of adolescents experiencing substance use problems. They were predominantly looking at courts or the criminal justice system applying pressure to enter treatment on those who have offended, or in the case of Nishimoto and Roberts, mothers whose access to children is under threat. In those cases, it could be argued that the ethics of overriding the individuals' autonomy by enforcing treatment is justifiable due to the harm they are causing to others through their criminal behaviours. This could be seen as being justified by the competing ethical principle of beneficence, or to do good. This is a far cry from the traditional psychiatric approach whereby someone is legally mandated to take treatment for their own good and has nothing to do with whether they have committed a crime.

We currently permit those experiencing mental ill health to be forced to have treatment against their will for their own good. Given the serious potential for physical, psychological and social harm from substance use why would we allow someone with a significant substance use problem to choose to not accept treatment? As pointed out in a review of mental health and substance use consenting laws in the US, adolescents rarely self-refer for substance use treatment but parents often report challenges in accessing treatment because the adolescent refuses (Kerwin et al. 2015). They further raise the concern that substance use impairs an individual's cognitive functioning to such a degree that their ability to consent is also impaired.

SELF-ASSESSMENT EXERCISE 16.4

Time: 15 minutes
- Is a person who smokes a few grams of cannabis a day really in a position to provide competent, informed consent?
- If this individual is a minor is it likely that the ability to consent is further eroded?

The fact that we deem it important to treat those experiencing mental health problems against their will but are often happy to allow those who use substances to live with the significant problems caused by their substance use, raises questions about society's view of and stigma towards substance users.

Some may feel that such enforced treatment would not work. As highlighted in the literature, there is some evidence that would lead us to believe that for at least some people there would be significant benefits. Let's imagine we allowed minors to be admitted for up to a month (for example) to receive residential treatment. For the duration of the treatment that young person would at least be safe as they would not be engaging in the risky substance use and associated behaviours. In addition, after a number of weeks in a residential facility, they would be less emotionally and psychologically effected from substances. At this stage they would be in a better position to objectively make decisions about their drug use and the need for treatment. If they slipped back into drug use at least we would have tried everything and a month off drugs is unlikely to have caused them harm. Furthermore, we would have made the same effort to help them with their substance use as we would have if they had a mental illness like schizophrenia. Is this not the essence of the ethical principle of justice – not treating them differently just because they have a substance use problem?

ETHICAL ISSUE 16.3: THE WITHHOLDING OF TREATMENT

Reviewing the concept of a depressive ill health and looking at criteria for depression we can see that the symptoms are not due: 'to the direct physiological effects of a substance' (American Psychiatric Association 2000). A similar statement is included for many disorders and makes sense as there is substantial research showing that various drugs can cause effects that mimic various different mental health problems. Stimulants can present similar to mania, Lysergic acid diethylamide (LSD) can lead to psychotic symptoms and alcohol can lead to depressive symptoms. It is worth noting that prescribed medications such as steroids can also lead to symptoms of mental health problems. On paper it seems sensible to suggest that if the mental health problem cannot be diagnosed properly because the person is taking a substance, then mental health treatment should be put on hold until the person has stopped using the substance and a clear assessment of symptoms undertaken. In reality many people with significant mental health problems do not simply stop the substance to aid the assessment and so the holding out for a period of abstinence is often futile in real world practice. It creates an artificial impression that mental health and substance use have a one-way relationship with substance use problems 'causing' mental health problems. In reality, there is a two-way relationship with many substances increasing the likelihood of developing a mental health problem but many mental health problems increase the likelihood of developing a substance use problem.

The main problem that seems to arise is that many mental health teams use the fact that a clear diagnosis is impossible as a reason to withdraw or withhold treatment. As outlined above the reason for this is often that they cannot be sure that the problem is not caused by the drug or that it would not be a good idea to give psychotropic medications to someone who is taking substances. Individuals are often referred to substance use services and advised to return once the substance use has been dealt with. This approach seems to fly in the face of best evidence based practice. For example, the National Institute of Clinical Excellence (NICE) guideline on treating co-occurring substance use and psychosis is that the normal, evidence based treatments for each disorder (i.e. the psychosis and the substance use disorder) should proceed at the same time (NICE 2011). A review of the treatment of Attention Deficit Hyperactivity Disorder (ADHD) with co-occurring substance use arrived at a similar finding, treat both the mental health and substance use problem concurrently (Edokpolo, Nkire & Smyth 2010). It has been recommended that when mental health and substance use problems co-occur, both: 'should be considered primary, and treatment of both should be integrated and simultaneous' (Minkoff 2013). So why might individuals experiencing mental health and substance use problems not receive treatment from mental health services? It is possible that many of the mental health professionals do not understand that evidence based treatment involves both being treated together. This would indicate that education and policies are needed on the appropriate treatment for these individuals. However, the reality is that it might be a deeper problem than this. Many professionals are aware that there are often negative views and stigma towards individuals using substances. Among professionals they are not always perceived as a popular group to work alongside but . . .

KEY POINT 16.5

Substance use problems are mental health or psychological problems.

As mentioned previously, the treatments for substance use and mental health problems overlap greatly . . . counselling type interventions with some medications at times. Furthermore, there is a large body of evidence showing that there is a significant overlap with anything from 50–90 percent of people experiencing substance use problems, having a mental health problem depending on the study taken (James et al. 2013). Yet for some reason most countries have established substance use and mental health services as completely separate organisations. This leads to an unsatisfactory situation where the person is bounced from service to service.

To summarise:

➤ If more often than not, individuals experiencing substance use problems also have a mental health problem why establish separate services?

➤ The overlap in the skills for treating these problems and the research highlighting the need for concurrent treatment, indicates that a single service treating both problems is preferable

➤ An important ethical concept is that of justice, that all individuals are treated equally and fairly. Is it fair that a person experiencing ADHD who also has depression has access to treatment but a person experiencing ADHD and cannabis use does not?

ETHICAL ISSUE 16.4: STIGMA IN SUBSTANCE USE

Stigma is a common problem for many groups within society and for the past 50 years or so it has been a major focus for those attending the mental health services. The concept of stigma was brought to the fore by the writings of the American Sociologist Erving Goffman in the 1960s. Goffman (1968) described a stigma as a:

KEY POINT 16.6

. . . personal characteristic which can lead others to see the person as different from 'normal' people and as less desirable, bad or weak.

Such stigmas can be based upon ethnic or cultural factors (*see* Chapters 4 and 7) such as nationality or religion but are often related to what could be seen as negative personal traits such as having a mental illness, criminal record or substance use problem. These views are often held by society and can be very powerful. If we focus on mental ill health we can clearly see the negative effect that stigma has on individuals. While it could be argued that attitudes towards those experiencing mental ill health have improved in recent decades there is no doubt that there has traditionally been a very negative stance taken by society towards those experiencing mental health problems. In general, society viewed those experiencing mental health problems as untrustworthy, dangerous, unpredictable and undesirable and consequently they were frequently detained and locked away or simply ignored. Once labelled these individuals would find it very difficult to integrate with society and find challenges in gaining employment, having relationships and generally being accepted by society. Their whole person was viewed in a negative light.

For those experiencing mental illnesses this stigma had a significant negative effect. Because they were terrified of being seen as less or in a negative light they were less likely to come forward for treatment. Why would one admit to having a disorder if this would mean you will be shunned? We now know the importance of early detection and intervention particularly for disorders such as schizophrenia.

KEY POINT 16.7

Stigma simply gets in the way of people accessing treatment early and has no positive benefit. People do not choose to become depressed, psychotic or anxious any more than they would choose to get cancer.

Therefore, stigma only causes problems by making the person feel worse about themselves and less likely to access help. Bad enough to hear distressing voices without having to believe that this means she or he are somehow less than others in society. Interestingly, research looking at mental health service users in the UK found that they were all affected by stigma but fear of stigma was more common than actual experiences of discrimination (Green et al. 2003). Research has found that as contact with people with mental health problems increases, negative and stigmatising attitudes tend to decrease (Alexander & Link 2003).

In recent years there have been concerted efforts and campaigns to destigmatise mental illness with many of these coming from various service user movements. In Goffman's terms people who knew people experiencing mental ill health and could see that they were just people were referred to as the knowing or wise. They saw past the so called stigma. De-stigmatisation campaigns encouraged people, particularly celebrities, to discuss their own challenges with mental health. This encouraged society to see past the stigma and realise that we all know people experiencing mental health problems and having a mental health problem hardly says something about the person.

This has had considerable success, and there is little doubt that now having depression or anxiety is more acceptable than even 20 years ago. It is debateable how more acceptable having disorders such as schizophrenia is but nevertheless progress is being made. Hopefully this reduction in stigma towards mental health will encourage people to access help sooner whether that be from friends, family or professionals but it will allow them to continue with their life more easily despite their mental health challenges.

As a result of the improvements gained by reductions in stigma it is easy to fall into a trap of seeing stigma as always a negative thing but this is not so. It could be argued that a variety of behaviours including drink driving, a man hitting his wife and even smoking are behaviours that were more acceptable half a century ago but now lead to the person being seen in a more negative light. This view of the behaviours as socially unacceptable has probably contributed to a decrease in these behaviours in society. A form of peer pressure has taken place with obvious benefits. Recently there has been an ongoing discussion in Ireland about the possibility of decriminalising all drug use . . . probably in a way similar to Portugal. Various arguments have been put forward for this including the diverting of efforts from a criminal justice to a health response and possible better outcomes that have been achieved in other countries that have introduced such an approach. However, one recent argument that has been introduced is the idea of destigmatising substance users. There is no doubt that those experiencing a known substance use problem are often viewed in a negative light by the general public, Accident and Emergency (A&E) professionals, mental health professionals, policing services etc (e.g. Rao et al. 2009, van Boekel et al. 2014). If the individual has a known substance use disorder it may be held against him or her in health care, for example, an alcohol problem may preclude the individual from a liver transplant, job applications and even social settings. In Ireland, the view seems to be that these stigmatising views are unfair and ought to be abolished. It has been suggested that destigmatising substance use may make it easier for someone to access treatment due to a decrease in concern about the negative views of others.

KEY POINT 16.8

This could be seen to be aligning neatly with the ethical principle of justice in that it treats those with substance use and mental health problems equally in terms of stigma.

There have already been publications on this that have recommended contact based interventions and communicating positive stories of those experiencing substance use problems to reduce stigma (Livingston et al. 2011).

However, there is a difference between mental health and substance use problems. As mentioned earlier those experiencing psychiatric problems such as schizophrenia, depression or obsessive compulsive disorder (OCD) do not choose to get these problems and there is little that they do that directly or deliberately contributes to the problem. On the other hand, those who have substance use problems did choose to engage in substance use at some point and it was this decision that has led to their current substance use problems. At the risk of stating the obvious, if people choose not to use drugs they would then not have to run the risk of suffering from some sort of substance related harm. There is an ethical onus on society to avoid doing things that might accidentally increase the likelihood of taking drugs in line with the non-maleficence principle.

Would the reduction in stigma towards drug use and drug users lead to an increase in drug use? Room (2005) described this phenomenon in great detail and points out that mental health services are solely the responsibility of one realm of government – the health department. In substance use there are numerous government departments involved in service delivery including education, criminal justice and health. Those on the side of prevention, particularly criminal justice services, want to use stigma as a form of social control to stop people using drugs in the first place thus reducing harm. Those working with drug users, often health services, tend to want to reduce the harm felt by individuals who are involved with drugs and within this framework stigma tends to cause significant difficulties. This leads to a perfect ethical dilemma where on the one hand stigma reduces the risk of some people taking up drug use due to fears of stigma and social exclusion. On the other hand this same stigma leads to the marginalisation of those who have developed drug problems and may be an impediment to them dealing with the problem by limiting their ability to gain employment or travel.

Many discussions in relation to stigma tend to come from one or other of these positions – stigma causing harm or stigma preventing harm. In reality the drug field is immensely complicated and we need to accept that they are both different sides of the same coin. Yes, the stigma associated with drug use does cause harm to some people but it protects others. The real question for society is to have this conversation in such a way so as to recognise this complicated phenomenon. We are left with the ethical dilemma of reducing harm to one group but increasing harm to another.

CONCLUSION

Here I have attempted to demonstrate some complicated ethical issues arising in relation to young people and substance use. We note that substance use is a complicated and emotional issue with many people taking entrenched positions based upon their ideology. While we must recognise the harmful effects of stigma and criminalisation as well as the need to fully understand the person's mental health needs, we must also recognise that these are complicated issues. The removal of criminal sanctions and stigma may have negative consequences attached. Similarly, we must accept that life and people are complicated.

KEY POINT 16.9

It is not always feasible to wait until the person has stopped taking substances before we treat their mental health problems. In most cases we will have to treat both together.

If we are to resolve these complicated debates, we need to fully review all sides of the debate.

REFERENCES

Alexander LA and BG Link. 2003. "The impact of contact on stigmatizing attitudes towards people with mental illness". *Journal of Mental Health.* 12: 271–89.

American Psychiatric Association. 2000. *Diagnostic and Statistical Manual of Mental Disorders.* 4th ed., Text Revision. Washington, DC: American Psychiatric Association.

Barry D, H Syed and BP Smyth. 2012. "The journey into injecting drug use". *Heroin Addiction & Related Clinical Problems.* 14: 89–100.

Brecht ML, MD Anglin and M Dylan. 2005. "Coerced treatment for methamphetamine abuse: differential patient characteristics and outcomes". *The American Journal of Drug & Alcohol Abuse.* 31: 337–56.

Burke AC and TK Gregoire. 2007. "Substance abuse treatment outcomes for coerced and noncoerced clients". *Health & Social Work.* 32: 7–15.

Callan JE and ME Callan. 2005. "An historical overview of basic approaches and issues in ethical and moral philosophy and principles: a foundation for understanding ethics in psychology". *Journal of Aggression, Maltreatment and Trauma.* 11: 11–26.

Edokpolo O, N Nkire and BP Smyth. 2010. "Irish adolescents with ADHD and comorbid substance use disorder". *Irish Journal of Psychological Medicine.* 27: 148–51.

Farabee D, M Prendergast and MD Anglin. 1998. "The effectiveness of coerced treatment for drug-abusing offenders". *Federal Probation.* 62: 3–10.

Goffman E. 1968. *Stigma: Notes on the Management of Spoiled Identity.* London: Penguin Books.

Goldstein RZ and ND Volkow. 2002. "Drug addiction and its underlying neurobiological basis: neuroimaging evidence for the involvement of the frontal cortex". *American Journal of Psychiatry.* 159: 1642–52.

Government of Ireland. 2001. *Mental Health Act.* Dublin: The Stationery Office.

Green G, C Hayes, D Dickinson, A Whittaker and B Gilheany. 2003. "A mental health users perspective of stigmatisation". *Journal of Mental Health.* 12: 223–34.

Hall W, M Farrell and A Carter. 2014. "Compulsory treatment of addiction in the patient's best interests: more rigorous evaluations are essential". *Drug and Alcohol Review.* 33: 268–71.

Hall W. 2015. "What has research over the past two decades revealed about the adverse health effects of recreational cannabis use?" *Addiction.* 110: 19–35.

Hibell B, U Guttormsson, S Ahlström, O Balakireva, T Bjarnason, A Kokkevi and L Kraus. 2012. *The 2011 ESPAD Report: Substance Use Among Students in 36 European Countries.* Stockholm: The Swedish Council for Information on Alcohol and Other Drugs (CAN).

James P, BP Smyth and T Apantaku-Olajide. 2013. "Substance use and psychiatric disorders in Irish Adolescents: a cross-sectional study of patients attending a substance abuse treatment service". *Mental Health & Substance Use.* 6: 124–32.

Kalivas PW and ND Volkow. 2005. "The neural basis of addiction: a pathology of motivation and choice". *American Journal of Psychiatry.* 162: 1403–13.

Kerwin ME, KC Kirby, D Speziali, M Duggan, C Mellitz, B Versek and A McNamara. 2015. "What can parents do? A review of state laws regarding decision making for adolescent drug abuse and mental health treatment". *Journal of Child & Adolescent Substance Abuse.* 24: 166–76.

Livingston JD, T Milne, ML Fang and E Amari. 2011. "The effectiveness of interventions for reducing stigma related to substance use disorders: a systematic review". *Addiction.* 107: 39–50.

Meier MH, A Caspi, A Ambler, H Harrington, R Houts, RSE O'Keefe, K McDonald, A Ward, R Poulton and TE Moffitt. 2012: "Persistent cannabis users show neuro-psychological decline from childhood to midlife". *Proceedings of the National Academy of Sciences of the United States of America.* 109: 2657–64.

Minkoff K. 2013. "Treating comorbid psychiatric and substance use disorders". *Psychiatric Times.* 30: www.psychiatrictimes.com/printpdf/160091.

National Association for the Reforming of Marijuana Laws (NORML). 2015. *Principles Governing Responsible Cannabis Regulation.* Adopted by NORML Board of Directors 5 September 2015. http://norml.org/about/intro/item/principles-governing-responsible-cannabis-regulation?category_id=811.

National Association for the Reforming of Marijuana Laws (NORML). 2016. *NORML Policy on Personal Use.* http://norml.org/about/item/norml-policy-on-personal-use?category_id=779.

National Institute for Clinical Excellence (NICE). 2011. *Psychosis and coexisting substance misuse: Assessment and management in adults and young people.* London: National Institute for Health and Clinical Excellence.

Nishimoto RH and AC Roberts. 2001. "Coercion and drug treatment for postpartum women". *The American Journal of Drug & Alcohol Abuse.* 27: 161–81.

Nutt DJ, LA King and LD Phillips. 2010. "Drug harms in the UK: a multicriteria decision analysis". *The Lancet.* 376: 1558–65.

Rao H, H Mahadevappa, P Pillay, M Sessay, A Abraham and J Luty. 2009. "A study of stigmatized attitudes towards people with mental health problems among health professionals". *Journal of Psychiatric & Mental Health Nursing.* 16: 279–84.

Richardson G. 2008. "Coercion and human rights: a European perspective". *Journal of Mental Health.* 17: 245–54.

Room R. 2005. "Stigma, social inequality and alcohol and drug use". *Drug & Alcohol Review.* 24: 143–55.

Shi Y, M Lenzi and R An. 2015. "Cannabis liberalisation and adolescent cannabis use: a cross-national study in 38 countries". *PLoS ONE.* 10: e0143562.

Smyth BP, P James, W Cullen and C Darker. 2015. "So prohibition can work? Changes in use of novel psychoactive substances among adolescents attending a drug and alcohol treatment service following a legislative ban". *International Journal of Drug Policy*. 26: 887–9.

Students for Sensible Drug Policies (SSDP). 2016. *Students for Sensible Drug Policies: Mission Statement*. http://ssdp.org/about/.

Van Boekel LC, EPM Brouwers, J Van Weekhel and HFL Garretsen. 2014. "Health care professionals' regard towards working with patients with substance use disorders: Comparison of primary care, psychiatry and specialist addiction services". *Drug and Alcohol Dependence*. 134: 92–8.

World Health Organisation (WHO). 2014. *Mental health: a state of wellbeing*. Geneva, World Health Organisation. www.who.int/features/factfiles/mental_health/en/.

CHAPTER 17

The older adult

Sarah Wadd

INTRODUCTION

As the number of older adults in the world's population is increasing, alcohol and drug use (including medication dependence) in older age groups is becoming an increasingly important issue. While many indicators of alcohol and drug use are decreasing in younger adults, they are increasing in older adults. For example, in the UK, the number of alcohol-related hospital admissions, alcohol-related deaths and drug-related deaths in older age groups has increased in recent years (Wadd 2014; Wadd and Papadopoulos 2014). The number of older adults in treatment for drug problems has also increased (Wadd 2014). In England, among men, the prevalence of drinking more than the recommended weekly drink limits (21 units; 210 ml or 168 g of pure alcohol) is highest among men aged 65–74, 30 percent of whom drink at this level (Health and Social Care Information Centre 2015). Among women, the proportion who drink more than 14 units (140 ml or 112 g of pure alcohol) is highest among women aged 55–64 (22 percent). The World Health Organisation (2012) has identified alcohol-related harm among older adults as an increasing concern.

Substance misuse can have devastating consequences for older adults including premature death, physical and mental health problems, self-neglect and withdrawal from family and friends. Older adults experiencing alcohol problems are more likely to be agitated, irritable and disinhibited and this has been shown to increase distress in caregivers (Sattar et al. 2007).

Some older adults have misused substances throughout their lives, often with periods of reduction, cessation and abstinence followed by cycles of relapse or escalation in consumption. Their relatively long history of substance misuse can mean that they are in poorer health, their social resources are depleted and their alcohol or drug use is entrenched. Others first develop problems in later life for reasons that can include stressful life events or a reduction in motivations for controlling substance use such as raising children or work responsibilities. Some older adults inadvertently become dependent to medicines such as benzodiazepines or opioid painkillers that they originally took as instructed by a doctor.

Chronological age is not a precise marker for changes that accompany ageing, there are dramatic variations in health status, levels of participation and independence among adults of the same age (World Health Organisation 1999). In the substance misuse research literature, the age cut-off for an 'older' substance user can be as low as 35 years (e.g. Shaw 2009). This may be partly due to the common age bias that alcohol and drug problems occur in the young but not the old. Others have argued that the ageing process among older people experiencing chronic alcohol and drug problems can be accelerated by at least 15 years (Beynon et al. 2009). However, using low age cut-offs creates even more heterogeneity in what is already a diverse demographic category and someone in their 30s or 40s is likely to have very different physiology, life circumstances and life experiences than someone in their 60s or 70s. For the purposes of this book chapter, an older adult is defined as someone aged 50 and over. It is important to keep in mind that there is still likely to be significant diversity in this group which, considering that some people live beyond the age of 100, potentially spans more than 50 years.

Age-related factors mean that older adults can have unique vulnerabilities and require different intervention strategies in relation to their substance use. For example:

➤ Older adults may have a reduced ability to metabolise and excrete alcohol and drugs potentially making them more vulnerable to the harmful effects even at low levels of use.

➤ Alcohol and drugs can exacerbate or accelerate the onset of conditions which are associated with ageing (e.g. cognitive impairment, falls).

➤ Older adults may be more likely to conceal substance misuse and less likely to ask for help because of high levels of shame and embarrassment and generational differences in terms of pride and disclosure of personal problems.

➤ Older adults may have different motivations for pursuing healthier behaviours e.g. maintaining independence and mental capacity.

➤ Losses, life changes and transitions associated with ageing can result in isolation, loss of independence, loneliness and psychological distress and may contribute to some people starting, recommencing or escalating substance misuse in later life.

➤ Older adults may have fewer or less active social roles (e.g. no longer employed, not raising children) therefore their substance misuse may be more likely to escape notice.

➤ Older adults may have extensive histories of substance misuse, multiple and complex needs and failed treatment attempts.

➤ Older adults may find it difficult to access services (e.g. due to decreased mobility or lack of transport).

There are also ethical concerns and dilemmas in terms of practice which are particularly relevant to older adults. Perhaps the most important ethical concern is the systemic ageism and age discrimination which permeates all levels of policy and practice in substance misuse, examples of which will be given in the first part of this chapter alongside recommendations for positive practice. The second part of this chapter will discuss some of the applied ethical dilemmas that may arise in practice with older adults which would benefit from consideration. The chapter draws on the author's research interviews with older adults with alcohol problems and specialist older adult's substance misuse practitioners.

ETHICAL CONCERNS

Prejudicial attitudes

SELF-ASSESSMENT EXERCISE 17.1

Time: 15 minutes

Consider to what extent you agree or disagree with the following statements:
- Older adults are too old to change their behaviour
- It is wrong to deprive older adults of one of their last pleasures in life
- It is disrespectful to ask older adults about alcohol and drug use
- It is not worth the time and energy for older adults because they are towards the end of their life

---

Ageism, a term first used by Robert Butler in 1969, is an attitude of mind which can lead to age discrimination (Butler 1969). Ageism can be either explicit or implicit, depending on intentionality. *Explicit ageism* is when there is a conscious awareness, intention or control in thoughts, feelings or actions in regards to the treatment or consideration of an older adult (Levy and Banaji 2004). Implicit ageism on the other hand includes thoughts, feelings and actions toward older adults that exist and operate without conscious awareness, intention or control. As this type of ageism is subconscious, it can be particularly difficult to identify and address.

You may not agree with some of the attitudes towards and values accorded to older adults described in the statements above, but professionals frequently don't intervene with older adults with alcohol and drug problems 'because they are old', 'may not have long to live' or 'drinking is one of their remaining pleasures in life' (Blow 2003; Dar 2006; Herring and Thom 1997; Wadd and Galvani, 2014). This is unacceptable and particularly regrettable because many of the ageist attitudes are based on myths. For example, despite the common misconception that older adults are 'too old to change their behaviour', older adults are actually more likely to be treated successfully for an alcohol problem than younger adults. In England, 63 percent of people aged 65 and over were treated successfully compared to 48 percent of those aged 18–64 (National Treatment Agency for Substance Misuse, Response to Freedom of Information request 2012). Similarly, in terms of drug use, 62 percent of people aged 60 and over completed treatment free of dependency compared to 47 percent of people aged 18–59 (Wadd 2014). Research in the United States has also shown that older adults are just as likely to benefit from alcohol treatment as younger adults (Lemke and Moos 2003; Oslin, Pettinati and Volpicelli 2002).

One older adults' substance misuse practitioner was keen to stress to the author that even those with a very long history of problem drinking could make changes.

> 'I have worked with clients who have had a 50 year drinking history and they are adamant that this is it and I have to stop and they do. And they do brilliant, every session they come to, I'm doing this now, I'm doing that. You know, for them within their head it is where they are at that moment and the service is there when they need it and they just take it and they go.'

It is also wrong to assume that intervention is inappropriate because 'it is wrong to deprive older people of their last pleasure in life'. Drinking is not a pleasure for many older adults, rather it is a maladaptive coping mechanism for stressful life circumstances or events. The author's interview with a 60-year old female who developed a drink problem when her mother who had Alzheimer's disease came to live with her illustrates this.

> 'She was bed-ridden. I had the nurse in four times a day. But once she started to have the Alzheimer's and I was looking after her, I was taking a drink and giving her a wee drink to be honest with you. She would be rambling on and it would be a story I had heard a thousand times . . . When I was coming home from work, I was starting to go to the off-licence and get a bottle of vodka. And then I would cook her dinner for the next couple of days and puree her food and wash her clothes, and line it all up for her. And then I was taking one to calm me down.'

These examples illustrate why it is so important that all decisions are properly informed with a full assessment – not made on the basis of ageist assumptions which may well be incorrect.

Discriminatory practices

Since discrimination of both older adults and people who misuse substances is commonplace, older adults with substance misuse problems are often doubly discriminated against. Age discrimination in substance misuse may occur at any point from screening, to referral for treatment, to delivery of substance misuse services. Older adults are less likely than younger adults to be screened for alcohol problems (Denny et al. 2016; Sorocco and Ferrell 2006) and, historically at least, less likely to have specialist alcohol treatment recommended by physicians (Curtis et al. 1989) and more likely to receive medical management for health problems caused by alcohol use rather than treatment for the alcohol problem itself (Moos et al. 1993). This phenomenon has also been observed in mental health services; compared to younger adults presenting with the same symptoms, older adults are referred less frequently for psychiatric assessments, and if they are assessed, they are more likely than younger adults to be prescribed psychoactive drugs and less likely than younger adults to receive counselling and other therapies (Spencer 2009).

Age discrimination can either be direct or indirect. Direct age discrimination occurs when a direct difference in practice or policy based on age cannot be justified. Direct age discrimination has become less common since the development of legislation to prevent this type of discriminatory practice. In the UK, for example, the government's Equality Act (2010) has placed a duty on health and social care services not to discriminate on age grounds. However, blatant examples of direct age discrimination can still be found. In a recent review of a national database for substance misuse detoxification and residential services in the UK, Dutton found that 11 of these services openly stated that they had an upper age threshold (in most cases 65) which would prevent older adults from accessing them (Dutton, personal communication, 2016).

Substance misuse services may indirectly discriminate against older adults even when, in theory, there is no obstruction to their access. Indirect age discrimination occurs when people from different age groups, with different needs, are treated in the same way, with the result that the needs of the older adult are not fully met. Most substance misuse services are geared towards younger people and in many cases do not meet the needs of older adults (Wadd et al. 2011). A review by the Healthcare Commission (2009) found that older adults were denied access to the full range of substance misuse services because:

> Even when they were theoretically available, they were either not offered in an age-appropriate way or were not available when staff attempted to refer to them. Many were geared towards younger people, usually males, and were felt not to be appropriate for older people, who could feel vulnerable in the atmosphere.

It is widely accepted that young people with alcohol and drug problems are entitled to specialist services because of their age and there is an argument that the same should apply to older adults. Evidence suggests that substance

Table 17.1 Positive practice in working with older adults and substance use

Do	Don't
Continually examine your attitude towards ageing and older adults and the impact that this might have on your practice	Assume that older adults are too old to change their behaviour
Challenge ageist attitudes and discrimination if you come across them	Assume that age doesn't matter in terms of services and interventions
Be flexible in recognising and responding appropriately to the age-specific needs of older adults	Treat people differently or unfairly because they are older
Recognise that older adults themselves may be a potential resource (e.g. as peer mentors in substance use services or peer educators in the community)	Allow a lack of confidence in working with older adults prevent you from taking action

misuse services specifically for older adults are linked to better treatment outcomes and adherence than mixed-age services (Atkinson 1995; Blow et al. 2000; Kashner et al. 1992; Kofoed et al. 1987; Slaymaker and Owen 2008). People who attend specialist older adults' substance misuse services also report feeling more comfortable in treatment settings with their peers (Wadd et al. 2011). Abuse of older residents by other residents in long-term care facilities (of any type) is now recognised as a problem that is more common than physical abuse by staff (Pillemer et al. 2012; Rosen et al. 2008) and the author's research suggests that some older adults are bullied and intimidated in mixed age residential substance misuse services. For example, in an interview with a 59-year old male, he told her:

> 'The [name of mixed age residential treatment centre] has a lot of frightful yobbos. They gang up against an educated man like me. They loathe my guts. I am just going to have to bear it you know. They have a vocabulary of about 700 words and half of them are expletives . . . But I just avoid them. I am allowed to eat out so I get away from them.'

Table 17.1 gives some hints and tips on positive practice in working with older adults and substance use.

Practices and policies that perpetuate stereotypes

Ageism includes 'age-blindness' – the belief that 'age doesn't really matter, and we should ignore age' (Calasanti 2008). But age does matter. As described previously, older adults have age-related vulnerabilities and needs which mean that they require different strategies in relation to substance misuse.

However, many substance misuse strategies make no mention or provision for older adults. Drink and drug public awareness campaigns are almost exclusively targeted at younger adults. There has been very little research on interventions and treatment for substance misuse in older populations. Many alcohol studies inappropriately exclude older adults and this is both unscientific and unethical. For example, trials of the feasibility of alcohol screening and treatment in dentist surgeries (Roked et al. 2015), a web-based cognitive bias modification for people with alcohol problems (van Deursen et al. 2013) and efficacy of acamprosate in the maintenance of abstinence in people who are alcohol-dependent (Scott et al. 2005), all excluded people over the age of 65.

Older adults are also often excluded from alcohol and drug prevalence studies. In Northern Ireland the Drinking Patterns Survey (DHSSPNI 2014) excludes people aged 75 and over. Similarly, the Crime Survey for England and Wales is the main source of data on the prevalence of illicit drug use in these countries. Although approximately 17,000 people aged 60 and over are interviewed for this survey each year, people aged 60 and over are not asked questions about drug use as an 'economy measure, reflecting their very low prevalence rates for the use of prohibited drugs' (Home Office 2013). The very limited data we do have on illicit drug use in people aged 60 and over showed that 1.1 percent of a small but random sample of people aged 60 and over in England had used illicit drugs in the last 12 months (Wadd 2014). This level of drug use is not insignificant and is likely to increase in the future as the 'baby-boomer' generation ages, because they grew up in a period of high levels of drug use and relatively liberal attitudes towards drugs. Unless repeat prevalence studies are carried out which do include older adults, the extent and nature of this trend will remain unclear.

As well as the obvious effects of excluding older adults from strategy, campaigns and clinical and social research, doing so is likely to perpetuate the myth among professionals and the wider public that alcohol and drug problems only affect young people.

ETHICAL DILEMMAS
Tensions between rights and risks

A tension can exist when alcohol misuse is identified in an older adult who is intellectually competent and wishes to drink alcohol despite a risk of serious harm. This dilemma comes into sharp focus when professionals are asked by older adults to help them obtain alcohol. For example, an older adults' substance misuse practitioner told the author.

> 'Sometimes they [home carers] take a client in a wheelchair to the off-sales. They aren't allowed to go personally and buy the alcohol.

Even if the client is intoxicated, if the client is saying I want to go to the off-sales, they will push them.'

Herring and Thom (1997) identified a case where a care worker had bought an older adult whisky and while he was intoxicated, he fell and broke his hip. As a result, the local authority had forbidden carers to purchase alcohol for service users. In contrast, in another local authority described in Herring and Thom's study, a care worker was dismissed for refusing to buy alcohol for service users.

These decisions are even more ethically challenging when there is a suggestion of cognitive impairment. Another substance misuse practitioner gave this example:

'I went to a review on Wednesday, mental health, and he is in sheltered housing, he is really quite an ill man, he is suffering from malnutrition. He was saying [he drank] about 3–4 cans of Tennents [extra strength lager] per day, but also his memory, he is suffering from early dementia as well, he said his wife died two weeks ago, she died in 2007, that kind of thing. So the manager of the mental health team from [name of psychiatric hospital] said "what if we bought a crate of beer a week and gave him two each day".'

However, buying alcohol for individuals experiencing alcohol problems is frowned upon by some substance misuse practitioners, one of whom told the author that he thought it was 'morally flawed' and described professionals who purchased alcohol for people with alcohol problems as 'drug-dealers with social responsibility'.

Case Study 17.1

Consider the following case study.

Danny (76) served 40 years in the RAF before retiring. He has had a very active retirement enjoying golf and travelling. Sadly, Danny lost his wife 10 years ago however he is close to his daughter Jane. She lives 20 miles away and has three teenage children. Danny and Jane decided six months ago that he should go into sheltered [assisted living] accommodation. Although still very fit, Danny was becoming increasingly forgetful and on one occasion there had been a fire in his kitchen when he forgot he had put on the chip pan. He was also forgetting to lock his front door and had been burgled.

He has settled well into the complex and is already a welcome regular in the pub down the road. He visits there every day at 4pm and is back home by 6 after having two pints of stout. Jane visits every Saturday with the grandchildren and always brings her dad a bottle of whiskey as she knows he loves a night cap. However, the staff at the sheltered complex have noticed in the past few weeks that Danny has been increasingly confused and agitated. On Saturday evening he was found wandering the corridors at 10pm. When approached by another resident he became very agitated and lashed out.

SELF-ASSESSMENT EXERCISE 17.2

Time: 20 minutes
- What (if any) action do you think the sheltered complex staff should take and why?
- Do you think that other residents in the sheltered complex have a right to be involved in discussions if Danny's drinking is having an impact on them?

This tension between rights and risks also extends to care homes. In recognition that alcohol consumption is a normal part of adult social life, many care homes provide on-site bars or other opportunities to consume/purchase alcohol. Others organise cocktail parties or beer and wine making as an opportunity for social interaction among residents. However, alcohol use can have a negative effect on health, physical and mental functioning, quality of life and social wellbeing in older adults living in care homes. It is associated with falls and accidents, confusion and forgetfulness, disturbed sleep, continence problems, harmful medication interactions, dehydration, depression, behavioural problems and poor management of conditions such as high blood pressure and diabetes. Even small amounts of alcohol can cause harm to older adults, particularly if they are frail, taking medications that interact negatively with alcohol or have medical conditions that are made worse by alcohol.

SELF-ASSESSMENT EXERCISE 17.3

Time: 30 minutes
- Do you think older adults have a right to have help purchasing alcohol if they are unable to do so themselves?
- If so, in what circumstances (if any) do you think this right should be rescinded?
- What are the risks to the older adult, to the staff member and to the organisation?
- How might these risks be mitigated?

In a free society, individuals have a right to make choices – even bad ones. People with capacity may make what some people would consider to be 'unwise' or eccentric decisions, but that does not mean that they do not have the capacity to make those decisions (*see* Chapter 10), even if practitioners and carers disagree with them. Most people would take the view that, in the majority of circumstances, the rights of older adults to drink alcohol and have help purchasing it if necessary should be respected even if it places them at risk of harm. There are, however, circumstances in which that right may have to be forfeited.

One such circumstance is when there is a significant risk of harming others. For example, an older adult living in sheltered accommodation might have a history of causing accidental fires when he or she is intoxicated. If that were the case, it would be reasonable for staff to try to limit the amount of alcohol that the resident is able to consume to ensure the safety of residents and staff. To aid decision making, service-level guidance can be useful. This could describe the provider's position on alcohol use, a reporting procedure for adverse events and case studies of ethical challenges and potential responses to guide ethical practice. It is important, however, that risks are considered on an individual basis, not from blanket practice or policies.

Sometimes the duty of care to protect the welfare of an older adult at risk means that interventions might have to be imposed. Consider an older adult living at home who has a chronic alcohol problem and where there is evidence of serious self-neglect. A number of older adults' substance misuse practitioners have articulated this dilemma in interviews with the author:

'Very often social services are called in to assess somebody and it could be because they have been deemed a vulnerable adult. If they go in and that person is really reluctant to engage, and very often older people are very suspicious of having their power taken away, they feel powerless as it is. Social services can go in and that person might be living in the most grotesque of circumstances but if that person is deemed to have capacity to make the choice then they withdraw and they just discharge them. So for me there is a huge issue there in terms of how social services really discharge people and let people get on with it.'

'The doctor says [the person] wants to commit suicide by drinking. They pretty much said "get lost" to me. Mental health says he has got mental capacity so just let him get on with it.'

The powerful ethical force of the statutory presumption of capacity can mean that practitioners are reluctant to question people's choices and uncertain how to balance protection of a capacitated adult with individual autonomy (Flynn 2007; Galpin 2010; Keywood 2010). In a review of 40 serious self-neglect case reviews, Preston-Shoot (2016) concludes that professionals should respond to individual wishes but recognise that refusal to accept intervention is not an automatic right to be protected at all costs. He suggests that appropriate actions could include:

➤ Assessment of capacity and the individual's ability to explain the different consequences of her/his choices
➤ Exploration and assessment of reasons for refusal
➤ Attempts to find a service option acceptable to the individual
➤ Ongoing monitoring of risks
➤ Involvement of other professionals
➤ Referral to a court

A decision about the perceived or actual risk should be taken in conjunction with the individual concerned, the family and the professionals involved. Levels of risk are subjective, therefore a judgement about an acceptable level of risk should be a joint decision. It is also important that accurate records are kept of discussions that take place and that the older adult is included in these discussions. Record keeping is critical in order to protect the person in making their choices, as well as the position of the service provider in the event of any complaints or litigation.

A harm reduction approach can also be highly beneficial in older adults who continue to misuse substances but decline other intervention. Harm reduction actions could include:

➤ Arranging home fire safety, physical and dental health check
➤ Speaking to GP (with the older adult's permission) about dangerous drug combinations or over-sedation
➤ Arranging for flu, tuberculosis (TB), Hepatitis A & B vaccination
➤ Arranging for the individual to carry identification and details of medical conditions and who to contact in case of collapse
➤ Arranging for a smoke alarm to be fitted
➤ Addressing trip hazards
➤ Encouraging him/her to make small changes (e.g. one alcohol-free day a week)
➤ Making sure reasons for drinking/drug use are addressed
➤ Exploring barriers to behaviour change
➤ Engaging with the family (with their consent and when it is safe to do so) and co-residents where appropriate

Alcohol and cognitive impairment

Older adults are the age group most likely to be affected by cognitive impairment and an estimated 5–25 percent of older adults are cognitively impaired (Kumar et al. 2005; Manly et al. 2005; Purser et al. 2005). Common causes of cognitive impairment in older adults are traumatic brain injury, stroke, degenerative neurological diseases such as Alzheimer's disease and alcohol and drug use. Between 50–80 percent of people of all ages with chronic alcohol problems experience cognitive impairment (Bates et al. 2002). Older adults are a high risk group for alcohol-related cognitive impairment because age-related physiological changes can make them particularly sensitive to the toxic effects of alcohol on the brain (Pierucci-Lagha and Derouesné 2003).

In contrast to progressive dementia such as that seen in Alzheimer's disease, alcohol-related cognitive impairment can in some cases be reversed. Most alcohol-related cognitive impairment recovers with abstinence or greatly reduced drinking (Volkow et al. 1995). Approximately one quarter of people experience a full recovery, one quarter experience significant recovery, one quarter experience slight recovery and one quarter experience no recovery at all (Smith and Hillman 1999). This means that it is vital that people experiencing alcohol-related cognitive impairment stop or greatly reduce their drinking so that they have the best chance of recovering their cognitive abilities.

However, being cognitively impaired reduces the chances that a person can be treated successfully for an alcohol problem (Fals-Stewart 1993; Fals-Stewart and Lucente 1994; Grohman and Fals-Stewart 2003). To improve the chances of successful alcohol treatment, the treatment needs to be tailored in accordance with the individual's cognitive strengths and weaknesses (*see* Wadd et al. 2013 for a review of ways in which substance misuse treatment can be adjusted for individuals with cognitive impairment). These adjustments can only be made if cognitive impairment is identified relatively early on in the treatment process. Studies have shown that people with alcohol and drug problems who have cognitive impairment cannot be adequately identified by substance misuse practitioners via clinical impression (Fals-Stewart 1997) or through self-report (Horner et al. 1999; Shelton and Parsons 1987). These findings have led to calls for routine screening for cognitive impairment in substance misuse services. Since older adults are the age group most likely to experience cognitive impairment, they are likely to be the group with the most to benefit from routine screening.

This creates an ethical challenge because screening for cognitive impairment also has the potential to cause psychological harm. A small study that the author carried out showed that cognitive screening in substance misuse services can be daunting and distressing for some older adults (Wadd et al. 2013). The Montreal Cognitive Assessment (Nasreddine et al. 2005) was used to screen 10 older adults attending a substance misuse service. Participants described a variety of feelings prior to the screening including 'nervous', 'fear of failure', 'needs to be done' and 'daunting'. One interviewee who had significant cognitive deficits, showed signs of distress during the screening process. At various times during the interview she said 'I feel terrible, I feel like a nine-year-old', 'I'll give myself a headache, that's the best I can do', 'oh here I'm getting agitated', 'I feel stupid' and 'don't think I'm illiterate because I'm not'. Similarly, initial findings from the Big Lottery funded Drink Wise, Age Well programme in the UK which is piloting screening for cognitive impairment in older adults receiving an alcohol intervention, have shown that some individuals have become distressed during screening (Julie Breslin, personal communication, 2016). A screening result which is indicative of cognitive impairment, no matter what the cause, is likely to be distressing, alarming and stigmatising, as well as costly if the individual is referred for further assessment. In some cases, false positives will lead to unnecessary distress.

A further concern is that, where screening is indicative of cognitive impairment, the older adult may not be able to access full neuropsychological assessment for a diagnosis and post-diagnostic support. Memory assessment services which are designed primarily for people with progressive cognitive impairment such as that seen in Alzheimer's disease, do not usually carry out full cognitive assessment in people with alcohol problems unless they are abstinent or have greatly reduced their drinking. This is because, as described previously, alcohol-related cognitive impairment can improve or recover spontaneously with reduced drinking/abstinence. Therefore, some services take the view that alcohol misuse should be addressed before assessment takes place. However, this means that older adults may find themselves in a catch 22 situation where they are unable to get a diagnosis, post-diagnostic support and treatment for their cognitive impairment until they stop or greatly reduce their drinking but their cognitive impairment may mean that their alcohol misuse cannot be treated successfully.

SELF-ASSESSMENT EXERCISE 17.4

Time: 40 minutes
- How does causing distress during cognitive screening in substance misuse services reconcile with the ethical principle of 'do no harm'?
- What could be done to reduce distress?
- Do you think that it is ethical for memory services to deny full assessment for cognitive impairment (and hence post-diagnostic support) in people who are unable or unwilling to reduce/stop drinking?

In the Drink Wise, Age Well programme, great efforts have been made to reduce distress which could occur as the result of screening. These include:
➤ Training staff who administer the screening tool
➤ Stressing to older adults that screening is optional
➤ Explaining to older adults that the tool is not an intelligence test and that screening cannot give a diagnosis of cognitive impairment, it can only indicate the need for further assessment
➤ Reassuring those undergoing the test that alcohol-related cognitive impairment may be reversible with reduced drinking or abstinence
➤ Working with other agencies to ensure that further assessment and support is available where the screen is indicative of cognitive impairment even where the older adult continues to misuse alcohol.

CONCLUSION

Age discrimination is damaging to the individual, is in some cases unlawful and is in all cases unacceptable. Treating people fairly, regardless of age is central to the principles of ethical health and social care and it is vital that we all work together to root out age discrimination in substance misuse policy and practice.

There is a delicate balance between empowerment and safeguarding, choice and risk. Professionals have a duty to consider the person's rights to self-determination alongside any risks that their choices might present. They also have a moral obligation to involve the individual concerned in decisions about their care. Professionals should look for the person behind the diagnosis of 'alcohol misuse' (or behind both diagnoses if they also have cognitive impairment) and attempt to understand and represent their views and wishes. These decisions are often complex and based on subjective views of what is an acceptable level risk. Individual practitioner's views are not necessarily right or wrong but joint-decision making is preferable to give a more rounded view.

REFERENCES

Atkinson RM. 1995. "Treatment programmes for aging alcoholics." In *Alcohol and Aging*, edited by T Beresford and E Gomberg, 191–211. New York: Oxford University Press.

Bates ME, SC Bowden and D Barry. 2002. "Neurocognitive impairment associated with alcohol use disorders: implications for treatment." *Experimental and Clinical Psychopharmacology* 10: 193–212.

Beynon CM, B Roe, P Duffy and L Pickering. 2009. "Self-reported health status, and health service contact, of illicit drug users aged 50 and over: a qualitative interview study in Merseyside, United Kingdom." *BMC Geriatrics* 9: 45.

Blow FC. 2003. "Special issues in treatment: older adults." In *Principles of Addiction Medicine*, 3rd ed., edited by A Graham, T Schultz, M Mayo-Smith and R Ries. 581–607. Chevy Chase, MD: American Society of Addiction Medicine.

Blow FC, MA Walton, ST Chermack, SA Mudd and KJ Brower. 2000. "Older adult treatment outcome following elder-specific inpatient alcoholism treatment." *Journal of Substance Abuse Treatment* 19: 67–75.

Breslin J. 2016. Personal Communication.

Butler RN. 1969. "Age-ism: another form of bigotry." *The Gerontologist* 9: 243–246.

Calasanti T. 2008. "A feminist confronts ageism." *Journal of Aging Studies* 22: 152–157.

Dar K. 2006. "Alcohol use disorders in elderly people: fact or fiction?" *Advances in Psychiatric Treatment* 12: 173–181.

Denny CH, DW Hungerford, LR McKnight-Eily, PP Green, EP Dang, MJ Cannon, NE Cheal and JE Sniezek. 2016. "Self-reported prevalence of alcohol screening among U.S. adults." *American Journal of Preventive Medicine* 50: 380–383.

DHSSPNI. 2014. Adult drinking patterns in Northern Ireland, 2013. www.health-ni. gov.uk/sites/default/files/publications/dhssps/adps-2013.pdf.

Dutton M. 2016. Personal Communication.

Equality Act 2010, c. 15. London: Stationery Office. www.legislation.gov.uk/ukpga/2010/15/contents.

Fals-Stewart W. 1993. "Neurocognitive defects and their impact on substance abuse treatment." *Journal of Addictions and Offender Counseling* 13: 46–57.

Fals-Stewart W. 1997. "Ability of counselors to detect cognitive impairment among substance-abusing patients: an examination of diagnostic efficiency." *Experimental and Clinical Psychopharmacology* 5: 39–50.

Fals-Stewart W and S Lucente. 1994. "Effect of neurocognitive status and personality functioning on length of stay in residential substance abuse treatment: an integrative study." *Psychology of Addictive Behaviors* 8: 179–190.

Flynn M. 2007. *The Murder of Steven Hoskin. A Serious Case Review.* Truro: Cornwall Adult Protection Committee.

Galpin D. 2010. "Policy and the protection of older people from abuse." *Journal of Social Welfare and Family Law* 32: 247–255.

Grohman K and W Fals-Stewart. 2003. "Computer-assisted cognitive rehabiliation with substance abusing patients: effects on treatment response." *Journal of Cognitive Rehabilitation* 21: 10–17.

Health and Social Care Information Centre. 2015. Health Survey for England. 2014: Chapter 8, Adult Alcohol Consumption. www.hscic.gov.uk/catalogue/PUB19295/HSE2014-ch8-adult-alc-con.pdf.

Healthcare Commission. 2009. Equality in later life: A national study of older people's mental health services. www.cqc.org.uk/sites/default/files/documents/equality_in_later_life.pdf.

Herring R and B Thom. 1997. "The right to take risks: alcohol and older people." *Social Policy & Administration* 31: 233–246.

Home Office. 2013. *User guide to drug misuse: findings from the Crime Survey for England and Wales.* London: Home Office.

Horner MD, RT Harvey and CA Denier. 1999. "Self-report and objective measures of cognitive deficit in patients entering substance abuse treatment." *Psychiatry Research* 86 (2):155–161.

Kashner TM, DE Rodell, SR Ogden, FG Guggenheim and CN Karson. 1992. "Outcomes and costs of two VA inpatient treatment programs for older alcoholic patients." *Psychiatric Services* 43: 985–989.

Keywood K. 2010. "Vulnerable adults, mental capacity and social care refusal." *Medical Law Review* 18: 103–110.

Kofoed LL, RL Tolson, RM Atkinson, RL Toth and JA Turner. 1987. "Treatment compliance of older alcoholics: an elder-specific approach is superior to "mainstreaming"." *Journal of Studies on Alcohol* 48: 47.

Kumar R, KBG Dear, H Christensen, S Ilschner, AF Jorm, C Meslin, SJ Rosenman and PS Sachdev. 2005. "Prevalence of mild cognitive impairment in 60- to 64-year-old community-dwelling individuals: The Personality and Total Health through Life 60+ Study." *Dementia and Geriatric Cognitive Disorders* 19: 67.

Lemke S and RH Moos. 2003. "Treatment and outcomes of older patients with alcohol use disorders in community residential programs." *Journal of Studies on Alcohol* 64: 219.

Levy BR and MR Banaji. 2004. "Implicit ageism". In *Ageism. Stereotyping and Prejudice Against Older Persons*, edited by TD Nelson, 49–75. Cambridge, MA: The MIT Press.

Manly JJ, S Bell-Mcginty, M-X Tang, N Schupf, Y Stern and R Mayeux. 2005. "Implementing diagnostic criteria and estimating frequency of mild cognitive impairment in an urban community." *Archives of Neurology* 62: 1739.

Moos RH, JR Mertens and PL Brennan. 1993. "Patterns of diagnosis and treatment among late-middle-aged and older substance abuse patients." *Journal of Studies on Alcohol* 54: 479.

Nasreddine ZS, NA Phillips, V Bédirian, S Charbonneau, V Whitehead, I Collin, JL Cummings and H Chertkow. 2005. "The Montreal Cognitive Assessment, MoCA: a brief screening tool for mild cognitive impairment". *Journal of the American Geriatrics Society* 53: 695–699.

National Treatment Agency for Substance Misuse, 2012. Fredoom of Information request [email]. Murray, T. 5 September.

Oslin DW, H Pettinati and JR Volpicelli. 2002. "Alcoholism treatment adherence: older age predicts better adherence and drinking outcomes." *The American Journal of Geriatric Psychiatry* 10: 740.

Pierucci-Lagha A and C Derouesné. 2003. "Alcoholism and aging. 2. Alcoholic dementia or alcoholic cognitive impairment?" *Psychologie & neuropsychiatrie du vieillissement* 1: 237.

Pillemer K, EK Chen, KS Van Haitsma, J Teresi, M Ramirez, S Silver, G Sukha and MS Lachs. 2012. "Resident-to-resident aggression in nursing homes: results from a qualitative event reconstruction study." *The Gerontologist* 52: 24–33.

Preston-Shoot M. 2016. "Towards explanations for the findings of serious case reviews: understanding what happens in self-neglect work." *The Journal of Adult Protection* 18: 131–148.

Purser JL, GG Fillenbaum, CF Pieper and RB Wallace. 2005. "Mild cognitive impairment and 10-year trajectories of disability in the Iowa established populations for epidemiologic studies of the elderly cohort." *Journal of the American Geriatrics Society* 53: 1966–1972.

Randall CJ, G Geller, EJ Stokes, DM Levine and RD Moore. 1989. "Characteristics, diagnosis, and treatment of alcoholism in elderly patients." *Journal of the American Geriatrics Society* 37: 310–316.

Roked Z, S Moore and J Shepherd. 2015. "Feasibility of alcohol misuse screening and treatment in the dental setting." *The Lancet* 385: S84.

Rosen T, K Pillemer and M Lachs. 2008. "Resident-to-resident aggression in long-term care facilities: an understudied problem." *Aggression and Violent Behavior* 13: 77–87.

Sattar SP, PR Padala, D McArthur-Miller, WH Roccaforte, SP Wengel and WJ Burke. 2007. "Impact of problem alcohol use on patient behavior and caregiver burden in a geriatric assessment clinic." *Journal of Geriatric Psychiatry and Neurology* 20: 120.

Scott LJ, DP Figgitt, SJ Keam and J Waugh. 2005. "Acamprosate: a review of its use in the maintenance of abstinence in patients with alcohol dependence." *CNS Drugs* 19: 445.

Shaw A. 2009. Senior Drug Dependents and Care Structures. Scotland and Glasgow Report. www.sdf.org.uk/index.php/download_file/view/145/167/.

Shelton MD and OA Parsons. 1987. "Alcoholics' self-assessment of their neuropsychological functioning in everyday life." *Journal of Clinical Psychology* 43: 395–403.

Slaymaker V and P Owen. 2008. "Alcohol and other drug dependence severity among older adults in treatment: measuring characteristics and outcomes." *Alcoholism Treatment Quarterly* 26: 259–273.

Smith I and A Hillman. 1999. "Management of Alcohol Korsakoff Syndrome." *Advances in Psychiatric Treatment* 5: 271–278.

Sorocco K and S Ferrell. 2006. "Alcohol use among older adults." *The Journal of General Psychology* 133: 453–467.

Spencer C. 2009. "Advancing substantive equality for older persons through law, policy and practice." www.lco-cdo.org/older-adults-commissioned-paper-spencer.pdf.

van Deursen DS, E Salemink, F Smit, J Kramer and RW Wiers. 2013. "Web-based cognitive bias modification for problem drinkers: protocol of a randomised controlled trial with a 2x2x2 factorial design." *BMC Public Health* 13: 674.

Volkow N and GJ Wang. 1995. "Monitoring the brain's response to alcohol with positron tomography". *Alcohol Health & Research World* 19(4): 296.

Wadd S. 2014. The Forgotten People: Drug Problems in Later Life. www.biglottery fund.org.uk/-/ . . ./Older%20People/the_forgotten_people.pdf.

Wadd S and S Galvani. 2014. "Working with older people with alcohol problems: insight from specialist substance misuse professionals and their service users." *Social Work Education* 33: 656–669.

Wadd S and C Papadopoulos. 2014. "Drinking behaviour and alcohol-related harm among older adults: analysis of existing UK datasets." *BMC Research Notes* 7: 741.

Wadd S, K Lapworth, M Sullivan, D Forrester and S Galvani. 2011. Working with Older Drinkers. http://alcoholresearchuk.org/downloads/finalReports/FinalReport_0085.

Wadd S, J Randall, A Thake, K Edwards, S Galvani, L McCabe and A Coleman. 2013. Alcohol Use and Cognitive Impairment in Older People. http://alcoholresearchuk.org/downloads/finalReports/FinalReport_0110.pdf.

World Health Organization. 1999. Aging: Exploding the Myths. http://apps.who.int/iris/bitstream/10665/66330/1/WHO_HSC_AHE_99.1.pdf.

World Health Organization. 2012. Global health adds life to years. Global brief for World Health Day. www.who.int/ageing/publications/global_health.pdf?ua=1.

TO LEARN MORE

Cooper DB and J Cooper. 2012. *Palliative Care within Mental Health: Principles and Philosophy*. Boca Raton, FL: CRC Press.

Cooper DB and J Cooper. 2014. *Palliative Care within Mental Health: Care and Practice*. Boca Raton, FL: CRC Press.

Royal College of Psychiatrists. 2011. Our Invisible Addicts. www.rcpsych.ac.uk/files/pdfversion/cr165.pdf.
Good summary of substance use in older adults.

Wadd S, K Lapworth, M Sullivan, D Forrester and S Galvani. 2011. *Working with Older Drinkers*. http://alcoholresearchuk.org/downloads/finalReports/FinalReport_0085.
Using interviews with older adults in treatment for alcohol problems and specialist older adults' substance misuse workers, describes the nature of the issue and tips for working with older adults with alcohol problems.

Wadd S, J Randall, A Thake, K Edwards, S Galvani, L McCabe and A Coleman. 2013. Alcohol Use and Cognitive Impairment in Older People. http://alcoholresearch uk.org/downloads/finalReports/FinalReport_0110.pdf.

Good practice advice for alcohol screening in older adults with cognitive impairment, screening for cognitive impairment in substance misuse services and working with older adults with cognitive impairment in substance misuse services.

Ward M and M Holmes. 2014. Alcohol Concern's Blue Light Project: Working with Change Resistant Drinkers. www.alcoholconcern.org.uk/wp-content/uploads/2015/01/Alcohol-Concern-Blue-Light-Project-Manual.pdf.

Not specifically about older adults but good practice advice on working with change resistant drinkers.

http://drinkwiseagewell.org.uk/

A website which provides good practice advice for professionals working with older adults (50+) who use alcohol, advice for older adults who are concerned about their drinking and for friends and family of older adults with alcohol problems.

CHAPTER 18

High risk sexual behaviour

Sunita Simon Kurpad

INTRODUCTION

There would be no ethical dilemmas if the 'right decision' was clear cut, easyand guaranteed a good outcome. For health professionals who have to regularly make decisions where the right thing to do may seemingly differ, according to different perspectives, or a long term good outcome may occur at the cost of a short term negative fallout, where the only certainty in health care is a degree of uncertainty, it is useful to realize that ethical dilemmas are inevitable when dealing with two emotive issues like substance use and high risk sexual behavior. This is especially so as issues of 'normality' or boundaries of what is culturally accepted (or even legal) may differ across societies, and indeed in the same society over time.

Meaning of high risk sexual behavior

High risk sexual behavior is usually defined as sexual behavior which increases the risk of sexually transmitted infections (STIs), unplanned pregnancies or sexual behavior while being too young/immature to understand how to be in a healthy relationship.

Some examples of high risk sexual behavior

Having multiple sexual partners, sexual intercourse with a person who practices high risk behavior and not using condoms especially if not in a steady long term relationship, are some examples of high risk behavior (HRB).

RELATIONSHIP BETWEEN SUBSTANCE USE AND HIGH RISK BEHAVIOR (HRB)

Despite the inherent difficulties in researching this issue, for more than two decades now most professionals have agreed that there is a relationship between HRB and substance use (Leigh and Stall, 1993; Graves and Leigh, 1995).

It is impossible, and perhaps inappropriate to imply a simple linear relation-ship between these two complex and multifactorial behaviors. While it would be difficult to say that substance use *causes* HRB, there is an association between the two. Many people who use substances may not enter into HRB, but for many who practice HRB, substance use has preceded it.

Substance use can impair judgement and put people at risk of high risk sexual behavior. Some exchange sex to support the drug habit. If intoxicated, people can put themselves in risky situations and be less able to protect themselves from sexual violence. In some persons with both substance use and HRB, the behavior could be a reflection of an underlying personality vulnerability like impulsivity and high 'sensation seeking' need.

ETHICAL IMPLICATIONS

Every person experiencing a substance use disorder (SUD) who has high risk sexual behavior puts him or herself into risk of greater medical and social complications of both problem behaviors. Several times, access to health care occurs in the context of 'crisis' circumstances (medical/social/legal) which push the person to seek help. These circumstances may affect motivation to take help, especially when the 'crisis' situation abates. It is important to also understand that the level of motivation to take this help may vary in persons over time. The well-known Prochaska and DiClemente's (1986) model for change, can help professionals understand how to help a person to move from current 'precontemplation' to future 'contemplation/action'. In some persons, final change in behavior may occur only after a few relapses.

When the person with HRB accesses health care, the other factor which can influence motivation is the attitude and manner of the health professional. A competent, well trained and compassionate health care professional is important in a person's journey to recovery/changing behavior. An under-standing of the ethical principles which underlie decision making is a useful guide, especially in crisis situations.

ETHICAL PRINCIPLES IN DECISION MAKING

For professionals working alongside people experiencing SUD and high risk sexual behavior, the same ethical principles which are used to guide health professionals form a useful framework to manage ethical dilemmas in high risk sexual behavior.

Respect for autonomy

Even in cultures where there is close family involvement and support, it is important to ask the person's permission before involving specific signifi-cant others in their care programme. Where there is a legal requirement (where permission is not necessary), it is still good practice to inform the person first.

Example

If disclosing about a minor's pregnancy to parents, it would be important to counsel and prepare the child for the possible reactions and first disclose it to the parent, whom the child asks for the information to be given first.

Non-maleficence (Do No Harm)

The fundamental principle in medicine. It is specifically important to bear this in mind in view of the fiduciary nature of the relationship between the health professional and the person who is in need of professional help. The latter is often in a vulnerable position due to the nature of their difficulties or the circumstances in which they are accessing help.

Example

There may be a situation where a person may confide that another health care professional is involved in a romantic or sexual relationship with the person. A person in such a situation is vulnerable to abuse and such a situation is invariably harmful to both in the long run. It would be important for the professional to be aware of the local 'reporting' procedure.

Beneficence (Do Good)

The reason the professional engages with a person who needs behavioral intervention, is to 'do good'. The ethical conflict arises when there is a clash of ethical principles depending on how one looks at the issue.

Example

If disclosing about a minor's pregnancy to parents, it would be important to counsel and prepare the child for the possible reactions and first disclose it to the parent, whom the child asks for the information to be given first.

The child may feel that telling the parents would not be 'doing good' to her, if she fears an angry backlash from the parents. But in such a situation, legally the child is not in a position to exert 'autonomy', and the parents need to be told. The child needs to be protected from further abuse and supported to manage the consequences of what has happened. It would be difficult to achieve this 'good' objective if parents are unaware of what has happened.

Justice

Sometimes, vulnerable persons are victims of abuse: physical, emotional or sexual. In most situations there are laws in place to protect their rights.

Example

In working alongside a transgender person, the therapist finds there has been violations of their human rights, it would be important to offer information on resources, such as legal help and advocacy groups.

Example

If disclosing about a minor's pregnancy to parents, it would be important to counsel and prepare the child for the possible reactions and first disclose it to the parent, whom the child asks for the information to be given first.

It would be important for the professional to be aware of local laws in place for the protection of children from child abuse. There is likely to be a requirement for mandatory reporting to Child Welfare services.

Case Study 18.1

A 40-year-old man, with a history of high risk sexual behavior has been admitted to the medical ward with tuberculosis. As his HIV test came in positive, the medical team need to test his wife. The man does not wish his HIV status to be known to his wife as he fears she will get very upset, so asks for immediate discharge from the ward. The medical team has asked for your intervention. How will you proceed?

Ethical dilemmas

The person has a right to autonomy. If he does not wish his HIV status to be known to someone else, he would be entitled to confidentiality. But confidentiality does not hold if there is risk of immediate harm to self or others.

Not telling the wife could 'benefit' the husband, but could harm her – as she could put herself at continued risk, if she is in an active sexual relationship with him. Telling her is the 'just' thing to do. Yet telling her just as the husband is getting discharged is not allowing enough time for her to handle her grief, and could lead to her getting 'very upset' and potentially put her at risk of 'self harm'. Going against the husband's wishes, could ensure he never comes back to see you again.

Suggested way to proceed

First, buy time, by delaying discharge if possible. It is very difficult to defuse a fraught situation if there is limited time.

Second, spend time counselling the husband. Ideally at the time of 'pretest HIV counselling', the need to disclose a positive report to the spouse and managing his anxieties, *before testing* should have been done. However, if for the sake of discussion, this was not done, explore the husband's concerns and anxieties. Explain that as the wife is at risk of this sexually transmitted illness, she has to be tested. In addition, as treatment is available, if she is actually HIV positive, the sooner it is started for her, the better it would be. And yes, she would be upset, but better to deal with this difficult situation now with help available for both to manage, than wait for the inevitable crisis at some point in the future.

Third, set up adequate time for the counselling session for the wife, having previously ascertained from the husband about her general coping style.

In all this remember, the law of the land takes precedence and if there is a need for mandatory contacting of sexual partners, that needs to be done. Sometimes, it may be difficult to know what is the best thing to do; for example, if the husband insists on discharge and his wife is contactable only by telephone. In these situations, it is best to discuss with a senior colleague/legal team and document the discussion, decision and its rationale in the case notes.

KEY POINT 18.1

In real life situations, the ethical principles may seemingly 'conflict'. When one is unsure what needs to be done, it is good to discuss with colleagues and to record the decision with its rationale in case notes. Where legal issues are anticipated, it would be important to get legal advice.

ETHICAL ISSUES IN HRB

The practical aspects of ethical issues for professionals working alongside people experiencing substance use problems with particular relevance to high risk sexual behavior are listed below.

Confidentiality and disclosure

Confidentiality is the obvious bedrock of good clinical practice. However, limits of confidentiality exist especially when there is immediate risk of harming self or others. It would be important to explain the limits of confidentiality before starting the session with the person, to avoid distress and misunderstandings later. In high risk sexual behavior where there is risk of transmitting infections to others, the law of the land must be followed regarding disclosure to partners. In clinical scenarios, it may be important for the person to have several counselling sessions before they garner the skills necessary for themselves to inform current or past partners of their infection status. This is important as STIs (sexually transmitted diseases) are treatable, and the earlier the partner with infections like HIV is under regular review, the better the outcome.

Unplanned pregnancies

It would not be appropriate to get into a discussion on the ethics of protection of life versus abortion and the rights of the mother versus that of a fertilized egg. Suffice to say an unplanned pregnancy need not be an unwanted one.

It would be important to counsel the person on the various options available to cope with the pregnancy. Adoption is also an option. It is important for health professionals to be aware of the law of the land regarding medical termination of pregnancy, especially if it is the result of sexual violence.

Professionals need to take care that their own personal views on this emotive subject do not affect or bias their interactions. If one's personal view would prevent one from having a professional stance on this issue, then the person's care should be transferred to another professional, in a sensitive manner.

Contraceptive use

Health education on effective and safe contraceptive use is important. Moreover, it is important for professionals to be aware of some of the ethical issues around contraceptive use. Some contraceptives prevent fusion of the sperm and ova to form a fertilized egg or zygote and there are those which prevent implantation of this zygote into the uterus. While the latter are marketed as contraceptives, there are groups who believe that life begins with the formation of a zygote, and would find this method of 'contraception' unacceptable. The question of when life begins or when personhood starts has been debated.

KEY POINT 18.2

With sexually transmitted infections like HIV, research evidence suggests that if condoms are used consistently and correctly, the risk of transmitting HIV is substantially reduced. However, many argue that it should be understood that when there is high risk behavior like multiple sexual partners' condoms will not guarantee safe sex, but relatively 'safer' sex.

It is not impossible for a person with HRB to be conflicted about contraceptive use for religious reasons. In this situation a referral to an appropriate person who can offer pastoral care would be useful. One needs to be aware of the need to be sensitive to religious diversity.

Expedited Partner Therapy (EPT)

Here, the physician prescribes treatment for the partner of the person with STI like gonorrhoea and chlamydia, without seeing or examining the partner. While this might have the advantage of possibly ensuring treatment to those who would not otherwise access treatment, it also raises some ethical concerns such as safety of the treatment, lack of informed consent from the partner and breaking the partner's right for confidentiality. Again one needs to be aware of local laws regarding this, which are listed in the Centre for Disease

Control (CDC) website (www.cdc.gov/). Some states in the USA allow this, some prohibit. However, the reality in clinical practice is that a treatment is unlikely to be efficacious if a person does not engage with it. In view of this, it might be more useful to have a few sessions with the person and help them gain the social skills to try and persuade the partner to come in for treatment (or at a minimum inform them of the need).

ETHICAL ISSUES IN SOME VULNERABLE GROUPS

A professional working with vulnerable persons, needs to be aware of the particular challenges that this poses, in order to ensure that ethical decisions are based on current scientific knowledge. It is possible that as scientific knowledge changes over the next few years, what is considered ethical may change over time. This is exemplified by the fact that the treatments prescribed by some mental health physicians some 40 years ago to try and 'change' sexual orientation, would now be considered unethical by that same group of physicians. In addition, it would be important to know the law of the land, as some of these groups have differing legal status depending on which country they live in.

Persons who need mental health care

Some people may exhibit high risk behavior as a temporary consequence of mental illness. For example, in the hypomania or manic phase of bipolar disorder. These phases of mood change can also be associated with substance use. Where the person is unwilling for voluntary mental health care, the mental health professional would need to evaluate the situation to assess whether mental illness warrants involuntary treatment. If so, the due legal process to initiate this process must be started.

Sometimes changes in sexual drive occur with damage to the brain

Though protecting the rights of each individual is extremely important, it can be considered unethical if we do not ensure treatment for mental illness that is known to respond to treatment (where there is risk to self or others). This is because some mental illnesses like mania or psychoses can temporarily cause the person to lose insight and awareness that they are unwell and subsequently need treatment.

SEXUAL ADDICTION AND ZOOPHILIA

Certain behaviors like sexual addiction and sexual acts with animals (zoophilia or bestiality) are known to put persons at risk of sexually transmitted and other diseases. The diagnostic validity of these terms have been debated. The tenth revision of ICD 10 International Classification of Disorders (ICD 10 – 2016), which is generally used worldwide, lists 'excessive sexual drive' and 'other disorders of sexual preference' to denote these problem behaviors. *The American Diagnostic and Statistical Manual*, 5th Edition (DSM 5 – 2016), lists hypersexual disorders as a condition which warrants further research, and paraphilic disorders as distinct from paraphilias (earlier called sexual 'deviances'). This is to try and ensure that just because a sexual preference is 'atypical', it is not classified as a disorder. To classify a sexual behavior as a disorder requires that distress is present (not just due to society's reaction) and that there is a threat to the psychological and physical well being of self or others.

KEY POINT 18.3

Whatever the state of current nomenclature, the professional should only use these terms to describe the behavior – not as a label to the person.

ADOLESCENTS

Recent brain developmental biology seems to be able to explain why adolescents think and behave differently from adults. Adolescents are less able than adults to plan and think through the consequences of their actions. As a group they are especially vulnerable to both substance use and high risk sexual behavior. Exposure to alcohol and drugs before birth can also adversely affect the developing brain.

The American Academy of Child and Adolescent Psychiatry (www.aacap. org/) has put out useful information on their website to aid all professionals working with adolescents. In the adolescent brain, the amygdala (part of the brain that deals with instinctual behavior) develops much earlier than the prefrontal cortex (the part of the brain which deals with planning and rational decision making). The prefrontal cortex matures into early adulthood. This is why adolescents as a group are more impulsive, putting themselves in risky situations and less able to modify behavior despite negative consequences. The Academy makes it clear that this does not mean they cannot make good choices or that they should not be held responsible for their actions.

WOMEN

It has been noted all over the world that women are less likely to access treatment for substance dependence. It has been noted that where treatment is not gender sensitive and tailored to the special needs of the woman, she would be at risk of continuing substance use and its attendant risk of commercial or forced sex work (Lal et al., 2015).

LESBIAN, GAY, BISEXUAL, TRANSGENDER, INTERSEX AND QUESTIONING (LGBTIQ) GROUP

Health professionals working alongside the lesbian, gay, bisexual, transgender, intersex and questioning group, need to be particularly aware of the challenges members of this group face. Over the years, members of this group have faced discrimination, unethical attempts at 'treatments', violence and even exclusion from religious support. Ethical professionals need to ensure that their own attitude is supportive and caring.

> **KEY POINT 18.4**
>
> While some individuals of homosexual or bisexual orientation have high risk sexual behavior (indeed as many with heterosexual orientation also do), variation in sexual orientation per se is no longer considered a mental illness.

In June 2016, the United Nations Human Rights Council (www.ohchr. org/EN/HRBodies/HRC/Pages/HRCIndex.aspx) passed a resolution on the human rights of lesbian, gay, bisexual and transgender (LGBT) persons by creating the post of an expert on violence and discrimination based on sexual orientation and gender identity. Despite this there are several countries in the world where it is considered illegal to be gay. Health professionals need to ensure that both access to health care and its effective utilization is not impaired in these groups, who remain vulnerable in some societies.

Increasingly some religious groups are wanting to 're-engage' with this group, noting the unfairness in trying to identify a person by sexual orientation or gender identity. This was exemplified by Pope Francis's now famous remark 'Who am I to judge?' in 2013. Indeed, accounts of the personal journeys of persons who have struggled with these two aspects of their identity, religion and sexuality, suggests that it is possible to reconcile both (Narrain and Chandran, 2016). Again this is an area where should the person perceive a need, a referral to a religious, diversity sensitive, pastoral care department can be made.

SEX WORKERS

The term sex worker has been used to denote a 'consenting' adult who is involved in sex work, as opposed to a child or adult woman, man or transgender who is 'trafficked' and exploited. Groups which have studied adult sex workers have suggested that it is better to move towards decriminalizing sex work (as opposed to those who suggest legalization). They have opined that it is the criminalization of this activity, which has led to their human rights violations. This makes sex workers a particularly vulnerable group in terms of limited access to health care. There can be complicated power structures and some exploited persons may not even have the choice to insist their client use a condom.

SEX OFFENDERS

The ethics of dealing with sex offenders is primarily around ensuring a proper informed consent for treatment and making sure there is no element of coercion. The ethical challenge would be balancing the risks to the community versus privacy of the person. A useful document which discusses the issues in some detail are available online at the website of the Centre for Sex Offender Management (CSOM – http://csom.org/), a project of the US department of justice. A detailed discussion would be outside the purview of this chapter but as recommended by CSOM, at a minimum, the sex offenders should have written information on the purpose and nature of treatment, anticipated risks, benefits and costs and the limits of confidentiality.

SOME ETHICAL ISSUES WITH RELEVANCE TO PROFESSIONALS

Sometimes professionals get into difficulties as they are unaware of the ethics around certain issues. Some of these are listed below.

Risks in dual relationships

As far as possible, professionals should maintain professional boundaries with persons under their care, especially in social and business arenas (Kurpad et al., 2012). This is to prevent any exploitation by the professional. All codes of practice prohibit a sexual relationship with a person under one's care (General Medical Council – GMC – 2013). Professionals are reminded that 'consent' for a sexual relationship in this power imbalanced relationship is not considered true consent (Kurpad et al., 2011).

Standards of care

It is important that the professional is aware of the standard of care that is expected from them. Team work, appropriate referrals and linking with other agencies like police or legal team, if required are important. Additionally, familiarize oneself with standard procedures, which should be followed in certain situations.

Example

A nurse drawing a blood sample from a person with HRB sustains a needle stick injury. As the nurse would be at risk of infectious disease and needs to follow appropriate post exposure prophylaxis for diseases like HIV, one needs to be aware of the ethical and legal issues, as well as the local policies around testing the individual.

Where the person consents for the testing, there is no problem. Where the person is unable to consent (for example, if unconscious), the British Medical Association (www.bma.org.uk/) has set down some useful guidelines. If it is possible to delay the testing until the person regains the capacity to give consent, that should be done. If not, the appropriate legal authority can take the decision. It is recommended that all testing without consent is done using pseudonyms and the person given the choice to be told the results of the testing or not, once they regain capacity. The rights of the health care professionals are important in this situation but the testing should not harm the individual.

Appropriate training and supervision for the professional

Sometimes, persons with HRB have personality vulnerabilities which can resurface in the professional person interaction. (Sometimes it is the professional who might have personality vulnerabilities.) Depending on the specific job description, the professional dealing with the person should be appropriately trained and qualified. It is always good practice for the professional to have access to supervision/discussion forum/or a colleague to discuss challenging situations or ethical dilemmas. Being up to date with the latest knowledge in the field is an important ethical requirement. For the individual or relative/care giver, it is extremely important to ensure that help is taken only from qualified people in centres which are registered appropriately.

Need for self-awareness in the professional

For any professional it is an ethical duty to be aware of one's own attitudes, beliefs, strengths and areas which need further work. This is especially important if one's attitudes and beliefs could get in the way of good therapeutic relationships with the person accessing help. For example, a homophobic attitude or difficulty in interacting with people from different cultures or religions would need to be effectively dealt with before dealing with these persons with HRB.

KEY POINT 18.5

For the professional, clinical work can be stressful and taking care of oneself to avoid burnout is also important. Sometimes specific issues like dealing with terminal illness and death in a person under our care can be particularly distressing for the professional.

Ethical research

As with research in any other group, it is important to take steps to protect the interest of the participant with proper informed consent and confidentiality. The local procedure for the approval research protocols before it is commenced must be followed.

When research is planned, the questions and interpretation of responses from participants should be considered carefully. When scales are used to measure substance use and sexual activity, the research investigator should assess the reliability of the information to be gathered due to the limitations of human memory and attributional bias. Importantly enough numbers of participants to ensure statistical power for the research should be studied.

A MODEL TO EVALUATE ETHICAL DILEMMAS IN CLINICAL PRACTICE

The National Association of Social Workers (NASW) in the US, has suggested a useful model to help make ethical decisions (TIPS manual – Batki and Selwyn, 2008).

1   Identify the clinical issues pertinent to the person
    For example, if the high risk behavior in a person is secondary to a mood disorder, that would need appropriate referral and management.

2   Identify the legal issues
    Whatever one's personal views on an issue, the law of the land needs to be adhered to. If the professional feels that the law has the potential to victimize the person, one can help the person access legal support and get in touch with advocacy groups.

3   Identify system issues
    If the centre where one works has a specific protocol to deal with a particular issue, it should be followed.

4   Identify cultural issues
    If the professional is not sensitive to cultural issues it can be distressing to the person and their family members.

5   Identify ethical issues
    If the professional recognizes that there is an ethical dilemma, it is important to acknowledge it and then take steps to deal with it. Discussion with an experienced colleague is always helpful and can reduce the professional's own anxiety in dealing with difficult situations.

6   Review the ethical principles at stake
    What are the various ethical principles that are relevant? Often on review, the dilemma is less than what seems on first count.

7   What are the possible options?
    Important to also take the person's opinion, as also the significant other/ care giver.

8   Review pros and cons of each option
    Not only for the person, but for the significant others in the person's family.

9   Act
    Document decision and its rationale.

10 Follow up and review situation

11 Further options

An ethics consultation is sometimes helpful, especially in dealing with an issue which could have some legal implications. This can be done before step 9 (action).

REFLECTIVE PRACTICE EXERCISE 18.1

Time: 40 minutes

As a health professional, reflect on your own attitude towards individuals with high risk sexual behavior. Will this attitude help or harm this person in their journey to address this behavior? If you should find anything that you feel you need to work on, how should you proceed?

This reflexive practice should be discussed with your supervisor. The supervisor should be able to support you to work through any issues that may arise, and allow a safe environment where any disclosure should not cause problems for you. You should ensure that your own attitude is not judgmental or prejudicial to persons experiencing substance use and/or high risk sexual behavior.

REFLECTIVE PRACTICE EXERCISE 18.2

Time: 50 minutes

How would you react if a person under your care told you that your colleague and good friend touched her inappropriately?

It is sometimes hard to believe that someone who you trust could behave inappropriately with someone else. You can watch an 18-minute video on sexual harassment titled, "Who would you believe?" which is freely available online at www.sjri.res.in/hhResources and discuss the issues it raises with colleagues (Simon Kurpad, 2015).

SELF-ASSESSMENT EXERCISE 18.1 – ANSWERS ON P. 268

Time: 30 minutes

1. If for your own religious beliefs get in the way of delivering current evidence based treatment for a person with a health problem due to HRB, what should you do?
2. As a health professional, what are the five focal virtues ethicists suggest you cultivate in yourself?
3. If you feel you have been given an unethical order, what should you do?
4. What are the ethical codes of practice you are expected to abide by?
5. What is Hebephilia?

REFERENCES

American Diagnostic and Statistical Manual, 5th ed. 2016. http://dsm.psychiatryonline. org/doi/book/10.1176/appi.books.9780890425596.

Batki SL and PA Selwyn. 2008. Consensus Panel Chair and Co-chair. (NASW's Ethical Issues, HIV/AIDS, and Social Work Practice training manual NASW, 1997 quoted in Chapter 8 Ethical Issues.) In Substance abuse treatment for persons with HIV / AIDS. Treatment Improvement Protocol (TIP) series 37. Centre for substance abuse treatment. p. 203. http://store.samhsa.gov/product/TIP-37-Substance-Abuse-Treatment-for-Persons-With-HIV-AIDS/SMA12–4137.

Beauchamp TL and JF Childress. 2001. *Principles of Biomedical Ethics*, 5th ed. Oxford University Press: Oxford.

General Medical Council. 2013. UK. *Good Medical Practice. Working with doctors working for patients. Maintaining a professional boundary between you and your patient.* www.gmc-uk.org/static/documents/content/Maintaining_a_professional_boundary_between_you_and_your_patient.pdf.

Graves KL and BC Leigh. 1995. "The relationship of substance use to sexual activity among young adults in the United States". *Family Planning Perspectives*. 27: 18–22, 33.

International Classification of Diseases (ICD10). 2016. http://apps.who.int/classifications/icd10/browse/2016/en.

Kurpad SS. 2015. *Sexual boundary violations: 'Who would you believe?'* An 18-minute film on sexual harassment, freely available online, with a list of FAQs at www.sjri.res.in/hhResources.

Kurpad SS, T Machado and RB Galgali. 2011. "'When a yes should mean no': doctors and boundaries". *Indian Journal of Medical Ethics*. 8: 126–127.

Kurpad SS, T Machado, RB Galgali and S Daniel. 2012. "All about elephants in rooms and dogs that do not bark in the night: boundary violations and the health professional in India". *Indian Journal of Psychiatry*. 54: 81–87.

Lal R, KS Deb and S Kedia. 2015. "Substance use in women: current status and future directions". *Indian Journal of Psychiatry*. 57: S275–S285.

Leigh BC and R Stall. 1993. "Substance use and risky sexual behavior for exposure to HIV: issues in methodology, interpretation, and prevention". *American Psychologist*. 48: 1035–1045.

Narrain A and V Chandran. 2016. "Religion and sexual orientation. Reconciling faith with same sex love". In *Nothing to fix. Medicalization of sexual orientation and gender identity.* Edited by Narrain A and V Chandran. Sage Yoda Press: India. pp. 285–301.

Prochaska JO and CC DiClemente. 1986. "Towards a comprehensive model of change". In *Treating addictive behaviours – process of change,* edited by WR Miller and N Heather. London: Plenum.

Sadock BJ, VA Sadock and P Ruiz (Eds.). 2014. *Kaplan and Sadock's Synopsis and Clinical Psychiatry. Behavioral Sciences/Clinical Psychiatry*, 11th ed. Chapters on Human sexuality and sexual dysfunctions, pp. 564–574; Sex addiction and compulsivity, pp. 590–592; Gender dysphoria, pp. 600–607. Wolters Kluwer: www.wolterskluwer.co.uk/.

TO LEARN MORE

Bloch S and C Paul. 1991. *Psychiatric Ethics*, 2nd ed. Oxford University Press: Oxford.

Christian Ethics. 2010. *A Very Short Introduction.* D. Stephen Long. Oxford University Press: Oxford.

Mela M and AG Ahmed. 2014. "Ethics and the treatment of sexual offenders". *Psychiatric Clinics of North America.* 37: 239–250.

Revathi A. 2016. *A Life in Transactivism.* As told to Nandini Murali. Zubaan Publishers: New Delhi.

Wakefield JC. 2011. "DSM-5 proposed diagnostic criteria for sexual paraphilias: tensions between diagnostic validity and forensic utility". *International Journal of Law and Psychiatry.* 34: 195–209.

Some Useful Documents at Websites

Expedited partner therapy (CDC) www.cdc.gov/std/ept/
>Working with adolescents (AACAP) www.aacap.org/AACAP/Families_and_Youth/Facts_for_Families/FFF-Guide/The-Teen-Brain-Behavior-Problem-Solving-and-Decision-Making-095.aspx

Working with sex offenders (CSOM)
www.csom.org/train/treatment/long/03/3_9.htm

On needlestick injuries (BMA)
www.bma.org.uk/news/2016/may/bma-sets-out-guidelines-on-needlestick-injuries

On sensitivity to religious diversity in health care (Penn Medicine. Hospitals of University of Pennsylvania)
www.uphs.upenn.edu/pastoral/resed/diversity_points.html

On professional boundaries (GMC)
www.gmc-uk.org/guidance/ethical_guidance/21170.asp

ANSWERS TO SELF-ASSESSMENT EXERCISE 18.1 – *SEE* P. 266

1 If your own religious beliefs get in the way of delivering current evidence based treatment for a person with high risk behaviour, you should hand over the person's care to another health professional. The person's wellbeing is always your primary concern, and it will be difficult for you to be at your best if you are troubled yourself.

2 The five focal virtues are compassion, discernment, trustworthiness, integrity and conscientiousness. (Beauchamp and Childress, 2001.)

3 In the rare situation where you feel that you have been given an unethical order, you can and should raise a conscientious objection. But it is good practice (and wiser) to do it respectfully.

4 The ethics codes of practice may differ according to the country in which one practices. It is good practice to familiarize yourself with the various codes and guidelines for practice that you are expected to abide by.

5 Hebephilia is sexual preference for children in early adolescence (approximately age 11–14 years). (Kaplan et al., 2014.)

CHAPTER 19

Medical cannabis in mental health–substance use

Kevin Reel, Jean-François Crépault,
Gavin S MacKenzie, and Bernard Le Foll

Cannabis is a substance that has been stigmatized for years, and that's why I'm so adamant about educating people on the health benefits of it.
(Eugene Monroe, quoted in Couric 2016)

Cannabis is not cannabis is not cannabis. It's made up of 130 different chemical compounds, some of which may have benefits for these folks and some of which may not. So it's really important to try to understand specifically what could help.
(Marcel Bonn-Miller, quoted in Couric 2016)

Cannabis is one of those topics that can inspire vastly differing moral responses, from deep resolve to redeem its reputation to equally deep repugnance for its potential to ruin lives. To varying degrees in between there is an acknowledgement of potential benefits, possible harms and growing recognition that polarized perspectives have done little to maximize the former and mitigate the latter. Our shifting regard for it has been influenced by politics, power, fear and race (Moscrop 2014; Rehm and Fischer 2015). This chapter will explore this history briefly in order to understand how the current complexities of medical cannabis evolved. It will then explore the ethical dimensions of the issue and the challenges that persist.

HISTORICALLY MORALIZED MESSAGES

The Canadian government criminalized cannabis in 1923, though it appears a true challenge to understand why (Schwartz 2014). More than a decade later, the film *Reefer Madness* conveyed an exceedingly alarmist portrayal of cannabis addiction (Sides 2015). Subsequently, absolutist declarations of 'wars on drugs' have shaped our views of cannabis so that they intersect with anxieties about mental illness, substance use and the unraveling of the fabric of society (Moscrop 2014; Philipsen et al. 2014). Clark (2000) noted the assertion of cannabis as a 'slippery slope' or 'gateway drug' while Room et al. (2010) have since demonstrated otherwise. A 2002 report prepared for the Canadian Senate Special Committee on Drugs examined the place of cannabis in cultures around the world and across time. With the increasingly multicultural context of many societies, the meanings and values associated with cannabis have become highly diverse. The report commented that: 'While on the surface the debate includes scientific arguments regarding the harms or benefits of marijuana, below the surface the debate is actually informed by preconceived cultural morals and values' (Spicer 2002).

Where *medical* cannabis is being discussed, the scientific arguments and clinical evidence obviously rank above others – albeit with certain caveats attached to how one defines 'scientific' and what one considers 'evidence'. Hathaway (2015) notes that professionals may feel threatened given that their training and authority operates from a philosophy that science, not individual experience, is what constitutes evidence. Equally, approaches to care in mental health and substance use embrace the philosophical perspectives of 'recovery' and 'harm reduction' in addition to other arguably conventional goals, often framed as abstinence and cure. Scientific study of clear empirical questions is hampered by agendas promoting preconceived judgements about cannabis. Kalant (2008) appeared to betray such preconceptions in concluding that: 'the lack of convincing evidence thus far makes it unlikely that future studies will demonstrate any significant advantage of smoked marijuana over oral or parenteral use of pure cannabinoids' (p. 518).

These attitudes and anxieties have hugely influenced the possibilities for rigorous research into the real harms and potential benefits of cannabis (Hathaway 2015; Rehm and Fischer 2015).

> '*I was eating 100 Percocets a month during my career, even up until five years after I retired. And it just made me feel bad. It made my head fuzzy. It screws up your insides*'
>
> – Jim McMahon (Couric 2016)

The United States has conducted its 'war on drugs' for decades, in part by including cannabis in the Federal Schedule I list of drugs (Drug Enforcement Agency 2016). This meant that funding for research was most often limited to studies seeking to affirm the danger of it, and little opportunity to explore the plant's constituent elements and their effects. Raphael Mechoulam, a less restricted Israeli researcher, was able to discover the chemical structure of the active ingredients and the primary mechanisms of their actions (O'Brien 2016). Of note, also, is the disproportionate effect that the ongoing enforcement of strict cannabis laws has on particular races over others. Some have noted the questionably rigorous enforcement of cannabis law for the disparity in arrests this creates along racial lines in North America (Golub et al. 2007; Spicer 2002) and the diversion of policing resources away from more serious crimes (Philipsen et al. 2014).

While the science of cannabis has slowly developed, public attitudes have evolved more swiftly (Fischer et al. 2016). Non-medical (i.e. 'recreational') use of cannabis became more common during the 1960s, most often associated with the 'hippie' demographic. The infamous *Reefer Madness* was sought out for its kitsch value. Some governments, too, have softened their stance with arguments in favour of its legalization and regulation. However, the prevailing pressures from the U.S. meant that official policy continued to be highly restrictive at the Federal level even while becoming more relaxed in many individual states (Philipsen et al. 2014). Clark (2000) outlines a history of highly convoluted U.S. Federal control of access to 'compassionate' cannabis and relative denial of those government funded studies that indicated its positive benefits.

Reports of the therapeutic properties of cannabis opened the minds of more people to the possibility that the vilified substance may have redeemable value. Among the drivers of this shift have been court cases that have challenged the constitutionality of the criminal statutes regarding possession or cultivation of marijuana, typically on grounds of compassion owed to those for whom the plant offered relief from symptoms associated with health problems such as seizures, pain and muscle wasting. Nevertheless, strict attitudes have remained and their influence manifests in such places as the United Nations *Convention on Psychotropic Drugs* (1971). This has been associated with a divide between those nations with powerful pharmaceutical sectors serving affluent health care systems and other developing nations that have historically relied on lower tech organic production of drugs (Spicer 2002).

REFLECTIVE PRACTICE EXERCISE 19.1

Time: 30 minutes

Consider the notions that come to mind when you think of the words cannabis, marijuana, ganja and weed.

- To what extent do you think the associations you make with these words have been shaped by images and ideas coming from media sources like film and journalism?
- How many of the associations you make with these words involve specific cultures and races?
- How many of them are comical?
- How many of them are characterized by some degree of negative regard?
- Are there any uncomplicated positive associations you can identify?
- How do you think your own associations would compare to those of others – colleagues, friends, strangers on a commuter train?

In 2001, Canada began regulating medicinal cannabis. The most recent version of these regulations was passed in 2015, with the curiously spelled title *Marihuana for Medical Purposes Regulations*. More curious were some of the restrictions still imposed, which have since been successfully challenged in court – among them the limitation of access to *dried* marijuana, excluding oils and fresh cannabis. It would seem that the prevailing moral resistance to cannabis found continuing, if subtle, expression in such seemingly arbitrary restrictions.

However, given the overall failure of severely restrictive policies criminalizing non-medical cannabis (Harcourt and Ludwig 2007), support is growing for its legalization and regulation as well (Parliament of Canada 2002). In Canada, the Centre for Addiction and Mental Health adopted a policy position in favour of this (Crépault, Rehm and Fischer 2016). In the 2015 Federal election campaign, the Liberal Party, led by Justin Trudeau, promised to legalize non-medical cannabis. Now in 2016, Prime Minister Trudeau's government has set about the task of making this happen. The context is currently an uncertain one with *medical* cannabis available to those individuals who are authorized as users by specific professionals and allowed to source it from licensed providers. In perhaps another year, there will be access to *non-medical* cannabis within a new regulatory system. This may reduce pressure on professionals to give authorizations, but it will also make it more likely that individuals will be using cannabis without the knowledge of the professionals who support them. This raises questions about how to frame policies and procedures on the use of medical cannabis in a manner that presents the least likely harm to therapeutic relationships. These relationships are primary factors in most individuals' recovery, but require openness and trust to take root and grow adequately to offer real benefits.

The remainder of this chapter will relate a summary of the exploration that has occurred in one organization as it responds to the changing landscapes around the availability and use of cannabis as Canadian law evolves. To illustrate some of the complexities that arise in practice, three brief individual illustrative vignettes will be used.

Case Study 19.1 – Reza

Reza (53) has a longstanding mood disorder and has lived with chronic diabetic neuropathy for the last six years. He has heard about the possibility that medical cannabis can help with pain and would like to know more. He asks about it on a regular visit to his diabetes clinic.

Case Study 19.2 – Edith

Edith (62) attends a clinic for people working to manage overuse of opioids. She has not been able to work since back surgery following a car accident 12 years ago. She still experiences chronic pain and has been unable to find another medication that offers satisfactory relief. Her primary goal now is to be able to play with her grandchildren as she did with her own children 40 years ago.

Case Study 19.3 – Peter

Peter (16) is currently a 'voluntary inpatient' in a specialist youth program after being transferred from his local rural hospital. He has experienced significant depression and anxiety for the past four years. He began using non-medical cannabis three years ago to help with his anxiety symptoms. He discloses that his mother is bringing him cannabis to smoke when off the hospital grounds. He is seeking authorization on medical grounds.

REFLECTIVE PRACTICE EXERCISE 19.2

Time: 40 minutes
- Make written notes on each of the individual stories above.
- Briefly describe your 'gut response' to each story.
- Identify the concerns you have regarding each person's potential use of medical cannabis.
- Make a list of questions you might ask each of them to explore these concerns.

NAVIGATING COMPLEX ETHICAL QUESTIONS

In Canada, regulated access to medical cannabis already exists. There is now the plan for regulated access to non-medical cannabis in the very near future. In the context of mental health and substance use, this means a complex and fluid policy and practice environment that requires simultaneous attention to a variety of laws, emerging research data, treatment approaches and fundamental ethical considerations that may appear to conflict more often than align.

In order to approach such a layered and at times counter-intuitive sphere of decision making, ethical tools and frameworks can help ensure that multiple concerns are addressed in the deliberations around treatment for individuals and policies for all. At the Centre for Addiction and Mental Health (CAMH), the myriad considerations that apply in such ethically complicated issues are highlighted in the idea of the 'e-GPS' or ethical guideposts for principled solutions (CAMH, undated – a). This framework includes a decision-making tool and guidance about the many relevant sources of information and direction that ought to be taken in account, including:

➤ extant policies
➤ professional codes, standards and regulations
➤ laws
➤ organizational values
➤ population specific factors
➤ organizational mandate or purpose.

Central to the e-GPS is the task of identifying the facts guided by the mnemonic 'CLEOS', which captures five domains considered essential to robustly circumspect decision-making in healthcare ethics:

1 clinical
2 legal
3 ethical
4 organizational
5 systemic (Russell 2008).

In the brief review of CLEOS factors that follows, some of the main facts are outlined. Critical unknowns should also be noted and factored into decision making accordingly.

Clinical

Our understanding of the functioning of the cannabinoid system has increased tremendously. An endogenous cannabinoid system has been discovered that consists of endocannabinoids (primarily anandamide and 2-arachidonoyl glycerol), two cannabinoid receptors (CB_1 in the brain and CB_2 mostly in the periphery), enzymatic degradation systems (through the fatty acid amide hydrolase enzyme for anandamide and the monoacylglycerol lipase enzyme for 2-arachidonoylglycerol) and cannabinoid transport reuptake system (Di Marzo 2006, Di Marzo et al. 2001, Piomelli 2003; Sugiura and Waku 2002).

The cannabinoid receptors are most extensive in the brain and widely present in the peripheral nervous system. Therefore, it is not surprising that exposure to cannabis will lead to pharmacological modulation of this endogenous system, which could lead to some therapeutic effects. In addition to the delta 9-Tetrahydrocannabinol (THC) that acts on the CB_1 receptors and on the CB_2 receptors as a partial agonist, some other components of cannabis may have some potential therapeutic utility. The most studied is cannabidiol, but a series of cannabinoid ligands (ex cannabidivarin, cannabinol . . .) have been also identified in cannabis. Their function still remains to be fully understood (Yücel et al. 2015).

According to a recent systematic review, there are just two medical conditions for which there is clear evidence of effectiveness: chronic pain (Savage et al. 2016) and spasticity (Koppel et al. 2014). There is some evidence for at least two other symptoms: reducing nausea and vomiting due to chemotherapy and aiding weight gain in HIV infection (Whiting et al. 2015). Claims have been made that cannabis can help with Post-Traumatic Stress Disorder (PTSD), although more research is needed to validate this (Betthauser et al. 2015). There is also evidence primarily from preclinical studies, but also from some clinical studies, that adding cannabinoid to opiate allows for the reduction in the dose of opioid needed for pain control (i.e. 'opioid sparing effect' of cannabinoid) (Elikottil Gupta and Gupta 2009; Meng et al. 2016).

Cannabidiol (CBD) is a CB_1 and CB_2 antagonist (Pertwee 2008) that is present is some cannabis strains. Interestingly, it has been suggested that THC and CBD may have opposite properties: THC produces psychotic-like and anxiogenic effects in humans (D'Souza et al. 2004, D'Souza et al. 2005, D'Souza et al. 2008), while CBD might modulate THC's euphoric (Dalton et al. 1976), appetitive (Morgan et al. 2010), anxiogenic, and other psychological/physical effects (Karniol et al. 1974, Nicholson et al. 2004, Zuardi et al. 1982). CBD may also have anti-seizure properties and a large clinical trial is currently underway in treatment resistant epilepsy in children (NCT02397863). CBD also showed great promise as an antipsychotic drug in pre-clinical and human studies as it was associated with fewer extrapyramidal side effects than conventional antipsychotics (Fakhoury 2016).

There is the potential for THC and CBD to alleviate symptoms of anxiety, but there is limited evidence obtained by clinical trials (Blessing et al. 2015). For mood regulation, the situation is very unclear. In clinical trials conducted mostly for pain control (Lynch and Ware 2015), users tend to show an improvement in mood ratings (Ware et al. 2010). Although this may be related to the improvement of their pain ratings, it is possible that cannabis exposure may have some benefit. However, some studies did not find benefit from THC exposure. There are also clear psychomimetic properties that are induced by THC exposure that suggest that the risk of psychosis may be due to overstimulation of CB_1 receptors (D'Souza et al. 2004). However, the finding that there was no improvement of psychotic symptoms by blockade of CB_1 with the use of an inverse agonist suggests that the situation is more complex than just a control of psychosis by CB_1 receptors (Meltzer et al. 2004).

While the evidence regarding the physical harms of cannabis might still be reported as somewhat equivocal (Meier et al. 2016), it is associated with a range of real harms. In summarizing a review of the literature, Crépault (2015) found that it may lead to cannabis use disorders (Lopez-Quintero et al. 2011) and both short term and chronic health problems (Hall and Degenhardt

2009; Volkow et al. 2014; World Health Organization 2016). From a public health perspective, they found reports of clear and concerning harms such as lung cancers from smoking it and traffic-related injuries when driving under its influence (Fischer et al. 2016, Imtiaz et al. 2016). The growing body of evidence indicates that younger individuals are most likely to be harmed. Notably, the risk of developing cannabis use disorder is increased if the exposure is started at early age (Le Strat, Dubertret, and Le Foll 2014). Regular cannabis use in adolescence can interfere with the normal development of the brain (George and Vaccarino 2015) with potentially permanent detrimental effects. Those who have a personal or family history of mental illness are more at risk (McLaren et al. 2009). Other key risk factors they found identified in the literature include earlier age and frequency of use, the potency of the product, its formulation and the manner in which it is used (Fischer et al. 2011).

Medical cannabis does not yet undergo the same approvals as regular pharmaceuticals and rigorous safety and quality considerations have not yet been established. Thus some professionals may be hesitant to recommend a "medicine" that is linked with so much uncertainty (Canadian Medical Association 2015; Rich 2014). In the face of this void, a recent safety study by Ware et al. (2015, p. 1233) did find that: 'Quality-controlled herbal cannabis, when used by patients with experience of cannabis use as part of a monitored treatment program over 1 year, appears to have a reasonable safety profile'.

More defiantly, Lake et al. (2015) assert that current prescribing practices are too cautious given the evidence that does exist. Even if our historical attitudes toward cannabis and those who use it reflect any bona fide concerns, the judicious use of medical cannabis might have a different risk profile than non-medical use that may challenge our prejudices (Savage et al. 2016).

REFLECTIVE PRACTICE EXERCISE 19.3

Time: 20 minutes

Recall the two quotes that began this chapter. How do you feel about their assertions after having read this brief clinical summary?

In practice, specific scenarios may arise. Individuals may request a prescription/authorization to begin using medical cannabis, or they may have already been prescribed/authorized to use medical cannabis by one professional and wish to continue doing so while being supported by other professionals. Conversely, the individual might be using cannabis outside of any legal arrangement, and this fact may or may not be shared with the professionals supporting them. Additionally, any individual may be using cannabis in any of the forms available – smoked, vaporized or edible preparations of leaves or oil – legally or not. Some professionals may well have concerns about individuals accessing less regulated products, and there may also be evidence of 'diversion' of the legally authorized cannabis to other individuals, as observed in opioid treatment (Venkat and Kim 2016).

SELF-ASSESSMENT EXERCISE 19.1 – ANSWERS ON P. 291

> **Time: 60 minutes**
> - Identify four different components of the cannabinoid system.
> - Explain what it meant by 'opioid sparing effect'.
> - Review the illustrative vignettes again. Which of those individuals may most benefit from the likely benefits of medical cannabis?
> - Do cautions arise in your mind for any of them?

Legal

The legal issues that must be addressed will vary between jurisdictions. The following discussion uses the current Canadian context to illustrate the potential complexity of laws regulating medical cannabis.

With regard to medical cannabis, Health Canada (2016) states:

> Dried marijuana is not an approved drug or medicine in Canada. The Government of Canada does not endorse the use of marijuana, but the courts have required reasonable access to a legal source of marijuana when authorized by a healthcare practitioner.
>
> The *Marihuana for Medical Purposes Regulations (MMPR)* came into force in June 2013. The regulations create conditions for a commercial industry that is responsible for the production and distribution of marijuana for medical purposes. They also make sure that Canadians with a medical need can access quality controlled marijuana grown under secure and sanitary conditions.

In a curious twist, the Federal Court declared the *MMPR* to be unconstitutional and invalid in February 2016 (*Allard v. Canada* [2016] FC236). The court found the *MMPR*'s regulatory restrictions arbitrarily limited the plaintiffs' ability to access cannabis in a manner that could potentially undermine their health care. However, the court delayed the declaration of invalidity for six months to allow the Federal government time to consider alternative regulations. The government indicated (Government of Canada 2016) it would amend the *MMPR* to comply with the court's ruling by August of 2016 (ahead of its stated intention to legalize marijuana in 2017) but at the time of writing it had not done so. Any policies and practices will thus be interim ones, given the prospect for significant changes in legal access to cannabis in the near future. At that point, there will be the possibility of separate regulations to govern medical and non-medical cannabis. The question of segregating these two markets is discussed in the 'systemic' section below.

Possession

The regulations allow for individuals to possess cannabis for medical purposes if a 'healthcare practitioner' completes necessary medical documentation (Health Canada Medical Practitioner's Form Category 1 2007; Medical Practitioner's Form Category 2 2007 – often referred to as an 'exemption' or 'authorization'). The maximum amount of dried cannabis individuals can possess at a time is 30 times the daily amount identified in the exemption documentation (up to 150 grams). The exemption lasts for up to 12 months and can be renewed. Additionally, the *MMPR* allows an individual to possess cannabis if it is provided to them by a 'healthcare practitioner in the course of treatment for a medical condition' or is provided to them by a hospital for a medical reason.

A 'healthcare practitioner' may possess cannabis for the 'practice of their profession', although this phrase is not defined. A 'healthcare practitioner' is defined in the *MMPR* as 'a medical practitioner or a nurse practitioner'. A hospital employee may also possess medical cannabis for the 'purposes of or in connection with their employment', presumably enabling the movement of the substance from one place to another within the hospital if necessary and dispensing to the person using it.

Prescribing

The *MMPR* permits either a medical or nurse practitioner to 'prescribe' cannabis. The scope of nurse practitioner roles varies among provinces with respect to prescribing controlled substances such as cannabis.

Providers

Government approved 'licensed producers' can be used by exemption holders to obtain their supplies. This is the single largest legal source of medical cannabis. The *MMPR* allows exemption holders to obtain cannabis directly from Health Canada; however, Health Canada does not currently sell marijuana. Storefront cannabis dispensaries and 'compassion clubs' are illegal.

Production

Who can produce medical cannabis?

Under the *MMPR*, licensed corporations and individuals can produce medical cannabis. The licensing process is outlined in the *MMPR*. At the time of writing, there are approximately 30 licensed corporate producers in Canada. Under the regulatory regime that preceded the *MMPR*, exemption holders could grow a certain quantity of marijuana for their own use if they obtained a Personal-Use Production License (PUPL). An exemption holder could also obtain medical cannabis from an individual that obtained a Designated Person Production License (DPPL), which allowed the producer to grow cannabis for up to two exemption holders. Although the *MMPR* eliminated PUPLs and DPPLs, some still remain active at this time as a result of a Federal Court order.

What can be produced?

The *MMPR* prohibits licensed producers from selling cannabis products other than 'dried marihuana'. However, in 2015 the Supreme Court of Canada ruled this prohibition was unconstitutional and violated section 7 of the *Charter of Rights and Freedoms* (*R. v. Smith* [2015] 2 SCR 602).

To date, Health Canada **has not** adopted the ruling in *Smith* to permit all forms of medical cannabis for purchase from licensed producers. However, it expanded the production and sale of medical cannabis by licensed producers beyond dried forms (as per the *MMPR*) by issuing a legal exemption (Health Canada 2015).

There are no restrictions in the *MMPR* on how dried cannabis is to be ingested or inhaled, and individuals may choose to use it, for example in foods or by vaporizing. Health Canada does not limit or recommend a particular method of administration.

It might be hard not to think of images of 'haze' and 'weeds' when trying to grasp the legal parameters outlined above. And other legislation must be considered. In Ontario, these include smoking laws, electronic cigarette laws and workplace health and safety laws among them. As mentioned previously, the U.S. has highly convoluted historical and current arrangements at multiple levels of government that affect access to and research into medical cannabis (Clark 2000).

SELF-ASSESSMENT EXERCISE 19.2 – ANSWERS ON P. 292

> **Time: 10 minutes**
> Identify four domains that would likely need to be addressed in any legal framework for the regulation of medical cannabis.

Ethical

While this whole chapter is an extended ethical exploration, this particular discussion of ethics will focus on how the CAMH organizational values (respect, courage and excellence) apply. Ethical discussions often refer to values and principles and the terms are sometimes used interchangeably. In one view, values are intangible things which we hope to increase in the world because they serve human interactions and flourishing. We do this by acting according to principles that promote them (College of Occupational Therapists of Ontario 2013).

Respect

> *Respect is a prerequisite for everything we do and aspire to be as an organization. It guides our interactions with each other, with patients and with partners. It models what we expect in return.*
> (Centre for Addiction and Mental Health 2012, 6)

Typically framed as 'respect for persons', this value encompasses considerations of maximizing autonomy and dignity as far as possible. It involves recognition of the individual's right to make choices for him or herself, according to their values and beliefs (within shared legal parameters). There may be concerns about the legitimacy of someone's request for a medical cannabis prescription. As with many medications, some of the requests may be premised on reasons other than the purported clinical need. It will be central to promoting respect that professionals reflect on that moralized and racialized history of cannabis and work to identify the 'implicit assumptions' that are embedded in our views on the matter, as with the many other biases we all typically carry (Banaji and Greenwald 2013).

Respect here applies to individuals who are living with mental health–substance use issues, and those who support them – professional or otherwise. It may be necessary to preserve and promote respect between providers where a decision to prescribe is questioned. Equally, some providers may hold profound moral hesitations about medical cannabis, despite the emerging evidence for its use. Even where a professional's hesitation may be premised on clinical rather than moral concerns, there is potential strain on therapeutic relationships (Eggertson 2014).

> *'I wouldn't be here today if it wasn't for cannabis, period. Cannabis has saved my life. I don't think of suicide anymore.'*
> – Kyle Turley (Couric 2016)

Any decision about medical cannabis initiation ought to be circumspect – with a clear clinical and ethical rationale, and within available practice guidelines that consider other medications including synthetic cannabinoids prior to initiating the use of medical cannabis. This process of trial and elimination of alternatives may be critical for some insurance coverage as well. It must also be cognizant of the experience of the individual requesting it. As Mark Ware says: 'It is time we begin to speak the language of cannabis, and discuss this with patients' (quoted by Rich 2014).

Hathaway (2015) also reminds us that the positivist philosophies of professionals, assuming science will offer clear evidence, may have to coexist with alternatives borne out of frustration and disappointment with conventional medicine. Such 'respect for lived experience, and a holistic view of illness, health and healing' may lead to the use of complementary therapies including cannabis.

Some general principles for promoting respect may be described as: maximizing collaborative communication; recognizing the expertise of lived experience (as seen in 'patient as teacher' paradigms in professional education (CAMH undated – b), and; being aware of our own, oral responses and hidden biases.

Courage

Courage is about standing up and being heard, about taking risks and doing what is right, not what is easy. It's about challenging prejudice and discrimination. It's about hope for the future.
(Centre for Addiction and Mental Health 2012, 6)

One way of seeing courage is as moral courage – the ability to act rightly in the face of popular opposition or the likelihood of controversy. Courage is one of the four cardinal virtues, along with its counterpart, prudence. The two ought to work together to produce a considered approach that recognizes, but does not necessarily bow to, any current *zeitgeist* around the issue.

Courage may also mean accepting that an initial position may require revision – in response to further information from stakeholders or changes in law or new clinical evidence. Reluctant professionals might have to accept that within the current parameters of practice and evidence for it, there is not much solid ground on which to refuse **all** medical uses of cannabis.

Principles which promote courage may include taking only well-reasoned risks and continuing to do the work required to further understanding of counter-intuitive treatment approaches like harm reduction. These principles for promoting courage apply to both individual and organizational decisions. The position taken by CAMH on decriminalizing and regulating non-medical cannabis was arguably one that required some courage – from those drafting the document through to the boardroom deliberations finalizing it. Adopting a positive stance toward medical cannabis still places any physician in clear opposition to the Canadian Medical Association's 2015 policy statement (CMA 2015). As emerging evidence gives more direction around the potential uses of medical cannabis, courage will be needed by all to regularly reflect upon and possibly revise their positions on the matter.

Excellence

Excellence drives us to raise the bar in all aspects of our work. It requires us to hold each other to the highest standards. It is about continuous improvement, accountability and transparency.
(Centre for Addiction and Mental Health 2012, 6)

Excellence demands approaching a complex issue like medical cannabis with the highest standard of ethical deliberation. For individual professionals, excellence is inextricably intertwined with transparency and communication. This requires that professionals create a therapeutic rapport and milieu in which those who may be using or wish to inquire about cannabis use for alleviating their symptoms are able to trust them. As quoted above, Mark Ware's assertion that professionals 'begin to speak the language of cannabis, and discuss this with patients' (Rich 2014) is a crucial foundation stone to that rapport.

For organizations creating policies that frame practice within their aegis, excellence is promoted by deliberating according to the principles of maximizing transparency, consulting broadly and explaining clearly and honestly the range of findings and considerations taken into account, including controversies and remaining unknown factors. At CAMH, this has meant the convening of an interdisciplinary group of individuals to lead the initial explorations, and taking the necessary time to reach the first iteration of a policy.

The next sections will explore the considerations at the organizational and systems levels with which any eventual policy will have to dovetail.

SELF-ASSESSMENT EXERCISE 19.3 – ANSWERS ON P. 292

> **Time: 10 minutes**
> - Describe the relationship between values and principles as described above.
> - Identify two principles that can promote each of the three values outlined above: respect, courage and excellence.

REFLECTIVE PRACTICE EXERCISE 19.4

> **Time: 40 minutes**
> Consider the organizational values at your place of employment.
> - How do they apply to thinking about a policy for medical cannabis?
> - What might promote those values required?
> - What three values would you say most characterize your personal ethics?
> - What would they demand of you in considering your own response to being involved with medical cannabis use or provision?

Organizational

In creating harmonized local policy and procedure, organizations will be in a position to impose restrictions on anyone wishing to use any cannabis product within their buildings and on their grounds. Any restrictions must align with the law – both the rights it protects and the restrictions it imposes. Cannabis is potentially subject to the same regulations as tobacco sales, smoking and the use of electronic cigarettes, in addition to others specific to medical or non-medical cannabis. These vary across jurisdictions. In some cases, as at CAMH, policy goes even further to create a tobacco-free environment (Centre for Addiction and Mental Health, undated – c).

Where local policies might go beyond the restrictions in law, a review of the principles underpinning those policies is advised. Simplistically equating cannabis and tobacco would be a mistake, given the therapeutic purpose of cannabis, for pain symptoms especially. Skepticism about the legitimacy of the therapeutic need or effectiveness for any individual ought to be explored transparently. Inpatient and outpatient contexts will present some of the same issues, and others specific to those contexts of service provision.

Cannabis (medical or otherwise) is most often smoked, but it can also be vaporized. Some vaporizing devices resemble and function like e-cigarettes, but not all do. Some involve neither combustion nor aerosols. These forms of cannabis use would be prohibited under Ontario law and thus also under CAMH's current tobacco-free policy, though edible forms of cannabis would not. Changes to legislation may follow from ongoing research, and perhaps advocacy.

Internal prescribing/authorizing guidelines would necessarily reference professional practice guidelines (CPSO and CFPC) and consider making use of implementation strategies such as the medical cannabis contract described by Wilsey et al. (2015) and Hill (2015). Other internal considerations include myriad regulations and operating procedures for hospital pharmacies, documentation in health records and operational arrangements on individual units.

Systemic

Health Canada estimates medical cannabis will involve $1.3 billion in annual sales by 2024, with approximately 450,000 registered users. There are currently an estimated 500,000 individuals using medical cannabis for health reasons, though not all are registered users (Canadian Press 2014). The growing level of need for professional support is evident.

Broader legalization

Legalization can take many forms, from an unfettered free market to a tightly regulated public health approach. A public health approach, carefully implemented, monitored, and enforced, can be a net benefit to society (via reductions in the social harms of criminalization and regulations on the product itself, as well as improved public awareness). A commercially oriented model can lead to increases in use and problematic use (e.g. frequent [daily/ near-daily] use, early onset, use while driving, etc.), and harms can increase as a result.

Merged or segregated approaches

There is already a blurry line between non-medical ('recreational') and medical use. Many people use cannabis for self-determined health-related purposes without the involvement of any professional. Under legalization, this line could disappear if the markets are not regulated separately. In Colorado they are separate; in Washington State they are merged. This will be a significant factor to consider as Canada moves into broader legalization of cannabis. As leaders in the field of addiction and mental health, CAMH will aim to bring the available evidence to deliberations on that matter. Maintaining regard for the benefits of harm reduction approaches will also be critical as CAMH fulfills its self-stated purpose to 'drive social change'.

The rise and regulation of dispensaries

In the current unusual context of flux in public opinion and legal regulation in Canada, illegal cannabis 'dispensaries' have been growing in number. They range from long-established compassion clubs aiming to facilitate access to cannabis for medical uses to shops that unapologetically sell cannabis to anyone over 19 with no other questions asked. These dispensaries may propagate misconceptions about both the current legal status of cannabis and its effectiveness as a medicine. The more commercially oriented shops may also contribute to a normalization of cannabis as a product like any other – which is the opposite of a public health approach. A significant systemic challenge is the need to improve the standardization of the dose strength of currently available products and the accuracy of their labeling (Vandrey et al. 2015). This may be maximized by precise regulation, keeping in mind the need to avoid arbitrary or burdensome requirements that ultimately restrict access unfairly.

By-laws associated with regulating outlets can include requirements that they be no less than a specified distance (e.g. 300 metres) from any school, community centre, or another dispensary (as in Vancouver, Canada). Hospitals and addiction treatment centres may also be included among such exclusion zones.

CONCLUSION

> There is no escape: we must decide as we decide; moral risk cannot, at times, be avoided. All we can ask for is that none of the relevant factors be ignored.
>
> (Berlin 2013, 19)

Cannabis remains the object of polarized opinions. Distinguishing its merits from the myths that surround it is a challenge as the benefits and harms evade simple understanding. Even as potentially safer synthetic derivatives are developed, the prescription opioid crisis (Born et al. 2014; Lake et al. 2015; United States Department of Health and Human Services 2016) indicates the need for ongoing evaluation. Most critically, we need to remain open to the possibility that good clinical and ethical reasons might exist for its use.

Deciding the parameters for access to medical cannabis is complex. We have a duty to those living with symptoms that it might improve. We also have a duty to those who may be harmed by it. Balancing such harms is an exercise in overcoming the fear of uncertainty. Incrementally, certitude will emerge . . . if we can shed the historical biases that have persisted for decades and let the power of evidence and lived experience lead us, cautiously and conscientiously.

REFERENCES

Allard et al. v. Canada. 2016. F.C.J. No. 195 http://cas-cdc-www02.cas-satj.gc.ca/rss/T-2030–13%20reasons%2024–02–2016%20(ENG).pdf.

Banaji MR and AG Greenwald. 2013. *Blind Spot: Hidden Biases of Good People.* New York: Delacorte Press.

Berlin I. 2013. "The pursuit of the ideal." In H. Hardy (ed.), *The Crooked Timber of Humanity: Chapters in the History of Ideas.* Princeton, NJ: Princeton University Press. pp. 1–20.

Betthauser K, J Pilz and LE Vollmer. 2015. "Use and effects of cannabinoids in military veterans with posttraumatic stress disorder." *American Journal of Health-System Pharmacy* 72: 1279–84.

Blessing EM, MM Steenkamp, J Manzanares and CR Marmar. 2015. "Cannabidiol as a potential treatment for anxiety disorders." *Neurotherapeutics* 12: 825–36.

Born K, G Cummings and A Laupacis. 2014. Canada's prescription opioid crisis. Healthy Debate. http://healthydebate.ca/2014/01/topic/politics-of-health-care/prescription-opioid-crisis-canada.

Canadian Medical Association. 2015. www.cma.ca/Assets/assets-library/document/en/advocacy/CMA_Policy_Authorizing_Marijuana_for_Medical_Purposes_Update_2015_PD15–04-e.pdf.

Canadian Press. 2014. "Health Canada swamped with medical marijuana business applications." www.cbc.ca/news/canada/health-canada-swamped-with-medical-marijuana-business-applications-1.2661070.

Centre for Addiction and Mental Health. Undated-a. www.camh.ca/en/hospital/care_program_and_services/hospital_services/Pages/guide_bioethics.aspx.

Centre for Addiction and Mental Health. Undated-b. www.camh.ca/en/hospital/about_camh/newsroom/CAMH_in_the_headlines/stories/Pages/The-Patient-as-Teacher.aspx.

Centre for Addiction and Mental Health. Undated-c. www.camh.ca/en/hospital/visiting_camh/Pages/Tobacco-Free-CAMH.aspx.

Centre for Addiction and Mental Health. 2012. *Tomorrow. Today: CAMH Strategic Plan 2020.* www.camh.ca/en/hospital/about_camh/mission_and_strategic_plan/Documents/StrategicPlan_Short_10May2012.PDF.

Clark PA. 2000. "The ethics of medical marijuana: government restrictions vs. medical necessity." *Journal of Public Health Policy* 21: 40–60.

College of Occupational Therapists of Ontario. 2013. *Guide to the Code of Ethics.* Toronto: College of Occupational Therapists of Ontario. www.coto.org/pdf/publications/Guide_to_Code_of_Ethics.pdf.

Convention on Psychotropic Substances. 1971. New York: United Nations. www.unodc.org/pdf/convention_1971_en.pdf.

Couric K. 2016. "For some NFL players, ban on medical marijuana is a real pain." PBS Newshour, July 4. www.pbs.org/newshour/bb/for-some-nfl-players-ban-on-medical-marijuana-is-a-real-pain/.

Crépault JF. 2015. *Cannabis Policy Framework.* Toronto: Centre for Addiction and Mental Health. www.camh.ca/en/hospital/about_camh/influencing_public_policy/Documents/CAMHCannabisPolicyFramework.pdf.

Crépault JF, J Rehm and B Fischer. 2016. The Cannabis Policy Framework by the Centre for Addiction and Mental Health: A proposal for a public health approach to cannabis policy in Canada. *International Journal of Drug Policy* 34 (August): 1–4.

D'Souza DC, WM Abi-Saab, S Madonick, K Forselius-Bielen, A Doersch, G Braley, R Gueorguieva, TB Cooper and JH Krystal. 2005. "Delta-9-tetrahydrocannabinol effects in schizophrenia: implications for cognition, psychosis, and addiction." *Biological Psychiatry* 57: 594–608.

D'Souza DC, E Perry, L MacDougall, Y Ammerman, T Cooper, YT Wu, G Braley, R Gueorguieva and JH Krystal. 2004. "The psychotomimetic effects of intravenous delta-9-tetrahydrocannabinol in healthy individuals: implications for psychosis." *Neuropsychopharmacology* 29: 1558–1572.

D'Souza DC, M Ranganathan, G Braley, R Gueorguieva, Z Zimolo, T Cooper, E Perry and J Krystal. 2008. "Blunted psychotomimetic and amnestic effects of delta-9-tetrahydrocannabinol in frequent users of cannabis." *Neuropsychopharmacology* 33: 2505–2516.

Dalton WS, R Martz, L Lemberger, BE Rodda and RB Forney. 1976. "Influence of cannabidiol on delta-9-tetrahydrocannabinol effects." *Clinical Pharmacology and Therapeutics* 19: 300–309.

Di Marzo V. 2006. "A brief history of cannabinoid and endocannabinoid pharmacology as inspired by the work of British scientists." *Trends in Pharmacological Sciences* 27: 134–140.

Di Marzo V, L De Petrocellis and T Bisogno. 2001. "Endocannabinoids Part I: molecular basis of endocannabinoid formation, action and inactivation and development of selective inhibitors." *Expert Opinion on Therapeutic Targets* 5: 241–265.

Drug Enforcement Agency. 2016. "DEA Announces Actions Related to Marijuana and Industrial Hemp." August 11. www.dea.gov/divisions/hq/2016/hq081116.shtml.

Eggertson L. 2014. "Marijuana strains doctor-patient relationship." *Canadian Medical Association Journal* 186: E511–E512.

Elikottil J, P Gupta and K Gupta. 2009. "The analgesic potential of Cannabinoids." *Journal of Opioid Management* 5: 341–357.

Fakhoury M. 2016. "Could cannabidiol be used as an alternative to antipsychotics?" *Journal of Psychiatric Research* 80: 14–21.

Fischer B, V Jeffries, W Hall, R Room, E Goldner and J Rehm. 2011. "Lower risk cannabis use guidelines: a narrative review of evidence and recommendations." *Canadian Journal of Public Health* 102: 324–327.

Fischer B, AR Ialomiteanu, C Russell, J Rehm and RE Mann. 2016. "Public opinion towards cannabis control in Ontario: strong but diversified support for reforming control of both use and supply." *Canadian Journal of Criminology and Criminal Justice* 58: 443–459.

Golub A, BD Johnson and E Dunlap. 2007. "The race/ethnicity disparity in misdemeanor marijuana arrests in New York City." *Criminology & Public Policy* 6: 131–164.

Gordon C, MJ Drolet and K Reel. 2015. "Facilitating interdisciplinary ethical decision making: occupational therapists as leaders in the emerging practice of professionally assisted dying." *Occupational Therapy Now* 17: 18–20.

Government of Canada. 2016. Statement from the Minister of Health – Minister Philpott confirms Canada's way forward on marijuana for medical purposes. March 24, 2016. http://news.gc.ca/web/article-en.do?nid=1042329.

Hall W and L Degenhardt. 2009. "Adverse health effects of nonmedical cannabis use." *The Lancet* 374: 1383–1391.

Hall W, M Renström and V Poznyak. 2016. *The Health and Social Effects of Nonmedical Cannabis Use.* Geneva: World Health Organization.

Harcourt BE and J Ludwig. 2007. "Reefer madness: broken windows policing and marijuana misdemeanor arrests in New York City, 1989–2000." *Criminology & Public Policy* 6: 165–182.

Hathaway A. 2015. "Regulating marijuana medicine in Canada: new challenges and prospects for meaningful reform." *Impact Ethics.* https://impactethics.ca/2015/08/04/regulating-marijuana-medicine-in-canada-new-challenges-and-prospects-for-meaningful-reform/.

Health Canada. 2015. Health Canada statement on Supreme Court of Canada Decision in *R v. Smith.* www.hc-sc.gc.ca/dhp-mps/marihuana/info/licencedproducer-product eurautorise/decision-r-v-smith-eng.php.

Health Canada. 2016. *Medical Use of Marijuana.* www.hc-sc.gc.ca/dhp-mps/marihuana/index-eng.php.

Health Canada's Medical Practitioner's Form for Category 1 Applicants. 2007. www.hc-sc.gc.ca/dhp-mps/alt_formats/pdf/marihuana/how-comment/form_b1-eng.pdf.

Health Canada's Medical Practitioner's Form for Category 2 Applicants. 2007. www.hc-sc.gc.ca/dhp-mps/alt_formats/pdf/marihuana/how-comment/form_b2-eng.pdf.

Hill KP. 2015. "Medical marijuana for treatment of chronic pain and other medical and psychiatric conditions: a clinical review." *Journal of the American Medical Association* 313: 2474–2483.

Hughes JC and C Baldwin. 2006. *Ethical Issues in Dementia Care: Making Difficult Decisions.* London: Jessica Kingsley.

Imtiaz S, KD Shield, M Roerecke, J Cheng, S Popova, P Kurdyak, B Fischer and J Rehm. 2016. "The burden of disease attributable to cannabis use in Canada in 2012." *Addiction* 111: 653–662.

Kalant H. 2008. "Smoked marijuana as medicine: not much future." *Clinical Pharmacology and Therapeutics* 83: 517–519.

Karniol IG, I Shirakawa, N Kasinski, A Pfeferman and EA Carlini. 1974. "Cannabidiol interferes with the effects of delta 9 – tetrahydrocannabinol in man." *European Journal of Pharmacology* 28: 172–177.

Koppel BS, JC Brust, T Fife, J Bronstein, S Youssof, G Gronseth and D Gloss. 2014. "Systematic review: Efficacy and safety of medical marijuana in selected neurologic disorders: Report of the Guideline Development Subcommittee of the American Academy of Neurology." *Neurology* 82: 1556–1563.

Lake S, T Kerr and J Montaner. 2015. "Prescribing medical cannabis in Canada: Are we being too cautious?" *Canadian Journal of Public Health* 106: e328-e330.

Le Strat Y, C Dubertret and B Le Foll. 2014. "Impact of age at onset of cannabis use on cannabis dependence and driving under the influence in the United States." *Accident Analysis and Prevention* 76 C:1–5.

Lopez-Quintero C, J Pérez de los Cobos, DS Hasin, M Okuda, S Wang, BF Grant and C Blancoa. 2011. "Probability and predictors of transition from first use to dependence on nicotine, alcohol, cannabis, and cocaine: Results of the National Epidemiologic Survey on Alcohol and Related Conditions (NESARC)." *Drug and Alcohol Dependence* 115: 120–130.

Lynch ME and MA Ware. 2015. "Cannabinoids for the treatment of chronic non-cancer pain: an updated systematic review of randomized controlled trials." *Journal of Neuroimmune Pharmacology* 10: 293–301.

McLaren JA, E Silins, D Hutchinson, RP Mattick and W Hall. 2010. "Assessing evidence for a causal link between cannabis and psychosis: A review of cohort studies." *Drug Policy* 21: 10–19.

Medical Practitioner's Form for Category 2 Applicants. www.hc-sc.gc.ca/dhp-mps/alt_formats/pdf/marihuana/how-comment/form_b2-eng.pdf.

Meier MH, A Caspi, M Cerda, RJ Hancox, HL Harrington, R Houts, R Poulton, S Ramrakha, W Murray Thomson and TE Moffitt. 2016. "Associations between cannabis use and physical health problems in early midlife: A longitudinal comparison of persistent cannabis vs tobacco users." *Journal of the American Medical Association of Psychiatry* 73: 731–740.

Meltzer HY, L Arvanitis, D Bauer and W Rein. 2004. "Placebo-controlled evaluation of four novel compounds for the treatment of schizophrenia and schizoaffective disorder." *American Journal of Psychiatry* 161: 975–984.

Meng H, JG Hanlon, R Katznelson, A Ghanekar, I McGilvray and H Clarke. 2016. "The prescription of medical cannabis by a transitional pain service to wean a patient with complex pain from opioid use following liver transplantation: A case report." *Canadian Journal of Anesthesia* 63: 307–310.

Morgan CJ, TP Freeman, GL Schafer and HV Curran. 2010. "Cannabidiol attenuates the appetitive effects of Delta 9-tetrahydrocannabinol in humans smoking their chosen cannabis." *Neuropsychopharmacology* 35: 1879–1885.

Moscrop, D. 2014. "Is medicinal marijuana bad medicine?" *Impact Ethics.* https://impactethics.ca/2014/10/20/is-medicinal-marijuana-bad-medicine/NCT02397863.

Nicholson AN, C Turner, BM Stone and PJ Robson. 2004. "Effect of Delta-9-tetra-hydrocannabinol and cannabidiol on nocturnal sleep and early-morning behavior in young adults." *Journal of Clinical Psychopharmacology* 24: 305–313.

O'Brien M. 2016. *Medical marijuana research comes out of the shadows.* PBS Newshour, July 13. www.pbs.org/newshour/bb/medical-marijuana-research-comes-shadows/.

Parliament of Canada. 2002. Cannabis: Our position for a Canadian public policy. Report of the Senate Special Committee on Illegal Drugs. www.parl.gc.ca/Content/SEN/Committee/371/ille/rep/repfinalvol3-e.htm.

Pertwee RG. 2008. "Ligands that target cannabinoid receptors in the brain: from THC to anandamide and beyond." *Addiction Biology* 13: 147–159.

Philipsen N, RD Butler, C Simon-Waterman and J Artis. 2014. Medical marijuana: A primer on ethics, evidence, and politics. *The Journal of Nurse Practitioners* 10: 633–640.

Piomelli D. 2003. "The molecular logic of endocannabinoid signalling." *Nature Reviews Neuroscience* 4: 873–884.

Rehm J and B Fischer. 2015. "Cannabis legalization with strict regulation, the overall superior policy option for public health." *Clinical Pharmacology and Therapeutics* 97: 541–544.

Rich P. 2014. *Sessions help clear the air on medical marijuana.* Canadian Medical Association. www.cma.ca/En/Pages/Sessions-helps-clear-air-on-medical-marijuana.aspx.

Room R, B Fischer, W Hall, S Lenton and P Reuter. 2010. *Cannabis Policy: Moving Beyond Stalemate*. Oxford: Oxford University Press.

Russell B. 2008. "An integrative and practical approach to ethics in everyday health care." *Risk Management in Canadian Health Care* 10: 9–13.

Savage SR, A Romero-Sandoval, M Schatman, M Wallace, G Fanciullo, B McCarberg and M Ware. 2016. "Cannabis in pain treatment: Clinical and research considerations." *Journal of Pain* 17: 654–668.

Schwartz D. 2014. "Marijuana was criminalized in 1923, but why?" *CBC News: Health*. Canadian Broadcasting Corporation. www.cbc.ca/news/health/marijuana-was-criminalized-in-1923-but-why-1.2630436.

Sides H. 2015. "Science seeks to unlock marijuana's secrets." *National Geographic. June*. http://ngm.nationalgeographic.com/2015/06/marijuana/sides-text.

Smith A. 2015. "What are the brain and behavioural effects of cannabis use in youth?" In *Substance Abuse in Canada: The Effects of Cannabis Use During Adolescence*. Edited by T George and F Vaccarino. 2015. Ottawa, ON: Canadian Centre on Substance Abuse. pp. 20–31.

Spicer, L. 2002. *Historical and Cultural Uses of Cannabis and the Canadian Marijuana Clash*. Report prepared for The Senate Special Committee on Illegal Drugs. Ottawa: Library of Parliament. www.parl.gc.ca/content/sen/committee/371/ille/library/spicer-e.htm.

Sugiura T and K Waku. 2002. "Cannabinoid receptors and their endogenous ligands." *Journal of Biochemistry* 132: 7–12.

United States Department of Health and Human Services. 2016. *Opioids: The Prescription Drug & Heroin Overdose Epidemic*. www.hhs.gov/opioids/index.html.

Vandrey R, JC Raber, ME Raber, B Douglass, C Miller and MO Bonn-Miller. 2015. "Cannabinoid dose and label accuracy in edible medical cannabis products." *Journal of the American Medical Association* 313: 2491–2493.

Venkat A and D Kim. 2016. "Ethical tensions in the pain management of an end-stage cancer patient with evidence of opioid medication diversion." *HEC Forum* 28: 95–101.

Volkow ND, RD Baler, WM Compton and SRB Weiss. 2014. "Adverse health effects of marijuana use." *New England Journal of Medicine* 370: 2219–2227.

Ware M, T Wang, S Shapiro and JP Collet for the COMPASS Study Team. 2015. "Cannabis for the management of pain: assessment of safety study." *The Journal of Pain* 16: 1233–1242.

Ware MA, T Wang, S Shapiro, A Robinson, T Ducruet, T Huynh, A Gamsa, GJ Bennett and JP Collet. 2010. "Smoked cannabis for chronic neuropathic pain: a randomized controlled trial." *Canadian Medical Association Journal* 182: E694–701.

Whiting PF, RF Wolff, S Deshpande, M Di Nisio, S Duffy, AV Hernandez, JC Keurentjes, S Lang, K Misso, S Ryder, S Schmidlkofer, M Westwood and J Kleijnen. 2015. "Cannabinoids for medical use: A systematic review and meta-analysis." *Journal of the American Medical Association* 313: 2456–2473. www.ncbi.nlm.nih.gov/pubmed/26103030.

Wilsey B, J Hampton Atkinson, TD Marcotte and I Grant. 2015. "The medical cannabis treatment agreement: Providing information to chronic pain patients through a written document." *Clinical Journal of Pain* 31: 1087–1096.

Yücel M, A Kandola and A Carter. 2015. "Remind me again, how does cannabis affect the brain?" *The Conversation*. http://theconversation.com/remind-me-again-how-does-cannabis-affect-the-brain-40641.

Zuardi AW, I Shirakawa, E Finkelfarb and IG Karniol. 1982. "Action of cannabidiol on the anxiety and other effects produced by delta 9-THC in normal subjects." *Psychopharmacology (Berl)* 76: 245–250.

TO LEARN MORE

Guidelines and policy statements

College of Family Physicians of Canada. 2014. *Authorizing Dried Cannabis for Chronic Pain Or Anxiety: Preliminary Guidance.* www.cfpc.ca/uploadedFiles/Resources/_PDFs/uthorizing%20Dried%20Cannabis%20for%20Chronic%20Pain%20or%20Anxiety.pdf.

College of Physicians and Surgeons of Ontario. 2015. *Marijuana for Medical Purposes. Policy Statement #1–15.* www.cpso.on.ca/policies-publications/policy/marijuana-for-medical-purposes.

Fischer B, V Jeffries, W Hall, R Room, E Goldner and J Rehm. 2011. "Lower risk cannabis use guidelines for Canada (LRCUG): a narrative review of evidence and recommendations." *Canadian Journal of Public Health* 102: 324–327.

Further details on legislative contexts

The Marihuana for Medical Purposes Regulations in more detail:

California's Medical Marijuana Morass: https://psmag.com/california-s-medical-marijuana-morass-b38172ce61e9#.u3xqh3qbi.

Ziemaski, D and MA Ware. 2015. "Canada's Marihuana for Medical Purposes Regulations: a synopsis for health professionals." *Journal of Hospital Administration* 4: 79–83.

Television/Internet Resources

PBS Newshour segments and stories on:

Medical cannabis www.pbs.org/newshour/bb/medical-marijuana-research-comes-shadows/ www.pbs.org/newshour/bb/until-research-unlocks-medical-understanding-of-marijuana-patients-experiment/

Prescription opioids www.pbs.org/newshour/rundown/opioid-dependence-leads-tsunami-medical-services-study-finds/www.pbs.org/newshour/rundown/montanas-pain-refugees-leave-state-get-prescribed-opioids/

CNN segments:

www.cnn.com/specials/health/medical-marijuana
www.cnn.com/2013/08/08/health/gupta-changed-mind-marijuana/
www.cnn.com/2015/04/16/opinions/medical-marijuana-revolution-sanjay-gupta/

A response to CNN's Sanjay Gupta on his position about medical cannabis:

www.asam.org/magazine/read/article/2015/05/01/sanjay-gupta-is-wrong-about-medical-marijuana

ANSWERS TO SELF-ASSESSMENT EXERCISES

ANSWERS TO SELF-ASSESSMENT EXERCISE 19.1 – *SEE* P. 277

Identify four different components of the cannabinoid system.
- endocannabinoids
- two cannabinoid receptors
- enzymatic degradation systems
- cannabinoid transport reuptake system

Explain what it meant by 'opioid sparing effect'.
- Adding cannabinoid to opiate allows for the reduction in the dose of opioid needed for pain control and thus may help manage overuse of opioids.

Review the illustrative vignettes again. Which of those individuals may most benefit from the likely benefits of medical cannabis?
- Reza's neuropathy may be helped by medical cannabis as relief of neuropathic pain has the most evidence behind it. See: Wallace MS, TD Marcotte, A Umlauf, B Gouaux and JH Atkinson. 2015. "Efficacy of inhaled cannabis on painful diabetic neuropathy." *Journal of Pain* 16: 616–627.
- Edith's pain may also be helped by medical cannabis, and her overuse of opioid medications might be reduced by the 'opioid sparing effect'.
- Peter's anxiety might be helped, although the evidence for this is not as strong.

Do cautions arise in your mind for any of them?
- Reza's diabetes will be accompanied by circulatory complications, which might be made worse over time by smoked cannabis. It may be that other forms of intake, such as vaporization, might be preferable.
- Edith's experience of overuse of opioids might suggest paying attention to her use of medical cannabis. If her goal is to spend better time with her grandchildren, there may be some discussion about how and when she uses cannabis so as to avoid any secondary risks to the children in her life.
- Peter is of an age that presents a particular risk of cannabis induced psychosis. His reported use of cannabis for some years already means he is not cannabis naive. Whether or not this suggests he is out of the risk zone is not necessarily clear. His still developing brain is also at risk of some of the effects of cannabis and this ought to be discussed. Given he has the support of his mother in providing cannabis, there is clear likelihood that he will use it regardless of medical authorization to do so. It would be advisable to approach his care planning in a manner that preserves trust in the therapeutic relationship and transparency about complementary therapies.

ANSWERS TO SELF-ASSESSMENT EXERCISE 19.2 – *SEE* P. 279

Identify four domains that would likely need to be addressed in any legal framework for the regulation of medical cannabis.
- possession
- prescription
- provision
- production

ANSWERS TO SELF-ASSESSMENT EXERCISE 19.3 – *SEE* P. 282

Describe the relationship between values and principles as described above.
- Principles are guides for acting in ways that promote (ethical) values. Values are intangible things generally considered to be good for human flourishing.
Identify two principles that can promote each of the three values outlined above: respect, courage and excellence.
- Respect can be promoted by communicating, seeing lived experience as a kind of expertise (reflecting some humility around our own limited experience), fostering awareness of our own moral responses (and containing these as appropriate) and working to recognize our own hidden biases or 'implicit assumptions'.
- Courage can be promoted by reasoning clearly about risk-taking and working to understand things that might seem counter-intuitive at first.
- Excellence can be promoted by transparency, consultation and honesty.

CHAPTER 20

Assisted death in mental health

Our last, best judgement – assisted death for intolerable, irremediable suffering in mental health–substance use

Kevin Reel, Rosanna Macri, Justine S Dembo, Sally Bean, Ruby Rajendra Shanker, Lucy Costa, and Robyn Waxman

It's 2016, and in Canada, the suicidally depressed still don't have the right to die. They still don't have the right to end their suffering with dignity; they still don't have the right to spare the people they love the shock of losing them, of knowing that they died alone in terrible pain.

(Bayliss 2016)

There is no situation in which depression – or any mental health problem – needs to be terminal, irremediable, or even nearly as disabling as it can be. . .There is no evidence that any mental health problem is irremediable in the same way as some physical ailments.

(Henick 2016)

These two sentiments represent the quoted authors' diverging viewpoints on assisted dying or medical aid in dying (MAID) in the context of mental illness. Both viewpoints are informed by their particular experience of illness and their interactions with mental health services, and each appears to have arrived at opposing conclusions. From an ethical deliberation perspective, it is important to consider that although these viewpoints may appear opposing, the wish to protect 'vulnerable' individuals may be a common thread.

The contrasting opinions on assisted dying in the mental health context are reflected in the various legal frameworks where assisted dying is allowed. Legislation on assisted dying around the world ranges from more restrictive (e.g. Oregon and Washington where it is limited to terminal illness, and only allows patient self-administration) to more liberal (e.g. Canada where access is effectively limited to individuals with terminal illness, but includes physician administration), to more permissive (e.g. Belgium and the Netherlands where individuals with mental illness and children are eligible). Regardless of mental illness being excluded, it is evident that some eligible individuals requesting assisted dying due to a grievous and irremediable physical condition will also be living with concurrent mental health conditions.

In Canada, there has been much deliberation on assisted dying in the context of mental health and substance use. What follows is a brief introduction to the complexity of some of the main concerns, considerations and conundrums that enter into the task of making a 'last, best judgement' (Grisez and Shaw 2004, 43) on this issue – at both macro and micro levels of law and individual interests.

Before exploring these dimensions of the issue, please take a moment to complete the first reflective exercise. Record your responses to these prompts for later reference.

REFLECTIVE PRACTICE EXERCISE 20.1

Time: 40 minutes
- Read the two quotes that are offered at the outset of this chapter. Make notes on your initial response to them.
- Describe briefly how you reacted emotionally to each quote.
- On a scale of 1–10, rate the extent to which you agree or disagree with each of them.
- Does either statement make assertions that are 'unproven', or that are likely difficult to 'prove'?
- Write down the terms that you might want to be defined more precisely.

This chapter assumes assisted dying within the context of mental health and substance use can be a legally and ethically defensible practice within specific parameters. Some of the principal ethical dimensions associated with assisted dying in such a context are clustered under four main themes to highlight how they manifest:
1 discrimination/stigma
2 counter-intuitions
3 uncertainties
4 conscientious persons and practice.

The aim of this chapter is to highlight these dimensions and to explore some of the less obvious details of implementing assisted dying within the mental health and substance use context.

Two illustrative individual stories will be used throughout this chapter – Prakesh and Cristina. These stories are fictional but informed by the experiences of real individuals.

Case Study 20.1 – Prakesh

Prakesh is in his late 70s with terminal metastatic prostate cancer and is requesting assisted dying. He has been taking anti-depressants since his early 20s. His depression became worse and more complex to manage after the death of his wife from cancer five years ago. Prakesh describes watching his wife's agonizing death from an inoperable brain tumour as devastating and disturbing. He wishes to avoid a similar fate, including what he considers a loss of dignity for no discernible benefit to anyone. He fears the likely loss of decision making capacity, which would lead to ineligibility for assisting dying in a jurisdiction where capacity is a criterion. Prakesh's two adult children have become increasingly estranged from him since the death of their mother. They both describe their relationship with their mother as more meaningful than their relationship with Prakesh. One child is more supportive of his request for assisted dying while the other completely objects.

Case Study 20.2 – Cristina

Cristina is in her late 40s and lives with schizophrenia. She has medications that help to treat her psychosis. As a long-term heavy smoker, she has developed chronic obstructive airway disease and has no interest in smoking cessation despite being aware that it could help prolong her life. She is on intermittent oxygen therapy and engages in unsafe practices, e.g. smoking while using the oxygen, despite repeated education on safe use. Due to the risk this presents, she is now being evicted from her housing and is having difficulty finding an appropriate living environment. She is alienated from her family and has no close friends, just a few acquaintances with whom she regularly smokes at her housing complex. She is considered to be socially isolated. She fears a slow and eventually painful death from her pulmonary disease and has requested assisted dying.

DISCRIMINATION/STIGMA

Inequitable access to a variety of services continues to exist for those experiencing mental health–substance use problems due to stigma, prejudice and discrimination (Thornicroft et al. 2007, Thornicroft 2010). Arguably, most people can empathize with physical symptoms far more easily than psychological ones. This ability to enter into the physical pain experience of others is possibly one factor in the growing acceptance of assisted dying. Attitudes toward mental illness are less informed by the personal experiences, stories and narratives of people experiencing mental health issues. These challenges of empathy and information can lead to a persistent inability to understand the sometimes relentlessly intense and painful psychological symptoms that people can experience despite years of treatments.

REFLECTIVE PRACTICE EXERCISE 20.2

Time: 30 minutes

Consider the lives of Prakesh and Cristina.

- With whose experience is it more likely that others can feel empathy?
- To whom might a neighbour, family member or healthcare provider find it more possible to extend an act of compassion such as a statement that recognizes their suffering and their struggle with their illness?
- What more do you need to know about each person's experience to better understand their suffering?

Although there are currently 12 jurisdictions around the world where assisted dying has been decriminalized or legalized, only four of those, Switzerland, the Netherlands, Belgium, and Luxembourg, permit assisted dying for persons with an irremediable mental disorder (Shaffer et al. 2016).

Some very uncomfortable questions lie at the heart of the debate about assisted dying being made accessible to people experiencing mental health–substance use problems. Misconceptions based on prejudicial and discriminatory assumptions still abound: these individuals are irrational or incapable, they have poor judgment, they are not suffering as much as their physically ill counterparts, they are not trying hard enough to get better, and they are likely to improve over time.

Individuals experiencing severe and persistent mental illness can indeed experience intolerable suffering (Berghmans et al. 2013). They can also be capable of understanding and appreciating the consequences of MAID and meet all legislated eligibility criteria (Neilson and Chaimowitz 2014). If we make a blanket assessment that all such individuals are 'too vulnerable' to be included among those potentially eligible to request assisted dying we create a class of fellow citizens that is then more vulnerable to enduring suffering, and possibly to feelings of abandonment and pressure. Rather than label, exclude and ultimately discriminate, efforts should be made to design and implement education and safeguards for any person requesting MAID (Shuklenk and van de Vathorst 2015).

SELF-ASSESSMENT EXERCISE 20.1 – ANSWERS ON P. 313

> **Time: 20 minutes**
> Describe two examples of potentially discriminatory assumptions that manifest in the context of assisted dying.

REFLECTIVE PRACTICE EXERCISE 20.3

> **Time: 40 minutes**
> - In what ways might mental health practitioners contribute to prejudicial attitudes and discriminatory decisions by asserting that individuals experiencing great suffering because of mental rather than physical illness ought to be deemed ineligible for assisted dying?
> - Recall the quotes that began this chapter.
> - What did you think of the assertion that 'there is no situation where depression needs to be as disabling as it is'?
> - What do you feel about the claim that 'the suicidally depressed still don't have the right to die'?
> - If it is acknowledged that some individuals might be experiencing intolerable suffering because of a grievous and irremediable mental illness or substance use, then what reasonable safeguards must be in place to ensure an assisted death would be the 'last, best judgement' by all involved in decision making?

COUNTER-INTUITIONS

In the next section we will explore some of the counter-intuitions that often appear when discussing assisted dying for those experiencing mental health–substance use related suffering.

Life is good; death is bad

The mere fact of wanting to die seems to fly in the face of a deep biological imperative to survive. Our compounded histories and cultural values also influence our attitudes towards death. For many, a 'death-wish' remains illogical, unthinkable. However, this idea is 'thinkable' and ultimately defensible for others, even if profoundly lamentable. The following counter-intuitions may help explain why we struggle with the prospect of death as a 'good', particularly in the context of mental health–substance use.

'Suicide' and 'rational suicide'

There is a need to distinguish conceptually between what might be considered conventional views of 'suicide' and a request for an assisted death – sometimes termed 'rational suicide'.

In what we might inelegantly call 'conventional' suicide, we conceive of a person in a crisis who takes action to end his or her life owing to a profound sense of despair and hopelessness, intersecting with experiences of stress, loss or other precipitating factors.

In the equally inelegant notion of 'rational' suicide, one must be open to the possibility that to feel hopeless and to consider ending one's life may be a reasonable option for some people given their experiences of any combination of symptoms that give rise to suffering and their understanding of their likely future (Hewitt 2009, Dembo 2010).

If the distinction between 'suicide' and 'rational suicide' is legitimate, as we believe it is, then it is easy to see that we need to embrace two distinct aims: diligently working towards preventing suicide while also allowing for the possibility of assisted death being someone's last, best judgement.

Disagreement about eligibility might bring tension into the therapeutic relationship. Similarly, conscientious opt outs by professionals present another possible point of tension. A strong therapeutic relationship is vital, since it is one of the most significant protective factors against suicide.

Therefore, it is important to consider if benefits may accrue from the chance to discuss death as an intervention without the historical scrutiny created by the absolute prohibition on assisting dying or 'counselling suicide'. It is important for physicians to have thoughtful discussions with individuals who request assisted death for psychiatric reasons. Some individuals may simply require information, and others may wish to pursue the option further. For this latter group, a willingness to consider assisted dying/MAID together with their care providers may, in fact, strengthen the therapeutic alliance, and can also help the individual find the will to pursue further treatment options and to continue living (Personal communication with psychiatrist Dr. Paulan Stärcke, Netherlands, End-of-Life Clinic, August 2015).

In the experience of some of the authors, the conversations about assisted dying deepened the therapeutic relationship. In some cases, the inquiring individuals self-assessed that they did not meet the criteria for assisted dying. In one published study, being eligible for assisted dying did not always result in its pursuit – it offered peace of mind enough knowing the option was available to enable continued living for the time being (Thienpont et al. 2015).

'Irremediability' amidst 'recovery' and 'hope'

In its initial public statement on assisted dying, the Centre for Addiction and Mental Health, Canada's largest mental health and addictions teaching hospital, recognized the possibility that in a minority of cases, mental illness may constitute an irremediable condition that causes intolerable suffering. The statement also asserts that 'safeguards must be in place to make sure that an individual truly has the capacity to consent to MAID' (Centre for Addiction and Mental Health 2016).

Noting the complexity of the irremediability criterion, the Canadian Psychiatric Association commented: 'The concept of irremediable should not be considered as simply identifying the diagnostic condition, but must be considered in the entire context of the expected illness course including considering the potential impact of possible treatment options on suffering and symptoms' (Canadian Psychiatric Association 2015, 4).

Among the reasons why assisted dying might seem unthinkable is the recovery paradigm that frames the thinking about mental health and substance use. The Mental Health Commission of Canada offers this definition of recovery: 'recovery involves a process of growth and transformation as the person moves beyond the acute distress often associated with a mental health problem or illness and develops new found strengths and ways of being' (Mental Health Commission of Canada 2009, 28). The Mental Health Foundation stopped short of offering a definition of 'recovery' but stated 'the guiding principle is hope – the belief that it is possible for someone to regain a meaningful life, despite serious mental illness' (Mental Health Foundation, undated).

Hope and assisted death might appear to be irreconcilable (Walker-Renshaw and Finley 2015). This apparent tension might be approached in two ways:
1 question the extent to which the idea of hope is promoted
2 and reconsider what is being hoped for and by whom.

Hope may not always be a benign entity. False hope may lead individuals with untreatable terminal illness to try increasingly painful and invasive treatments that may detract significantly from their quality of life (Bernacki and Block 2014). The appropriate place of hope in mental health care is worthy of reflection and debate, bearing in mind that, as Dembo suggests, 'Taken too far, hope and positive illusions can become harmful' (Dembo 2013, 4). She suggests that unfounded hope and the endless pursuit of further treatments (all of which have significant side effects and risks), in situations where available treatments have proven inadequate, could lead to more prolonged suffering, loss of dignity and self, and fractures in the therapeutic alliance. Gupta (2016) goes as far as broaching, though not espousing, the possibility that an individual living with mental illness who makes repeated attempts to end their own life *could* be argued to be in a terminal phase of the disease, at least probabilistically.

While cure or recovery are typically default goals in all health care, where illnesses have no cure or treatment is ineffective, symptom relief and comfort care become a worthwhile goal – lesser, but more likely achievable. Thus, the definition of recovery and what is being hoped for, and by whom, may shift throughout the course of an individual's illness. Equally, professionals may have to shift their own expectations and be cognizant of their own hopes and vulnerabilities in the face of their inability to help further. This self-awareness is critical in responding to individuals seeking assisted dying.

Vulnerability

Protecting the 'vulnerable' has figured prominently in Canadian debates on the laws surrounding assisted dying. The preamble to the final bill states 'Whereas vulnerable persons must be protected from being induced, in moments of weakness, to end their lives . . .' The assumption appears to be that anyone other than terminally ill individuals is too susceptible to coercion and social role devaluation to risk offering them potential access to assisted death, notwithstanding any other safeguards. In the vast majority of discussions wherein 'vulnerability' was a central concern, there was a significant omission: no definition of terms. The spectre of vulnerability was placed front and centre, but never explored in its own right. To help redress this, we propose adopting the definition used by Incardona et al. (2015, 22):

> A common and essential feature of human nature that highlights our shared experience and reciprocal responsibility to each other. It does not only refer to a person's characteristics but also to the situation encountered as a result of determinants such as health, access to support and potential to participate in community life. Vulnerabilities should be seen in their broader social and political context to highlight the potential for mitigation by addressing health, social and economic factors affecting individuals or groups.

A key consideration with respect to vulnerability is that the label should not be applied broadly – in isolation of individual factors. Labelling others as vulnerable may create an increased likelihood that they become vulnerable to something. In the context of assisted dying, a blanket judgement that 'mental illness makes anyone vulnerable' becomes a self-fulfilling prophecy – they become vulnerable to discriminatory restrictions of rights afforded to others (Lenihan 2016).

Data alone, even alarming data, does not meaningful evidence make

Among the counter-intuitive dimensions of the debates in Canada has been the need to resist drawing conclusions where data can prompt highly distressing emotions. There is a clear need to engage in circumspect consideration of the safeguards to be created when making assisted dying available. However, some data has been repeatedly cited as evidence that means individuals with mental illness ought to be excluded, when that data actually supports no such conclusion. A recent example of this phenomenon is the review by Kim, De Vries and Peteet (2016) of online case summaries of individuals receiving assisted dying for psychiatric conditions in the Netherlands.

The report's objectives were 'to describe the characteristics' of people receiving assisted dying for psychiatric conditions and 'how the practice is regulated in the Netherlands' (p. 362). The conclusion summarizes the findings on the first objective by stating the people receiving assisted dying are 'complicated, suffering patients'. As for the adequacy of the system of regulatory oversight, it 'remains an open question that will require further study' (p. 367).

Between posing its objectives and the findings on them, the report includes much simple descriptive data that raise many questions and suggests further exploration is needed. However, the limited summary documents reviewed are unlikely to reveal much of the depth of the individual experiences, thera-peutic relationships and clinical processes that would shed true light on those individuals' lives beyond the forms. Nonetheless, the data has been cited repeatedly to support the position that mental illness ought to be an ineligible condition for assisted dying (Kim and Lemmens 2016), including one ironically published in a series entitled 'Making Evidence Matter' (Chochinov 2016). A more recent counterpoint to these writings is the review by Ezekiel et al. (2016) which arrived at similar conclusions to those of Kim, De Vries and Peteet (2016) without the alarmist conjecture.

In what is often referred to as 'opinion based evidence making', stories or observations with high emotional impact – or high 'yuck factor' – can be readily enlisted to bolster convictions that there is a clear right and wrong. There are complexities, no doubt. However, it remains to be argued conv-incingly that uncomfortable data is evidence that assisted dying should be denied to those with intolerable suffering because of mental illness.

Other unsettling data might also need to be collected and analysed. Where individuals make successful or unsuccessful attempts to end their own lives, there is the potential for multiple layers of harm. Unsuccessful attempts can lead to increased suffering – physically and psychologically, for the person who tried to die and for those around them. Even a well-planned self-effected death can leave harm behind when it must be implemented in secret (Supreme Court of British Columbia, Hollis Johnson Affidavit Case No. Sl12688). There is little or no opportunity to say goodbye to others, no chance to prepare loved ones for a death they may not be anticipating. In other situations, one's inability to proceed with a plan from fear or uncertainty does not necessarily make for less suffering in future if the treatment pros-pects have proven to be inadequate. It may be the case that in many such situations assisted dying might limit further damage to people's lives. Only when we include such harms and their potential avoidance in an overall calculus of a capable person's decision to pursue assisted dying can we begin to truly discern how distressing data translates into real life risks and benefits for real people.

REFLECTIVE PRACTICE EXERCISE 20.4

Time: 45 minutes
- Make notes of your thoughts on each of these counter-intuitions:
- Use a sheet with two columns headed 'Prakesh' and 'Cristina' (Case Studies 20.1 and 20.2).
- In each column, consider how each of the five tensions described above may contribute to perpetuating discrimination/stigma or promoting individual-centred practice in working with each of Prakesh and Cristina.
- Describe how you might approach these tensions in a manner that maximizes individual-centred practice and minimizes discrimination/stigma for each of them.

SELF-ASSESSMENT EXERCISE 20.2 – ANSWERS ON P. 313

Time: 15 minutes
Identify three terms that might best be distinguished or clarified very specifically in the context of assisted dying

UNCERTAINTIES

There is no escape. Moral risk cannot, at times, be avoided. All we can ask for is that none of the relevant factors be ignored.

(Berlin 2013, 19)

In this next section we identify some of the ongoing uncertainties that will need to be managed as assisted dying practice evolves. The idea of collaboratively reaching that last, best judgement about whether to pursue assisted dying carries a weight that is perhaps incomparable to almost any other decision. Uncertainties exist in most areas of health care, but their gravity is amplified in the context of assisted dying based on the fact that the outcome is final and irreversible.

Ir/remediability

In order to be eligible to request an assisted death, the condition producing the suffering must be grievous and irremediable. While suffering is evidently a subjective judgement, and grievousness might be seen as an objective judgement, it is likely that the question of ir/remediability may be a more complex hybrid of subjective and objective. It is also a hybrid of **quantitative futility** (less than 2–5 percent chance of 'recovery') (Hebert and Weingarten 1991) and **qualitative futility** (treatment will not allow for an individual to live her life according to her goals and values) (Swetz et al. 2014).

As discussed above, there is clear recognition that some experiences of mental illness can be considered irremediable. How and when to settle on a last, best judgement about irremediability remains a profoundly uncomfortable decision. However, that does not mean the decision is to be left forever unmade, as this would arguably perpetuate the experience of intolerable suffering and give rise to other harms and risks that might be of a more significant order.

An added ethical dimension in assisted dying is the fact of it involving not only a refusal, but also a request for another intervention. Thus practitioners are placed in a position of being asked to do something they may feel deeply is not (yet) their last best judgement of what should be done (*see* Chapters 10 and 13). While it is the individual's life, and his or her lived experience, at the centre of this decision, the professional's obligation to participate remains worthy of discussion. Is it legitimate for a professional to require, prior to their involvement in any assisted dying process, that the individual trial those treatments for which they believe evidence is considered 'strong'? Could there be consensus about the criteria for such 'strong evidence'? Would an individual's experience of significant side-effects mitigate the level of remediation any treatment is deemed to achieve for them?

Capacity assessment

A subject of great debate, capacity assessment is arguably the most fundamental of all the current eligibility criteria in Canada's legal framework. Many professionals worry that they do not have the experience or guidelines/standards to assess capacity for assisted dying. The question of whether current clinical and legal standards and tests for capacity suffice is still being considered (Canadian Psychiatric Association 2016). It is important to recall that within many legal systems capacity to consent to treatment is assumed until there is good reason to question it and it must then be proven to be lacking (Canadian Psychiatric Association 2015). Equally, many if not most individuals who live with mental illness are indeed capable as determined by conventional assessments for treatments other than assisted dying (Grisso and Applebaum 1998; Weinstock et al. 1984).

A recent review of the literature on capacity assessment tools used in mental health practice found that of the 24 different tools described in the literature, 12 were developed for use within mental health practice (Shanker 2016). Most tools test four domains of capacity following legal standards (i.e., understanding, appreciation, reasoning, and communicating a choice), however they neither define nor interpret the domains consistently. The tools heavily rely on the skills of the assessor, and the results can be vulnerable to assessor bias particularly if conducted within a risk-averse clinical environment. There was also insufficient data across tools to suggest that the psychosocial context of the individual was adequately considered in the capacity assessment process, with the exception of two tools:

1 the Regional Capacity Assessment Tool (RCAT)
2 the Assessment of Capacity to Consent to Treatment (ACCT – Pachet et al. 2007; Moye et al. 2007).

Most capacity assessment tools were developed to interpret capacity where the consequences of a treatment/intervention favour life (Grisso and Applebaum 1998). This urges reflection about the nature of some mental health conditions that may make it impossible to use a commonly held understanding of capacity, particularly in the context of assisted dying. As a minimum, it is advised to use capacity assessment tools as part of a multi-faceted process rather than a standalone test for capacity (Werth et al. 2000).

Family involvement

Eligibility for assisted dying requires first and foremost a capable, voluntary individual making the request. Thus, in most jurisdictions where assisted dying is available, the family's opinions likely have little or no 'legal' standing. That being said, is it prudent to involve them to inform the eligibility assessment (*see* Chapter 15)? Many challenges exist where an individual and family are in any degree of disagreement about end-of-life decisions. Most healthcare professionals are familiar with the potential for highly complex family dynamics. It is likely that the high stakes – moral and clinical – of assisted dying will heighten the prospects of such complexity.

Support for individual peers (and caregivers) where assisted dying is being explored/pursued

While fully supporting an individual's wish to explore and possibly pursue an assisted death, it is difficult to imagine that it will not have some effect, perhaps significant, on peers and caregivers. A collaborative network that can immediately share experiences and strategies for support may identify promising and best practices.

REFLECTIVE PRACTICE EXERCISE 20.5

Time: 60 minutes
- Consider the way in which the social determinants of health (e.g. employment, housing, sexuality (*see* Chapter 14), etc.) have been at play in the lives of Prakesh and Cristina (Case Study 20.1 and 20.2). Think about how often you are willing or able to address the social determinants of health on your practice.
- Make a list of the sorts of 'symptoms' Prakesh and Cristina might experience.
- Now make notes on how these may have an impact upon their self-esteem.
- Consider the medications each of them may be prescribed.
- List the effects these have on the body and self-identity.
- How do these effects potentially affect one's experience in terms of social determinants of health?

SELF-ASSESSMENT EXERCISE 20.3 – ANSWERS ON P. 314

> **Time: 10 minutes**
> Identify three examples of uncertainty that are typical in mental health and substance use practice

CONSCIENTIOUS PERSONS AND PRACTICE

Matters of individual and collective conscience are central to assisted dying. The term 'conscience' typically arises in the context of conscientious refusal, opt-out or objection. The protection of individual conscience rights allows professionals to practice within their own values systems, and the collective conscience protects all involved from any sort of stigmatization regarding their involvement or refusal. Ideally, conscience should underpin all elements of the practice and process of assisted dying – contemplation, participation, facilitation and objection.

As with many ethically sensitive matters, assisted death intersects with fundamental ideas about the value, meaning and purpose of life. Whether these ideas are explicitly linked to religion, faith or more general values, they are thoroughly grounded in one's sense of spirituality – a term used here in the broad sense, as captured by the Canadian Association of Occupational Therapists (Canadian Association of Occupational Therapists 2002, 182): 'a pervasive life force, manifestation of a higher self, source of will and self-determination, and a sense of meaning and purpose, and connectedness that people experience in the context of their environment'.

Regulating practice, respecting conscience

All regulated professionals have a code of ethics and most organizations espouse values in addition to codes of conduct. These values and codes of conduct reflect more precise practice expectations.

Individuals considering assisted dying are also making decisions with their own conscience. It is likely that most individuals who would be eligible for assisted dying would also be cognizant of the matters of conscience involved for their service providers (Reel 2016).

The primacy of trust in the individual-professional relationship is pivotal. There is the need for trust in the society-professional relationship. Regulated health professionals are given broad privileges of access to people, their information and their bodies. This privilege is granted and maintained based on the professional's behaviour and practice, and is accompanied by other duties. Professionals must always reflect on their own competency and scope of practice. This trust relationship currently guides many end-of-life decisions and significantly life-altering decisions.

Monitoring incidence and potential contributing/mitigating factors to address in future

As assisted dying becomes legal and part of practice, there is a corresponding legal and ethical duty to create a rigorous and detailed system for reporting, tracking and monitoring to help understand the range of requests received and the associated outcomes. This will help identify specific remedies and supports that could subsequently become priorities for development or implementation – especially those addressing social determinants of health, which may be addressed with sufficient resourcing of extant but inadequately funded services.

REFLECTIVE PRACTICE EXERCISE 20.6

Time: 60 minutes

Return to the quotes that began this chapter and the notes you made at the outset.

- Describe how you now react to each quote.
- On a scale of 1–10, rate the extent to which you agree or disagree with each of them.
- Does either statement make assertions that are 'unproven'? Describe what proof or argument you might expect to see on those points.
- Do they make assertions that are likely difficult to 'prove'? Can you imagine how to resolve these ideas that may be beyond proof?
- Which of the uncertainties outlined above enter into these areas of argument/opinion, and how?
- Write down the terms that you feel remain to be defined more precisely.

SELF-ASSESSMENT EXERCISES 20.4 – ANSWERS ON P. 314

Time: 10 minutes

Describe three possible sources of individual moral direction

CONCLUSION

This chapter has explored some of the most demanding dimensions of assisted dying in the context of mental health and substance use problems. Four themes were identified:

1 discrimination/stigma
2 counter-intuitions
3 uncertainties
4 conscientious persons and practice.

The issues are profound and complex and have been explored only minimally here. Wherever assisted dying is permitted or is being contemplated, these issues must be explored in depth and in perpetuity as they manifest within the particular social, regulatory and professional cultures of the jurisdiction.

While undertaking this exploration and deliberation, it is likely useful to focus on the existence of great overlap in values and aims – principally those of caring and alleviating suffering. Useful reporting systems would help identify specific remedies and supports that could subsequently become priority for development or implementation – especially those addressing social determinants of health. It should be conceivable to simultaneously adopt a 'prevention program' while also embedding assisted dying into practice – much like efforts to minimize, prevent and end practices of restraint and seclusion.

As in all healthcare practice, complexity and uncertainty can lead to distress, anxiety and fear. Conscience and reason must mitigate these tendencies, while acknowledging the strong values and emotion-based responses that exist as well. Only with enduring attention to conscientious practice will those involved in this highly sensitive decision-making find their way at last, to the best judgement possible.

KEY POINT 20.1

Discrimination/stigma

Prejudicial attitudes and discriminatory eligibility criteria directed toward excluding those with psychiatric illness complicate discussions and decisions about MAID.

KEY POINT 20.2

Conscientious practice

Despite apparent differences of opinion, there is likely an overlapping consensus on overarching aims to reduce suffering and preventing vulnerability in an ethics of care.

The preservation of relationships is of the utmost importance to quality care.

KEY POINT 20.3

Counter-intuitions

Many terms need to be defined clearly and applied circumspectly – avoid classifying whole groups of people as one thing or another, and keep an acute awareness of the potential for certain moral inclinations and assumptions to be at play.

> **KEY POINT 20.4**
>
> **Uncertainties**
>
> Making peace with uncertainty is a significant challenge for most people, and for practitioners with duties of care this carries particular weight. Focussing on high quality communication and collaboration can help with making a last, best judgement in assisted dying – where uncertainties are bound to be present.

REFERENCES

Bayliss G. 2016. It doesn't get better: the mentally ill deserve the right to die with dignity. *The Walrus*, April 14. https://thewalrus.ca/suicide-is-not-painless/.

Berghmans R, G Widdershoven and I Widdershoven-Heerding. 2013. Physician-assisted suicide in psychiatry and loss of hope. *International Journal of Law and Psychiatry*, 36: 436–43.

Berlin I. 2013. "The Pursuit of the Ideal". In: H Hardy (ed.) *The Crooked Timber of Humanity: Chapters in the History of Ideas*. Princeton, NJ: Princeton University Press. pp. 1–20.

Bernacki RE and SD Block, for the American College of Physicians High Value Care Task Force. 2014. "Communication about serious illness care goals: a review and synthesis of best practices". *Journal of the American Medical Association Internal Medicine*, 174: 1994–2003.

Canadian Association of Occupational Therapists. 2002. *Enabling Occupation: An Occupational Therapy Perspective*. Ottawa: CAOT Publications ACE. www.cpa-apc.org/media.php?mid=1471.

Canadian Psychiatric Association. 2015. "Informed consent to treatment in psychiatry". *Canadian Journal of Psychiatry*, 60(4): 1–11. www.ncbi.nlm.nih.gov/pmc/articles/PMC4459249/pdf/cjp-2015-vol60-april-positionpaper-insert-eng.pdf.

Canadian Psychiatric Association. 2016. "CPA interim response to Report of the Special Joint Committee on PAD". www.cpa-apc.org/media.php?mid=2441 http://groups.cpa-apc.org/email/display.php?M=527591&C=70e1a2b8628c4481bd5e1fc13bbadc79&L=675&N=726.

Centre for Addiction and Mental Health. 2016. *CAMH statement: Assisted dying legislation and mental illness*. www.camh.ca/en/hospital/about_camh/newsroom/CAMH_in_the_headlines/stories/Pages/CAMH-statement-Assisted-dying-legislation-and-mental-illness.aspx.

Chochinov HM 2016. Assisted suicide for those with mental illness a risky proposition. http://umanitoba.ca/outreach/evidencenetwork/archives/28386.

Dembo JS 2013. "The ethics of providing hope in psychotherapy". *Journal of Psychiatric Practice*, 19: 316–22.

Dembo JS 2010. "Addressing treatment futility and assisted suicide in psychiatry". *Journal of Ethics and Mental Health*, 5: 1–3.

Ezekiel J, EJ Emanuel, BD Onwuteaka-Philipsen, JW Urwin, J. Cohen. 2016. Attitudes and practices of euthanasia and physician-assisted suicide in the United States, Canada, and Europe. *Journal of the American Medical Association*, 316(1): 79–90.

Grisez G and R Shaw. 2004. "Conscience: knowledge of moral truth". In C Curran (ed.) *Conscience*. New York: Paulist Press. p. 43.

Grisso T and PS Appelbaum. 1998. *Assessing Competence to Consent to Treatment: A Guide For Physicians and Other Health Professionals.* Cary, NC: Oxford University Press.

Gupta M. 2016. "A response to 'Assisted Death in Canada for Persons with Active Psychiatric Disorders'". *Journal of Ethics in Mental Health.* Open Volume. www.jemh. ca/issues/open/documents/JEMH_Open-Volume_Commentary_Response_ Assisted_Death_in_Canada-June2016.pdf.

Hebert PC and MA Weingarten. 1991. The ethics of forced feeding in anorexia nervosa. *Canadian Medical Association Journal,* 144: 141–4.

Henick M. 2016. Letter to Justin Trudeau. https://markhenick.wordpress.com/2016/04/11/ a-letter-to-justin-trudeau.

Hewitt J. 2009. "Rational suicide: philosophical perspectives on schizophrenia". *Medicine, Health Care and Philosophy,* 13: 25–31.

Incardona N, S Bean, K Reel and F Wagner. 2015. An Ethics-based Analysis & Recommendations for Implementing Physician-Assisted Dying in Canada. http://jcb. utoronto.ca/news/documents/JCB-PAD-Discussion-Paper-2016.pdf.

Kim S, RG De Vries and JR Peteet. 2016. "Euthanasia and assisted suicide of patients with psychiatric disorders in the Netherlands 2011 to 2014". *Journal of the American Medical Association Psychiatry,* 73: 362–8.

Kim S and T Lemmens. 2016. "Should assisted dying for psychiatric disorders be legalized in Canada?" *Canadian Medical Association Journal,* 188: E337–E339.

Lenihan D. 2016. Assisted Dying – Who is vulnerable to whom? *National Newswatch.* www.nationalnewswatch.com/2016/05/09/assisted-dying-who-is-vulnerable-to- whom/#.VzJLVqPD-1u.

Mental Health Commission of Canada. 2009. *Toward Recovery and Well-Being.* Ottawa, ON: Mental Health Commission of Canada. www.mentalhealthcommission.ca/sites/ default/files/FNIM_Toward_Recovery_and_Well_Being_ENG_0_1.pdf.

Mental Health Foundation. [no date]. "Recovery". www.mentalhealth.org.uk/a-to-z/r/ recovery.

Moye J, MJ Karel, B Edelstein, B Hicken, JC Armesto and RJ Gurrera. 2007. "Assessment of capacity to consent to treatment: challenges, the 'ACCT' approach, directions". *Clinical Gerontologist,* 31: 37–66.

Neilson G and G Chaimowitz. 2014. "Informed consent to treatment in psychiatry (Position Statement)". *The Canadian Journal of Psychiatry,* 60. www.ncbi.nlm.nih. gov/pmc/articles/PMC4459249/pdf/cjp-2015-vol60-april-positionpaper-insert-eng. pdf.

Pachet A, A Newberry and L Erskine. 2007. "Assessing capacity in the complex patient: RCAT's unique evaluation and consultation model". *Canadian Psychology/Psychologie canadienne,* 48: 174.

Reel K. 2016. "Matters of conscience and end-of-life care." *Hospital News,* 5 July. http://hospitalnews.com/matters-conscience-end-life-care/.

Shaffer CS, AN Cook and DA Connolly. 2016. "A conceptual framework for thinking about physician-assisted death for persons with a mental disorder". *Psychology, Public Policy, and Law,* 22: May: 141–57. http://dx.doi.org/10.1037/law0000082.

Shanker R. 2016. *A Review of the Literature on Capacity Assessment Tools within Mental Health Practice.* Toronto: Joint Centre for Bioethics. http://reportal.jointcentre forbioethics.ca/news/maid-briefing-document.shtml.

Shuklenk U and S van de Vathorst. 2015. Treatment-resistant major depressive disorder and assisted dying. *Journal of Medical Ethics,* 41: 577–83.

Supreme Court of British Columbia, Hollis Johnson Affidavit Case No. Sl12688. 2011. https://bccla.org/wp-content/uploads/2012/06/20110824-Affidavit-Carter-Hollis-Johnson.pdf.

Swetz KM, CM Burkle, KH Berge and WL Lanier. 2014. Ten common questions (and their answers) on medical futility. *Mayo Clinic Proceedings*, Jul. 89: 943–59.

Thienpont L, M Verhofstadt, T Van Loon, W. Distelmans, K Audenaert and PP De Deyn. 2015. "Euthanasia requests, procedures and outcomes for 100 Belgian patients suffering from psychiatric disorders: a retrospective, descriptive study". *British Medical Journal Open*. http://bmjopen.bmj.com/content/5/7/e007454.

Thornicroft G. 2010. "Shunned: evidence for improving stigma and discrimination." In workshop proceedings of: *Ending Stigma and Achieving Parity in Mental Health: A Physician Perspective.* 11–12. Prepared by Chenier Consulting. www.cpa-apc.org/media.php?mid=1471.

Thornicroft G, D Rose, A Kassam and N Sartorius. 2007. "Stigma: ignorance, prejudice or discrimination?" *British Journal of Psychiatry*, 190: 192–3.

Walker-Renshaw B and M Finley. 2015. "Carter v. Canada (Attorney General): Will the Supreme Court of Canada's Decision on Physician-assisted Death Apply to Persons Suffering from Severe Mental Illness?" *Journal of Ethics in Mental Health, Open Volume*. www.jemh.ca/issues/open/documents/JEMH_Open-Volume_Benchmark_Assisted%20Death-Nov20-2015.pdf.

Weinstock R, R Copelan and A Bagheri. 1984. "Competence to give informed consent for medical procedures". *Bulletin American Academy of Psychiatry and the Law*, 12: 117–25.

Werth Jr JL, GA Benjamin and T Farrenkopf. 2000. "Requests for physician-assisted death: guidelines for assessing mental capacity and impaired judgment". *Psychology, Public Policy, and Law*, 6: 348.

TO LEARN MORE

Reflections and stories from individuals living with mental illness can offer specific insights into the debate around its availability for mental illness and addiction related suffering.

"An open, 'uncomfortable' conversation on mental health, suicide and doctor-assisted death." A radio interview with Graeme Bayliss, the person behind the quote that opened this chapter. Canadian Broadcasting Corporation, *The Current*, Monday April 25, 2016. www.cbc.ca/radio/thecurrent/the-current-for-april-25-2016-1.3551316/an-open-uncomfortable-conversation-on-mental-health-suicide-and-doctor-assisted-death-1.3551346

"As a person with mental illness, here's why I support medically assisted death." Adam Maier-Clayton, *The Globe and Mail*, May 8 2016. A personal story supporting the option of MAID in mental health related suffering. www.theglobeandmail.com/life/health-and-fitness/health/as-a-person-with-mental-illness-heres-why-i-support-medically-assisted-death/article29912835/

"People With Mental Illness Deserve To Die With Dignity, Too." Arthur Gallant, *The Huffington Post*, April 4, 2016. A personal take on the need for better services as well as equitable access to assisted dying. www.huffingtonpost.ca/arthur-gallant/mental-illness-suicide-_b_6637866.html.

An award-winning book of fiction based on the story of the author's sister is *All My Puny Sorrows* by Miriam Toews (published by Knopf/Doubleday). She is part of a panel discussion on the topic of assisted dying and mental health held at University College at the University of Toronto and available for viewing on YouTube here:

A Conversation About Assisted Death with Author Miriam Toews. www.youtube.com/watch?v=7Iu-RY5_T9I

There are increasing numbers of video documentaries available online in which people share their stories of exploring and opting for assisted death.

Eva's GP visits to perform the assisted death she has been seeking for some time: www.pbs.org/newshour/bb/right-die-belgium-inside-worlds-liberal-euthanasia-laws-2/.

Emily is 24 and has been asking for an assisted death for two years now . . . the request/review/approval process is nearing completion: www.youtube.com/watch?v=SWWkUzkfJ4M.

Sanne and her father describe the experience of her opting for an assisted death: https://aeon.co/videos/what-it-s-like-to-stand-by-your-daughter-in-her-choice-to-die.

A professional reflection and stories from a professional very involved in this matter is:

Libera Me, by Lieve Thienpont. It has been translated into English and is available as an e-book. www.witsand.be/store/p61/Libera_Me_E-BOOK_ENGLISH.html.

The Joint Centre for Bioethics, University of Toronto, has numerous open access Medical Assistance in Dying Ethics Resources. One can sign onto the mailing list for updates:

http://jcb.utoronto.ca/news/physician-assisted-death-resources.shtml
http://jcb.utoronto.ca/news/maid-draft-policy-template.shtml

The Joint Centre for Bioethics also holds public seminars that are archived for later viewing:

http://jcb.utoronto.ca/tools/seminars.shtml.

Many have addressed various aspects of assisted dying and related topics:

Nov 19, 2014, Aart Hendricks: Physician assisted suicide: challenges the Dutch Euthanasia Act failed to address

Nov 18, 2015, Daniel Weinstock: Harm Reduction as Overlapping Consensus

Feb 3, 2016, Trudo Lemmens: Why Physician-Assisted Dying Can and Should Remain Restricted After Carter: Lessons from the Belgian Experience Fe

Feb 24, 2016, Kevin Reel: A Final Enablement? A Survey of Canadian Occupational Therapists' Perspectives on and their Role in Supporting "Physician-Assisted Death"

Apr 20, 2016, Ruby Rajendra Shanker: Making Peace with Clinical Uncertainty: Ethical Implications for the Clinician and for the Practicing Healthcare Ethicist

Another very complex aspect of assisted dying not covered in this chapter is the question of advance directives. Two stories that raise the issues involved are those of Gillian Bennett and Margot Bentley.

www.cbc.ca/news/canada/british-columbia/gillian-bennett-s-family-scatters-her-ashes-after-public-goodbye-1.2752596

www.cbc.ca/radio/thesundayedition/in-the-presence-of-a-spoon-a-karin-wells-documentary-1.3111456

Think Carefully About Advance Requests for Medical Assistance in Dying. Ethicist Jonathan Breslin explores some of the considerations of advance directives for assisted dying in this blog on the Canadian Medical Association Journal website:

http://cmajblogs.com/think-carefully-about-advance-requests-for-medical-assistance-in-dying/

It might be useful to watch a very brief online video in which Brené Brown explores empathy versus sympathy – particularly her comments about "At least . . ." www.thersa.org/discover/videos/rsa-shorts/2013/12/Brene-Brown-on-Empathy.

The new Canadian law and related resources.

> Canada's Bill C-14: www.parl.gc.ca/HousePublications/Publication.aspx?Language=E&Mode=1&DocId=8384014

There were a number of reports produced in advance of the Canadian law:

> The External Panel on Options for a Legislative Response to Carter v. Canada made no recommendations but collected many perspectives from various contributors. *External Panel on Options for a Legislative Response to Carter v. Canada. 2015. Consultations on Physician-Assisted Dying: Summary of Results and Key Findings.* Final Report. www.justice.gc.ca/eng/rp-pr/other-autre/pad-amm/pad.pdf.

> The Provincial Territorial Expert Advisory Group on Physician-Assisted Dying sought structured submissions to a series of questions and made a range of recommendations in its final report: www.health.gov.on.ca/en/news/bulletin/2015/docs/eagreport_20151214_en.pdf.

> The Special Joint Committee on Physician-Assisted Dying also received many submissions and made many recommendations in its report *Medical Assistance in Dying: A Patient-Centred Approach.* www.parl.gc.ca/content/hoc/Committee/421/PDAM/Reports/RP8120006/pdamrp01/pdamrp01-e.pdf.

> "Alberta court ruling at odds with federal assisted-dying bill." Sean Fine, *The Globe and Mail,* May 18 2016. Article on the Alberta Court of Appeal case of a woman with psychiatric illness seeking MAID. www.theglobeandmail.com/news/national/alberta-appeal-court-shoots-down-federal-rationale-for-assisted-death-limits/article30074138/.

There are several advocacy and lobby groups in Canada addressing the issue of assisted dying from different perspectives. These are just a few:

> The British Columbia Civil Liberties Association – advocacy group supporting the successful court challenge of the blanket ban on assisted dying in Canada. https://bccla.org/.

> The Vulnerable Persons Standard – advocating for limiting access to only those who are dying of a terminal illness. www.vps-npv.ca/.

> Dying With Dignity – longstanding advocacy group in favour of assisted dying. www.dyingwithdignity.ca/.

> Euthanasia Prevention Coalition – longstanding advocacy group opposed to assisted dying. www.epcc.ca/.

A series of professional body resources has been published as the law changed in Canada. These will likely be updated over time as provincial and territorial legislation is created.

> Time Needed to Establish Standards and Guidelines Around PAD Says CPA President. http://groups.cpa-apc.org/email/display.php?M=527591&C=70e1a2b8628c4481bd5e1fc13bbadc79&L=675&N=726.

Systematic/ Literature Reviews of Capacity Assessment Tools:

> Sturman ED. 2005. "The capacity to consent to treatment and research: a review of standardized assessment tools". *Clinical Psychology Review,* 25: 954–74.

Dunn LB, MA Nowrangi, M Be, BW Palmer, DV Jeste and ER Saks. 2006. "Assessing decisional capacity for clinical research or treatment: a review of instruments". *American Journal of Psychiatry*, 163: 1323–34.

Okai D, G Owen, H McGuire, S Singh, R Churchill and M Hotopf. 2007. "Mental capacity in psychiatric patients". *The British Journal of Psychiatry*, 191: 291–7.

Racine CW and SB Billick. 2012. "Assessment instruments of decision-making capacity". *The Journal of Psychiatry & Law*, 40: 243–63.

Lamont S, YH Jeon and M Chiarella. 2013. "Assessing patient capacity to consent to treatment: An integrative review of instruments and tools". *Journal of Clinical Nursing*, 22: 2387–403.

Resources supporting reducing prejudice, discrimination and stigma abound.

The Centre for Addiction and Mental Health has one program focussing on making attitudinal changes in primary care. http://bit.ly/1a9MB1e

ANSWERS TO SELF-ASSESSMENT EXERCISES

ANSWERS TO SELF-ASSESSMENT EXERCISE 20.1 – P. 297

Describe two examples of potentially discriminatory assumptions that manifest in the context of assisted dying
- All individuals with mental health conditions are vulnerable.
- All individuals with mental health conditions are at risk of dying by suicide.
- All individuals with mental health conditions are incapable.
- The suffering of individuals with mental health conditions is less than that of individuals with somatic illness.

ANSWERS TO SELF-ASSESSMENT EXERCISE 20.2 – P. 302

Identify three terms that might best be distinguished or clarified very specifically in the context of assisted dying
- suicide/assisted dying
- treatment/intervention/service
- effecting/hastening
- inquiries/requests
- options/choices
- medical/physician/legal assistance in dying

ANSWERS TO SELF-ASSESSMENT EXERCISE 20.3 – P. 305

> Identify three examples of uncertainty that are typical in mental health and substance use practice
> - Remediability
> - Precision of capacity assessments
> - Involving family
> - Supporting peer individuals

ANSWERS TO SELF-ASSESSMENT EXERCISES 20.4 – P. 306

> Describe three possible sources of individual moral direction
> - values/ethics/principles
> - religion-based teaching/law/doctrine
> - faith-based beliefs
> - professional ethics

CHAPTER 21

End-of-life
An exercise in comprehension

Jo Cooper

INTRODUCTION

This chapter was not originally written with specific ethical principles highlighted. However, there are ethical implications and considerations throughout. The reader is requested to read this chapter as an exercise in itself, using the knowledge and comprehension gained throughout this book. When reading, apply your skills to identify potential and actual ethical dilemmas, giving consideration to how you would manage these. There is not an immediate solution to an ethical predicament; the situation will involve full and open discussion with colleagues and others, and there is always a way forward with the issues raised, despite the difficulties that are revealed. In all medical and nursing spheres, decisions regarding moral dilemmas may need to be taken on a daily basis. It is extraordinarily difficult to make a rational decision within an emotional context; it is not a question of right versus wrong: 'Feelings and emotions are entirely distinct from reason and rationality' (Broom, 2003). Exploring demanding end-of-life issues is intrinsic to palliative medicine and nursing.

There is often no right or wrong answer, but by using a frame of reference made on the basis of a clear and defined axiom will help to provide sound judgement. The most widely used structure comprises of four ethical principles, identified by Beauchamp and Childress (2012). The principles comprise:

1 Autonomy: regarding the person as an autonomous being; able to be involved in making decisions.
2 Beneficence: to do good; to provide benefit.
3 Non-maleficence: to do no harm.
4 Justice: being fair, with the provision of equity.

We all have a moral conscience, but none of us necessarily think or feel the same about any given situation. Therefore, it is useful to have a set of principles with which to deal with an ethical predicament. Jeffrey (2006) reminds us that although the four principles assist in clarifying our thinking and the identification of ethical issues, the principles may clash. The scenario concerning 'Grace' (later in the chapter), demonstrates the differing positions of family members, even though their intent is unanimously to provide the highest quality care for their very much loved mother.

In every situation ethics expresses a respect for life, at the same time accepting that death is unavoidable. Twycross suggests that the principle aim of treatment is not to prolong life, but to make the life that is left, as comfortable and as meaningful as possible (Twycross, 1997). I would like to express here, to my clinical colleagues working within mental health–substance use, that this, for you, must be much easier said than done. Particularly in the field in which you work. Helping the person who feels that their life is no longer worth living, and that they have nothing of value left to offer must surely represent the most difficult of challenges. To provide this care, to 'do' this work, to offer yourself, is the greatest gift you can give. To be able to identify the problems disclosed and to sit quietly alongside the distress of the individual, with genuine empathy, compassion and understanding, while engaging in respect for life, and for the humanness of the individual, is my personal view of an ethical human being.

What follows is revised and adapted with kind permission from © Cooper J. 2014. 'End of Life'. In: *Palliative Care Within Mental Health: Care and Practice*, edited by DB Cooper and J Cooper. Boca Raton; Florida: CRC Press.

This chapter will discuss end-of-life care in its broadest sense, regardless of diagnosis or place of death. The chapter reviews aspects of a 'good death', place of death and some of the difficulties presented to health professionals and families at the end-of-life.

REFLECTIVE PRACTICE EXERCISE 21.1

Time: 20 minutes
- What do you think constitutes a good death?
- Consider physical, psychological, spiritual, social and family elements.

A good death will mean different things to different people. Such factors as:
➤ choosing the place of death – **autonomy**
➤ good pain and symptom management – **beneficence**
➤ mending of relationships that may have been difficult or broken – **non-maleficence**

➤ being spiritually at peace with oneself
➤ availability of resources, such as appropriate and timely medications, practical aids to enhance comfort and human resources – **justice and fairness**
➤ effective communication between Inter- Intra-disciplinary team members.

These are some of the principles representing the features of a good death. Certain factors such as poor pain and symptom management, lack of choice of place of death, lack of professional teamwork and feelings of a lack of control can lead to a poor or unsuccessful death (Griggs, 2010). As professionals, we may feel that the death of an individual we had cared for had gone particularly well. Pain and distressing symptoms had been managed effectively, the family had been kept well informed by the supporting teams and the individual had died at home – their chosen place of death. However, the family may not feel that this was a good death. It may have been untimely; diagnosis may have been late or mismanaged; poor symptom management and damaged relationships all constitute a suboptimal death. Numerous variables come into play and could cause the family to feel that the death was not as they had planned. A distressing death can also be characterised by the person dying alone, particularly if the family had planned or expected to be present, causing untold anguish for those family members.

REFLECTIVE PRACTICE EXERCISE 21.2

> **Time: 10 minutes**
> • Do you feel that 'a good death' is a responsible term for professionals to use?

Masson (2002), suggests that the term is inappropriate and idealised and using the term 'good enough death' may be more achievable and realistic. It is a useful phrase to consider and may be helpful for us to remember when things do not always go to plan. However, we should always aim for the best possible care at the end-of-life, using our knowledge, skills and attitudes in order to prevent unplanned problems.

SELF-ASSESSMENT EXERCISE 21.1

> **Time: 25 minutes**
> • Think about the kind of care that you (or someone close to you) would like to have at the end-of-life.
> • Make a list of what you feel would be important and meaningful for you.

The National End-of-Life Care Strategy for England (Department of Health, 2008), defines a good death as:

➤ being treated as an individual with dignity and respect
➤ being without pain and other symptoms
➤ being in familiar surroundings
➤ being in the company of close family or friends.

SELF-ASSESSMENT EXERCISE 21.2

Time: 10 minutes
● Does this resonate with you?
● Is there anything you would like to add?

THE CONCEPT OF A GOOD DEATH

The concept of a good death has provoked a great deal of attention in recent months. Governmental (UK) pressures are currently to improve end-of-life care (The National Council for Palliative Care, 2006). This leads primarily to the individual having more choice about place of death and to promote a good death, which is paramount not only to the individual themselves and their family, but also for the health professional and teams managing care at the end-of-life.

For many – but not all – individuals, death occurs at the end of a long or chronic period of ill health, and is therefore often expected. However, death is still an emotional and physical shock when it happens and the family need ongoing and intensive support at this distressing time. The professional team are present to support and to smooth the way forward for the family who undergo mounting pressures before, during and after the death. It may be more difficult for the family if their relative has not been able to die in their place of choice and this may leave them with an acute sense of guilt, making the bereavement process prolonged and difficult. Moreover, death by suicide, or stigma related ill health, ending in death (e.g. HIV and AIDS) will cause further family distress. Additionally, the family will remember this death, and the professional team caring for them, for the rest of their lives, such is the impact at this time. Negative situations may hinder their road to recovery for months or even years. Self-help groups are offered to the bereaved family, but if in the case of suicide or stigma related deaths, it is far less easy for a family member to attend a group and disclose their feelings.

Since the essence of nursing is to relieve suffering (Beauchamp and Childress, 2012), professionals who continuously witness unrelieved pain or distressing symptoms can feel inadequate, as if they have failed the individual and the family. Professionals involved with caring for those people who are dying may need specialist education, guidance and ongoing support. We have no way of truly knowing the world of the person who is dying and their family, no way of knowing their past, their experiences, their distress, their losses and sometimes, however much we plan, things do go wrong. For that family, the death may never be a good one.

EARLY ASSESSMENT

Early assessment, identification and rapid response to symptoms remain paramount when planning for a good death. Pain and there are many different types, all requiring different approaches and analgesics, can escalate rapidly, requiring rapid response on the part of the supporting team. People who are dying do not tolerate symptoms easily, due to progressive weakness. This causes undue distress to the person, their family and to the health professional. Continuous review and assessment of pain and symptoms should be regular and ongoing. Situations can change very quickly, in just a few hours, and the team must be prepared for this. Explanations at this time should be given both to the individual and to their family as to why a certain medication is used, what the response might be, and when they can expect palliation. Ensure that the whole intra-/inter-disciplinary team are informed of changes in both condition and medication, so that they are aware of the current situation.

REFLECTIVE PRACTICE EXERCISE 21.3

Time: 40 minutes
- Does the individual truly have a choice in the type of care and treatment they receive?
- Does the individual have a choice as to the place in which they would like to die?
- Reflect on the last person you cared for at the end-of-life (or that you saw being cared for): were they given a choice about place of death, or the type of care they would like to receive? If so, was this achievable for them?

CHOICES

There are times when the wishes and choices of the individual are different to those of their family. Each family member may have a different viewpoint. This is when it is important to bring the family members together to facilitate an empathetic and helpful discussion, in a caring and non-threatening environment. Each person has a story to tell and each person's view is valuable and important. There are occasions when family conflict can arise over aspects of care and/or treatment, and what the family perceive to be the best type of care. This can happen regardless of the place of death.

Case Study 21.1.1 – Grace

Grace (72) was dying. She was in a nursing home, a widow with five adult children. The home staff were happy to keep Grace 'at home', providing they, together with Grace, were supported by the healthcare team. Grace had been comfortable, with minimal pain – managed with a transdermal fentanyl patch. Nausea and vomiting were successfully managed with oral cyclizine. Grace gradually began to lose consciousness – expected by the home staff, but not expected or accepted by some of her family. A syringe driver providing anti-emetics was prescribed, resulting in good management of her symptoms of intractable nausea.

Three members of Grace's family felt that she should have 'a drip' (intravenous fluid), as her mouth was dry, her lips starting to crack and her skin was becoming flaky. Understandably, they felt that she was dehydrated. Grace's two other daughters felt that Grace was comfortable, that she was being well cared for by professionals who knew her and the family well, and that a 'drip' would not help her at this stage of her dying.

Family conflict made it difficult for the home staff to cope, to know what to do, or for them to make a decision alone regarding Grace's care. They contacted the hospice team for help and support.

SELF-ASSESSMENT EXERCISE 21.3

Time: 30 minutes
- As a professional, how would you manage this situation?
- Can you identify the ethical challenges?
- How might you help Grace's family to understand that she was dying and that at this stage intravenous fluids would be more burdensome than helpful?

Case Study 21.1.2 – Grace

A very simple question in this case was all it took to resolve family conflict. The question asked by the health professional was . . . 'You know your mum better than anyone? What do you think she would have wanted'? Almost immediately, the family agreed that mum would have wanted to be left in peace – to die in a peaceful and dignified way, with no prolongation of her suffering, with no tubes or drips, unless this would improve her well-being.

However, the questions and answers did not just happen! The professional sat, with the family, in Grace's room while she slept. They 'chatted' over a cup of tea, getting to know a little about Grace, her life and her loves, from each family member in turn. Each little piece of information built a picture of Grace and reminded the family of past times, and of Grace's character, which sometimes is briefly forgotten or lost in the midst of ongoing distress.

The family, together, understood that a 'drip' would not help Grace. It may even add to her symptoms of nausea and vomiting and the tubes could easily get in the way of getting physically close to Grace. There were other ways the home staff could overcome her dry lips, mouth and flaky skin and the family accepted this, and subsequently became involved with some of these aspects of care. As soon as they realised what 'mum' would have chosen, their decision was easy, and family unity restored.

Dealing with life, and decisions around death and choice, is not always this simple or easy, but it is a good question to remember to ask. It will not fit all situations. However, in most situations, there is a question that guides us . . . so we can help those involved. The emphasis is on 'listening' and acting on what we hear. The answer is not obvious, it is in the exploration of the problem, uncovering the top layers, and delving underneath. It may involve us taking risks, but unless we do so, we will not help and we will not learn. We cannot 'fix' people's lives, or change them, we can only do our very best to help. Often, as professionals, we enter into complex situations, not knowing what we may find. If we truly listen – and listening is always the key – something happens! We just have to tune in, forget our own concerns and we will find an answer. Often, just by exploring the problem, the person will find his or her own answer. This takes time and skill, but it is a skill that experience brings. The important thing is never to give up.

SELF-ASSESSMENT EXERCISE 21.4

Time: 15 minutes
- How honest are we when people ask us questions about dying?

Most people, but not all, prefer to know, to understand what is happening, so that they are prepared for difficulties that arise during the end-of-life. However, we come back to 'choice'. Not everyone will want candid responses. People have the right to choose how much or how little information they want. If we go too far, they will soon tell us, or show us in their body language. Again, this may cause family conflict. Some families will feel that their relative should not be told the diagnosis, or that they only have 'so long' to live. They feel that the person will not be able to cope. Sometimes this is their own fear and reluctance to deal with the issues that this will bring. During this time, the relatives need just as much support and attention as the individual. Again, it is about exploring, gently and kindly, family perceptions and why they feel as they do; understanding each individual, and taking the time to 'be with'; working alongside the family as the unit of care is an integral part of the essence of caring.

COMMUNICATION STRATEGY

Below are some examples of questions that have been asked by individuals or family members in this author's experience. Guidance is offered as to how the questions could be managed. We all have our own strategies to help, so these are not definitive.

Question 1: How long have I got?

➤ Explore what the person is actually asking you.
➤ Watch their body language, particularly visual expression.
➤ Ask: 'How long do you think you may have?' This opens up the question so that you can talk it through and not just give an arbitrary answer.

Question 2: Am I dying?

➤ Ask: 'What makes you ask that question; what's going through your mind?'
➤ Find out what has led up to this – has the person spoken to the doctor recently?
➤ Is it something that has been said, or just thought about?
➤ Ask the person what they think – gives us time to think, to listen and open up discussion.

Question 3: How will I die?

➤ Some people want to know what to expect. You could ask if they would like to know what to expect.
➤ What are their own expectations? What are they thinking? What are they feeling? What a person feels or thinks may be different.
➤ Do they mean what physical symptoms or emotional feelings they might experience, or both of these?
➤ Make sure you have clarified this before talking – explore first.

Question 4: I'm worried about my family. How will they cope?

➤ Find out what the actual and real fear is.
➤ How has the family member coped before when there has been a crisis?
➤ Who will their main support person be?
➤ Be prepared to listen, rather than giving hurried placations.

Question 5: Will I die in pain?

➤ Use exploratory questions.

➤ Tell me about some of your worries about pain.

➤ Is there someone you know who has died in pain?

➤ Is the person talking about physical, emotional or spiritual pain, or all of these?

➤ We can explain about the many and varied types of pharmacological and non-pharmacological methods we use in managing pain.

Question 6: Would you let a dog suffer like this?

➤ Be prepared to sit with this distress and just listen.

➤ Ensure that they feel they have been heard by clarifying some of their thoughts and feelings.

➤ Acknowledge how hard it is for them to watch the person they love die.

REFLECTIVE PRACTICE EXERCISE 21.4

Time: 20 minutes
* For a moment, consider yourself as a spiritual and ethical human being . . . and your own thoughts on the meaning of suffering.

SPIRITUALITY

Spirituality often carries a reference to feelings of 'peace' and dying with 'dignity' (Griggs, 2010), with the feelings of being at peace with oneself as a core feature of a good death (Masson, 2002). Relationships and conflicts from the past can remain distressing for all involved and some form of resolution at the end-of-life is important. This is difficult to achieve but it is implicit, if the individual consents, that we attempt to help. Often, at this time, the individual is more concerned about their family than about themselves, and if they have chosen to receive information regarding their condition, they have time to plan and prepare for their family as well as themselves. We all have our own ideas about dignity, which can mean different things to different people, and we know when we are being treated with respect. Loss of body image, complex and difficult pain problems, loss of independence can all be linked to a loss of dignity (Jeffrey, 2006).

Dignity can be difficult to characterise, but part of caring for each individual means that we must establish how each perceives their own dignity (*see* Chapter 6).

REFLECTIVE PRACTICE EXERCISE 21.5

Time: 40 minutes

Just think how you would like to be treated, for example:

- How would you like to be addressed?
- Would you expect the professional to introduce her/himself?
- Would you appreciate the professional saying 'thank you for sharing that with me'?
- If you were in a side room, would you appreciate the professional knocking, or asking if it was all right to enter, particularly if family were present?

DYING AT HOME

SELF-ASSESSMENT EXERCISE 21.5

Time: 20 minutes

- Consider the potential barriers to dying at home.
- How might these compare with dying in hospital, or nursing and residential care?

Many people choose to die at home. Very few actually do so. 'Home' is the place that the person considers to be his or her home. This may be their own personal home, a nursing or residential home, a family member's home or a hostel where the person has been cared for when experiencing substance use problems.

One of the problems of end-of-life care at home is the potential lack of resources and rapid responses to symptoms, particularly in rural areas. Insightful community teams will approach the general practitioner/medical doctor and request that drugs needed for end-of-life care are pre-emptively prescribed for the individual, taken to the home and kept in a locked box, ready for use when the time comes. This is especially helpful in terms of 'out of hours' services, when professionals visiting the person may be different from those visiting during normal working hours. Moreover, it can be extremely difficult and frustrating trying to obtain drugs quickly at the weekend when time is of the essence. Symptoms can change rapidly, from hour to hour, and local chemists do not always stock drugs needed for end-of-life care (Griggs, 2010). Keeping drugs at home reassures the individual and the family that they will not be kept waiting in pain or with other symptoms. This also provides the additional benefit of providing peace of mind and reassurance for the visiting professionals. The family should be fully supported at this time and if they 'feel' supported by a trusted team, then dying at home has a much better chance of running smoothly and being successful. If the family want it to work, then it will work. If they are left isolated, feeling unsupported and frightened, then the person is likely to need an admission. However, we need to consider that not all people are going to be cared for at home at the very end, however much they or the family want this. Often people with brain tumours, dementia, difficult chronic illnesses, or where the family is elderly, may prevent a home death. Each situation is different and there is no 'blanket' policy when managing care at the end-of-life.

Wherever a person eventually dies, most time will be spent at home in the last year of life, so providing the best care at home for the final stages will always be important (Social Care Institute for Excellence – SCIE – 2013). In addition, the person may have chosen to die at home, but symptoms have become complex and unmanageable and hospital admission is necessary. This can cause an enormous amount of guilt for the family who may have been emotionally planning and preparing for their loved one to die at home. It is important that we listen and acknowledge their feelings of distress and concern, and that they feel heard.

It is not uncommon for people to change their minds when death approaches or if symptoms become difficult for that person to cope with. Home may become a frightening place to be and dying at home becomes less important than when they were well.

Case Study 21.2 – Joyce

Joyce (74) was suffering from intractable chest pain, shortness of breath, nausea and agitation. She was cared for at home by her family and recently commenced professional carers. Joyce was told after her hospital admission that she had a chest infection and was given antibiotics, steroids and inhalers, with a transdermal fentanyl patch for pain relief. This was difficult for the family to comprehend as Joyce remained very poorly at home. Joyce had no appetite; she had lost weight, and did not respond to medications for her breathlessness. Her chest and now back pain were well managed using prescribed fentanyl, with OxyNorm for breakthrough pain. Her general practitioner visited when requested and no further hospital admissions were felt necessary. The community nurses provided pressure-relieving aids and Joyce remained physically comfortable with care from her family.

At 0500 one morning, Joyce called for her family. She had struggled out of bed to use the commode, was extremely breathless, pale and feeling agitated and unwell. The family asked her if they could call the paramedics, to which Joyce agreed. Joyce was taken to hospital and admitted under the medical team. The family were told that Joyce was very ill, and would need palliative care, as there was no treatment as such that could be offered 'at this stage'. Although the word 'dying' was not used per se, the family acknowledged and understood that this may be the case. Joyce was diagnosed with a pleural effusion. Her lung was drained and her fentanyl patch increased to compensate for escalating pain.

Joyce had never been able to talk about death or dying. It seemed to frighten her. She had often mentioned in the past that she did not want to die in hospital, but that was as far as her communication went. At this stage, Joyce was happy and content to remain in hospital. She never asked to go home, or protested about where she was. Joyce had always lived in the present moment, was active, a loving mother, mother in law, and grandmother.

Because there had been no other diagnosis given, difficult conversations had not taken place with Joyce. Three days before her death she was diagnosed as having lymphoma, with secondary deposits in the lung. For those last three days, Joyce was able to communicate with her family, but still chose not to talk fully or express her feelings around dying. What she did tell her family was that she 'wanted to be with Dad now', so the family knew that she had accepted the fact that she was dying. The day prior to her death, she became restless and agitated, with accompanying breathlessness and distress. A syringe driver with analgesia was given, with a sedative to reduce her agitation and feelings of breathlessness. Her symptoms were well managed and Joyce died peacefully in her sleep in the early morning, three days following her diagnosis.

Not knowing her diagnosis until late in her disease did not mean that Joyce did not know that she was dying. She had always been a very strong individual and she died as she had lived, with courage and a strong faith. It was not possible for Joyce to go home to die. Everything happened so quickly, time was very short. Joyce never requested to go home . . . neither did her family. At the end, Joyce was made physically comfortable and emotionally settled with her family around her for most of the time. Medication was readily available, as was specialist equipment, specialist knowledge and support. The barrier to Joyce dying at home was probably herself. It did not become important to her any more. What was important for Joyce was that her complex symptoms were well managed, her pain, agitation and breathlessness were all reduced, and those whom she loved and who loved her surrounded her. For Joyce – she understood that she was going to 'a better place'.

RELATIONSHIPS AND COMMUNICATION

Relationships underpin everything that we do . . . in life generally, personally and professionally. The relationships we form with our colleagues, regardless of what team they represent, the individual for whom we care and the family remain paramount within the practice of ethical caring.

Relationships are built on trust and honesty with each other. They are sometimes fragile and can be broken easily. It takes time, attention and hard work to build good working relationships, but in end-of-life care it is vital that we take the time and effort to make the relationship work. It has many benefits for all concerned and can help to ensure that we all feel trusted, valued and secure.

SELF-ASSESSMENT EXERCISE 21.6

> What do you think we need to do to ensure we maintain effective working relationships?

Working with and caring for people who are dying can be distressing and stressful for the health professional. Sitting with a person's distress and feeling their pain can be one of the most difficult aspects of what we do. To make relationships work better, thereby offering a whole team approach providing optimal care to those within our care, we need to:

➤ communicate regularly, openly and effectively with each other. Speak well of our team colleagues and with confidence in their strengths and abilities. If you show the family that you have faith in colleagues, this promotes a good beginning for them

➤ get to know each other as well as possible. Set up regular meetings – these can be brief, but face-to-face meetings are more meaningful than a quick phone call or message. Get to know each other on a human, spiritual level as well as a professional level

➤ acknowledge that we can achieve much more for the person and their family by working cohesively together than we can as individuals

➤ share our mistakes. We all make them. Talking them through helps others and ourselves to learn. Often our vulnerability is our strength.

Communicating openly with the person who is dying and their family is paramount – each person needs to know what to expect and how we are able to help. Often people tell us that the hospital has said 'there is nothing more we can do'. This causes feelings of rejection and hopelessness. In palliative care, there is always something we can do . . . it is a treatment in itself. The goal is **not** to prolong suffering, but to do everything in our knowledge and power that we can to make that person's journey comfortable and well managed. The Gold Standards Framework (GSF) for use in the community has improved communication and teamwork between general practitioners and health professionals (Mahmood-Yousuf et al., 2008), the primary aim being to improve organisation and increase quality of care for individuals at the end-of-life. The GSF is recommended as a model of good practice. Sometimes we can feel unsure and frightened of open and transparent communication, not just with the person who is dying and their family, but also within the clinical team itself. We may have many concerns that we will not know the answers to the questions we are asked. There is no shame in saying something like 'I don't know the answer to that, but will take it back to my team and someone will be able to help'. If we do this, it shows that we are acknowledging their difficulty and we are going to do something positive and remedial. Make sure we do go back with the answer – do not keep the person waiting.

Ways of communicating with people who are dying can be learned. Hospices often run study days and workshops and there is always something we can learn. For health professionals who are inexperienced (and we have all been there) we do not always know what we need to know. An experienced colleague can act as a helpful and critical 'friend', reviewing difficult situations and ways of dealing with distress. Clinical supervision is the term used, but this can suggest that only clinical situations need reviewing, and the term 'supervision' can be inappropriate. The relationship we have with a trusted mentor will help us to acknowledge that it is often the dialogue we need to have with people, individuals and family that will smooth the way forward, more than what we actually 'do' in a clinical, hands-on sense. Never be afraid to ask questions yourself. It is the only way we will learn. If **you** need to ask it, then you can be sure that you will not be the only one wanting to know.

SELF-ASSESSMENT EXERCISE 21.7

> **Time: 30 minutes**
> Consider that you are caring for a person at the end-of-life, regardless of their diagnosis.
> - What questions are you comfortable with?
> - What questions might make you feel uncomfortable or awkward?
> - Whom might you approach for help?
>
> Think carefully about your responses.

Acknowledging the culture of the person and their family is important (SCIE, 2013). If you are unsure about this, ask them. People are not offended if they know we need that information in order to help them. People are more likely to feel offended if we *do not* ask. People all differ in their needs regarding family involvement; some will accept help from the family, others may not. It is important that we show respect, sensitivity and acknowledge the person's choice. Cultural issues may create barriers to good communication, which can lead to feelings of discrimination and lack of empathy (Eshiett and Perry, 2003). Everyone will have their own traditional values, and we must have respect and understanding when caring for people from different cultures (*see* Chapters 4 and 7).

When we talk about 'the family', this can mean different things to different people. It does not necessarily mean blood relatives. It could be same sex partners, close friends or a neighbour but they may be considered to be that person's family (*see* Chapter 15). It is always prudent to check just how much information the family want. Some families will want to know everything, others virtually nothing. Take a systematic approach, just a little at a time, and gauge the reactions. Again, never be afraid to ask. Most will choose to have information, given in lay terms, so that they know what to expect. Our presence within the home is valuable, in terms of supportive and empathic care, whatever position in the team we are. We may not always be needed to perform 'a task', but being ourselves and being alongside the family is of paramount importance when giving end-of-life care.

There is often a long and unpredictable journey for people experiencing mental health–substance use problems, with many setbacks on their road to recovery. Providing care at the end-of-life for people experiencing dementia and other mental health problems can present a raft of challenging situations, involving the individual, the family and the professional teams. Communication can be stressful and constrained for the individual, who may forget facts or be unable to express them. People with dementia can experience problems comparable with those of people who have a cancer diagnosis, but the former experience a lower quality of care at the end-of-life (Mitchell et al., 2004; Sampson et al., 2006). The ability to make an informed choice and decisions about type and place of care may be denied. The family need to be involved at every point in their journey and looked upon as experts in that person's care (*see* Chapter 15). Ongoing assessment and review of symptoms is just as important as with any ill health, and changes managed appropriately and responsibly. A slow decline in physical function and ability enables general practitioners/medical doctors to recognise the nearness of end-of-life (Grisaffi and Robinson, 2010). The family often express fears about the person's diminishing food intake, how the person will die and how they will recognise that the end-of-life is approaching. These issues will need exploration with the family and time and advice should be given to help them to understand what it is they will be facing. The needs of the family are sometimes overlooked and a conscious effort to talk – and to listen – regularly is needed wherever end-of-life care is taking place. If admission to hospital is needed, the family should be invited to help with care, if they choose and are willing to do so.

END-OF-LIFE

SELF-ASSESSMENT EXERCISE 21.8

Time: 15 minutes
Can you identify some of the common features indicating that the end-of-life is approaching?

It is often difficult to know just when the end-of-life is near. Some people will exhibit the classic signs, others may not. The following is a guide and is considered normal progression. However, this can be a frightening time for the family if they have not been well prepared:

- loss of appetite
- reduction in oral intake
- loss of interest in their surroundings and social withdrawal
- continuing weight loss
- wanting to remain in bed
- decline in the ability to communicate.

Some people at the end-of-life will be too ill, or otherwise unable, to make decisions about their care. However, Jeffries (2006) reminds us that the end-of-life offers a last opportunity to make choices. It is important to remember that even if communication is difficult, we must try to obtain the individual's agreement for care required. As the person becomes less attentive, the family will become more involved, acting on that person's behalf.

CONCLUSION

Good end-of-life care should be available in all settings, regardless of diagnosis. The individual and the family remain the central focus of care with therapeutic relationships and effective communication as the foundation for providing this care. We need knowledge, skills, the right attitude, and attention to the smallest detail to make someone's care at the end-of-life a 'good' experience. Families need and deserve help with preparation in knowing what to expect when a person dies, both emotionally and physically. An important point for us to consider is that each individual should feel heard, their views valued, so taking time to listen and act on what we hear, plays an important role for each person and family member. We need to be able to respond quickly to physical and emotional symptoms, with understanding, kindness and compassion.

We must, in doing this work, also take care of each other and ourselves. This is not being narrow; it has far-reaching and positive effects for those within our care. Treat ourselves with compassion – know our colleagues and ourselves – learn about who we are, for working with people, human being to human being, teaches us much about ourselves. We can consciously use this learning to help others, giving the best possible care to those individuals who are entering the final stage in the journey of life.

© Cooper J. 2014. "End-of-Life". *In: Palliative Care within Mental Health: care and practice*, edited by DB Cooper and J Cooper. Boca Raton, FL: CRC Press.

REFERENCES

Beauchamp TL and JF Childress. 2012. *Principles of Biomedical Ethics.* 7th ed. New York: Oxford University Press.

Broom DM. 2003. *The Evolution of Morality and Religion.* Cambridge: Cambridge University Press. p. 100.

Department of Health. 2008. *End of Life Care Strategy: promoting high quality care for all adults at the end of life.* London: Department of Health. www.gov.uk/government/ publications/end-of-life-care-strategy-promoting-high-quality-care-for-adults-at-the-end-of-their-life.

Eshiett MA and EHO Parry. 2003. "Migrants and health: a cultural dilemma". *Clinical Medicine.* 3: 229–31.

Griggs C. 2010. "Community nurses' perception of a good death: a qualitative exploratory study". *International Journal of Palliative Nursing.* 16: 139–48.

Grisaffi K and L Robinson. 2010. "Timing of end of life care in dementia: difficulties and dilemmas for GPs". *Journal of Dementia Care.* 18: 36–9.

Jeffrey D. 2006. *Patient-centred Ethics and Communication at the End of Life.* Abingdon: Radcliffe Publishing. pp. 24, 28.

Mahmood-Yousuf K, D Munday, N King and J Dale. 2008. "Interprofessional relationships and communication in primary palliative care: impact of the Gold Standard Framework". *British Journal of General Practice.* 58: 256–63.

Masson JD. 2002. "Non-professional perceptions of 'good death': a study of the views of hospice care patients and relatives of deceased hospice care patients". *Mortality.* 7: 191–209.

Mitchell S, D Kiely and MB Hamel. 2004. "Dying with advanced dementia in the nursing home". *Archives of Internal Medicine.* 164: 321–6.

The National Council for Palliative Care. 2006. *End of life care strategy.* London: The National Council for Palliative Care. www.ncpc.org.uk/sites/default/files/NCPC_ EoLC_Submission.pdf.

Sampson EL, V Gould, D Lee and MR Blanchard. 2006. "Differences in care received by patients with and without dementia who died during acute hospital admission: a retrospective case note study". *Age and Ageing.* 35: 187–9.

Social Care Institute for Excellence, Rutter D and P Holmes. 2013. *Dying Well at Home: the case for integrated working.* London: Social Care Institute for Excellence. www.scie.org.uk/publications/guides/guide48/files/guide48.pdf.

Twycross R. 1997. *Introducing palliative care,* 2nd ed. Oxford: Radcliffe Medical Press, p. 9.

TO LEARN MORE

Cooper DB and J Cooper. 2012. *Palliative Care within Mental Health: principles and philosophy.* London: Radcliffe Publishing.

Cooper J. 2006. *Stepping in to Palliative Care: care and practice.* 2nd ed. Oxford: Radcliffe Publishing.

Cooper J. 2006. *Stepping in to Palliative Care: relationships and responses.* 2nd ed. Oxford: Radcliffe Publishing.

Jeffrey D. 2006. *Patient-centred Ethics and Communication at the End of Life.* Oxford: Radcliffe Publishing.

Rinpoche S. 2008. *The Tibetan Book of Living and Dying: a spiritual classic from one of the foremost interpreters of Tibetan Buddhism to the West.* Edited by Gaffney P, Harvey A. London/Sydney/Auckland/Johannesburg: Rider.

CHAPTER 22

Small changes

David B Cooper

REFLECTIVE PRACTICE EXERCISE 22.1

Time: 60 minutes
- Now you have read this book do you feel you have a better understanding of ethics within mental health–substance use in your life and work environment?
- Think! How can you apply this ethical knowledge into your own area of care and practice?
- Who can you approach in order to instigate what you have learned into your own and others practice?
- When will you do this?
- Make an action plan and deadlines for your actions and stick to them.

INTRODUCTION

Ethics and ethical care and praxis run throughout our work, and our personal and professional practice. It is not always clear as to what is meant by ethics, and here we anticipate that this book has gone some way to add clarification to both practice and thinking. Moral values and philosophy must be at the heart of everything that we do . . . it is pivotal to our daily lives and practice. The importance cannot be over emphasised, to stray from ethical practice can do untold harm to the individual, the family and fellow professionals.

To be ethically competent we must communicate effectively and efficiently with all those we come into contact with in our daily lives.

REFLECTIVE PRACTICE EXERCISE 22.2

> **Time: 30 minutes**
>
> Take time to reflect on your life and your place in the world. When you commenced your education and training . . . what did you hope to achieve for the person within your care? Now go back to that place . . .
> - Are you currently achieving these aims?
> - If not, why not?
> - How can you bring about the changes in your practice?
> - How can you share this new knowledge and skill with your fellow professionals?
> - What do you hope to achieve now?

COMMUNICATION

All the above is meaningless without effective communication between professionals and the person and family receiving compassionate care. What follows concentrates on effective communication . . . which is at the heart of care and caring.

KEY POINT 22.1

Effective communication is a master key . . . it fits all locks and opens all doors . . . (Cooper 2011).

SELF-ASSESSMENT EXERCISE 22.1

> **Time: 10 minutes**
>
> Consider the following
> - When was the last time you wished communication within or outwith your team could be improved?
> - What steps do you think you could take to improve communication?

Effective communication can reduce the level of stress and burnout experienced by the professional. Sadly, burnout is no longer rare but an increasing level of risk for the professional in health and social care (Davidson 2014).

Communication is pivotal when avoiding increased levels of stress and burnout. However, if this is the case – why do we often get it wrong? If effective communication is easy – why do we not practice it? If we are pleased when communication has gone well and angry when it has not – why do we have high expectations of other's effective communication and not pay attention to our own practices? If we are experiencing the effects of stress and burnout ourselves why are we so unsympathetic to others when they experience the same (Davidson 2014)?

As individuals, we should know what to do and how to do it – there are no excuses. Yet, we remain ineffective communicators – unless, it impacts on us directly. Then we become experts – we notice how ineffective communication damages our day!

Here we provide a foundation for common courtesy and good practice that should be part of our professional and personal lives. We have become too familiar with poor communication and easily over-simplify or underestimate its ethical, professional and personal importance. Consequently, we miss the value it holds for individuals, groups, and ourselves.

WHAT IS EFFECTIVE COMMUNICATION?

Communication can be subdivided into seven parts . . .

1 individual, family and carers
2 junior team
3 peers
4 intra-disciplinary team
5 inter-disciplinary team
6 middle management
7 senior management

. . . each is interdependent and interrelated – none stand alone.

> **KEY POINT 22.2**
>
> Integral to, and at the centre of all our actions, is effective communication with the individual, family, and carers (Cooper 2012).

Each person individually experiences the negative consequence of ineffective communication. Therefore, effective communication is like the ripples in a pond, flowing effortlessly between each part.

Communication pond?

Water is made up of millions of individual molecules that collectively give water its fluidity (Cooper 2012). Individuals within an organisation, or inter-linked fields, are like the individual molecules of water. Each is interdependent on the other to provide the best possible quality of care for the individual, family, and carers.

Imagine a stone landing in a pond. The ripples move seamlessly through the water until the pond is smooth, ready for the next stone. In this analogy, you are the stone. It is your responsibility to ensure your communication flows effectively and effortlessly through the organisation.

Therefore, effective communication emanates like the ripples on a pond, flowing effortlessly. Each professional having an equal responsibility to effectively communicate with the other: each intra- and inter-dependent. Only then can communication, ethical and professional practice . . . and the care of the individual, family, and carers . . . be effective.

INDIVIDUAL, FAMILY AND CARERS

The individual, family, and carers are central in any care environment (*see* Chapter 15). Every action, act, or omission, from the junior member to the most senior manager, impacts on these individuals. Ineffective communication makes the treatment and intervention experience devastating and destructive.

The impact of verbal communication between professionals cannot be over-emphasised.

KEY POINT 22.3

How professionals share important, and routine information related to the individual, family and carers, does have a major impact on the successful outcome of any therapeutic intervention (Cooper 2012).

With the individuals' permission, information relating to past and present health or social problems can be discussed with each professional or agency. Just as important is the information available from family and/or carers relating to the individuals concerns. The individual may forget or be unable to express important facts and information relevant to the presenting problem. Often, individuals and family can feel intimidated by the 'knowledgeable professional'.

The individual, family, and carers can become dependent on the professional. This is not a deliberate act. It is easy to feel safe in the hands of a competent professional. The individual comes to depend on immediate access and consequently, sudden unexpected and unplanned withdrawal is disruptive and unethical. The individual, family, and carers should be informed at the outset about the level and extent of your involvement in their care. This should be periodically reinforced so the individual is aware of your end-date.

Moreover, it is possible for the professional to extend contact with the individual, family, and carers beyond that which is therapeutic. We gain subconscious reward from their dependence on us – the professional (Cooper 2012)!

Careful monitoring and clinical supervision will aid awareness of such instances so that effective addressing of the negative aspects can be worked through . . . and overcome.

> **KEY POINT 22.4**
>
> Clinical supervision aids identification of over involvement and dependence, as well as, exploration of our actions and omissions within care and caring.

Individuals do progress without our watchful eye if appropriate and effective intervention and treatment is managed effectively. We cannot protect them from all ills or dangers. Being aware of our limitations, intervention and the extent of the therapeutic value, takes experience. Close monitoring of our actions is essential. A good indicator would be . . . when we come to write the legal records related to the individual and we have little to say about the person's progress – it is time to evaluate ones effectiveness. Ineffective communication is damaging and destructive.

> **KEY POINT 22.5**
>
> Common sense, courtesy and good manners form the basis of effective communication (Cooper 2012).

Setting an example

During times of pressure and stress, effective communication is the first thing to suffer, yet it reduces pressure and stress. Effective communication frees time to deal with other matters that are important to individualised care. Effective communication comes from the top. Senior managers lead by example: only then will the employee find the tasks that he or she is set easier to work with and control. However, a lack of such leadership is not an excuse for one's actions, inactions, or omissions.

There is plethora of ineffective communication examples that one could describe: each one of us has our own personal story! This chapter aims to demonstrate that, with a little work from you, some new small steps in effective communication leading to a good quality standard of ethical and professional care and caring can happen within and outwith your organisation: you just have to give it brain space and effort. It is not a thing to do later but an instrument to use constantly – always at the forefront of everyday activities.

Effective communication costs nothing. Misunderstanding, anger, frustration, complaints and worry . . . for the individual, family and carers, other professionals and oneself . . . can be avoided.

Having cited all the above, none of this holds any importance if the receiver of communication does not listen. This two-way process is imperative if com–munication is to be effective.

No professional wants the individual, family, or carers to suffer as a conse-quence of his or her inaction – yet, we risk this every day through poor communication. It is not their responsibility – it is our responsibility to make communication effective and meaningful to the best of our ability and under-standing.

SUPERVISION AND SUPPORT

The professional needs to self-confirm that supervision is not about the manager spying on the professional's practice. Moreover, that to seek support is not a weakness but a willingness to learn and improve your professional human care and caring. How can we try to manage situations differently, producing a more desirable outcome for all concerned? Good reflective supervision can help endorse our functioning as an ethical human being, maintaining the moral value of human conduct, and the principles which underpin it.

Clinical supervision and support is designed to help us to reflect deeply on the work we are doing, and how we do it. How it makes us feel and whether our practice could be undertaken in a more meaningful and caring way. Per-haps 'supervision' should be renamed to 'helpfulness programme'.

Each of us, when undertaking this work, needs to acknowledge that we are all dependent on each other, whether we are junior or senior members of the care team. To share such knowledge enables us to care and work with compassion (*see* Chapter 6). However, it is not merely about being compassionate to others . . . we need to be compassionate to ourselves. If we are not, then we will fail to be compassionate to those we care for and our fellow professionals.

WHAT WE HAVE LEARNED

As we have seen throughout these chapters, ethics, ethical and professional care and practice demonstrates many parallels with the care given in mental health–substance use practice. Therefore, it is not always obvious . . . we just need to look for it when working on a busy ward, within the home and community or the care home environment to see that parallels exist. However, because of their co-existence it should not be too difficult to adapt the processes, programmes and aspects of care that run like a thread through many of these chapters. When reflecting on what you have read, remember that it is just as important to look after yourself. This is something we often fail at, which can lead to a painful and distressing personal and professional environment. Caring for ourselves needs inclusion in our daily life and practice 'never assume people know . . . they do not!' (Cooper 2011).

The authors and editor hope that this book, and the earlier six books, have offered some insight to the application of introducing ethical, professional practice within mental health-substance use care and practice. The hope is that it has stimulated and motivated the reader on to good practice and further reading.

We have attempted to address the heart of ethical and professional care and caring throughout this book and hope that it may lead on to implementation. This chapter forms the final piece of effective and meaningful care and caring by addressing the importance of communication which is placed as high in importance as any other care and practice covered in this book. Feasibly, this jigsaw is complete and we all can now progress to the heart of ethical and professional care and caring in our daily lives and practice.

REFERENCES

Cooper DB. 2011. Communication: the essence of good practice, management and leadership. In *Developing services in Mental Health–Substance Use,* edited by DB Cooper. Boca Raton, FL: CRC Press. pp. 161–70.

Cooper DB. 2012. Looking after yourself and colleagues. In *Palliative Care within Mental Health: principles and philosophy,* edited by DB Cooper and J Cooper. Boca Raton, FL: CRC Press. pp. 265–87.

Davidson R. 2006. Stress issues in palliative care. In *Stepping into Palliative Care 1: relationships and responses* edited by J Cooper. 2nd ed. Oxon: Radcliffe Publishing. pp. 135–45.

Index